Secret War in Shanghai

Secret War in Shanghai

Bernard Wasserstein

P

PROFILE BOOKS

First published in Great Britain in 1998 by
Profile Books Ltd
58A Hatton Garden
London EC1N 8LX

Typeset in Lapidary 333 by MacGuru
macguru@pavilion.co.uk

Printed and bound in Great Britain by Bookmarque Ltd, Croydon

A CIP catalogue record for this book is available from the British Library.

ISBN 1 86197 091 9

Contents

Abbreviations

See also p. 293 for list of abbreviations used in endnotes.

CCG   China Commando Group (British)

KMA   Kailan Mining Administration

OM   Oriental Mission (Far East section of SOE)

OSS   Office of Strategic Services (USA)

RII   Research and Investment Institute *or* Resources Investigation
Institute (Chinese)

SACO   Sino-American Cooperative Organization

SIS   (British) Secret Intelligence Service (MI6)

SMP   Shanghai Municipal Police

SOE   Special Operations Executive (British)

Maps

1 The Far East, 1941

2 China, 1941

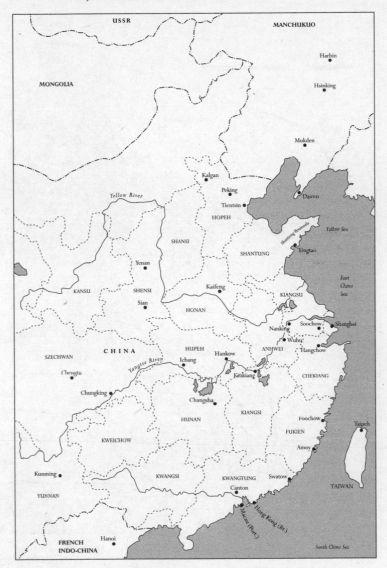

3 Shanghai during the Second World War

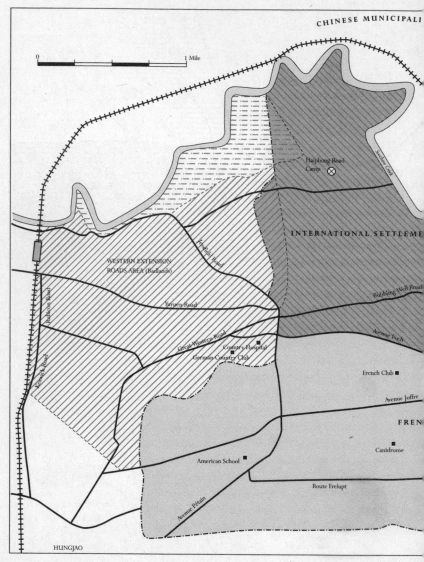

CHINESE MUNICIPALI

Haiphong Road
Camp

INTERNATIONAL SETTLEME

0   1 Mile

WESTERN EXTENSION
ROADS AREA (Badlands)

Jessfield Road

Yuyuen Road

Hungjao Road

Jessfield Road

Bubbling Well Road

Avenue Foch

Great Western Road

Country Hospital

German Country Club

French Club

Avenue Joffre

FREN

American School

Canidrome

Avenue Pétain

Route Frelupt

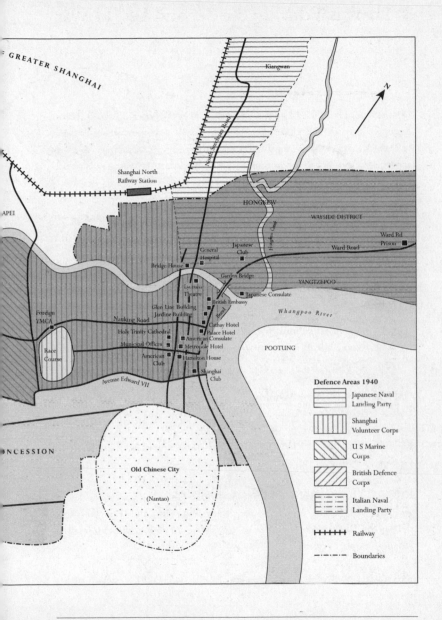

GREATER SHANGHAI

Kiangwan

N

APEI

Shanghai North
Railway Station

HONGKEW

WAYSIDE DISTRICT

Ward Rd
Prison

General
Hospital

Japanese
Club

Ward Road

Bridge House

Garden Bridge

YANGTZEPOO

Lyceum
Theatre

Japanese Consulate

British Embassy

Glen Line Building

Whangpoo River

Foreign
YMCA

Jardine Building

Nanking Road

POOTUNG

Holy Trinity Cathedral

Cathay Hotel
Palace Hotel

Race
Course

Municipal Offices

American Consulate

American
Club

Metropole Hotel
Hamilton House

Avenue Edward VII

Shanghai
Club

Defence Areas 1940

Japanese Naval
Landing Party

Shanghai
Volunteer Corps

U S Marine
Corps

ONCESSION

Old Chinese City

(Nantao)

British Defence
Corps

Italian Naval
Landing Party

+++++ Railway

— · — · — Boundaries

Who Was Who

Designations such as '0.113' were code-names used by the British Special Operations Executive during the war. Other aliases given here were nicknames applied by friends or enemies, cover-names deployed by intelligence agents or pseudonyms adopted by criminals. Chinese names in this book are generally rendered according to the Wade-Giles system commonly used in the period.

BERRIER, 'Count' HILAIRE du (American): Adventurer, aviator, journalist; Japanese agent in Shanghai.

EISENTRAEGER, Colonel LOTHAR (German): Abwehr officer; a.k.a. 'Ludwig Ehrhardt'; head of Abwehr station in Shanghai, 1942–45.

ERBEN, 'Dr' HERMANN (Austrian-American): Adventurer and ship's doctor (unqualified); monkey expert; friend of Errol Flynn as well as of Dr Albert von Miorini (*q.v.*); low-grade German agent in Shanghai during the war.

GANDE, W. J. (British): Wholesale liquor merchant; head of Shanghai section of Oriental Mission, Special Operations Executive, 1941.

KAHNER, Major GERHARD (German): Policeman; head of Shanghai Gestapo, 1940–43.

KENTWELL, LAWRENCE KLINDT (British-Chinese): Disbarred lawyer and journalist; a.k.a. 'Kan Teh-yun', 'Kum Tuck-yen', and 'Ken Wen-loo'; during the Pacific War member of Legislative Yuan (parliament) of pro-Japanese puppet régime.

KESWICK, JOHN H. (British): a.k.a. '0.113' and 'AD/O'; Taipan of Jardine, Matheson trading company in Shanghai; senior official of Special Operations Executive, 1942–45.

KESWICK, W. J. (British): a.k.a. 'Tony' and 'AD/U'; brother of the above; Jardine, Matheson taipan; Chairman of Shanghai Municipal Council, 1940–41; during the war served as Director (in London) of Far East section of the Special Operations Executive.

KILLERY, VALENTINE ST JOHN (British): Businessman; a.k.a. 'O.100'; on eve of war chief representative of ICI in Far East; head of Oriental Mission of Special Operations Executive, May 1941 to June 1942.

MEISINGER, Colonel JOSEF (German): War criminal; head of SS in Far East, 1941–45.

MILES, Lieutenant-Commander (later Admiral) MILTON (American): Naval officer; a.k.a. 'Mary', 'Trout' and 'O.610'; Director of Operations of Office of Strategic Services in China, 1942–45.

MIORINI, Dr ALBERT von (Austrian): Doctor and extortionist; shady operator in Shanghai before and during the war.

MOY, HERBERT ERASMUS (Chinese-American): Broadcaster; worked for German and later for Japanese radio stations in Shanghai during the war.

NATHAN, EDWARD JONAH (British): Businessman; chief manager of the Kailan Mining Administration to February 1943.

OTANI, INAHO (Japanese): Assistant naval attaché and head of the Foreign Affairs section of the Japanese Naval Intelligence Bureau in Shanghai from August 1941.

PICK, 'Captain' EUGENE (White Russian): Actor, gangster and political adventurer; born Evgeny Mihailovich Kojevnikoff, a.k.a 'Hovans', 'Doctor

Clige', and many other aliases; employed during the war by Foreign Affairs section of Japanese Naval Intelligence Bureau in Shanghai.

RAYMOND, ALAN (Australian): Horse-racing enthusiast; headed collaborationist 'Independent Australia League' in Shanghai during the war.

RUFFE, Baron, R. AUXION de (French): Advocate and author in Shanghai.

SIEFKEN, Captain LOUIS THEODOR (German): Naval officer; a.k.a. 'Smith'; head of Abwehr station in Shanghai, 1940–42.

SUMAIRE (RAJKUMARI SUMAIR APJIT SINGH) 'Princess' (Indian): Fashion model and adventuress; perhaps niece of Maharajah of Patiala.

TAI LI (Chinese): Head of the Military Bureau of Investigation of Statistics; a.k.a. 'the Himmler of China' and 'O.601'.

TU YUEH-SHENG (Chinese): Gangster, politician and philanthropist; head of the 'Green Gang' in Shanghai to 1937; during the war moved to Chungking.

Introduction

The Second World War began in the Far East on 7 July 1937 with the Japanese onslaught on China. The battle of Shanghai in the autumn of that year marked the bloody climax of the first phase of the conflict. Britain and the United States were not drawn in formally until December 1941, the Soviet Union only in the final days in 1945. Yet in reality all the major powers found themselves embroiled from the outset in one way or another in the struggle for mastery of the Asiatic mainland. All had vital economic or strategic interests there. All maintained significant intelligence establishments there. Between 1937 and 1945 all sought to advance their interests, at times by applying brute force, more commonly by subtler, undercover means. The cockpit of this war was the intelligence capital of the Far East – Shanghai. This book tells the story of that secret war. It is an enquiry into the interstices of espionage, subversion, deception and terror; into a murky political netherworld that produced strange, cross-cutting alliances and enmities, that evoked both heroism and treachery, and that reflected in microcosm the global war of nations.

With its lurid vice, savage criminality and conspiratorial politics, no place on earth in the 1930s and 1940s better exemplified the twilight zone of clandestine warfare than Shanghai. The wealth and sophistication of China's largest, most cosmopolitan and most dangerous city rendered it a killing-field of brutal economic competition, ideological struggle and murderous political intrigue.

Shanghai's ever-open door attracted an extraordinary agglomeration of ill-assorted foreign communities: 'White' and 'Red' Russians imported their fierce mutual animosities from their homeland and perpetuated them in their exotic exile; German businessmen dutifully celebrated Hitler's birthday at the German Garden Club but found to their dismay that they were outnumbered in Shanghai by thousands of 'non-Aryan' German-speaking refugees from Nazi persecution; upper-crust 'Shanghailander'

Britons rubbed shoulders with Baghdadi Jewish property tycoons; Korean gangsters, Filipino musicians, low-life cardsharps, pickpockets and assorted con-men plied their various trades. So too did *demi-mondaines* of various nationalities who preyed on tourists at the Park, the Metropole and the Cathay hotels as well as on naval and military men of half a dozen countries in other, more questionable, haunts. Even in superficially respectable areas of the city meretricious glamour and horrific poverty, filth and squalor intertwined symbiotically. At Ciro's night-club, the first in the city to enjoy full air-conditioning, British taipans and Chinese mobsters tangoed with their wives or mistresses into the small hours. Outside, uniformed Russian doormen – self-appointed ex-Tsarist 'generals' whose spurious medals could be purchased by the dozen in the Hongkew market – held at bay importuning hordes of deformed Chinese beggars. In less salubrious dance-halls, bars and 'joints', lines of Russian 'taxi-dancers' and Chinese 'sing-song girls' sat waiting for customers. In 1935 one in every thirteen women in Shanghai was reckoned to be a prostitute[1].

Throughout the city violence was a constant threat whether in the form of political assassinations, gang warfare or lovers' fights. The stained cobbles of Blood Alley (rue Chu Pao-san) in Frenchtown bore witness to the frequency of brawls among foreign soldiers and sailors. God, who allowed Shanghai to endure, owed an apology to Sodom and Gomorrah – so said the American Christian missionaries who strove to combat the devil in his own habitation. A Chinese journalist agreed: Shanghai, he wrote, was 'a city of forty-eight-storey skyscrapers built upon twenty-four layers of hell'.[2]

The imposing European-style buildings of the banks and merchant houses on the Bund, Shanghai's famous waterfront on the Whangpoo River, gave an appearance of solidity and permanence. But the city was constructed on what were literally shaky foundations. Many of its towering structures were built on concrete rafts that floated on mud flats.

上海

Modern Shanghai was to a large extent a foreign, not Chinese, creation. The old 'native city' of Nantao had, it is true, been an important port and market town for several centuries. But significant urban development began only after the signature of the Treaty of Nanking between Britain and China in 1842, at the conclusion of the first Opium War. With that and subsequent agreements with the USA and France, China agreed to open Shanghai and certain other ports to foreign commerce. Building on these 'unequal treaties' and interpreting them in a far-reaching way, the foreign powers gradually extended the privileges accorded to their merchants in the 'treaty ports'. Parts of these cities were appropriated as 'concessions' ruled directly by the powers as quasi-colonies. Within these enclaves foreigners could conduct business according to their own laws, exempt from taxation by the Chinese and immune from interference by Chinese courts or officials. Within half a century Shanghai grew to be the central clearing-house of waterborne trade between the entire Yangtse river system and the rest of the world. The port's 35 miles of wharves could accommodate over 170 ships and 500 sea-going junks at a time. Half of all China's foreign trade was cleared through Shanghai.

By the late 1930s Shanghai had sprouted into one of the urban wonders of the world. China's most dynamic city, her economic, cultural and political hub, Shanghai was the supreme prize awaiting the victor in the struggle for power among the would-be heirs of the Manchu emperors who had been overthrown in the Chinese revolution of 1911 but not replaced by any stable form of national government. With a population of more than 5 million, Shanghai was the sixth largest city in the world, the greatest commercial entrepôt in the Far East and a magnet for foreign, particularly British, investment.

Like Gaul, Shanghai was divided into three parts (see map on pp. x–xi). Each was a virtually sovereign jurisdiction with its own government, armed force and police. The largest, in both area and population, was the Chinese Municipality of Greater Shanghai which formed part of the Republic of China. This, however, constituted only the outer periphery of the city proper. Since the suppression of a communist revolt in the city in 1927, the central government at Nanking, headed by General Chiang Kai-shek, had sought to consolidate its authority over the whole of Shanghai. Chiang's Kuomintang party ran what amounted to a one-party police state. But it found that, notwithstanding its formal sovereignty, its writ did not run very far even in the Chinese municipality. Warlords and gangster-politicians competed for power with one another, with the central government and with new-style Chinese capitalists. And all of them regarded with rapacious envy the two prosperous foreign enclaves in the centre of the city.

The smaller of these, the French Concession, was a mainly residential district abutting on to part of the river foreshore. It had a population of half a million in 1936; a small fraction were foreigners, and of these only 2,342 were French civilians. They were outnumbered by 11,628 Russian residents (mainly anti-Bolshevik Whites who had fled from Siberia at the end of the Russian Civil War) and 2,468 British. The concession was ruled as an almost absolute monarchy by the French Consul-General. He was nominally assisted by a municipal council appointed by himself, but his relationship with them was akin to that between Louis XIV and the court of Versailles. For security the Consul-General could call on a force of 4,000 gendarmes, under 300 of whom were French, the remainder Chinese or Vietnamese. The French police maintained a supremely well-informed political section and supremely corrupt departments supposedly devoted to the suppression of drugs and vice – in reality much more devoted to the illicit profits to be derived from these and other rackets.

The heart of Shanghai, its commercial and industrial core, encompassing hundreds of factories, miles of quays and godowns (warehouses), as well as parks and pleasure-grounds, fashionable clubs and hotels, and the consulates of the great powers, formed an entity unique in world politics – the International Settlement. This area had a population of about 1.2 million in 1936 of whom only about 40,000 were foreigners. Yet this minority had been the settlement's rulers since its foundation.

Unlike most of the other foreign concessions in China, the International Settlement did not belong to any one power. The settlement's constitution, the Land Regulations, first issued by the local Chinese authority in 1845 and subsequently revised several times, took final form in 1898. This peculiar document, although recognized as binding in treaties between the major powers and China, left several issues unclear – notably the question of sovereignty. Although the settlement was in every real political sense a foreign colonial enclave, sovereignty over it remained theoretically Chinese. The ruling body, the Shanghai Municipal Council, was limited from above by the residual authority of the 'Consular Body' and from below by the 'ratepayers'. These were a small group of property-owners, mainly British and Americans (in later years also Japanese), dominated by the taipans, heads of the great British merchant houses and banks. The ratepayers met in a public meeting once a year to decide major issues of policy and to elect the council. The council's chief civil servant, Godfrey Phillips, a former president of the Cambridge Union, was one of the most powerful men in Shanghai. A high property qualification restricted voting rights to a small minority of the European population. In 1935, only 3,852 out of the 38,940 foreign residents in the settlement had the right to vote. Until the Second World War this alien oligarchy effectively controlled the destiny of Shanghai. If the French Concession was pre-revolutionary France in exotic miniature, the International Settlement was an oriental echo of England before the Reform Act.

At the apex of Anglo-Saxon society in Shanghai stood the Keswick brothers, Tony and John, taipans of the great Jardine, Matheson trading concern. Known as the 'muckle house' on account of its Scottish origins, Jardine, Matheson employed over 100,000 workers in its mills, factories and godowns, and owned a fleet of more than 30 merchant and passenger ships. Tony Keswick exercised political as well as economic leadership of the settlement, since he also served as chairman of the Shanghai Municipal Council. His brother John's academic performance at Cambridge had been poor (a third class in the historical tripos at Trinity College) but he learned fluent Chinese in Shanghai, both Mandarin and the Shanghai dialect. A friendly, outgoing character, John had what was described as 'a remarkably pronounced back to his head which so resembled the statues of the Chinese god of happiness, Fu Shen, that in the country Chinese often touched him in the belief that some of his happiness would rub off. It usually did.'[3] The brothers would be seen at all the major social events of the Shanghai season – charity balls, club dinners, race meetings and the 'paper hunt' in which the rituals of English rural sportsmanship were refashioned to conform to the topography of the surrounding Chinese countryside where canals rather than hedges were the main challenges to horsemanship. The Keswicks' peacetime role was extended, in a different form, during the Second World War when they took charge of the British subversive warfare effort in China.

There were no political parties in municipal affairs but political struggle in the settlement was nevertheless intense. In the 1930s it took two main forms: resistance by the foreign communities to the Chinese government's demands for the effective recognition and exercise of Chinese sovereignty in the settlement; and growing conflict between Japan and the Anglo-Saxon powers for control of the affairs of the settlement.

Although to outward appearance 'international', the settlement's Municipal Council was really governed by British interests during most of its history. Until the early 1930s British and American councillors were always a majority on the council. The Germans had had one seat until the First World War but were excluded thereafter and replaced by Japan, whose citizens by that time formed the largest single community in foreign Shanghai. A second Japanese seat was added in 1927 but the Japanese pressed hard for greater representation. With their growing population and investment in the settlement they obviously constituted the wave of the future. As for the Chinese majority of the population, they had no say at all in the government of the settlement until 1928 when three Chinese members were added for the first time to the nine foreign members of the Council. Two more joined them in 1930. But in keeping with the council's undemocratic nature, the Chinese members were not directly elected but were nominated by the Chinese Ratepayers' Association, a body representing wealthy Chinese business interests.

The settlement's political structure reflected the economic reality of Britain's supremacy in the city – and of her quasi-imperial dominance in China as a whole. Thirty-eight per cent of all foreign holdings in China in 1931 were British; and three-quarters of Britain's $963 million stake in the country was invested in Shanghai. The British controlled more than half of all China's shipping. The inspector-general of the Chinese customs and most of his senior staff were British citizens. In China, as elsewhere, the British, conscious of the dangers of what we would now call 'imperial overstretch', eschewed formal annexation. Instead, they opted for an informal imperialism of which Shanghai was a pre-eminent model.

上海

Protecting and perpetuating alien predominance in Shanghai was a complex security system. The settlement's chief protectors of law and order, the Shanghai Municipal Police (SMP), had been established soon after the council's inauguration in 1853. The 5,000 members of the force included Chinese, Sikh, and later also Japanese and Russian personnel; but the commissioner and senior officers were always British – at any rate until the eve of the outbreak of the Pacific War in December 1941. In its early years the settlement police had a turbulent history: in 1860 its superintendent was dismissed 'on charges indicating systematic fraud and extortion'.[4] Less corrupt than the French Concession police and better trained than those of the Chinese Municipality, the settlement's police in the 1930s were probably the most efficient in China.

Police in Shanghai were less hampered by libertarian niceties than their confrères at the Sûreté or Scotland Yard. The Municipal Police Special Branch, for example, was apparently quite prepared to cooperate with a British military intelligence officer in arranging for the murder of a local American communist – an incident later described with relish in the officer's unpublished memoirs.[5] The French Concession police were notorious in the late 1920s for being under the thumb of the all-powerful boss of the Chinese Green Gang, Tu Yueh-sheng. As a leading French lawyer in the city once put it, 'China is not France and what may be true in Paris is not necessarily so in Shanghai.'[6]

The division of Shanghai into separate police jurisdictions created fertile conditions for large-scale international criminality. A wanted man who wished to escape the attentions of the police in one of the three jurisdictions in the city could simply hop over into a neighbouring section, since cooperation among the Chinese, French and settlement police forces was seldom intimate – except in the suppression of communism.[7]

In the inter-war period gangsters, both Chinese and foreign, turned Shanghai into the world's wholesale drug hypermarket. More illegal drugs were seized in Shanghai each year than in the entire United States. Where the American authorities captured pounds, their Shanghai counterparts uncovered tons – or often turned the other way with a venal wink, 'squeeze' being an accepted part of the Shanghai way of life. In Shanghai the drug trade had been largely controlled since the mid-1920s by Tu Yueh-sheng's Green Gang.

With an estimated 20,000 gangsters at his beck and call, Tu was a formidable political presence in the city. An orphaned former fruit-stall apprentice, he was a highly sophisticated political operator. He deserves, indeed, to be classified as an outstandingly gifted entrepreneur, probably the greatest racketeer in modern China. In 1927 he was said to have collaborated with the settlement authorities and Chiang Kai-shek in the suppression of communists in Shanghai. Later he achieved a *modus vivendi* with the rulers of the concession who for a while gave him a free hand to traffic in the area in return for a rake-off. As the British consul-general put it in 1930, the Green Gang bosses were

> extremely useful intermediaries in dealing by Chinese
> methods with any Chinese troubles which arise [in the French
> Concession] ... They can continue their opium dealings just so
> long as the concession benefits – very materially – and is
> spared much of the trouble to which foreign authorities in
> China are so often heirs.[8]

In 1932 the concession administration finally summoned up the courage to eliminate Tu's narcotics operation from the area. Then he simply moved his base to the neighbouring Chinese city, building an extensive network of influence within the ruling Kuomintang hierarchy.

Tu's case illustrates the often close connections between the criminal and political classes in Shanghai. As the Shanghai rackets, particularly gambling, vice and drugs, developed in the 1930s into monstrous industries, foreign criminals, 'bad hats' and confidence tricksters were attracted to the city in droves, turning it into a veritable 'paradise of adventurers'.[9] These aliens, like their Chinese counterparts, often combined racketeering with quasi-political activity on behalf of local or foreign powers.

Among the foreign rogues of the Shanghai underworld were the British gun-runner General 'One-Arm' Sutton and the American 'Peg-Leg' Kearney. 'Strictly speaking', as Kearney put it, he was 'only half an American', since he was only 3 feet tall, having had both his legs amputated. He had two wooden legs but travelled everywhere by rickshaw. A former arms salesman, he claimed to have served as an admiral in the Chilean navy.[10]

The generation of Sutton and Kearney had mostly faded out by the late 1930s but their successors, bit-players in the Shanghai game of nations during the Second World War, were no less colourful. Chief among them were a White Russian opera singer, theatrical impresario and gang boss 'Captain' Pick, a fraudulent Indian 'Princess' Sumaire, an abortionist, brothel-owner and sexual extortionist Dr Albert von Miorini, a monkey expert, narcotics dealer and unqualified 'Doctor' Hermann Erben, and a shady Franco-American journalist, aviator and pimp Hilaire du Berrier. In addition to their regular criminal avocations, all of them also served as low-level intelligence agents, usually offering their services to the highest bidder.

The movements, correspondence, connections and activities of such figures were closely monitored by the police forces in all three sections of the city – most intently by the 'Special Branch' (political police) of the Shanghai Municipal Police, one of whose functions was an information-gathering arm in the Far East for the British Secret Intelligence Service (later known as MI6 or SIS). The head of the Special Branch was guided in these duties by an MI6 representative attached to the staff of the British consulate. For much of the inter-war period this was Harry Steptoe, an 'old China hand'.

The British intelligence operation in Shanghai was probably second to none in the 1930s but it had formidable rivals: Russians, Japanese, French, Germans and (a little late off the mark) Americans. All these powers and some others maintained intelligence stations in the city in the 1930s: Japan alone was said to have as many as 20 different units by 1938.[11] Shanghai consequently became the main intelligence marketplace for the entire Far East. As the centre of political activity in China, particularly of left-wing propaganda, and the home of a cosmopolitan population that included tens of thousands of political émigrés, Shanghai was a natural focus for espionage, both Chinese and foreign.

The settlement and concession police could normally deal with crime, riots, strikes and also (relying on the SMP Special Branch and the French political police) with political subversion. But they were inadequate in dealing with full-scale Chinese revolts or military threats. To meet these dangers the settlement had its own little army, the Shanghai Volunteer Corps, about 2,500 strong, recruited mainly from the local foreign population. The corps was divided into companies organized on a national basis, among them British (the largest), American, Filipino, Portuguese, Jewish and a small Chinese detachment. The corps had a proud record of defending the settlement against external (that is, Chinese) threats. Formally established in 1870, the force grew out of a foreign citizens' militia that beat off imperial Chinese troops in the Battle of Muddy Flat in 1854. Between then and 1938 the corps was mobilized 25 times to deal with internal or external threats to the security of the settlement.

The only permanently mobilized and paid unit of the volunteer corps was the Russian regiment, founded in 1927 and recruited from the large community of White Russians in Shanghai. The regiment was fully motorized: its 20 fast Chevrolet lorries each had a Lewis gun mounted above the driver's cab. The Russians were used in peacetime for riot duty and as guards in the municipal prison in Ward Road. Two platoons stood by, day and night, to answer police riot calls. Although the regiment had a Russian officer-in-charge, it was effectively controlled by a British 'adviser'. 'They are a fine force', wrote one of the unit's British officers in October 1937, 'and act as a spearhead whilst the remainder of the corps is mobilizing. With a British officer to tell them what to do, they would go anywhere and do anything. Real tough nuts.'[12]

To intimidate potential enemies further, the foreign powers maintained garrisons of professional troops in Shanghai. Foreign troops and warships had intervened in China repeatedly over the previous century and the right of the powers to station forces in China had been secured by treaty following the Boxer rebellion of 1900. Gunboats of several powers, particularly Britain and the United States, patrolled frequently up and down the Yangtse and larger vessels often showed the flag on Warship Row opposite the Bund on the Whangpoo. In the crisis of 1927 Britain dispatched a major force of 20,000 men to Shanghai; America, Japan, France, Italy, the Netherlands, Spain and Portugal together sent a further 20,000. Most of these troops were withdrawn when the crisis passed but some remained. In 1937 the American garrison at Shanghai consisted of 150 officers and 2,600 men; the British had 90 officers and 2,500 men; the French 50 officers and 2,000 men; and the Italians 20 officers and 750 men.

Japanese warships had appeared at Shanghai in 1884 and a small detachment of soldiers landed in 1897, but it was not until 1927 that a significant Japanese military presence was established with the arrival of the Special Naval Landing Party. They came to the settlement initially as defenders rather than aggressors, participating with other foreign forces in the protection of the enclave against the threat of attack or subversion by Chinese nationalists and communists. On that occasion their arrival was at the urgent request of the British government – fearful for the huge British investment stake in China, yet reluctant to commit larger numbers of troops to its defence. In 1931 the Japanese again participated in a joint defence of the settlement and were assigned responsibility for defending zone 'A' which covered the Hongkew and Yangtsepoo areas north of the Soochow Creek (see map on pp. x–xi).

In January 1932, following their invasion of Manchuria and a growth in Chinese-Japanese acrimony in Shanghai, the Japanese landed 20,000 troops in the city and, after a bitter battle with the Chinese 19th Route Army, occupied its Chinese section. This 'Shanghai incident' alarmed the British who began to worry about Japanese designs on the International Settlement. Diplomatic pressure by the Western powers produced a Chinese-Japanese peace agreement in May 1932 under which the bulk of Japanese forces withdrew from the city. But the Naval Landing Party kept a garrison of 1,800 men in barracks in Hongkew. The majority of the Japanese civilian population also lived in this area, so Hongkew came to be known informally as the 'Japanese Concession'. After 1932 the authority of the Municipal Police in this area was increasingly challenged by Japanese security organs.

上海

Politics in Shanghai, like business, was played by cutthroat rules in which the normal codes of polite society, whether Chinese or foreign, were loosened and coarsened. European Shanghai imported its own quasi-colonial attitudes and prejudices. But without the constraining influence of a governing imperial power, the 'Shanghailanders', often saw themselves as aboard a little ship cast out on its own in a hostile sea. They developed an outlook that, in its blinkered arrogance, set them apart even from the normal run of colonial populations.

The 'Shanghai mind' was the pregnant – and to the British ruling class in Shanghai deeply offensive – coinage of Arthur Ransome in a report from Shanghai for the *Manchester Guardian* in 1927 in which he denounced those British who 'look round on their magnificent buildings and are surprised that China is not grateful to them for these gifts'. The complex of values that Ransome pinned down with cruel precision was an extreme version of the colonialist mentality – it lacked only a Kipling or Maugham to capture its supremely philistine cultural parochialism and the snootiness of its social pretensions. But the Shanghai mind was also something more – and Ransome was perceptive enough to notice it: the British in Shanghai regarded their own economic interests not merely as synonymous with but as the defining criterion of British national interests in the Far East. 'Unless British policy coincides with their own', wrote Ransome, 'they are prepared at any moment to be the Ulster of the East.'[13] The unique constitutional status of Shanghai, an imperial outpost in fact that was not a colony in name, had given its British ruling class delusions of grandeur and a collective self-importance that accorded ill with the diminishing power Britain could muster, militarily, diplomatically and politically in the city and in East Asia in general.

The Shanghai mind flourished in its natural habitat at No. 3, the Bund, the splendid premises of the Shanghai Club. This mainly British, all-male institution applied rigorous racial and social conditions for membership. Chinese, of course, were not admitted. Nor, in general, were Japanese – though occasional exceptions were made in the 1930s. The sacred heart of the club was the 'longest bar in the world', at which a strictly graduated protocol was observed. The end near the window, looking out on to the Bund, was the preserve of the river pilots; next to them at the head of the bar stood the grandest taipans, such as the Keswick brothers, and directors of banks; lesser fry occupied positions further back, ending with the newly-arrived young 'griffins' at the far end. Even in the sweltering heat of the Shanghai summer the rule requiring jackets and ties to be worn was observed with a punctiliousness worthy of Pall Mall.

The British expressed their true feelings about the Chinese more freely in private than in public. An extreme example of such attitudes is the correspondence of a British police officer in Shanghai with his relatives in England, who wrote in 1921 that orientals 'should only be treated as the animals they are'. In 1926 the same officer complained to his sister that 'the way the foreign powers are "crawling" to these damned yellow pigs is nauseating'. Two years later, in a letter to his aunt, he described the Chinese as 'this bunch of worthless, treacherous, yellow-skinned reptiles'.[14] These were not merely the ravings of a disgruntled individual. They echoed a general opinion in the expatriate community – and in official circles. An official memorandum, entitled 'Notes on Shanghai 1928', produced for the guidance of the British army in India, appended the following notes on 'Some Chinese Characteristics':

> Probably the outstanding feature of the Chinese mind is its passivity. He [sic] is incapable of producing any active constructional [sic] doctrine and is full of contradictions …
>
> It has been well said of the Chinaman that 'he is out of step with the world'; western standards are inapplicable to him. Civic or national duties in the sense that we accept them are unknown to him …
>
> Of the Chinese as a soldier, there is little to say, except that he is utterly useless compared with western standards. There is very little difference between the ordinary soldier and the ordinary bandit.[15]

If the British nevertheless found themselves fighting as allies of the Chinese in both world wars, they did so very much *de haut en bas*.

The conventional Japanese view of the Chinese was strikingly similar. In 1932 a Japanese observer commented:

> It would appear a gross exaggeration to say that Chinese soldiers are bandits in official uniforms and that bandits are disbanded soldiers but this is one of the incredible truths about China. Soldiers to all appearances, [Chinese troops] in fact are a uniformed rabble … They are untrained, cowardly, unpatriotic, treacherous, mercenary, and everything else a soldier should not be.[16]

A Japanese guidebook declared candidly in 1940 that 'up to the present the feeling of Japanese towards whatever Chinese might be living near them has been to have as little to do with them [as possible], and their [i.e. Japanese] attitudes of racial superiority are quite overbearing'.[17]

Not all Japanese and not all British in China exhibited such attitudes. Some, in both cases, made notable efforts to achieve a sympathetic understanding of Chinese culture and society. But the dominant tone in the foreign communities was one of ethnic contempt towards the surrounding native population.

Little wonder, then, that in their struggle for power in China both the Japanese and their chief great-power competitors tended to regard and treat the Chinese in purely instrumental terms. The game of nations in Shanghai during the Second World War was enacted on a stage where the Chinese appeared mainly as puppets or in crowd scenes.

This book is set in China but it is not primarily about China. The strange little war of worlds in the foreign enclaves of Shanghai was a projection on to a Chinese screen of the larger ideological and strategic rivalries of the world powers. But this is not an exercise in military history. It is an examination, in an occluded, microcosmic setting, of the conduct of war by other means: propaganda of word and deed; conflicts between and within intelligence organizations; the dilemmas of conscience and interest that led some of the foreign residents of Shanghai into resistance to the Japanese occupation and others over the abyss into treason; and the bizarre synergy between criminal and political underworlds of which even an Orpheus could not have calmed the infernal spirits.

1 Solitary Island

On the night of 7 July 1937 Japanese soldiers staged a provocative incident at the Lukouchiao (Marco Polo) bridge near the old imperial capital of Peking – or Peiping as it was known at the time. The episode was probably not part of a premeditated plan of aggression but it was nevertheless seized upon by the Japanese army as the pretext for launching a large-scale invasion of China. In the initial onslaught the Japanese swept all before them. By the end of the month Chinese forces were compelled to withdraw from Peking and soon afterwards from Tientsin.

A month later the war shifted to Shanghai. On this front the initiative for the outbreak of hostilities was taken by the Chinese. At a council of war on 7 August Chiang Kai-shek and his chief military advisers decided to launch a counter-offensive at Shanghai. Their reasons were both military and political. They believed that their great local superiority in numbers over the Japanese would enable them to score a swift, dramatic victory in Shanghai; and they further hoped that warfare within sight of the foreign concessions would arouse the sympathy, perhaps even the intervention, of the foreign powers. On 11 August Chiang moved three crack divisions to the city. Large-scale fighting erupted two days later when about 80,000 Chinese troops attacked the Japanese garrison of 5,000 men.

During the first few days of the battle in Shanghai the Japanese were almost driven into the Whangpoo, but they soon recovered ground when reinforcements arrived. On 23 August thousands of infantry and marines under General Matsui Iwane landed near the city. Altogether in the course of the fighting in Shanghai the Japanese ferried in 90,000 troops who confronted a Chinese force that eventually numbered over 300,000. The Japanese made up for their inferiority in manpower by superior tactics, training and equipment. The guns of the Japanese Third Fleet, moored in the Whangpoo, pounded the Chinese-held districts of the city mercilessly. The climax of the battle came at the end of October when a lone battalion of 800 Chinese set up defensive positions in Chapei and stood their ground for four days against a devastating Japanese barrage. Estimates of Chinese casualties ranged from 100,000 to as many as 250,000. Whatever the exact number, the Chinese lost the cream of their officer corps; their most effective fighting units were decimated. The Japanese lost about 40,000 men.

On 10 November the mayor of the Chinese municipality convened a defiant press conference, promising a fight to the death. Before dawn the next day, he fled in an aeroplane in which, so it was said, he had stowed his large stock of gold bars. The Japanese proceeded to occupy the whole of the Chinese municipality, celebrating their triumph with a victory parade. General Matsui insisted on exercising the right to march his men through the International settlement. They were prevented from continuing into the French Concession only by a show of strength by the French garrison.

The foreign concessions remained relatively intact during the battle, 'like a postage stamp with the edges torn off', as a French journalist put it.[1] In the settlement the Volunteer Corps had been mobilized on 12 August in response to Chinese military actions seen as threatening the integrity of the district. But the corps remained on the sidelines throughout the ensuing campaign which was fought almost entirely outside the foreign enclaves. The brutality of the war nevertheless reached into the very heart of the settlement in a horrific manner. On 14 August Chinese warplanes attempted to bomb the flagship of the Japanese China Seas Fleet, *Idzumo*, stationed on the Whangpoo, opposite the Bund. Four bombs missed their target and landed instead on the nearby city streets. Two exploded on Nanking Road, Shanghai's most crowded thoroughfare, two others in front of the Great World Amusement Centre on Avenue Edward VII at the border between the concession and the settlement. The bombs caused mayhem, scattering dead bodies and limbs in all directions. An estimated 2,000 shoppers and passers-by were killed.

The battle of Shanghai had further catastrophic effects on the city. Destruction of property was massive, particularly in Chapei. In a letter home at the end of December an American resident described some of the physical damage:

Shanghai has changed greatly. While all sand bags are removed from the Bund and from most of the downtown streets, barbed-wire entanglements are still around, in short, portable lengths, that can be put in place quickly at almost any street intersection. On the perimeter of the settlement and Concession not only do barricades and entanglements remain in place, but all posts are manned still, day and night ... I have seen a part of the destruction in Chapei ... south of Soochow Creek. No devastation that I saw in France [during the First World War] was more complete. I have seen the same thing in Nantao from Siccawei Road, within the Concession. It is not good to look at.[2]

The immediate economic consequences of the fighting were disastrous. The value of Shanghai's foreign trade fell by 76 per cent between July and December. Even after the conflict in the city itself ended, Shanghai's waterborne connections with the 'outports' higher up the Yangtse continued to be disrupted, causing a further decline in trade in 1938. Japanese requisitions in the fertile Yangtse delta near the city raised the price of rice, leading to food riots. Many Chinese industrial enterprises were moved wholesale to the interior of China. Others sought the protective umbrella of foreign flags and moved to the concession or the settlement.

The foreign enclaves also became havens to hundreds of thousands of refugees from elsewhere in the city and from the war in the interior. An American newspaper correspondent compared the influx to birds fleeing from a storm or 'creatures of the forest ... from some major catastrophe which they sense':

They came in seemingly endless streams – in motor cars, buses, trucks, handcarts, wheelbarrows, rickshaws, on foot. The weak and aged and very young were carried on the backs or in the arms of others. Babies were packed into baskets which swung from the carrying poles over the shoulders of coolies. Boys of eleven or twelve struggled with the burden of their aged grandmothers ... A million destitute refugees settled down over the foreign settlements in a vast swarm and took possession. Every nook and corner which could receive man, woman or child was occupied. They sank down on the grassplots and landscaped flower gardens of the Bund. Every doorway, window ledge, vacant bit of ground, alleyway in the downtown districts was appropriated ... They even invaded the coffin shops which sprang up like mushrooms, and slept at nights in the wooden coffins.[3]

In November 1937 Father Jacquinot de Basange, a 'tall, gaunt, bulbous-nosed Catholic priest, who had lost an arm fighting Germans in the Great War',[4] established a neutral 'Refugee Safety Zone' in the Nantao district next to the concession. The *mutilé de guerre* was quite fearless in the face of armed men: he would use his wooden arm to knock Japanese soldiers on the head.[5] A quarter of a million refugees soon took shelter there as Catholic relief organizations, the International Red Cross and the Red Swastika Society struggled against impossible odds to care for them.

The battle of Shanghai strengthened the *de facto* authority of the Japanese in Hongkew and adjacent areas in the north-east corner of the settlement above the Soochow Creek. Altogether they now exercised effective control over more than half the area of the settlement. The Garden Bridge, which formed the main link across the creek between the Japanese-occupied area and the rest of the settlement, was heavily guarded by Japanese troops and became a virtual frontier post. Until February 1938 the 'Japanese Concession' was virtually sealed off. After that Chinese residents were allowed passage on a limited basis. But Chinese and foreigners alike who attempted to cross the bridge were subjected to humiliating searches and occasional ill-treatment by Japanese guards.

In late November 1937 the conquerors established a new government for the Chinese municipality. This was reorganized in April 1938 as the 'Special Municipality of Shanghai'. For the next four years the contiguous foreign concessions, surrounded and threatened by hostile forces, became a solitary island in the sea of Japanese occupation.

Following their victory in Shanghai, the Japanese swept through much of eastern China, conquering the capital, Nanking, on 12 December. The victors sacked the city, indulging in massacre, looting and rape on a horrifying scale. More than 40,000 Chinese civilians were slaughtered and 20,000 women were raped. Even the Japanese commander, General Matsui, felt ashamed and later retired to a temple to do penance.

The Chinese government, hoping, in Chiang Kai-shek's phrase, to 'trade space for time', fled first to Hankow, later to the remote western city of Chungking, some 1,600 miles west of Shanghai, where they maintained a shaky semblance of national sovereignty.

In 1938 the Japanese advance resumed: in October they captured Canton and Hankow. Thereafter a stalemate developed. It endured for the next six years. The Chinese regrouped and changed their strategy. They adopted a more cautious defensive posture, while harassing the enemy with guerrilla attacks behind the lines, particularly in the countryside, where Japanese control was far from total. But the Chinese army was rent by factional disputes and the rivalries of regional warlords. Moreover, behind the facade of a united front against Japan, Chinese resistance was hampered by the long-standing antagonism and suspicion between the Kuomintang government of Chiang Kai-shek and the communist forces in Yenan commanded by Mao Tse-tung. The Japanese, enjoying great aerial superiority, gained Ichang in June 1940. In October 1941 they succeeded in crossing the Yellow River though they were driven back later in the year. By late 1941 about a quarter of the land area of China proper (excluding, that is, such regions as Tibet) lay behind Japanese lines. The occupied lands included most of China's industry, her greatest cities and her richest agricultural provinces.

At first the Japanese were uncertain how to govern their newly-acquired territories. In December 1937 they established a 'Provisional Government of China' at Peking (the city's old name was restored under the occupation). In March 1938 they sponsored another puppet régime, the 'Reformed Government' at Nanking. But they accorded formal recognition to neither government, treating both with contempt. A more serious effort at the formation of a collaborationist régime was made by a prominent Kuomintang politician, Wang Ching-wei, who eventually succeeded in March 1940 in establishing a new Chinese administration at Nanking. Its authority was also tenuous and its area of administrative power undetermined. The Japanese did not formally recognize it until the following November. The relationships of Wang and other Chinese collaborationists with the Japanese were complex and often far from harmonious. Many Chinese warlords pursued ambiguous policies, shifting with the wind of military expediency.

The lines between Japanese-controlled and 'free' China were fuzzy through much of the war. The vast size of the country defeated Japanese attempts to impose an economic blockade against the nationalist-held areas. Commerce between occupied and unoccupied China continued at a brisk pace. Chinese capitalists in Shanghai often traded with the Japanese and with Chungking simultaneously. Remarkably, a letter posted in Japanese-occupied areas would generally reach Chungking and vice versa.

Guerrilla attacks on the Japanese in the countryside around Shanghai continued throughout 1938 and 1939. In the city, resistance to the Japanese and their Chinese collaborators took the form of terrorist and counter-terrorist violence. Among the many victims was the pro-Japanese mayor of the Chinese municipality of Shanghai, assassinated in October 1940 by members of the semi-fascist Blue Shirt society. Reciprocal killings of pro- and anti-Japanese citizens led local wags to suggest that 'the Shanghai equivalent of the Biblical eye for an eye was a "banker for a banker, an editor for an editor"'.[6]

Some 150 such murders between 1937 and 1941 were laid at the door of the Chinese government's Military Bureau of Investigation and Statistics. Its head, General Tai Li, earned a sinister reputation for dark, behind-the-scenes political manipulation. An amalgam of secret police, espionage service and old-style Chinese brotherhood, his organization was connected with the Blue Shirt movement. Tai Li combined a moralistic puritanism (agents were forbidden to marry during the war or to gamble, smoke or play mah-jong) with a ruthless brutality towards deviants and enemies. Yet China's torturer-in-chief had an engaging smile and, when he chose, could charm foreign visitors. Journalists and diplomats often compared Tai Li's organization with the Gestapo but its chief's amiable mask earned him surprising accolades: 'Although I disapproved of nearly everything Tai Li did ... [as] the Himmler of China ... he was one of my warmest friends,' wrote

the British ambassador, Sir Archibald Clark Kerr.[7] Tai Li's underground
network remained a force to be reckoned with throughout the war. As time
went on, however, his capacity to project his organization deep into Japanese-occupied territories diminished. In October 1941 his Shanghai station
was blown up by agents of the Wang Ching-wei puppet régime and the station chief was captured.[8]

Although the British and American governments disapproved of Japanese actions in China, their citizens in Shanghai had mixed feelings. Some
vigorously denounced Japanese expansion, likening it to Nazi aggression in
Europe. But few Shanghailanders had much liking for the Kuomintang government. In the early stages of the Japanese invasion of China foreign businessmen in Shanghai clubs could be heard expressing the hope that the
Japanese would 'clean up the country'.[9]

Whatever the ambiguities of the Shanghailanders' response to the war in
general, British public opinion was outraged by Japanese attacks on British
targets in China. On 24 August 1937 Clark Kerr's predecessor, Sir Hughe
Knatchbull-Hugessen, was wounded when his car was attacked on the
Nanking-Shanghai road by Japanese aircraft. In December two British gunboats, HMS *Ladybird* and the *Bee*, were shelled on the Yangtse. Over the following two years the Japanese applied steadily growing pressure on British
interests in China, on the British-controlled customs, on railways and navigation rights – and on British supremacy in Shanghai.

As the nation with the largest investment stake in Shanghai, the British
had traditionally taken the lead in its defence. But the British government,
increasingly preoccupied with the menacing situation in Europe, could not
afford to risk large-scale military involvement in the Far East. They
therefore persisted in a policy of appeasement of Japan. In deference to
Japanese susceptibilities, the Shanghai Municipal Police suppressed anti-
Japanese activity in the settlement after July 1937. Anti-Japanese terrorists
were turned over to the Japanese. Chinese 'national salvation societies'
were suppressed. In October 1938 Clark Kerr, opposing the withdrawal of
one of the two remaining British battalions in Shanghai, reported that the
Japanese reaction to the Munich accord was that the British were 'prepared
to put up with almost any indignity rather than fight'.[10] But British military
planners had recognized for years that the settlement was indefensible

against any determined Japanese effort to occupy it. In May 1939 instructions to the remaining token British contingent of troops in Shanghai were 'not to resist' in the event of a Japanese attack on the settlement.[11] Meanwhile, Clark Kerr's warning turned out to be a prophecy when, in December 1938, the Japanese subjected the British concession in Tientsin to a humiliating siege. An Anglo-Japanese agreement over Tientsin in July 1939 constituted, in the eyes of many observers, a 'Far Eastern Munich'.

American policy was similar. When the USS *Panay* was sunk by the Japanese on the Yangtse in December 1937, American opinion was shocked. There were calls for retaliation. But the Japanese apologized and American policy reverted to isolationism. Admiral H.E. Yarnell, who was Commander-in-Chief of the US Asiatic Fleet, personally favoured a stronger American line, but he recognized that the Anglo-American position in Shanghai would be untenable in the event of a full-scale Japanese attack. In February 1939 he told a private gathering of British and American members of the Shanghai Municipal Council: 'Their [the Japanese] intention is to take over the settlement and they have boiled up a case ready for when the time comes … If they come in force we shall not try to stop them.'[12]

For the time being, the Japanese limited themselves to consolidating their control over the Chinese area of the city and attempting to extend their influence within the settlement by a mixture of intimidation and guile. They had long complained bitterly over their exclusion from real power in the government of the settlement. They could claim some quasi-democratic basis for their complaints in the relative population figures of foreigners. By 1935 more than half of the foreign population of the settlement was Japanese. Yet they held only two out of the nine foreign seats on the Municipal Council. To some extent they could hope to acquire dominance in the settlement by legitimate means in the course of time, since further growth in their population and property holdings was slowly but inexorably increasing their voting power in council elections. They were not, however, prepared to wait patiently.

British business leaders in the settlement, fearful that, even without a formal Japanese occupation, the area would by stages fall under Japanese control, began to weigh possible counter-measures. One device for thwarting Japanese ambitions that they considered – and eventually adopted – was manipulation of the complex voting system for the Municipal Council. Many of the British ratepayers represented large business interests which, if legally separated into small parcels, could multiply their votes. In April 1939, therefore, the London head office of the major British trading firm Butterfield & Swire wrote to its Shanghai representative: 'If the British landowners do not take the necessary steps to divide up their votes as the Japanese are doing, the latter will soon dominate the Council by constitutional means. We have no doubt you are doing your best to drive this in.'[13] The following month the firm's Shanghai representative wrote back that it was 'safe to assume' that the Japanese were aiming at 'control of the entire administration'. The appeasing tendency and atmosphere of pessimism among British taipans was evident in the proposal made in the same letter that 'a form of gentleman's agreement might be reached for dividing the settlement into a series of wards or parishes, each with its own small committee of administration, but acting in collaboration with the central authority of the Council proper.' The hope was that such a quasi-partition of the settlement would 'allow the Japanese to retain a fairly important measure of influence in the Northern areas' and might enable the British to 'suspend the inevitable consequences of the operation of the present franchise until such time as we are in a better position to negotiate a new constitution'. 'With the Japs?', was the marginal comment added by a recipient at the London office next to the words 'gentleman's agreement'.[14] The proposal was not adopted but it was a sign of the gradual loss of confidence of the British business class in the city.

The Achilles' heel of the settlement lay in the Western Extension Roads district. These roads had been constructed over the years by the Municipal Council and were patrolled by the Municipal Police. The area, comprising 7,640 acres, just outside the settlement boundary, had a foreign population of more than 10,000. Many of Shanghai's wealthiest foreign residents owned luxurious homes in the district. Although outside the settlement, they paid local taxes to the council under penalty of suspension of power and water supplies in the event of default.

Following the withdrawal of Chinese nationalist forces from Shanghai in November 1937, the Japanese sponsored the creation of a Chinese police force in the Western Roads area, which was placed under the control of the puppet municipality. Offices for tax collection on behalf of the puppet authorities were also set up. Plans for the further exploitation of the zone moved into high gear when, in late 1938, the Japanese general-politician, Doihara Kenji, famous for his exploits in Manchuria, held a conference in Shanghai with renegades from the Chinese secret service. This resulted in the creation in early 1939 of a security apparatus designed to terrorize Shanghai into submission. With Japanese help, Wang Ching-wei's movement set up a police headquarters at 76 Jessfield Road in the Western Roads area in July 1939. The building became a virtual fortress and its interrogation chambers and torture apparatus acquired a dark celebrity.

A Municipal Police report described the transformation of the Western Roads district:

> From February 1938 gambling dens commenced to spring up on the extra-Settlement roads, established by Chinese loafer leaders with the assistance of Japanese of like character, while Hwo Wei Lottery, much favoured by the lower class of Chinese, became rife. In May of the same year the Japanese Military established a Shanghai Amusement Supervision Department in the area under the charge of a Japanese for the collection of a daily 'protection' fee from the gambling houses.
>
> Opium dens and shops retailing this drug were later established under the guidance of the Japanese authorities, each paying a monthly levy to the Japanese, monopoly for the supply of the drug being held by the Special Service Section of the Japanese Military, with a Japanese advisor to the local Japanese-sponsored government in charge.
>
> As Japanese control over the Western area became more complete, so conditions deteriorated until the district became the haunt of every type of undesirable character and a haven of armed robbers who did not hesitate to fire on the Municipal Police whenever opportunity presented itself.[15]

By late 1939 the Western Roads area was estimated to harbour 24 gambling dens, 200 Hwo Wei Lottery dens, 42 opium hongs and 100 opium smoking dens.[16] Some of the drug and gambling establishments boasted large private armies. For example, the 'Hollywood' opium and heroin hong, located on property belonging to Wang Ching-wei, claimed to have 400 armed guards. It operated 24 hours a day.

The heavy involvement of the Japanese and their collaborators in the drug trade ended the reign of the Green Gang chieftain, Tu Yueh-sheng, over the Shanghai narcotics industry. In November 1937 he found himself humiliatingly driven out of business and out of town by the racketeers protected by the Japanese. He retreated to Kuomintang-held China and ostensibly devoted himself to good works as head of the Chinese Red Cross. His less patriotic successors were cast in a different mould. One was later described in an American intelligence report as 'a 300-odd pound gangster [who] made his headquarters in the New Asia Hotel in Hongkew where he used the bathroom for the decapitation of Chinese who refused to play ball with the conquerors and puppets'.[17]

Japanese political pressure on the settlement meanwhile increased. In November 1937 they succeeded in installing censors in the Chinese Telegraph Administration offices in the settlement. In January 1938 they took over the Wireless Administration, the foreign cable offices and the Chinese Post Office.

The Japanese also sought to win control of Chinese newspapers in the foreign enclaves. Before the war Shanghai had been the broadcasting and press centre of the Far East. Its newspapers, both Chinese and foreign, had enjoyed relative freedom from censorship in the settlement. The only exceptions were those suspected of communist leanings. In early 1938 the Municipal Council gave way to some extent and placed restrictions on the press. But they resisted Japanese efforts to achieve full control. The problem became acute as anti-Japanese newspapers and magazines moved from occupied areas of the city to the settlement or the French Concession. Chinese publishers managed to circumvent the new limitations by registering their papers under the names of sympathetic foreign front men. The comparative freedom of press and broadcasting in the settlement between 1937 and 1941 infuriated the Japanese and they used every possible means, including violence, to suppress hostile propaganda. Many newspaper offices were bombed several times.

Such outbreaks of anti-Japanese terrorism in the course of 1938 led to Japanese calls for resolute police counter-action and a renewal of their long-standing demand for greater Japanese participation in the Municipal Police, particularly at senior levels. The British and Americans drew the line at this. 'Our view', the American councillor Norwood Allman later wrote, 'was that we had an adequate force, nor would we fire anyone to make room for a Jap.'[18] The (British) Commissioner of Police had put it more diplomatically in a submission to the Municipal Council some years earlier:

> The fact that the administrative control of the force and its
> general working has been in the hands of British officers since
> its inception to the present day has given a deep-rooted
> character to the force that cannot be altered now without
> creating complications, which are more likely than not to
> react adversely on the well-being of the force ... The Japanese
> branch is of very recent origin ... Members of the Japanese
> branch do not readily submit to control by members of the
> foreign branch ... Members of the other branches definitely
> resent control by Japanese officers mainly because they have
> not been accustomed to it.

As an expression of axiomatic conservativism this could hardly be bettered. Lest he be suspected of imperialist or racial arrogance, the commissioner added that if the situation were reversed, and the British were now seeking to displace long-established Japanese officers, 'I should give the same answer as I do now.' Yet he drew a racial distinction when he argued:

> The present senior police officers in the council's service are
> solely the council's servants. I doubt if any Japanese officer
> can be the free agent of the council, however ardently he may
> wish to be so, and therefore the position of a Japanese officer
> in one of the key posts would be a difficult one.'[19]

Given the traditionally close relationship between the head of the Municipal Police Special Branch and the local representative of the British Secret Intelligence Service, the implication that British, unlike Japanese, officers were above national loyalties was, to say the least, disingenuous.

In March 1939 an 'understanding' was reached between the Japanese Gendarmerie and the Municipal Council whereby the council promised that the settlement police would cooperate with the Japanese in the detection of terrorism. The Council announced that it had recruited 45 new Japanese policemen that year and that 'it was already taking steps to bring the Japanese branch up to budget's strength by obtaining 33 more recruits from Japan'. The press communiqué added that the police commissioner was 'prepared to give sympathetic attention to the suggestion of placing a senior Japanese officer with several selected Japanese subordinates in a composite section within the present framework of the crime branch' but denied press reports 'that officers of the Japanese Gendarmerie are to be established in Shanghai Municipal Police stations'.[20] For all their confident demeanour, however, British officials in Shanghai were conscious that they were standing on quicksand.

上海

Two years after the outbreak of the Sino-Japanese war, China's leading city seemed half-dead. The English poets W. H. Auden and Christopher Isherwood, who visited Shanghai in May 1939, described the foreign concessions as:

> an island, an oasis in the midst of the stark, frightful
> wilderness which was once the Chinese city. Your car crosses
> the Soochow Creek: on one side are streets and houses,
> swarming with life; on the other is a cratered and barren
> moon-landscape, intersected by empty, clean-swept roads ...
> formidable, excluded watchdogs, the real masters of Shanghai
> inhabit the dark, deserted Japanese Concession, or roam the
> lunar wilderness of Chapei, looking down hungrily upon the
> lighted, populous, international town ... In this city –
> conquered, yet unoccupied by its conquerors – the

mechanism of the old life is still ticking, but seems doomed to stop, like a watch dropped in the desert.[21]

Yet all the while, as the visible military and political struggle continued in this urban wasteland, another kind of war was being waged by shadowy figures in the city's nether regions.

2 Bad Hats

If, as an American diplomat allegedly once said, gentlemen do not read each other's mail, then Shanghai was no gentlemen's club. There is evidence that in the period before the outbreak of the Pacific War Japanese intelligence penetrated the British and American consulates and captured coded materials. At the same period the Italians appear to have gained access to the Japanese Naval Headquarters in Shanghai and were intercepting its communications. Meanwhile the British wireless monitoring station, headed by James H. Smart, was reading radiotelegrams on the Shanghai-Berlin and Mukden-Berlin circuits. German military signals traffic was decrypted by the British and passed on to the United States.[1] In addition, Soviet activities, mainly organized through the local office of the TASS news agency, were monitored by the Japanese and the British. And all of the above were closely observed by the ubiquitous agents of Tai Li.

In the late 1930s the Japanese greatly expanded their security operations in Shanghai. Several Japanese intelligence bodies functioned in the city, gathering information on Chinese nationalists and communists as well as on the activities of other foreign powers in Shanghai. The most important Japanese secret organization was the Naval Intelligence Bureau – reflecting the primacy of the navy among Japanese organs in the city. The army's Second Department was also active and the Foreign Ministry established its own agency, the Special Investigation Unit. This worked under the aegis of the Consulate-General in Shanghai and was responsible for gathering and analyzing intelligence from all over China. It had a staff of more than 60 Japanese and a network of Chinese agents throughout the country.

In their choice of European agents in Shanghai, the Japanese displayed an astonishing lack of discrimination – or from another point of view a supreme realism. Many of their employees were well-known figures in the Shanghai underworld. One such recruit to the Japanese cause was an unemployed soldier of fortune whose activities, even before his arrival in the

Far East, had engaged the interest of the British authorities.

Hilaire du Berrier was born in 1906 of Franco-American parentage in Flasher, North Dakota. A gregarious and, to some eyes, attractive young man, he combined the promiscuous sociability of a billy-goat with the predatory viciousness of a rattlesnake. According to his own later account, he 'studied art, journalism, [and] aviation in America' and in 1931 moved to Paris where he joined the monarchist-fascist Action Française movement. At about that time his mother died, leaving him a substantial amount of money which he used for a while as a financial safety cushion.[2] Over the next few years Berrier dabbled in self-promoting literary activity and prowled on the fringes of respectable society.

The Shanghai Municipal Police Special Branch ascertained that Berrier had flown for the Negus (Emperor) of Abyssinia in the war against the Italians in 1935–36 'as pilot of reconnaissance and bombing planes'. (The plural may have been an exaggeration since the Imperial Abyssinian Air Force at the time is said to have consisted of exactly one aeroplane.) Berrier boasted of having been awarded the Star of Ethiopia and the Order of St George and the Dragon in Abyssinia. He also claimed to have served as 'chief of protocol and advisor to H. H. Yissaf, Nawaub of Tygre'. At the beginning of the Spanish Civil War in the summer of 1936 Berrier was reported to have joined the Republican government's air force 'and took part in many air fights and skirmishes against fascist machines'.[3]

In October 1936 Guy Liddell, a senior officer of MI5, the British internal security agency, informed the Home Office of the recent arrival in London of 'one Hilaire du Berrier, describing himself as an American journalist' and 'giving as his address Barclays Bank, 1 Pall Mall'. Two days after reaching London, Berrier wrote to the Air Ministry inquiring about the possibility of purchasing aircraft. He gave as a reference 'Barclays Bank, Monte Carlo'. The Air Ministry suspected Berrier of seeking warplanes to be used in the Civil War in Spain. His inquiry appears to have received no answer.[4]

Berrier had been well paid for his service in both the Abyssinian and the Spanish air forces. Leaving London, he embarked on travels (again according to his own account) to 'Central Europe and the Balkans, representing [a] Dutch aircraft firm'. A few months later, Berrier turned up in Shanghai.

He now gave his profession as 'aviator' rather than journalist. The Municipal Police Special Branch reported:

> Nothing can be learned locally of his background save that he is conversant with the Gaelic tongue, but he is regarded by a number of people who came in contact with him here as a very reserved type of person of charming disposition with the breeding of a gentleman.

The Special Branch could find out nothing about his political beliefs and concluded that his motivations were financial rather than ideological: 'It would seem that du Berrier is a mercenary adventurer who is prepared to sell his qualities as an aviator to the highest bidder.'[5] These suspicions were well founded. The picture of du Berrier that emerges from the Special Branch reports is of a peculiarly nasty example of the species of political adventurer, many of whom were drawn to Shanghai at this period.

Berrier's initial purpose in coming to China seems to have been to try to sell aeroplanes – though he met with little success in this enterprise. In letters to his sister in America in the summer of 1937, he complained of being at a loose end in China:

> The trouble is trying to decide who to tie up with. My old friend, Colonel Schmidt, who was with me in Addis Abeba, Paris, and Spain, once said: 'Make your friends on one side of the river, Hal, make them good and strong … ' Well, Schmitty was right, only the difficulty is knowing which side of the river. It's like a parachute jump. You have to be right the first time.[6]

A little later he wrote: 'I don't know what I'll be doing now, Helen, as our business here has flopped. We can sell the stuff alright, but they want it on credit – and the answer is "NO". I'm bored and looking for some excitement anyway.'[7] In his search for violent stimulation, Berrier had, it turned out, chosen a suitable landing-ground. A week after he wrote those words, fate obliged and provided him with what he craved: a small war – or so it seemed, at any rate at the outset.

Having failed to find any cash buyers for planes, Berrier decided to return to Europe. On 13 July 1937 he boarded the Japanese liner *Haruna Maru* as a second-class passenger. His ticket was booked through to London. As he bought the ticket, Berrier remarked, 'Well! I shall have to watch out when the steamer calls at Naples, for if the Italians know I am on board they will come and drag me off and put me up against a wall.' Perhaps sobered by this prospect or, alternatively, sensing new opportunities as a result of the outbreak of the Sino-Japanese War a few days earlier, Berrier disembarked at Hong Kong and returned to the Chinese mainland. Shortly afterwards he volunteered to join the Chinese air force which was seeking trained pilots to confront the Japanese.

In desperate military straits, the Chinese were willing to turn to anyone for assistance in the air. From the autumn of 1937 until mid-1938 the USSR rotated four fighter and two bomber squadrons of 'volunteer' airmen in China who engaged in combat missions for the Chinese air force. They were some help but their numbers were limited and their loyalty suspect. The Chinese air force, like all branches of the government, was riddled with corruption and inefficiency. Nor did Chiang Kai-shek's appointment of his wife as head of the force do much to restore morale. Later in the course of the conflict, the American Claire Chennault served as the real air force chief but his famous 'Flying Tigers' unit of American volunteers did not arrive until September 1941. Hence the readiness of the Chinese in the autumn of 1937 to turn to adventurers such as Berrier.

Berrier's tour of duty was short-lived. Not long after he enlisted, his plane crashed at Hankow. He sustained a minor knee injury and decided to give up flying for the time being. At any rate, that was the version told in Shanghai. In an account of his activities he sent to his sister some time later, Berrier admitted what was probably the real reason for the sudden end to his service: 'Charged with being a Japanese spy, was sacrificed in a typical Chinese political passe-passe in Hankow, November 1937, and dismissed from Central Government service. Barely escaped from the interior.'[8]

On his return to Shanghai, Berrier was closely watched by the Municipal Police who reported that he 'expressed considerable resentment at the treatment – in the monetary sense – meted out to him by the Central Government Air Force'. The report continued:

However he still appears to be in possession of ample funds as may be exemplified by the fact that he recently gave a large dinner party at the French Club; among the guests were such well known persons as Vice Admiral Le Bigot [of the French Navy] and Mr M. Speelman, director of the International Savings Society. Nevertheless, it is learned from a reliable source that du Berrier has cabled to the Paris office of Barclay's Bank (Dominion, Colonial and Overseas) Ltd., requesting the remittance of further funds.

Meanwhile, Berrier's political views seemed to be swinging back from left to right, since he now expressed regret for his support for the Republican cause in Spain and declared 'in no uncertain terms that, as a result of his own experiences in Spain when fighting for the "Loyalists", he considered it a great pity that France and Great Britain had not assisted General Franco in his campaign against the "Leftist" Government'.[9]

Although he had no ostensible source of earned income, Berrier maintained a luxurious lifestyle. He lodged first at the Metropole Hotel and then at the Cathay Mansions. He was photographed at the French Club, where he attended a dinner as guest of the prominent French advocate Baron Auxion de Ruffe. In a letter to his sister, Berrier noted that the lawyer was an aristocrat and further promoted him to the non-existent position of 'mayor of the French Concession'.[10] Fascinated by titles, he decided to adopt one himself and added the handle 'Count' to his name. A little later, he had private notepaper printed bearing his monogram and – as if to suggest even higher rank – a coronet.[11]

By early 1938 Berrier's continued affluence was ascribed to a sinister source. The Municipal Police reported that he had become friendly with an agent of the Japanese Intelligence Service, Fred Vernon Wagner.[12] He was further said to have obtained Chinese aeronautical information, which he passed on to the Japanese, including plans of aerodromes and details of the location of Chinese bases and aircraft.[13] Life as a spy seemed to affect Berrier's nerves. He wrote to his sister:

It's hot, I'm tired. Shanghai is full of jews, japs, and gunmen, and it's about a toss-up which are worse. Law and order have gone with the winds and gambling joints and opium dives have taken their place. Shanghai has gone mad; everybody hippity-hoppin riotously down the primrose path and running debts to the skies, because tomorrow the whole works may go up in smoke taking banks, book-keeping systems and over-drafts with it.[14]

Berrier's mental agitation was, perhaps, hardly surprising, given the dangerous nature of his new political alignment.

An anonymous memorandum in the confidential files of the Municipal Police Special Branch records the next phase of Berrier's Shanghai career. The document bears no date but was probably written some time in 1939. Berrier, it appears, had now joined the Japanese puppet movement headed by Wang Ching-wei:

International Secret Service Organized by
Wang Ching-wei's Group in Shanghai

Mr Wang Ching-wei's traitorous campaign in this part of China is becoming internationalized according to exclusive information secured from a reliable foreign source in close touch with the situation. Mr Chow Fu-hai, formerly minister of propaganda of Central Kuomintang headquarters and a trusted agent of Mr Wang Ching-wei, had been active in Shanghai for the past three months, as previously reported. He organized for Mr Wang's campaign a secret service network in Shanghai and entrusted the job to a Mr Liu Shou-kwei, alias Gen. Liu Hai-cheng, a military man from Szechuen. This Gen. Liu is reported to have drawn a subsidy of $400,000 per month from the various gambling dens in the west district of Shanghai through special arrangements made by the Japanese Special Service Organ. It is also learned that several of Mr Wang Ching-wei's leading subordinates have also invested heavily in these gambling houses, hence the subsidy. Another Cantonese called Mr Chu Ting collects money from these gambling houses for Gen. Liu regularly. With this huge amount of money, Gen. Liu is maintaining a force of 900 Chinese and foreign agents engaged in various kinds of secret activities ...

My foreign informant, after mixing with this group, found out that Mr Li has under him a big number of foreign agents, among whom there are a Ing. Nino J. Brondello, an Italian air officer, a Count du Berrier, a French munition salesman, a Mr Wright, a Canadian young man and a certain German staying at the Palace Hotel. Their secret headquarters are at Mr Li's residence situated at Flat D21, Sun Court Apartments, 621 Weihaiwei Road. But these first three foreigners have their own quarters somewhere at Route Père Robert. My informant believes that these foreigners, besides doing intelligence service for Mr Wang Ching-wei, also purchase arms and munitions for their leader. Their houses are well guarded with armed men and they carry pistols with them wherever they go. They claim that they have good connections with both the SMP [Shanghai Municipal Police] and FMP [French Municipal Police], that is why they are able to get licences for their pistols from the police. Mr Brondello told my informant that Mr Wang Ching-wei is receiving a subsidy of $5,000,000 from the Japanese every month. From the observations made by my informant it is believed that these men are also engaged in the assassination of Wang Ching-wei's enemies. At least they are preparing to do so.

Mr Li Lien-fang is reported to have decided to send Mr Wright to Hankow, Count du Berrier to Nanking and Ing. Brondello to Wuhu for important mission[s]. They are to help in 'reconstruction' of these cities, Mr Li said.

My informant is working hard to find out the whole situation as she has the trust of these foreigners. If she has the necessary backing, it is believed that she will be able to unearth a most alarming story of international significance.[15]

The obscure provenance of this document might tempt one to dismiss it as an unproven anonymous denunciation, typical of many that reached the Shanghai police at this period – were it not that its essential elements are corroborated by Berrier himself.

In a letter to his sister in May 1939, Berrier confirmed the connection with Brondello – 'just come out from Abyssinia. (We never argue about it.)' He also referred to a friend of the Italian, 'a rich divorcee who sends her car for him every day', on whom Berrier and another foreign friend called for 'tiffin' – much to the annoyance of Brondello.[16] Was this unnamed woman perhaps the mysterious female informant referred to in the Special Branch report?

More first-hand evidence of Berrier's activities is available in a memorandum, written by Berrier in 1941 for the 'family record', in which Berrier boasted of his accomplishments as an adventurer. This confirms that he had decided to ignore the advice of his old friend 'Schmitty' and to cross to the other 'side of the river'. According to this account, Berrier was appointed 'Lieutenant-General and Chief of Staff for Air under General Yeh Pang in the army of Wang Ching-wei'. The rank, like other titles awarded by Berrier to himself, can probably be dismissed as self-aggrandizing fiction, but his confession that he had switched from the anti- to the pro-Japanese side in the war may be taken at face value. Berrier added, however, that he resigned his position with Wang 'at the end of one year', explaining that decision as follows:

> The rumour of espionage is enough to ruin a soldier all over
> the world, even though the rumour is only the idle concoction
> of anti-foreign Chinese in a little Yangtse village. American
> consulates and intelligence services lent their efforts to
> proving the Japanese were right. All efforts to rise again were
> frustrated in China.'[17]

With his service in the Japanese puppet regime's air force at an end, du Berrier was reported by the Shanghai Municipal Police (which monitored his activities closely) to be enjoying the society of a squalid circle of Axis agents and sympathizers in Shanghai.

上海

Among Berrier's early acquaintances in this arena was another foreign adventurer with whom he came to share business interests and leisure activities. Dr Albert von Miorini was a well-established Shanghai physician. A specialist in gynaecology, he had left Vienna several years earlier, after carrying out a botched abortion. Miorini prospered in his new milieu, setting up residence in a luxurious apartment with a rooftop garden at 934 Bubbling Well Road. The doctor was a keen photographer, traveller and sportsman. A lover of music, he hosted soirées when he played the cello with members of the Shanghai Symphony Orchestra. He also participated in amateur theatricals: in 1940 he both directed and acted in the play *He is Not Jealous*. The *Ostasiatischer Lloyd* gave the production a rave review, congratulating Miorini on the 'effervescent gaiety' he brought to the piece.[18]

Behind the cultivated mask lay a poisonous character. According to a post-war American intelligence report, Miorini was 'suspected very strongly of illegal abortions, dope peddling, and specializing in cure for venereal diseases … Said to be a collector of intelligence items. He is technically a good surgeon, but an unpleasant personality.'[19]

A man of broad tastes, Miorini cultivated not only political and cultural but also commercial, narcotic and sexual pursuits. In 1933 he was reported to be involved with a group known as the Spider Club, which installed a gambling den at a rented house at 72 West End Gardens. According to a police report, the society:

> was nothing more than a rendezvous where wealthy foreigners
> and Chinese met to drink, dance, take drugs etc. These
> meetings often ended in orgies. Dr Miorini … introduced
> many female visitors to the Club. It was also reported at that
> time that Dr Miorini met at the club many Chinese interested
> in drug trafficking on a large scale with whom he dealt later in
> the privacy of his office.[20]

In 1936 Miorini had been implicated in a case of murder in the French Concession: a Municipal Police report stated that he was 'strongly rumoured' to have 'administered a poisonous injection … at the instigation of [a] gang of international drug traffickers with whom Miorini was affiliated ... Although no direct evidence could be obtained to substantiate this rumour there was every reason to believe that [it] contained the truth.'[21]

Miorini lived with a Eurasian woman, Ruby Edwards. The wife of an Englishman, she spoke excellent English. According to the Municipal Police, she was 'morally unscrupulous and acts as a procuress who obtained young Chinese girls for Miorini's pleasure in addition to acting as his interim mistress'.[22] Miorini supported not only her but also her husband and children. By all accounts a man of strong sexual urges, the doctor was accused by a female employee of 'overwhelming' her. The woman was paid off, but on this and other accounts Miorini was refused admission to the German Medical Association in Shanghai.

Miorini's intelligence connections probably dated back at least to early 1939 when he embarked on a trans-Asiatic motor journey from Palestine to Shanghai. American intelligence later concluded that as of April 1939 he was working:

> for the Jap. Sp[ecial] Service Corps and his job is to lure
> wealthy Chinese into their hands to be held for ransom ...
> Miorini brings his Chinese victims to a high-class gambling
> house established by Cpt. Kuwahata on the corner of Haining
> and North Chekiang Rd. and from there they are spirited
> away.[23]

Notwithstanding his varied criminal activities, Miorini never faced prosecution and was said to enjoy a considerable reputation as a doctor.

Another member of Miorini's circle was his oldest and dearest friend, a bosom companion since medical school days in Vienna, Hermann Erben. An Austrian-American, Erben had enjoyed a colourful career, even before becoming a full-fledged player in the game of nations in Shanghai in 1941.[24] He was described in an FBI report as 'a strongly built, affable sort of fellow with hornrimmed glasses'.[25] Over 6 feet tall, he had blond hair, blue eyes, a ruddy complexion, a scar on his left cheek and another on his right thumb.

Erben was born in Vienna in 1897 and studied medicine at Vienna University but did not qualify with a degree. For a while he worked in Vienna as a doctor's assistant. In 1924 he won a Rockefeller Fellowship for study at the Psychiatric Institute for Medical Research in Morristown, New Jersey. He moved to the United States, acquiring American citizenship in San Francisco six years later. From 1926 onwards he lived a wandering life. For some years he worked as a ship's doctor on the American Dollar and President lines. In 1934 he visited New Guinea, following reports of the discovery of goldfields. While there he struck up an acquaintance with the Hollywood film star Errol Flynn. The two men subsequently 'bummed around together, travelling finally from New Guinea to India, to Abyssinia, and then to Vienna'.[26] In 1935 Erben took part in a trans-Asiatic motor expedition but was arrested in Calcutta on suspicion of opium smuggling; he was charged with possession of an unlicensed revolver and cartridges, fined 300 rupees and deported to the United States.

On 23 November that year the *New York Herald Tribune* reported his arrival in New York aboard the freighter *City of Rayville* in the company of 1,100 monkeys that he was importing from Calcutta. A further 100 monkeys had died en route. Erben had performed autopsies on the carcasses and preserved 30 of the skulls which he said had research value. Upon disembarkation in New York, he encountered some difficulties with the US customs authorities. Eventually he secured admission with his simian charges and took lodging at the Seamen's Annex of the YMCA. He left soon afterwards, following a difference over his bill.

In the course of the next few years, Erben travelled to Palestine, China, and north and south America. In 1936 he talked of going to Ethiopia to work in a Swedish Red Cross unit – but instead he visited Spain during the Civil War in the company of his friend Flynn. In 1937 he was reported 'to have been engaged in inciting a mutiny' aboard an American passenger liner, the SS *West Mahwah*, on which he was working. Although it was decided not to prosecute him, FBI inquiries revealed a pattern of bizarre behaviour aboard the ship: he had allegedly 'wiped his hands on the American flag after taking food from the ice box', had given a Nazi salute to a passing German ship, and had threatened anyone criticizing Adolf Hitler that he would 'crush and sink my teeth into his throat'.[27] Later that year he worked for a time for the Chinese government in a hospital in Nanking.

Erben joined the Nazi Party in May 1938, shortly after the Anschluss, receiving membership number 6,378,730. In November 1939 he obtained a passport from the German embassy in Buenos Aires and travelled to New York. He had meanwhile come under suspicion of espionage and was subjected to close surveillance by the FBI. Federal agents questioned several of Erben's acquaintances, including Flynn, who declared that Erben had 'a very brilliant mind' and was 'the type of person who would do everything in his power to make it appear that he was in fact an espionage agent'. Flynn added that Erben had a 'propensity for getting into trouble'. While vouching for Erben's uprightness of character, Flynn said that he often 'created a bad impression on those who did not know him very well'. The investigation report continues:

> As for being a German agent, he [Flynn] stated that Dr Erben
> would probably make the worst agent in the world for any
> nation, since they have the finger on him in every port of the
> world. He explained that by this he meant that in a great many
> places Dr Erben had been guilty of some minor infraction of
> local rules, such as not having the proper papers at the proper
> time, or saying the wrong thing at the wrong time.

The word that best described Erben, declared the film star, was 'screwball'.[28]

In January 1940 Leslie Farmer of the British Naval Control Service in Buenos Aires visited the US consulate-general in that city and said that 'the British intelligence service had information concerning Dr Erben's activities as a German agent, especially during the time he was on the Austro-American Trans-Asiatic Expedition'. He also said that the British considered Erben a 'bad man', although 'not as dangerous as he might be' because he 'talks too much'.[29] Erben first secured employment as a German agent in Mexico City in January 1941. At the German embassy there he received a new passport, made out in the name Alois Ecker, musician. Under this name, he travelled to Japan and presented himself at the German embassy in Tokyo, where the naval attaché instructed him to proceed to Shanghai.

Erben had visited Shanghai for the first time in 1928 in order to call on his 'classmate and lifelong friend' from Vienna, Miorini.[30] Miorini's criminal ventures were probably facilitated by his relationship of trust with Erben, who came under renewed suspicion of drug trafficking in the late 1930s and was closely watched on that account by the US authorities.

上海

In the summer of 1940 a fresh and exotic face enlivened this happy little society. The 'Princess' Sumaire, aged 22, stepped off a boat from India and reserved a suite at the Cathay Hotel. She immediately attracted attention on account of her elegant appearance, her scandalous behaviour and her mysterious origins. Within a short time Sumaire had won a wide, multinational circle of friends. Among them were Vicki Burkhardt ('Countess Victoria Lea') and her mother Mrs Oleaga, Hilaire du Berrier, the property tycoon Sir Victor Sassoon, officers of the local Italian garrison, a number of English and American society girls, the American journalist and gossipmonger Don Chisholm and a couple of professional dancers who went by the stage names 'Don and Dolly'. The princess was also 'seen constantly in the company of Helen Bascha', described in a police report as 'fairly attractive, usually drunk'.[31] A later American intelligence report pruriently observed that 'there is little doubt but that they were physically intimate'.[32] This 'comprehensive international circle of acquaintance' aroused the interest of the Municipal Police. Detective Sub-Inspector McKeown, whose special beat was Indian affairs, was assigned to report on the antecedents, activities, connections and intentions of the 'princess'.

McKeown reported that Sumaire claimed to be the daughter of the late Maharajah of Patiala. Her past life as well as her conduct during her stay in Shanghai made her in McKeown's judgement 'open to suspicion either on moral or political grounds'. After a few weeks in Shanghai, she went on holiday to the beach resort of Tsingtao. At the end of the summer she returned and took up residence at the Park Hotel, the most modern and sumptuously appointed in the city. A man described in McKeown's report as 'a prominent person in the local French community' – in fact, Berrier's friend the advocate Auxion de Ruffe – visited her in her suite at the Park. 'Finding that she was in very scanty negligée, he is supposed [as McKeown delicately put it] to have left immediately.' A strange sort of Frenchman this, to be scared away by the sight of a young woman *en déshabille*! As will be seen shortly, there may have been another reason for the lawyer's precipitate withdrawal.

Unable to decide whether her activities had any political significance, Detective McKeown kept Sumaire under observation and produced a second report. This stated that she had been married as a child to a senior official of the Indian State Railways but later separated from him. Her family were said to have disowned her 'owing to her loose morals'. From an Indian source McKeown ascertained that she was 'a follower of the Lesbian cult'.[33] The detective's findings were submitted to his superiors, who placed one copy in the confidential drawer and passed another on to Harry Steptoe, the British Secret Intelligence Service representative in Shanghai. Meanwhile, the 'princess' was kept under continued surveillance.

Who was Sumaire? Why had she come to Shanghai? Was she really a princess? The answers to these questions may be pieced together from subsequent Shanghai police reports as well as from evidence that became available as a result of post-war investigation of Sumaire's activities during the Japanese occupation.

Sumaire's full name was Rajkumari Sumair Apjit Singh. She was never a princess. She was indeed a member of the princely Patiala family, though the exact nature of her relationship to the Maharajah was never firmly established by the investigating authorities. That potentate himself, when told by a visitor that his daughter had been seen, asked 'Which one?' The visitor replied, 'A girl who calls herself Sumair claims to be your daughter.' Whereupon the Maharajah answered, 'It is quite possible. I have twenty-three daughters.'[34] One report had it that Sumaire was the Maharajah's illegitimate daughter and that he had had her legitimized shortly before his death in 1938. The Municipal Police concluded, after inquiries in India, that she was the Maharajah's niece. Detective McKeown, a stolid British policeman not given to sensationalism, added: 'Although she was the niece of the late Maharajah, she was probably his mistress also.'[35]

The Maharajahs of Patiala ruled a territory the size of Yorkshire. They ranked first in the order of precedence of rulers of native states in the Punjab and were entitled to a salute of 17 guns. The Maharajah was among the richest men in the world, with an annual revenue officially calculated in 1918 at £640,000. When he visited England in 1925 he took with him 200 pieces of luggage each stamped with his elephant coat of arms. One hundred rooms at the Savoy Hotel were engaged for him and his retinue. Three of his 20 motor cars were permanently ready outside the hotel in case he emerged.[36]

Sumaire was born in 1918. Little is known of her early life which was presumably spent in or near the princely seat, Motibagh Palace at Patiala. The family were Sikhs among whom arranged marriages at a young age were not uncommon. Sumaire was married, apparently in her early teens, to Sirdah Apjit Singh, an official of the Indian State Railways. The union was not a success and the couple soon separated. In about 1937 Sumaire travelled to England with her father. While there they quarrelled and as a result Sumaire severed relations with him and most other members of her family except her mother.

At the age of 20, in 1938, Sumaire was living in Paris with her mother. She worked there as a model for the fashion designer Elsa Schiaparelli. Meanwhile the old Maharajah died and was succeeded by his son Yodavindra Singh, a former All-India cricket captain. When the European war broke out in 1939, the young Maharajah ordered both Sumaire and her mother to return home. Sumaire did so, but her mother who was ill went to the United States.

The young woman did not adjust well to the sudden transition from the glamour of the French capital to the stuffy provincial atmosphere of Patiala. True, it too was a capital – 'sports capital of India', as a modern guidebook has it.[37] But polo and cricket, the stuff of conversation in the princely household, could hold little attraction for the ex-mannequin. No doubt what she wrote some years later was already true at this time: 'Excepting for my sentiments and emotions that are still so sensitively Oriental, I am in every sense of the word completely Westernized.'[38] When her mother wrote suggesting they meet in Los Angeles, Sumaire seized the opportunity to leave her native country. She set out by sea, arriving in Shanghai, as we have seen, in July 1940. Instead of rejoining her mother, however, she remained in the 'Paris of the East', relishing its cosmopolitan night life and lively café society.

By all accounts Sumaire was not conventionally beautiful. She had a podgy face and snub nose, and was somewhat short for a model. On the other hand she dressed elegantly in oriental-style robes and carried herself with poise and a certain dignity. She soon acquired the reputation of a nymphomaniac. Even the bellboys at the Park Hotel, it was said, were not safe from her attentions. Like a voracious spider, she attracted first one, then another, eventually a buzzing swarm of admirers who found that, once enmeshed, they could not escape.

Baron Auxion de Ruffe was one among her many conquests. Described as 'a tall, well-built man of imposing appearance', he was 65 years old at the time.[39] A war hero, collector of antiques and political writer, the baron had a number of published works to his name, including *Is China Mad?* (1928) and *Femmes d'Asie et d'ailleurs* (1929). In the 1930s he had often played a delicate role in negotiations among the French, the Japanese and local business/criminal interests. Following Berrier's arrival in Shanghai he had, as we have noticed, entertained the aviator at the French Club.

Auxion de Ruffe's reasons for getting involved with the Indian 'princess' remain unclear. Perhaps, on his part, it was a straightforward sexual liaison. Sumaire's interest in him, however, was more than merely social. She had discovered that his wife, Selina, was carrying on an affair with a Greek. Sumaire, it was said, tried to blackmail Selina by threatening to reveal the secret to the baron. Selina refused to pay and even made a counter-threat of physical violence against Sumaire.[40]

上海

Berrier, Miorini, Erben and Sumaire formed one little circle of Japanese supporters and criminal-political intriguers in Shanghai. Another revolved around a man whose multiplicity of identities and monstrosity of behaviour outclassed all possible competitors, 'Captain' Eugene Pick, alias Hovans, alias 'Doctor' Clige – to mention only three of his *noms de guerre*. Pick, as we shall call him, was born Evgeny Mihailovich Kojevnikoff in 1899 or 1900 in Riga, Latvia, son of a Cossack army colonel. His early life is obscure. During the First World War he fought in the Russian army. He later claimed that he had been captured 11 times by the Germans and escaped back to the Russian lines on each occasion. From 1919 to 1922 he studied at the Military Academy and at the Academy for Music and Drama in Moscow. After graduation he was said to have worked as an assistant military attaché in the Soviet embassies in Afghanistan and Turkey.

Pick arrived in China in 1925 as an assistant to the Russian military mission there. Over the next two years he worked for the Comintern in China, acquiring a close knowledge of its inner workings. In 1927, however, he turned coat and furnished the British intelligence authorities with what purported to be a detailed breakdown of the entire Comintern apparatus in China. The then British ambassador, Sir Miles Lampson, in a dispatch to the Foreign Office, in August 1927, enclosed one of Pick's memoranda with the comment that it deserved 'particular attention' and 'while its accuracy cannot be guaranteed, it has the ring of truth and is considered to be substantially accurate'.[41] Pick's report was received with great respect in the Foreign Office, which decided to print and circulate it to other White-hall offices as well as to the prime ministers of the dominions.[42] According to a later US intelligence report, Pick:

> bled them [the British] for large sums of money for long and devious reports on communist activities in China. When he had exhausted the British, subject [Pick] went to work for the U.S. Treasury Department and double-crossed them out of US$600 and sold a tip-off to the group the Department was after on his first assignment for $2,000.[43]

Pick also published a series of articles in the *North China Daily News*, containing some of the more sensational of his revelations concerning Soviet subversion in China.

Over the next decade Pick became a well-known figure in the Russian theatre world in Shanghai, as stage manager, actor, opera singer and ballet dancer. During this period he was best known under his stage name Eugene Hovans. He also worked as an impresario, running his own theatre with the grandiose title of the Far Eastern Grand Opera. At the same time he found rich pickings in the Shanghai politico-criminal underworld as a professional informer and small-time racketeer. According to one account he blackmailed an American judge whom he had discovered was a homosexual; the judge's body was later found in the Whangpoo. In 1929 Pick was sentenced to nine months in jail for forgery. Two years later a Chinese court convicted him of fraud and extortion and condemned him to a year in prison: he had falsely represented himself as a military adviser to the Chinese government in Canton and in that capacity had secured million-dollar arms contracts. Later he was said to be hawking around pamphlets and books stolen for him by coolies from the Soviet consulate. In 1937 a Russian newspaper in Harbin accused Pick, together with a woman described as his 'common-law wife of Georgian origin who owned a small boarding-house at Taydong Road behind the Astor House Hotel at Shanghai', of white-slaving and keeping a house of assignation.[44]

Pick was always the life and soul of any party he attended. He had a good singing voice and when out for an evening with friends at a restaurant would give sonorous renderings of Russian folk songs. An acquaintance described him as having 'a Mongolian cast of countenance ... no hair at all, wears a black skull cap, has burned scars on his head ... a heavy vodka drinker ... a flashy dresser ... usually went armed with a pearl handled revolver'.[45] The scars on his head were rumoured to be the result of burning oil which had been poured on him during torture sessions by communists angry at his turncoat activities. Another acquaintance gave this picture of him:

> He was a highly emotional individual and gave vent to his
> emotions easily. He had a great deal of self-respect and an
> overbearing superior air. He wasn't anxious for material
> wealth but desired position and honor in life. He was very
> compassionate and always helped any beggar that he
> encountered on the street. He was, at times, very trusting. On
> the other hand, he could be very suspicious. He met many
> people but quickly tired of them. Therefore he had many
> enemies and no intimate friends ... He used to say 'Drama
> and music are my best friends and the stage is my entire
> life.'[46]

A post-war American intelligence report described Pick as 'well-educated, a good linguist, an accomplished actor and a facile writer. He is also a competent murderer, intelligence agent, agent provocateur and smuggler of arms.'[47]

Pick began work as an agent for the Japanese Naval Intelligence Bureau in Shanghai in 1937. He organized a ring of European agents whose primary task was to engage in counter-intelligence against foreign, particularly British and American, targets.

In August 1940 Pick visited Japan for a holiday. There he met Commander Otani Inaho, the Japanese officer who later headed the Naval Intelligence Bureau in Shanghai and became Pick's chief Japanese patron. In a post-war interrogation Otani recalled that Pick's driving emotion seemed to be hatred of the Russian communists. 'When he spoke about the Soviets it was as though he were possessed of a consuming hate. His face flushed, he became highly emotional, and gesticulated wildly like a dramatic actor completely gripped by the role he was playing.'[48] According to Otani, Pick 'tended to be unstable and childlike in many of his habits and actions' and 'remarkable for his ups and downs. He would one day be throwing money right and left and the next day would be just another little Russian professional actor.'[49]

Pick's circle of more than 40 paid agents, informers or associates constituted a *Who's Who* of the foreign underworld in Shanghai. One of his employees was the hit-man Nathan Rabin. A former member of the Purple Gang in Detroit, Rabin had a sideline as a professional trombonist. By 1937 he was said to be functioning as a Japanese agent. An American intelligence source later described him as 5 feet, 9 inches tall, strongly built, with a 'Polish face, crude expression' and a swagger. The report stated that he became 'one of the most notorious Japanese gang members in Shanghai. Extortionist and blackmailer. Killer when drunk. His sole aim with the Japanese: obtain as much money as possible by criminal means and hide behind Japanese officials.'[50] Other figures in Pick's entourage included 'Count' Vladimir Tatischeff, blackmailer, swindler and informer for the Japanese Gendarmerie and the Gestapo, 'Baron' N.N. Tipolt, a former Russian naval officer, as well as numerous young Russian women.[51]

All these people were the most prominent of the politico-criminal amphibians spawned in the mud of Shanghai's secret wars. Plucking from the gutter a small army of such low-life operatives, Chinese as well as European, the Japanese gradually extended their influence in the unoccupied areas of the settlement and in the concession. Meanwhile, as the Japanese vice slowly tightened around the foreign enclaves of Shanghai, a new impetus was given to local rivalries by the outbreak of war in Europe.

3 Phony War in the International Settlement

The European war opened in Shanghai with the battle of the flags. The International Settlement, which belonged to no nation and to every nation, took national symbols very seriously. As one old resident wrote:

> All of us leaned on the flag and advertised our nationality.
> There are probably more flag poles per capita in Shanghai than
> in any other city in the world. The visitor who comes up the
> Whangpoo past the Bund usually thinks that some holiday is
> being celebrated, for a flag of some nation is flying from every
> roof. Hundreds of them fly daily in the residence sections.
> One gets so used to seeing them that a foreign house without
> a flag looks naked.[1]

The first skirmish took place in early September 1939 at the mat-sheds of the German tennis club: two swastika banners were hauled down by persons unknown. In the process the sheds were wrecked. The club's premises were on the city recreation ground and race course which also housed other sports clubs of various nationalities. To avoid further conflict and to ensure that the war in Europe would not cause any interruption in all-important sporting activities and horse-racing, the ground trustees asked all members not to fly national flags.[2]

Meanwhile the German embassy and consulate, which occupied part of the British-owned Glen Line building, were instructed by the management on the first day of the war to remove the German flag from the building. The Germans appealed for reconsideration of the ruling and the owners referred the matter to the British embassy. The ambassador, true to the traditional neutrality of the settlement and evidently not yet attuned to the principles of total war, told the landlords 'that he thought no great harm would be done, and that we might allow them to display the flag as they have always done'.[3]

The committees of the British and French clubs were reported to be 'scratching their heads over the position of "enemy" members'.[4] Eventually the head of the Nazi Party Foreign Organization in China, Ernst Wilhelm Bohle, solved the problem for them by issuing an order to all Germans in the country to withdraw from enemy clubs and to exclude enemy members from German clubs.[5]

In the French Concession Germans were refused building permits and commercial licences. Those affected turned out to be mainly Jewish refugees rather than Nazis. Officials promised to investigate individual cases to ensure that the innocent did not suffer; but at the same time it was reported that the French authorities 'had solid grounds for suspecting that non-Jewish Germans, members of the intelligence service, have had their passports stamped with the glaring red "J" which designates German Jews, in order to avert suspicion'.[6] Germans employed in British and French firms were dismissed: those whose passports were marked 'J' were eventually taken back by British firms – but not by French. Apart from these episodes, Germans were not molested, apart from one German resident who booed when King George VI appeared on the screen during a showing of *The Lion Has Wings* at the Cathay Theatre.

上海

The Germans in Shanghai had long had something of a chip on their shoulder. Although Germany had well-established ties with China, her position in Shanghai had always been secondary in comparison with that of Britain or the United States. Her investments there were dwarfed by those of the Anglo-Saxon powers and her shipping and other interests in the region were also far smaller. In addition to their general antagonism to the Anglo-Saxon democracies, Germans in Shanghai harboured a special, local grievance: during the First World War, they had been deprived of their privileges, including judicial extraterritoriality. After the war most had been deported from China – a measure that they saw, not without reason, as an act of petty vengeance by the victorious powers. In the inter-war period

German merchants re-established themselves but they remained deeply resentful of what they saw as the unfair treatment they had received.

The loss of Germany's Far Eastern and Pacific dependencies after the First World War had diminished but not eradicated its interest in China. Its most important manifestation in the inter-war period was military: German officers played a major role as advisers to the Chinese army. Headed by General von Falkenhausen, they remained influential during the early stages of the Sino-Japanese War, though the budding alliance between the Germans and the Japanese led to the repatriation of most of them in mid-1938. At that time too the Germans withdrew their ambassador from Chungking, although for a while they kept some informal lines of communication open to the Chiang Kai-shek régime.

German foreign policy in the Far East in the period 1939–41 had a dual aspect. On the one hand, the Germans were eager to see the United States, Britain and France embroiled in conflict with Japan, since that would divert Allied resources from Europe. For this reason they backed a forward policy to the south by Japan – though they were less keen on further Japanese advances into the interior of China than on a Japanese push against Allied interests in places such as Shanghai, Indo-China and Singapore. On the other hand, Japan was seen by Germany as a strategic constraint on the Soviet Union. To that extent the Germans wanted Russia's attention to be diverted from Europe by the simmering territorial disputes with Japan in the Soviet Far East. This would dictate a forward policy by Japan in the north. For a long time the Germans could not be entirely sure in which direction the Japanese would turn. At the local level in Shanghai, the Germans aligned themselves squarely with the Japanese in municipal politics, hoping, with misplaced optimism, that their ally would generously share whatever spoils might be forthcoming.

The Nazi party had been active among the German community in Shanghai since 1933 and by the outbreak of the war had succeeded in converting or neutralizing most non-Nazi influences – except, of course, among the German-Jewish refugees. Party branches also existed in Tientsin, Peking and other Chinese cities. Various subsidiary organizations, such as the Hitler Youth, a Nazi cultural bureau and a medical organization, were also formed. The Shanghai SA, a uniformed body, had about 100 members who occupied themselves in guarding the German radio station and other institutions and in intimidating local non-Nazi Germans.

The Shanghai Germans included a few non-Nazis, among them Pastor Fritz Maas of the Evangelical Lutheran church, who was dismissed for administering sacraments to 'non-Aryan' German refugees. With the outbreak of the war in Europe, German businessmen in Shanghai, most of whom had hitherto been lukewarm towards Nazism, found that party membership was an essential prerequisite to the securing of German government contracts. After September 1939 German, like British, firms in Shanghai enjoyed a tremendous boom as a result of government purchase orders. Under Nazi pressure, companies such as Agfa and I. G. Farben dismissed Jewish employees from their Shanghai offices and adjusted their policies to meet the national interest – or at any rate the Nazi interest.[7]

The Nazi leader in China, Siegfried Lahrmann, was a former commercial clerk who had joined the party in 1931 and secured the sinecure position of 'Director of German State Railways, China Branch'. He was a heavily-built, ruddy-faced man with a large belly, whom a German diplomat recalled as looking 'a bit brutal'.[8] Lahrmann was recognized as Landesgruppenleiter for the whole of China. He intrigued against non-Nazi German diplomats, among them Consul-General Martin Fischer, whom he accused of lacking the 'Hitler spirit'. But Lahrmann himself faced opposition from more extreme Nazis who considered him unqualified for leadership.[9]

While both the consulate-general and the Nazi party maintained intelligence sections of their own, the most important German intelligence organ in the city was the local branch of the Abwehr, the main foreign espionage organization of the armed forces, headed by Admiral Canaris. The Shanghai office was established by Captain Louis Theodor Siefken. A stout, broad-shouldered man in his mid-40s, he arrived in Shanghai in August 1940. After serving in the German air force in the First World War, Siefken had worked for Junkers Airways and for various shipping firms in foreign countries. In June 1940 he was recalled to Berlin and assigned to the Abwehr where he was trained 'in codes, use of secret inks, and micro-photography'.[10] He was nominally assigned to the German Consulate-General in Shanghai as a 'commercial adviser', but he acted directly under the orders of the naval intelligence section of the Abwehr in Berlin. In communications with Berlin he generally used the cover name 'Smith'.

The chief task of Siefken's office was to provide Berlin with information on ships' movements throughout the Pacific region. In particular, he sought information that would be useful for German raiders in attacks on Allied shipping. The bureau also acted as a central post office for reports received in drop boxes in Shanghai from the Philippines, South America and other places. Agents' reports, often in the form of microdots, were placed in these boxes in envelopes which Siefken then forwarded to Berlin; according to his own account he was often unaware of their contents. His staff took photographs of Allied ships in Shanghai. They prepared photostats of navigation charts. Local agents picked up gossip and secured information on the location of minefields in Hong Kong and Singapore harbours. German shipping firms such as Melchers & Co and the Hamburg-Amerika Line donated facilities and expertise to Siefken's organization. Under his direct control a network of agents and sub-agents was established in other places, including Tientsin, Peking and Bangkok. In addition to the collection of data on the Allies, Siefken's office also assembled delicate information concerning Germany's ally, Japan. Of special interest to Berlin were reports on suspected deliveries of war materials by the Japanese to the Russians.

Most importantly, Siefken established a wireless listening team for the interception and decoding of ships' messages. The team worked in cooperation with Italian radio experts. German shipping firms in Shanghai were ordered to help in setting up the organization and a front company, known as 'Astra Electrical Appliances' was formed, with an office on the corner of Kiangsi and Kiukiang Roads. As the radio work grew, it became necessary to rent a house on Columbia Road and the German and Italian experts consolidated their activities there.

One of the Abwehr's most effective agents in Shanghai was Carl Jochheim, described in a German intelligence report as an international swindler and ex-convict who had been accused of stealing aluminium ingots from the Swiss Aluminium Rolling Mill in Shanghai. The Germans, like the Japanese, had little compunction about making use of men with criminal backgrounds. When Jochheim's history was brought to the attention of the German naval attaché in Tokyo, he recorded in his diary that he did 'not take it too much to heart':

> I myself have long been under the impression that Jochheim
> has an adventurous kind of character. Such characteristics
> should not matter particularly if we weigh his past against his
> potential for acquiring useful intelligence. People employed in
> the secret intelligence service are often, even if not
> predominantly, of such a kind. So far, Jochheim has proved to
> be extremely useful in picking up information.[11]

Siefken employed a number of such agents, generally for low-grade assignments such as watching ships' movements on the river or chatting up sailors in bars.

The Siefken bureau followed standard Abwehr regulations that forbade any open connection with the Nazi party. The rule was strictly observed by the Shanghai office, except that 'for health reasons' they were allowed to belong to the SA sports section.[12] Siefken travelled a great deal to Nanking, Tientsin, Peking and Tokyo, so much so that one of his subordinates complained that he was able to see him only three or four times a year. All this activity yielded a stream of intelligence that was relayed to Berlin. Much of this was of only marginal value but on at least one occasion the results were spectacular.

In November 1940, German signals intelligence achieved a notable coup when a German commerce raider, *Atlantis*, captured the British Blue Funnel liner *Automedon* off Singapore. The ship, which had been converted into a frozen meat and stores carrier, was sailing from Liverpool to Hong Kong and Shanghai. On 11 November, when she was about 250 miles south-west of Sumatra, she came under attack. The vessel was rocked by explosions and the master was killed immediately. The surviving senior officer rushed to the captain's cabin which had been 'reduced to a shambles' and struggled desperately to find the key to the strong room where secret mail was held. He failed. The captors subsequently discovered a treasure trove of confidential official communications, including secret codes and correspondence destined for various British military and intelligence offices in the Far East. Among these was mail addressed to the Secret Intelligence Service station in Shanghai.[13] The delighted German naval attaché in Tokyo declared that the captured documents 'exceeded our highest expectations'.[14]

From the outset of his activities, Siefken encountered what he regarded as obstruction from the consulate and embassy officials in Shanghai. There existed almost congenital suspicion between the diplomats and security personnel. Friction arose particularly from the fact that Siefken, as an employee of the German general staff, was allowed to use his own code in communications with Berlin. His messages were thus indecipherable by the consular officials. Partly because of such tensions, the Siefken bureau's headquarters were moved from the German consulate building to the fifth floor of the Defag (Deutsche Farben-Handelsgesellschaft Waibel & Co, a subsidiary of the giant industrial trust I. G. Farben) building at 261 Szechwan Road.

Siefken's difficulties were compounded by the existence of a separate and rival German secret organization: the local branch of the Gestapo headed by Gerhard Kahner, a malevolent ruffian whose behaviour earned him a reputation for domineering brutality. The secretary of the German embassy in Tokyo considered him dishonest and a liar, 'sexually dissatisfied', and with an 'inclination to sadism', though he added that Kahner took a 'strong stand for Germany'.[15]

Kahner arrived in Shanghai in 1940, charged with the tasks of observing Jewish emigrants in the city and conducting counter-espionage against the British intelligence apparatus there. His installation in Shanghai had evoked a protest from Consul-General Fischer, who argued that the first sphere was already covered by the consulate. The SS chief, Heinrich Himmler, insisted that Kahner's work necessarily included investigation of Jewish emigrants. At the same time, he proposed that, as a cover, Kahner be attached to the embassy press office.[16] Fischer reluctantly consented but, in a private comment for the eyes of the Foreign Ministry only, he pointed out that the proposed arrangement would have the advantage that Kahner would fall under diplomatic authority, which would facilitate the 'supervision' of his activities.[17] The remark was diplomatically omitted from the version of Fischer's message that was forwarded by the German Foreign Office to Kahner's superior, Oberführer Müller, a senior SS official.[18]

A post-war report on Kahner's activities as Gestapo chief in Shanghai noted that several Germans in the city '"who were not satisfied with the way things were going" simply "disappeared" and later their bodies were found floating in the Whangpoo River. The rest of the German community believed – not without reason – that Kahner had had them kidnapped and killed.'[19]

上海

Although the Germans built up a substantial undercover apparatus in Shanghai, they remained hamstrung by the fact that since the First World War they had been denied the right to station troops or naval units there. When Britain declared war on Germany on 3 September 1939, there were still 1,496 British regular troops and 1,234 US marines in Shanghai, as well as over 4,000 British and American troops stationed elsewhere in China. There were also 1,714 French troops (mainly Annamites) and 214 Italian marines in the city.[20] Yet in spite of the war against Germany in Europe, the dominant note in British and French policy in the Far East continued to be one of appeasement. The need to concentrate resources in Europe made the Allies all the more anxious to make almost any concession in order to prevent the Japanese entering the war on the side of Germany. Japan had already signed a five-year Anti-Comintern Pact with Germany in 1936 and the British had no desire to afford her any ground for moving into a still closer alignment with the Nazi régime.

Major British enterprises accordingly received official guidance to apply the Trading with the Enemy Regulations very flexibly in Shanghai 'so as to give the Germans as little handle as possible for enlisting Japanese sympathy or support against us' – as a report for Butterfield & Swire put it. The same report added: 'Our instructions are to complete all contracts already entered into with Germans, to pay debts due to them before the outbreak of war, to deliver cargo held in German names prior to the outbreak of war, and generally to round off all existing engagements but not to enter into new ones.'[21]

Having already concluded that the settlement was militarily indefensible, the British now took an explicit decision not to resist in the event of a Japanese attempt to complete their conquest of the city. In December 1939 the British army commander in Shanghai was instructed that in the event of a Japanese occupation of the settlement, 'British troops will not resist but will allow themselves to be interned, either by the Americans or the French, preferably the former, since the latter are likely to be involved in operations also.'[22] British officials in the Far East did not relish the policy of appeasing Japan but could do nothing about it. 'It has been a jolly humiliating mission, my time in Tokyo', Sir Robert Craigie, the British ambassador to Japan, confessed in September 1940 at a garden party given at the British ambassador's residence in Peking. Pronouncing himself 'nauseated with being polite to the little blighters', Craigie declared, 'Once we have Hitler trounced we will drive the Nips back to where they belong.'[23]

Against this background, the Japanese had only to push, by gentle and not so gentle means, for the whole Anglo-American house of cards in the settlement to totter. The pressure came at the weakest point – the Western Extension Roads area. The ominous prospect was described by the Swire representative on 15 September 1939:

> The Japanese have lost no time in starting an attempt to exploit the preoccupation of the Western Powers. During the past ten days armed Ta Tao [puppet] police have been entering the Western Outside Roads Area in large numbers and they have commenced patrolling the Council's roads, building sandbag posts etc., and generally displaying a most truculent attitude. In the meantime, the Council has been inundated with reports from reliable sources that the Japanese military have the bit in their teeth and are determined to secure full control over this area, including the roads.
>
> ...
>
> Godfrey Phillips, the Municipal Council Secretary and Commissioner General ... reported ... to a meeting consisting of the British Ambassador, the American Consul-General, Major-General Simmonds [the senior British military officer in Shanghai], and representative members of the Council, to the effect that he was convinced that we should be faced by a forceful attempt to oust our police and gain control

of the area unless we were willing to negotiate immediately,
and this meeting reached the unanimous conclusion that, in
the new circumstances created by the European war, there is
no alternative but to try to come to some sort of an
arrangement.[24]

Negotiations began immediately but soon bogged down on the stipulation
by the Chinese puppet régime that its police be given full control of the
whole Western Roads area.[25]

No doubt as a stimulant to these discussions, the Japanese began applying pressure by violent means. On 22 September the Swire representative
noted that 'Ta Tao [Chinese puppet] police recently drafted into the area
are displaying increasing truculence, and several of the Council's Chinese
and Sikh police have been disarmed by strong gangs of Ta Tao people
dressed as civilians.'[26] A month later he reported 'two nasty shooting incidents' in the area, one of which amounted to 'a small pitched battle in Jessfield Road, involving the throwing of hand-grenades and the use of
Thomson guns'. In the face of such violence the Municipal Police abandoned some of their posts in the area and reduced their profile. The British
military commander refused to assist the Municipal Police in reclaiming
their positions 'because it was feared that this might be provocative and involve a clash with the Japanese Gendarmerie'. As for the Municipal Police
commanders, they worried that their Chinese subordinates, 'already rather
demoralized by weeks of playing second fiddle to the Ta Tao people', might
refuse duty in the area. They could hardly be blamed for this, commented
the Swire representative, 'as no one can reasonably be expected to relish
the job of standing in the middle of the road to be shot at by any passing
gangster'. Anglo-American dissension did not help matters:

The Americans [the Swire report continued] characteristically
continue to talk big but act small; they press for firm action by
the Council and the British Military, but decline to send a man
into the area to help, though they are now talking about
sending some Marines to protect American lives and property,
which would doubtless mean putting their men on specific

American properties, and would not serve to give the general
support to the Council's police which is so badly needed.

Not surprisingly, the Municipal Council was said to be 'virtually distraught
in its efforts to find a solution to the problem other than withdrawal from
the area'.[27]

Dissatisfied with the pace of the talks, the Japanese resorted to even
more direct methods. On 6 January 1940 an unsuccessful assassination attempt by six men armed with pistols was made on Godfrey Phillips as he
was driving along the Avenue Haig on his way to work at the Municipal
Council offices. 'Discreet enquiries' by Detective Inspector Crawford of
the Municipal Police disclosed that the crime 'was instigated by Wang
Ching-wei's party and the Japanese Military Police'. Three of the would-be
assassins were traced to the Intelligence Section of the Japanese Military
Police while another three were Chinese puppet 'Special Service Corps'.
The Japanese had fired on Phillips while their Chinese coadjutors had kept
watch. Inspector Crawford reported that after the attack the three Japanese had run into an alleyway:

> but were halted by the armed guards of the Sun Sun Gambling
> Den, no. 30 Tsu Ka So, who mistook them for armed robbers.
> They told the armed guards that they came from 'Kung Kwan'
> (a courtesy name for the residence of a high class Chinese and
> here indicating 76 Jessfield Road) and were handed over to
> the … Special Service Corps … The three were later
> transported to 76 Jessfield Road, the headquarters of the
> Special Service Corps, and thence taken away by the Japanese
> Gendarmerie. It is reported that they are at present detained
> at 94 Jessfield Road, the premises of the Western District
> Section of the Japanese Military Police, who are stated to have
> demanded a statement from them as to why they failed in
> their mission after coming so close to their object.

Crawford surmised that the purpose of the attack had been threefold: first,
to prevent the conclusion of an agreement over the policing of the Western

Roads; second, to bring about the replacement of the puppet mayor of the Chinese municipality; third:

> and the most important reason – after the assassination which was expected to be successful, to lay the blame on the Chungking Government by fostering propaganda to the effect that the case was perpetrated by agents of [the] Chungking Government on account of Mr Phillips' attempt to conclude an agreement with the puppet régime which is opposed to [the] Chungking Government and which is not recognized by foreign powers. By means of such propaganda it was expected that [the] sympathy of the foreign community, at least a section of it, would turn from the Chungking Government towards Wang Ching Wei.[28]

As the British and French position in the Far East weakened, law and order in the Western Roads area continued to deteriorate. In February 1940 a French police report stated:

> the audacity of the bandits no longer knows any limits. They attack foreigners and Chinese alike in full daylight, even in the most frequented streets in the vicinity of the 'badlands' to which they flee after their attacks. Sixty percent of all armed robberies in the Settlement are committed in the immediate vicinity of the 'badlands'.

The same report estimated that the proprietors of gaming establishments in the area were paying more than $1 million a month in 'squeeze' to the Japanese.[29]

In the meantime the gambling operators and their Japanese patrons had extended their area of operations, thanks to an agreement mediated in December 1939 by the French lawyer Auxion de Ruffe. A deal was struck whereby the Japanese agreed to open the gates between the concession and the old Chinese district, Nantao, to permit the quarter's former residents to return. As a kind of *quid pro quo*, a group of Chinese gambling promoters was granted a licence to operate a large gambling house in Nantao.[30] Father Jacquinot's 'Refugee Safety Zone' in Nantao was dissolved in June 1940; its remaining 19,000 residents were given a month's supply of victuals and left to fend for themselves.

A *modus vivendi* on the policing of the Western Roads area was reached between the Shanghai Municipal Council and the Japanese-controlled Chinese municipality on 16 February 1940, but it was not until the following December that the two sides finally settled on regulations for implementing the agreement. These provided for the creation of a new body, to be known as the Western Shanghai Area Special Police Force, which would have charge of the entire Western Extension Roads area. The force would be composed partly of officers nominated by the Municipal Police and partly of nominees of the (Japanese-sponsored) Chinese municipality's police and would operate under the aegis of the puppet municipality. The settlement authorities were far from happy with the arrangement but, as Phillips told the British consul-general, the deal was 'as satisfactory as can be obtained by negotiation with the (puppet) Special City Government in existing circumstances'.[31] Further wrangling delayed the establishment of the new force until 15 March 1941.

Although the British gave way on this point and also yielded to demands for an increase in the number of Japanese officers in the Municipal Police, they were determined at all costs to maintain control over the Municipal Police Special Branch because of its role in intelligence-gathering. The department's former concentration on tracking communists had by now been replaced by broader preoccupations.

In December 1939, for example, a Special Branch report was submitted on 'certain activities' at an office building at 17 Foochow Road, following a complaint from the executive manager of William Hunt & Co Steamship Corporation which owned the building. The manager expressed suspicion that the office block 'had been taken over by pro-Japanese elements'. One of the sub-tenants in the building was a pro-Wang-Ching-wei Chinese newspaper owned by A. M. Kiehn, an American 'well known in Shanghai for his attempts to pass bad cheques'. Kiehn was also known to be a Japanese agent and had recently returned from a visit to Japan. Nothing untoward could be discovered by the Settlement police at 17 Foochow Road, but shortly afterwards the concession police obtained evidence suggesting that William Hunt & Co themselves were engaged in questionable dealings and might be trying to throw smoke in the eyes of investigators. From the inquiries of the French police it emerged that the enterprise was American in name only. In reality it was a front for the interests of the China Merchant Steam Navigation Company, controlled by the Chungking government. In order to prevent the Japanese from seizing their property at the time of the occupation of Chinese Shanghai in 1937, the owners had transferred nominal control to William Hunt, a former American vice-consul at Tientsin who had had to resign from his consular position in 1927 as a result of a financial scandal. Behind the 'double control' of the Chinese shipping interests, it appeared that 'certain Chinese enterprises were ... in close contact with German houses'. The French police concluded that Hunt, who was 'in close contact with certain high officials of the Chungking Government', was 'utiliz[ing] the neutral status of his house to "favour" the despatch into "Free China", via Indo-China, of German merchandise ordered by Chinese firms controlled by him or his Chinese friends'.[32] Such complex multinational business manoeuvres, for which the settlement was the perfect setting, rendered ineffective Anglo-French efforts to enforce the trading blockade against Germany.

As this episode illustrates, the French police cooperated with the British on political cases in the period from the outbreak of the war to the fall of France in June 1940. This was a break with past practice. With the exception of the First World War period, the two neighbouring police authorities had frequently behaved more like enemies than allies. While there was some exchange of information on routine criminal matters, coordination in political cases was much less common. The French police were, in any case, regarded with disdain and suspicion by the British on account of their notorious susceptibility to 'squeeze' and their old association with gangsters such as the former Green Gang boss, Tu Yueh-sheng.

上海

Given the impossibility, as it seemed, of combating the enemy by force of arms or even by economic warfare, the British and French were reduced to one weapon: words. In Shanghai, as in Europe, the phony war was more a matter of gestures and propaganda than of fighting. Its main battlefields, apart from flagpoles, were newsprint and the airwaves. The British and American press in Shanghai before the war had enjoyed a high reputation. Among the four English-language dailies, the *North China Daily News*, known as 'the Old Lady of the Bund', held an unquestioned primacy. The foremost British newspaper in the Far East and the oldest in any language in China, it was a kind of Far Eastern equivalent of *The Times* of London. The paper represented British business interests and for much of its history faithfully reflected the thought processes of the 'Shanghai mind'. It had a circulation of about 10,000. Much less influential was the *Shanghai Times*, which sold between 6,000–7,000 copies. Since 1915 it had belonged to an Englishman, E. A. Nottingham. In 1924, he had fallen into financial difficulties. After appealing for help in vain to a number of British banks, he turned to the Yokohama Specie Bank which not only advanced him the required sum but arranged a subvention by the Japanese government. Thenceforth the paper pursued a barely-disguised pro-Japanese line. In the years 1939–41 it gave patriotic support to the British war effort against Germany while urging a conciliatory attitude towards Japan. By contrast, the *Shanghai Evening Post and Mercury*, a lively, American-owned popular paper, was strongly anti-Japanese. The *China Press*, although nominally an American company, was in reality owned by interests close to Dr H. H. Kung, a senior Chinese nationalist politician. It hoed a pro-Kuomintang line – and consequently suffered frequent bomb attacks.

Some Anglo-Saxon journalists were well known public figures. Two, in particular, were thorns in the flesh of the Japanese: J. B. Powell, editor of the *China Weekly Review*, an American who received an indirect subsidy from the Chinese nationalists in the form of bulk subscription orders for his journal; and H. G. W. Woodhead, a British citizen, who was editor of *Oriental Affairs* and also wrote a regular column in the *Evening Post and Mercury*. Both wrote vigorous denunciations of Japanese aggression in China; both were to suffer terribly as a result.

In July 1940 puppet organs published a 'blacklist' of seven foreign and 87 Chinese journalists, all of whom were targeted for assassination. The foreigners included Cornelius V. Starr and Randall Gould, respectively proprietor and editor of the *Shanghai Evening Post and Mercury*, J. B. Powell and Norwood F. Allman, an American lawyer who was the registered owner of a pro-Kuomintang Chinese newspaper. Allman was a leading figure in settlement politics and business life. In addition to his legal duties and his management of the Chinese *Shun Pao* newspaper, he also served as honorary Mexican consul, ran a paper mill, was director of a cinema chain, commanded the American company of the Shanghai Volunteer Corps and served as a member of the Municipal Council. Few of the blacklisted men were intimidated by death threats though most took defensive precautions.

The foreign community was also served by a number of papers in other languages. The *Journal de Shanghai*, edited by Jean Fontanel, had a circulation of a little over 2,000 and received a substantial annual subsidy from the French consulate-general. In 1936 the local Shanghai German newspaper, *Deutsche Shanghai Zeitung*, was taken over by the Nazi party and renamed *Ostasiatischer Lloyd* (the title of an older, defunct German paper). Although purporting to be still independent, the paper became the leading organ of Nazi propaganda in the Far East under the editorial control of Dr Horst Ley, a long-time and faithful Nazi.

The *Lloyd's* donkey-like adherence to the party line involved a painful sacrifice of potential revenues: it was compelled to refuse not only advertisements from the large German-Jewish refugee population in Shanghai but also announcements from the German Evangelical Church which, in its local manifestation, was deemed politically unreliable. In the winter of 1940–41 Ley agreed, at a meeting with the German consul-general, Martin Fischer, and A. Henschel, Landesgruppenleiter of the Nazi Foreign Organization in Shanghai, that the paper would henceforth exercise strict control over the acceptance of advertisements. When Ley nevertheless printed two pages of church announcements, Henschel issued a peremptory order to the German press attaché insisting that henceforth the paper must not accept any more announcements from the church.[33] The exasperated Ley pointed out that it was well-nigh impossible to check the 'Aryan' credentials of every person who bought a small classified advertisement. The paper's staff, he claimed, had in fact tried to carry out such checks but when a Chinese clerk presumed to question the racial antecedents of customers, the procedure had been considered 'an offensive impertinence'. Ley's protest led Henschel to accuse him menacingly of 'un-National-Socialist conduct'.[34] Such squabbles notwithstanding, the *Lloyd* generally served the Nazi cause with unswerving faith. For a time the *Lloyd* also put out an English-language paper, *Noon Extra*. A more openly Nazi publication, *Ostasiatischer Beobachter*, appeared monthly under the editorship of S. Lahrmann, head of the Nazi party in China, but its indigestible ideological diatribes were attractive only to hard-core fanatics.

Whereas the pro-Nazi German press in Shanghai could survive only with official backing, the German-Jewish émigré press, which had a much larger potential audience, flourished without subsidies – to the great annoyance of the local German authorities. By 1940 there were 17 Jewish periodicals in Shanghai, including two daily newspapers: the *Shanghai Jewish Chronicle* (circulation around 3,000), edited by a Polish Jew, Ossi Lewin, and the *Gelbe Post* (circulation around 2,000), edited by A. J. Storfer.[35] The German consulate-general took legal advice when one paper called Hitler 'Germany's hangman', suggested that Rudolf Hess was a 'Hamitic crossbreed' and printed other disobliging comments on Nazi leaders. But since the Municipal Police's censorship apparatus was effectively under British control, such attacks could not be prevented from appearing.[36] Some prominent local Jewish journalists were deprived of their German nationality – but this sanction had little effect.[37]

After the outbreak of the European war, the German government decided to enhance its propaganda effort in Shanghai. A big well-financed press bureau was established on the sixteenth floor of the Park Hotel. Headed by Baron Jesco von Puttkamer, it operated under Goebbels' Propaganda Ministry and worked in cooperation with the local branch of the Nazi party. An animated, bespectacled, middle-aged man, Puttkamer was described as 'of the old-fashioned Junker type'.[38] His father had been a major-general, his mother a romantic novelist. Puttkamer had joined the Nazi party at an early stage, attracted by its violent nationalism. He was the author of a number of books of xenophobic inspiration, among them *Wahr bleibt Wahr: deutsch die Saar!* (1934). He also wrote articles for the Nazi press. He left his wife and children behind in Germany but, as a post-war US intelligence report put it, 'had a girl secretary and travelling companion who kept him happy in China'.[39]

Under Puttkamer's direction, Shanghai became the centre of the German propaganda effort for much of the Far East: material was sent not only throughout China but to the Philippines, the Dutch East Indies – and even to North and South America and Europe, since mail from China was not strictly censored when arriving in neutral countries.[40]

The Allies soon noted with concern the heightened effectiveness of German propaganda in the region. In February 1940 a British intelligence report stated that the German Trans-Ocean agency was supplying 100–200 pictures a month in Shanghai as against a dozen or so made available by the British Ministry of Information. The result was that even Russian newspapers that were 'pro-Allied in tone' were compelled to rely on these free German photographs.[41] By contrast, some Allied propaganda did not produce the desired effect. For example, when the violently anti-Nazi film *Confessions of a Nazi Spy* was shown to packed houses at the Astor Cinema in the concession in May 1940, a British intelligence report noted that Chinese spectators who did not understand the dialogue 'were merely impressed with the display of massed German troops goose-stepping into Czechoslovakia'.[42] The Allied counter-propaganda effort was jeopardized by German penetration of the office of the British press attaché in Shanghai – though the Nazis seem not to have utilized this source effectively.[43]

At first the Allies enjoyed greater fortune in the war over the airwaves. Shanghai's 40 or so radio stations, some of them very powerful, broadcast in many languages to the entire region. In addition to the large number of Chinese transmitters, most of the major European languages and ideologies were represented. Each of the major powers had its own broadcasting station: for example, XQHA (Japanese), FFZ (French), XIRS (Italian) and XRVN (Russia). The main pro-Allied ones were the British-owned XMHA and XCDN, the broadcasting arm of the *North China Daily News*. Typical of the output of these stations were such programmes as the BBC serial play *Shadow of the Swastika* (broadcast in January 1941), a talk by the journalist Stefan Lorant entitled 'I Was Hitler's Prisoner' (February 1941) and recordings of speeches by Winston Churchill.

Probably the most effective English-language broadcaster in the Far East at this period was the American journalist Carroll Alcott. A British intelligence report called him 'our most useful propagandist in Shanghai'.[44] His talks on XMHA angered the Japanese to such an extent that they used naval wireless equipment to try to jam them. The 'bulldog-voiced but soft-hearted' Alcott was repeatedly threatened and lived in constant fear of kidnapping or assassination.[45] Suspecting that he had been 'fingered' for treatment by Captain Pick's 'hit-man', Nathan Rabin, Alcott hired a bodyguard, wore a bullet-proof vest and avoided entering public places other than the foreign clubs.[46] Perhaps because of these precautions the attack never came.

The German counter-offensive in the radio war was at first rather ineffectual. Before 1939 the Germans had had only a minor presence on the Shanghai airwaves and at the outbreak of the European war they were compelled to stop broadcasting 'German hours' from a station in the concession. The Japanese then placed at their disposal a first-class transmitter with comfortable studio facilities attached. But this was also a Japanese military transmitter and since the Germans were still formally neutral in the Sino-Japanese conflict they felt obliged to decline the offer. For a while they rented a local Chinese station which broadcast news and commentaries in German and English. But a British intelligence report in the spring of 1940 noted that station XHHB's 'libellous' anti-British propaganda was not very successful:

> The tone of the news comments is vituperative but not very imaginative. The propaganda talk is presented with a sort of bespectacled German earnestness, and the obviously thought-up comments on the local British press are no match for the apparently artless humour of Carroll Alcott.[47]

After a time, however, the Germans improved the technical quality of their broadcast propaganda effort and eventually built up an impressive wireless establishment in Shanghai.

German radio propaganda came into its own with the opening of a new station, XGRS, with the most powerful transmitters in the Far East. Situated near the Kaiser Wilhelm School on the Great Western Road, this was initially a medium- and long-wave station only, but early in 1941 it started short-wave transmissions which made it audible throughout much of the

East Asian region. The manager of the station, Carl Flick-Steger, was a German-American who had studied at Brown University in Rhode Island and worked for several years for the Hearst newspapers as a correspondent in Berlin and Vienna. After a spell as Hearst correspondent in Shanghai, he took up his position at XGRS in December 1940, renouncing his American citizenship at the outbreak of the Pacific War. The station's staff included other Americans: Robert Fockler, a former trombone player who had headed the band at 'Demon' Hyde's Del Monte café, and Val Honeycutt, divorced wife of an American sailor. Unlike most German radio stations abroad, XGRS was not run by Goebbels' Propaganda Ministry but was under the authority of the Foreign Ministry. Flick-Steger called it 'Ribbentrop's personal baby'.[48] The British succeeded for a while in hampering XGRS by secretly blocking its requests for increased power from the American-owned Shanghai Power Company.[49] But the delicacy of Britain's strategic and diplomatic position in the Far East in general, and in Shanghai in particular, precluded more public or forceful counter-measures.

By far the most intellectually impressive and polished propaganda vehicle in any language produced in Shanghai during the war was the German-controlled English-language literary and political monthly *XX Century*. This journal, produced from October 1941 until the summer of 1945, was funded by the propaganda section of the German Foreign Ministry. Its editor, Klaus Mehnert, became a well-known personality in wartime Shanghai.

Born in Moscow in 1906 of German parentage, Mehnert was a relative of the German ambassador in Tokyo, Eugen Ott. Mehnert studied at various German universities and was awarded a Ph.D. in Berlin in 1930. He also spent a year as an exchange student at the University of California at Berkeley where he married an American co-ed. After working for two years as a German foreign correspondent in Moscow, he moved to Honolulu where he taught from 1938 to 1941 at the University of Hawaii. An ambitious, energetic, intelligent and gregarious man, with glasses and large, protruding ears, Mehnert was a popular figure in pro-Axis café society in Shanghai. At the same time he did not inspire trust. A post-war acquaintance said of him that he knew 'how to skirt the truth and make it look like truth'.[50]

According to Mehnert's post-war account, in a memorandum submitted to US Army Intelligence, he was recommended for the job in Shanghai by the diplomat Adam von Trott zu Solz who was an old friend.[51] Trott, a leading figure in the German resistance, was executed in 1944 for his participation in the July plot against Hitler. Mehnert's claim may well have been a self-serving attempt at exculpation. As editor of *XX Century*, he was paid the high salary of RM2,000 per month – in his memoirs, published in 1981, he recalled that when offered this amount he was unsure whether it was per month or per year.[52] But Mehnert may have been colouring the truth on this point too. A post-war American intelligence report stated that he had been paid the regal amount of RM5,000 per month for the first three months and RM3,000 thereafter. Whatever the salary, he had no compunction about accepting it.

Upon Mehnert's arrival in Shanghai in July 1941, the Municipal Police Special Branch instituted a watch on him. They reported that he was 'an enthusiastic Nazi' (contrary to Mehnert's post-war claims that he was lukewarm in his allegiance). His projected magazine, the police report continued, 'is being financed, according to reliable information, by Nazi funds, the real aims of the publication being closely connected with pro-Nazi and anti-Allied propaganda'.[53] Over the next four years Mehnert steered his publication cunningly along a sophisticated path that eschewed overt pro-Axis advocacy. *XX Century* attracted a wide range of contributors, few of whom were publicly identified with Nazism. Thanks to its official subsidy, the magazine cost very little and although it had only 3,500 subscribers was considered one of the most influential propaganda outlets in the Far East. A post-war American intelligence appreciation called the magazine 'one of the slickest bits of propaganda work that has been done anywhere'.[54]

上海

Among Mehnert's contributors was Hilaire du Berrier. The retired aviator plainly felt a certain awkwardness in associating with the Nazi journalist, but he explained the connection away happily enough in a letter to his sister in September 1941:

> Much to my embarrassment, between the time when I agreed
> to write them a short article and the time when the magazine

came out with said article in it, Axis money exerted pressure
on Dr Mehnert (and perhaps a threat or too [sic]) so that
when it came out I suddenly found it had swung from a 100%
neutral, cultural, far-eastern journal to an Axis propaganda
sheet, with me sharing honors in it alongside the former
German ambassador to China and the Italian military attaché
to Nanking. Too bad too. Not only for the chagrin this first
issue is going to cause me, but Mehnert had given me carte-
blanche to write a short thing a month for him, any subject I
wished to cho[o]se – with $600 (Chinese money) on delivery.
Now I fear I shall have to drop him. He's a nice fellow ... He
is not Nazi so he hoped to make a living for himself in
Shanghai with this magazine, thought he could keep it neutral.
I told him it was impossible: Gestapo would shake the club
over him if he didn't swing with them, the allies would force
him out of publication if he didn't swing their way, but he
determined to try. It seems I was right.[55]

Although this letter shows that Berrier was aware of the magazine's real
backers, he did not drop Mehnert and, in fact, continued to contribute to
the journal.

Meanwhile, things had been looking up for Berrier on another level. He
had made the acquaintance of an interesting young woman, Rosalynd
Kadoorie. For a fortune-hunting wastrel whose funds were running low,
she was a wonderful catch. Her family were part of the old-established
Baghdadi Jewish merchant community in Shanghai and were fabulously
wealthy. The attachment prospered and Berrier boasted to his sister that he
and Rosalynd were engaged to be married.

The start of the European war, however, led to an abrupt change in
Berrier's plans. He wrote to his sister announcing that he had volunteered
for the French army and would shortly sail from Shanghai. 'Too bad! I was
coming along well with my writing, had taken a new apartment and was
going to marry Rosal[y]nd this month. She is upset about it and the General I have been working for is annoyed, as I was under a contract with
him.'[56] The French, however, took their time in mobilizing him. In May

1940 he was still in Shanghai and advised his sister:

> In case you should get a cable from me stating that I have left
> China for points West ... you can always write Rosa ... her
> address is: Mlle Rosalynd Kadoorie, 8 Edinburgh Road,
> Shanghai. Yes, Rosa and I are still as one. She is a great girl and
> more fun than a circus ... Rosa is a scream, full of all the
> supersticion [sic] of the Orient, and at regular intervals when
> the family ghosts, pursued by wild or homeless spirits, come
> back for a meal or a night's frolic in the old home, Rosa sees
> them and can't sleep for nights.[57]

In the summer of 1940 Berrier's apparent readiness to serve the Allied cause was overtaken by events: 'France collapsed while preparations were being made to take over a command in Somaliland', he later explained to his sister.[58] In July that year Berrier volunteered for the British forces but was rejected.[59] Shortly afterwards the Municipal Police reported that Berrier had recently attempted to steal some documents from a room at the Park Hotel occupied by Chiang Kai-shek's German former bodyguard, Captain Walter Stennes, but had been caught in the act.* Stennes kept the matter quiet but Berrier was said to be 'afraid that he may yet suffer in some way for his temerity'.[61]

The same report noted a change in Berrier's social life. The vivacious Rosalynd Kadoorie seemed to have been forgotten, for Berrier was now 'co-habiting with a Mrs Oleaga who was formerly Mrs Burkhardt'.[62] Evelyn

---

* Stennes had been a close confidant of Hitler in the 1920s but in 1931 he participated in an abortive party revolt against Hitler in the course of which he was said to have given Goebbels 'a good sound hourse whipping'. After Hitler's assumption of power, Stennes was arrested and tortured. Thanks to the intervention of President Hindenburg, he was released upon giving a written promise not to engage in anti-Nazi propaganda abroad. He went to China with a letter of introduction from General Ludendorff, as a result of which he served as head of Chiang Kai-shek's personal bodyguard from 1934 to 1940. He then moved to Shanghai, installed himself in the luxurious Park Hotel, notorious as a base for Nazi agents, and 'led a very extravagant life there',[60] Stennes's loyalties thereafter remained unclear, but he was widely suspected of having enrolled in the Nazi cause.

Oleaga had been born to British parents named Buchan. Her first marriage had been to a Swiss national, G. J. Burkhardt, a partner in the British firm Burkhardt, Buchan & Co. According to a Municipal Police Special Branch report, this firm had been closely connected with the local branch of a Soviet trading company 'and was also known to have been financed by funds from Moscow'. The Soviets were said to use the firm to conduct business 'when it was not convenient for a Soviet concern to act directly'. In 1933 Burkhardt committed suicide by shooting. Three years later, Burkhardt, Buchan & Co went into liquidation, 'the directors owing money widely in Shanghai'. Meanwhile Evelyn had gone to Manila where she married a Spaniard, Francisco Oleaga. Around the time of his marriage, Oleaga abruptly left his job and it subsequently emerged that a large amount of money could not be accounted for.[63]

Berrier's motive for moving in on Mrs Oleaga, who was already of a certain age, is suspect. It may be that he was attracted to Evelyn's daughter, Vicki, who moved in a fast social set in Shanghai expatriate society. But Vicki went off on an extended visit to Hong Kong. When she returned to Shanghai some months later, she followed Berrier's example and added a spurious handle to her name. Henceforth she styled herself 'Countess Victoria Lea'. Meanwhile her mother tired of Berrier's company and was reported to be associating with an Italian officer.[64] Mrs Oleaga was regarded by the Municipal Police as 'politically suspect'. They watched her movements and reported that she 'attempts to peddle information to various consular authorities in Shanghai'.[65]

The Special Branch kept Berrier under even closer observation. They ascribed his interest in Mrs Oleaga to squalid mercenary motives:

> It is said that he is endeavouring to establish a male brothel somewhere on Avenue Joffre to which rich women will be recommended by Dr von Miorini (Austrian) and Mrs Ruby Edwards and that when the time is ripe du Berrier will attempt to blackmail such women as will appear to be 'easy' victims. Du Berrier is stated to be without funds at present and to be subsisting on money provided by Mrs Oleaga.[66]

What might appear as a joking aside in a letter from Berrier to his sister shortly afterwards provides some confirmation of at least one of these extraordinary charges:

> Husbands are running wild these days since their families left Shanghai. You know, Shanghai's Russian girls are famous the world over. For years they have huddled dejectedly in Shanghai night clubs all the way from Blood Alley to Hungjau, fighting over any lonely males that come their way like lions over a lost straggler – always hungry, broke, tired, homeless. Now all of them have homes and none of them are hungry. Like Mercury, the messenger of the Gods, I propose to live the rest of my life on blackmail ...[67]

As this letter half-indicated, Berrier had plunged deep into a moral abyss.

'Count' du Berrier, Evelyn Oleaga, her daughter 'Countess' Victoria Lea, Dr von Miorini and Ruby Edwards all formed part of a meretriciously smart, if dangerous, circle in which lack of respectability was redeemed by liberal spending of large amounts of (sometimes non-existent) money, in which life histories and titles were fabricated, and political and sexual loyalties were commodities for sale to the highest bidder. The broadening of the international conflict in the course of 1940 and 1941 soon offered this set and their ilk scope for profitable speculation.

上海

After France fell in June 1940, its empire in the Far East crumbled to dust. Indo-China was swallowed up by the Japanese 'Co-Prosperity Sphere', although the French were permitted to save a measure of spurious dignity by continuing to exercise administrative and police duties in the colony. The United States, increasingly perturbed by Japanese expansionism, reacted by freezing Japanese assets but the move did nothing to moderate Japanese policy. In their concession in Tientsin the French agreed to accept 'supervision' over all their activities by Japanese gendarmes. The effects of the catastrophe in France were soon felt in Shanghai too. On 25 June the

French defence sector next to their concession was handed over to the Japanese and the Wang Ching-wei régime. Then, two days later a Franco-Japanese agreement was signed providing for police collaboration: Chinese political suspects found in the concession would henceforth be handed over to the Japanese.

Some French citizens in Shanghai rallied to de Gaulle; most adopted a wait-and-see attitude; a few identified openly and strongly with the Vichy régime. One who did so with particular gusto was the lawyer Auxion de Ruffe. He was unusual, even among devotees of Marshal Pétain, in acting as a propagandist for the Japanese. In his journal *Extrême Orient* he repeatedly published articles attacking British and American privileges in Shanghai.[68]

The French collapse left the British in the Far East, as elsewhere, in something of a quandary how to regard their former allies. The French community in Shanghai 'needed careful nursing', wrote a British diplomat in August 1940. 'The collapse of France rather unhinged them and little [Henri] Cosme, the Ambassador, though he is amiable enough, has neither the character nor the guts to give them the lead that they needed.' A new French consul-general, Roland de Margerie, arrived in Shanghai in September. He was the former *chef de cabinet* of Paul Reynaud, the last democratic premier of the Third Republic. The view at the British embassy was that Margerie might 'not be too much tarred with the Pétain brush'.[69] According to later information from the Foreign Office, Margerie had been notably pro-British and 'all out for the continuation of the war'. But he incurred the enmity of Reynaud's influential mistress who 'did her best to get rid of him'. After the armistice, the report continued,

> those who were in charge of the French Foreign Office had the decency to try to have the better men who were not in sympathy with the armistice policy sent to posts abroad, so that they would be available to help France again when the time came. Margerie was consequently appointed to Shanghai.

He travelled to China via London and while there considered momentarily 'throwing his hand in' – but decided to continue his journey. British diplomats seemed of two minds about him. On the one hand, he seemed to be 'still an out and outer'. On the other, he was felt to be not altogether trust-worthy 'unless his interests happened to coincide with ours'.[70] The German consul-general in Shanghai, Martin Fischer, who got to know Margerie well, later came to similarly ambivalent conclusions, classifying him as an 'attentiste'.[71]

British reservations about Margerie turned out to be justified: he served his Vichy masters with unwavering loyalty in Shanghai and was later rewarded with the ambassadorship to China. He struck the authentically confessional Vichy note in a speech delivered at the French community's New Year celebration in January 1941: 'In truth we must not hesitate, given the situation, to recognize the facts in all their cruelty, to weigh the consequences of our frailties and our errors. Each of us can be one of the humble artisans of the work of national reconstruction.'[72] Margerie's wife, who came from a prominent banking family, was considered 'tiresome and a climber' at the British Foreign Office. While in Shanghai he consoled himself for his political and marital travails by taking as mistress the wife of a local American doctor.[73]

A test of the attitude of the local French authorities presented itself soon after Margerie's arrival. From mid-1940 until early 1941 a Free French group in Shanghai, headed by Roderick Egal, a local wine merchant, disseminated Gaullist propaganda and recruited 65 men to fight in de Gaulle's forces. The recruits included 24 French policemen, among them Robert Jobez, the number two man in the concession's police force. Initially Egal's activities were welcomed by the British embassy; a British diplomat considered that he had a 'brave but not lighthearted optimism and moral courage coupled with a sympathetic understanding of the difficulties of others, which is pretty rare'. The diplomat added: 'He runs his own show and rightly does not look to us for any direct support for fear of compromising his own position; but he keeps in close touch with us and we help him whenever we can. It would be very difficult to find anyone better suited to this delicate work.'[74]

These warm feelings were short-lived. Just as his master in London proved to be a tiresome headache to Churchill and Roosevelt, so Egal's own 'headstrong behaviour' came to be considered an embarrassment by some British officials. He was said to have used 'very violent' language and the

Foreign Office suggested that de Gaulle might be asked to send a message to him urging 'restraint and forbearance'.[75] There was a palpable sense of relief in British official circles in April 1941 when pro-Vichy elements engineered Egal's arrest on a charge of inciting French sailors to desert. He was removed from Shanghai to Hanoi to await trial. The arrest produced 'great indignation' in the French community and a 'tremendous outburst of pro-De Gaulle sentiment' manifested itself at the French Club.[76] De Gaulle sent a message to Margerie appealing to his sense of honour and asking for Egal to be freed.[77] The British eventually secured his release on condition that he furnish an undertaking not to engage in political activities. Although Egal returned to Shanghai briefly the following autumn, he was unable to enter the concession since Margerie telephoned his British counterpart to emphasize that Egal would be deported if he set foot there.[78] The British considered threatening, by way of reprisal, to arrest the French consul-general in Hong Kong as well as other pro-Vichy Frenchmen there and in Singapore. But such forceful proposals were soon abandoned as impractical.

Meanwhile the pro-Vichy French ambassador to China, Cosme, issued an order to all French municipal officials and policemen in Shanghai to sign oaths of allegiance to Marshal Pétain. Those who refused to give the pledge would be dismissed. There was no report of any refusal. Although another French businessman took over leadership of the local Gaullists, Free French activity in the city was henceforth more or less snuffed out.

The entry of Italy into the war in June 1940 also had repercussions in Shanghai. US marines had to be redeployed between the Italian and British defence areas in the settlement to prevent untoward incidents between soldiers of the two countries now at war yet strangely still cooperating in the defence of the foreign enclave. The 17,000-ton Italian luxury liner, *Conte Verde*, which had carried large numbers of German-Jewish refugees to Shanghai over the previous few years, happened to be in port at the time and could not leave for fear of encountering enemy warships. As a result she remained moored in the Whangpoo for the duration.

The desperate military straits in which Britain found herself in the summer of 1940 inevitably impaired her position in the Far East. In July the prime minister, Winston Churchill, announced that the government would be ready to negotiate with the Chinese the abolition of extraterritoriality and the return of concessions – but he added the proviso that such negotiations would take place only when peace had been restored.[79] A pamphlet circulated in Shanghai in July 1940 by the 'Chinese Corps for Riddance of Britains [*sic*]' called on the British army and navy 'to consider the odious situation of your own country' and recommended: 'Better withdraw from Shanghai immediately. Otherwise you will involve yourself into annihilation.'[80] The ill-meant advice was taken. On 7 August the British cabinet decided to withdraw all British troops from Shanghai, Tientsin and Peking. A 'most immediate most secret warning order' was issued to the garrison commanders explaining that the units were to be withdrawn for three reasons:

a) They are of little military value.
b) The Japanese are out to force a quarrel leading to hostilities.
c) Failure to withdraw now might lead to an ultimate withdrawal in humiliating circumstances.[81]

The decision was implemented on 20 August when the last British troops left Shanghai. Japanese forces took up positions in defence sector 'D' (the Western Roads). Their demand for control over sector 'B', however, was resisted and responsibility for that area was assumed, for the time being, by the Shanghai Volunteer Corps.

But the settlement's little army itself was slowly disintegrating. At full strength in October 1937 it had comprised about 2,500 men. By November 1939 it had been reduced to 2,057, of whom 323 were members of the permanent Russian detachment. In 1940 the Municipal Council decided, 'in the interests of economy', to incorporate the Russians in the Municipal Police. A small crowd watched the unit's last ceremonial parade at the Race Course in January 1941.

The fading away of Britain's token military presence in the city was a green light for Japanese expansionism. Meanwhile, Japan's decision in September 1940 to throw in her lot with the Axis and sign a tripartite pact with Germany and Italy was soon felt in Shanghai. In November 1940 a senior Japanese officer, Major-General Miura Saburo, spoke semi-publicly about plans for seizure of the international section of the city. In a speech to a

Japanese audience at the Concordia Club, Miura disclosed that the settlement would be blockaded whereupon the Municipal Council would be compelled to cooperate unconditionally with the Japanese. Foreigners would thereafter be registered in two classes: 1) enemy belligerents; 2) neutrals and Axis subjects.[82]

For the time being, the Japanese contented themselves with political pressure. This made sense, as they had good reason to believe that they might gain control of the levers of power in the settlement by constitutional means, relying on their continued growth in numbers. By September 1939 there were 1,827 Japanese qualified to vote in the settlement as against 1,118 British. While the British might generally rely on the 387 Americans voters to side with them, the 419 Germans would be expected to support the Japanese. The 345 Russians might thus hold the balance of voting strength. These figures, as the Swire representative put it, made 'grim reading' and British business circles began to fear the worst.[83]

In the Municipal Council election in 1940 the Japanese refused to collude in the traditional gentleman's agreement whereby seats were, in effect, allocated in advance according to the fixed national quotas. Instead of nominating their customary two members, they put forward five candidates and set about campaigning vigorously for support. With their increased numerical and commercial strength the Japanese had serious hopes of winning all five seats and thus overturning Anglo-Saxon predominance on the council. In response, the British and Americans resorted to what even Caroll Alcott called 'legal ballot-box stuffing'.[84] To counter the Japanese numerical advantage, the large British and American business firms made an organized effort to subdivide their properties into small lots, thereby multiplying their votes. The result of the election on 10 and 11 April was a crushing defeat for the Japanese. The American Norwood Allman headed the poll with 8,000 votes, the largest number ever cast for a candidate in the settlement's history. Three of the five Japanese candidates were defeated. The resulting council, the last ever elected in the settlement, contained five British, two American and two Japanese members (as well as the five Chinese elected by the Chinese Ratepayers' Association).

Local Japanese political leaders felt humiliated by this defeat and pondered revenge. An opportunity came at the annual ratepayers' meeting, held at the racecourse, in January 1941. Among the 2,000 people attending was the 70-year-old chairman of the Japanese Ratepayers' Association, Hayashi Yukichi. Norwood Allman recalled Hayashi as 'a nearsighted little man who seemed to be hiding behind his huge, horn-rimmed spectacles'.[85] A British intelligence report noted 'in passing – and without any attempt to be scurrilous – that Hayashi ... laid the foundation of his fortunes in running a brothel'.[86] He had first come to political prominence at the time of the municipal council election of 1936. On that occasion too the Japanese had failed in an attempt to increase their representation – whereupon Hayashi, at a post-election dinner at the Japanese Club, picked up a knife, slashed his finger and wrote in his own blood: 'I assume responsibility for what has happened.'[87] Afflicted again by a mortified sense of personal responsibility, Hayashi mounted the platform at the ratepayers' meeting and, 'in a high Hitler-like voice he harangued in Japanese for almost half an hour'. Shortly afterwards he rose from his seat in the audience, raised a gun and shot W. J. Keswick, the Jardine taipan and new chairman of the municipal council. The Japanese seated around Hayashi 'rose as one man with shouts of "Banzai! Banzai!"'.[88] Keswick suffered only flesh wounds; a Japanese councillor and a Japanese municipal official were also lightly injured. A riot erupted as the infuriated crowd hurled chairs, photographic flashbulbs and wooden boards at the platform. The would-be assassin stood calmly for several minutes after the shooting with his hands in his pockets, surveying the imbroglio, until he was carried away on the shoulders of Japanese supporters.

Hayashi was eventually arrested by the Japanese Consular Police but released under bond pending a trial. He made no bones about admitting his guilt. In accordance with established procedures in the settlement, Hayashi had the right to be tried before a Japanese court. Rather than consider the case in Shanghai, the Japanese moved him to Nagasaki. A court there found him guilty and sentenced him to two years' hard labour, suspended for five years. The sentence was later reduced to one year suspended. He therefore got off virtually scot-free and returned to Shanghai in August 1941.

There was a certain irony (noted at the time in the pro-Chungking press) in the Japanese choice of Keswick as a target for assassination, since he was regarded as an appeaser of the Japanese for having handed over to the Chinese puppet municipality land records that had been lodged in the Settlement for safe-keeping.[89] The shooting did not deflect Keswick from his accommodationist course. On 2 February 1941, his arm in a sling, he signed the latest reinterpretation of the Western Roads policing agreement with the mayor of the Chinese municipality. The document provided that the Special Political Police operating out of 76 Jessfield Road would cease their activities. As agreed in principle a year earlier, the 'Western Area Special Police Force' was to be established under a cooperative arrangement between the Municipal Police and the puppet municipal authorities. Gambling and opium dens in the area were to close or transfer to Nantao. Many in fact moved there but two, Farren's Night Club and L'Eventail, both frequented by Europeans, continued to function in spite of orders from the Chinese police to close. After a time others opened again in the district – one, it was rumoured, in the presence of the puppet deputy minister of police himself.[90]

A few days after the agreement was signed, the meeting of the ratepayers, so rudely interrupted by the Keswick shooting, was resumed and passed without incident. Following the meeting, Godfrey Phillips held a press conference. According to a report in the pro-Japanese *Shanghai Times*, the council's senior official was forced into a public confession of the extent to which the British business firms had manipulated the voting system to ensure continued British-American control:

> On being asked how many registered ratepayers there were,
> Mr Phillips replied that there were about 9,000. It was then
> put to him by one of the press representatives present that
> according to the list issued by the SMC, six men represented
> 4,310 votes, another eight men 800 votes, making a total of
> 5,110 votes or more than half the total. The questioner then
> asked why the Council went to the expense of holding a
> meeting when these fourteen men could get together and
> decide on Council policies.

This apparently innocent question, of course, exposed the procedural sham into which the representatives of the Anglo-Saxon powers had been driven in their desperate desire to preserve their dominance on the council. True to the best British civil service traditions, Phillips had a ready response to the awkward questioner: 'I won't answer any constitutional or political questions.'[91]

As the annual spring election period again approached, the Japanese made it clear that they were in no mood to brook a repetition of the previous year's loss of face. They warned the British that they could not guarantee to maintain order or restrain the indignation of the local Japanese community if Japanese representation on the council were not somehow increased. The British and Americans now had few bargaining chips left. Negotiations among the powers eventually produced agreement to suspend parts of the land regulations and create a provisional council by appointment rather than election. Each power was to nominate its own representatives under an agreed numerical quota. Japanese representation was increased to three, as was American. The number of British councillors was reduced from five to three and of Chinese from five to four. Germany, Italy, the Netherlands and Switzerland would each have one councillor. This produced a council in which the Anglo-Americans were a minority: six out of 17. The Axis powers together now held five seats. As Allman, who was reappointed, put it delicately, 'the 1941 election was omitted'.[92] The arrangement was rubber-stamped by a meeting of the ratepayers on 17 April 1941.

In spite of the war clouds over the Pacific, Shanghai's frenzied nightlife continued as if there were no tomorrow. So did popular sporting activities. British horsemen rode their small Asiatic ponies at the municipal racecourse. Dog-racing proceeded as usual at the Canidrome. Jai Alai, the Basque game that was a Shanghai fad, attracted large crowds. And the 'Miss China 1941' competition delighted patrons of the Argentina night club. Chinese and foreigners alike took a more than merely sporting interest in all of these contests. As inflation ate away at the value of the Chinese currency (it shrank in value from about 3 to US$1 to 1,875 to US$1 between 1937 and May 1941) betting stakes reached astronomical heights. But behind the neon façade, the century-old Anglo-American domination of the International Settlement was dissolving.

4 Waiting for the Barbarians

The German invasion of the Soviet Union on 22 June 1941 added a new dimension to the conflict in the Far East – and to the political role of its largest European community: the 25,000 Russians in Shanghai. They were mainly remnants of anti-Bolshevik forces that had been active in Siberia during the Russian Civil War. They had arrived, a rabble of soldiers, sailors and assorted hangers-on, aboard a fleet of Russian warships that fled Vladivostok in December 1922. Following the Japanese occupation of Manchuria in 1931, more Russians fled from cities such as Mukden and Harbin to the apparently greater security of the foreign enclaves in Shanghai.

A large number settled in the French Concession. Avenue Joffre, lined with Russian cafés serving blinis, bortsch and black bread, and stores selling Siberian furs and mementoes of 'la vieille Russie', became known as 'Little Moscow'. In Shanghai, as in Berlin, Paris and New York, the refugees set up their own institutions – schools, churches, clubs – to perpetuate in exile the lost world of pre-revolutionary Russia.

Russia was the only great power other than Germany whose citizens did not enjoy special legal privileges in Shanghai. The Soviet Union had voluntarily abandoned its extraterritorial rights after the revolution. It lost little by this, as most of the Shanghai Russians were, in any case, not Soviet citizens. Technically stateless, they were represented by a Russian Emigrants' Committee headed by former imperial Russian consular officials. The committee had no diplomatic standing and was repeatedly challenged by rival bodies claiming to represent the community.

The Shanghai Russians imported in their mental baggage the conspiratorial political culture of their homeland – exacerbated by the introverted and paranoid style common among émigré communities. Political opponents were routinely castigated as traitors, Bolshevik agents, freemasons or Jews. The local Russian leaders, such as the former Tsarist general Theodore L. Glebov, tended to be suspicious of everything around them, uncompromising in their hostility to the Soviet régime and deeply resentful of what they saw as their betrayal by the Allied powers. The Russian press in Shanghai provided a forum for the often rancorous political debates of the community, though the most widely read Russian paper, the *Shanghai Zaria*, stood somewhat aloof from ideological controversy: while, of course, anti-Soviet, it tried, under its founding editor L. V. Arnoldov, to cater for all sections of the White Russian population.

Unemployment was a major problem in the community. In 1927, 150 former soldiers were recruited to form the Russian unit of the Shanghai Volunteer Corps. In the crisis of that year they contributed to the defence of the International Settlement against the threatened communist insurrection. Other Russians were recruited into the Shanghai Municipal Police and in a few cases were promoted to senior positions, particularly in the Special Branch. A few of the emigrants had managed to salvage capital from Russia and set up in business in Shanghai. A handful lived by selling off pieces of jewellery one by one. The majority were penniless and many drifted into a life on the margins of respectable European society. Many of the women had been camp-followers of the armed forces and became a notorious and conspicuous element in Shanghai nightlife, working as bar-girls, taxi-dancers and whores.

The heyday of Russian influence in China had been the early 1920s. For a time the Kuomintang hoed a leftist line and Soviet advisers headed by Mikhail Borodin and Adolf Ioffe sought to steer China towards a communist millennium. But alien dominance came to be resented and the Soviet-Kuomintang alliance ended abruptly. The turning-point came in Shanghai in 1927: the Chinese communists were crushed by an unholy alliance of forces loyal to Chiang Kai-shek and local gangster elements under the control of the Green Gang boss Tu Yueh-sheng. The authorities in the concessions winked as the anti-communist troops passed through their districts. In this crisis the White Russian community too played a part – its members' last, and for once successful, stand against bolshevism.

Throughout the following decade the Special Branch of the Municipal Police fixed on the suppression of communism as its first priority. In 1931 it scored a further significant victory when, with the help of the French Concession police force, it broke apart the main Far Eastern network of

Comintern in the so-called 'Noulens case'. 'Hilaire Noulens' and his wife (their real names have only recently become known: Yakov Rudnik and Tatyana Moiseenko[1]) headed a large group of Soviet agents operating throughout the Far East. The couple's arrest led to the virtual collapse of the network and constituted a severe setback for Soviet intelligence and subversion in the region. Meanwhile Chiang Kai-shek pursued a savage purge of communists. The results in Shanghai were impressive. By 1935 there were estimated to be no more than 100 active party members left in the city. It took a long time for the party to regroup and recover its influence among Shanghai's industrial workers.

After 1927 and particularly after Mao Tse-tung led his army on the Long March into the hills of Yenan in 1934–35, the Chinese communists shook off Comintern, that is Russian, control to a considerable degree. In Shanghai, however, the party remained more susceptible to Comintern influence than the independent-minded comrades in Yenan. One consequence was the greater readiness of the Shanghai party to collaborate both with 'progressive' elements in the Chinese business community and with powerful local gangster elements. The party's call in 1935 for a 'united front' of communists with the Kuomintang against the Japanese represented a victory over Mao Tse-tung for so-called 'internationalist' elements headed by Wang Ming, a Moscow-trained Comintern loyalist. Although Stalin gave the nod to Mao as party leader in 1937, Wang Ming's influence remained perceptible in the underground Shanghai party for many years.[2]

The outbreak of the Sino-Japanese war led to a renewed warming of relations between the Chinese nationalists and the USSR. In July 1938 serious clashes between Soviet and Japanese forces broke out on the Soviet-Manchurian border. The following summer renewed fighting erupted on the border between Mongolia and Manchuria and continued until an armistice was agreed on 16 September 1939.

Building on the temporary alignment of Soviet and Chinese policies, Soviet propagandists in Shanghai moved cautiously above ground. In the autumn of 1937 a Repatriation Union of Russian Emigrants in Shanghai was established with the declared object of promoting pro-Soviet propaganda and assisting local Russians to obtain Soviet citizenship and return to their homeland. The union organized public meetings and published a weekly newspaper. The French authorities refused to allow the organization to operate in the concession, whereupon it established its office at 105 Love Lane in the settlement. Detective Inspector A. Prokofiev, one of the most experienced and reliable Russian officers of the Municipal Police Special Branch, was assigned to report on the union. He ascertained that although the union engaged in considerable publicity and activity, it attracted little support. Like many such bodies, the union was a far from spontaneous growth. In reality, it was closely controlled by official Soviet agents.

Predictably the union attracted hostility from right-wing circles:

> It was not [wrote Prokofiev] because anybody objected to
> their intention of departing for the USSR. On the contrary, it
> was often said in those circles that departure of pro-Soviet
> elements from Shanghai would only 'purify the atmosphere'
> here. However, suspicion was openly expressed that, instead
> of granting them permission to return to Soviet Russia, the
> Soviet Government would prefer to keep them where they are
> in order to utilize these elements for their own ends as an
> instrument of propaganda, willing informers and agents. In
> this connection references were made to the activities of a
> similar organization in Paris, members of which, it was
> alleged, were involved in political assassinations and
> kidnappings. The animosity towards the local Repatriation
> Union found its expression in a bomb attack on 22 December
> 1937, presumably by a group of Russian political extremists,
> and in an attack on 5 September 1938 against N. Svinyin-
> Svetloff, Chairman of the Union, by a member of the local
> group of the Russian Fascist Party.[3]

The Russian fascist party was one of several extreme-right groups sponsored by the Japanese with a view to possible use against the Soviets in Siberia. Founded at Harbin in 1931, it was led by a fanatical adventurer, Konstantin Vladimirovich Rodzaevsky. The party's Shanghai branch organized Christmas parties decorated with swastikas and balloons, but otherwise achieved little. Since the 1920s the Japanese had also supported a

⌐ Russian force headed by a Cossack Ataman, Grigorii Semenov.
⌐anese kept Semenov in reserve in case of a Russo-Japanese war in
⌐ia. Using Japanese funds, Semenov recruited a number of White Rus-
⌐ns from north China into a small military unit based in Tientsin (later in
Dairen) which trained in readiness for the day when it could participate in
the liberation of the homeland as an ally of the Japanese army. Semenov's
son, a fluent speaker of Japanese and French, served as a Japanese nominee
in the Foreign Affairs section of the Shanghai Municipal Police until 1944,
reporting on the French community in Shanghai.

Rumours that the Japanese were using White Russian forces against the
Soviets in frontier battles were exploited by Soviet propagandists in Shanghai. Those Russians who allowed themselves to be used on the battlefield
against their fellow-countrymen were denounced by a pro-Soviet weekly as:

> ugly vampires who keep themselves alive by sucking the blood
> of their brothers. Of course, these pitiful individuals are not
> an asset to the Japanese Army, but the mere fact of their
> presence in the enemy ranks (and that presence is absolutely
> voluntary) arouses in us a feeling of high indignation. We are
> sure the Japanese have the same feeling of contempt and
> squeamishness towards those renegades and consider them
> mercenaries who crawl on their bellies in front of their
> masters or hateful degenerates with crooked brains.[4]

In the poisonous vein characteristic of the Shanghai press wars, the White
Russian press responded with equally abusive counter-accusations.

The divisions within the Russian community had bloody consequences.
By 1939 the Japanese had taken the Russian Emigrants' Committee, headed
by Charles Metzler, under their wing. Using a mixture of threats and patronage, they reduced it to virtual servitude. But they were disappointed by
Metzler's failure to secure Russian votes in support of Japanese candidates
in the elections to the Municipal Council in the spring of 1940. Metzler's
Japanese patrons lost patience with him shortly afterwards when he resisted
pressure to hand over funds under his control. They seem to have decided
to make an example of him. In August 1940 Metzler was murdered.

His successor, Nikolai A. Ivanov, a 'stocky, bald lawyer', was appointed at a closed meeting with Bishop John, spiritual head of the Russian Orthodox Church in Shanghai, and Colonel Lu Ying, police commissioner of the puppet municipality. The new leader of the White Russian community conformed more precisely than Metzler to the demands of the Japanese and their Chinese puppets.[5] Ivanov sought to consolidate the control of the Emigrants' Committee over all White Russian institutions in Shanghai. He announced a '"self-imposed" obligatory tax' to be paid to the Committee by all members of the community. A diehard conservative, he also ordered a return to the Julian calendar, prevalent in Russia before 1917, which differed from the Gregorian calendar by 13 days. All letters emanating from the committee were dated according to the old calendar, causing considerable confusion to recipients. In January 1941 the Russian Orthodox Confraternity Hospital, the largest in the city, was taken over by Ivanov's committee, 'reportedly "not by deed of purchase"'.[6] Ivanov next eyed the Russian Club in Avenue Foch. This was a non-political cultural and social institution where theatrical performances were staged. The committee took advantage of complaints of 'communistic themes' in plays presented in the club to launch 'investigations' – though, meeting some resistance from the club's leaders, Ivanov drew back from seeking to take it over.[7]

The following September, Ivanov too was murdered. His assassins were reported by the French political police to have been 'Chinese terrorists' – although, of course, that proved nothing as to the original source of the attack.[8] Ivanov's disappearance only strengthened the dictatorial tendency in the Russian community. Reflecting the militarist mood, the committee was henceforth headed by an army officer, first by a colonel, and then by General Glebov who remained in charge until his death in October 1945.

The Shanghai White Russians were deeply divided by the German attack on the Soviet Union in June 1941. The majority, particularly older elements, remained hostile to the Soviet régime and regarded its defeat in war as the only hope of bringing about the fall of communism. They tended almost instinctively to see the Nazis as liberators rather than invaders of their homeland. Although Japan was neutral in the German-Soviet War, its status as an Axis ally of Germany earned it sympathy among Shanghai Russians. The *Shanghai Zaria* expressed the general feeling when it supported pro-

Japanese statements by Ataman Semenov and declared: 'Russian immigrants [in Shanghai] are for the New Order and demonstrate full loyalty to the Nipponese Empire'.[9] In October 1941 the Emigrants' Committee decided to expel all members suspected of working for or even sympathizing with the Soviets. At the same time, in an effort to counter Soviet propaganda, 30 Russian organizations in Shanghai, including the Union of Russian Veterans and the Cossacks' Union, formed a Supreme National-Ideological Russian Grand Council.

Some younger elements in the community, assiduously courted by Soviet propagandists, argued that the Stalin régime should be regarded as temporary and that all Russians should rally to the defence of the national hearth. About 1,500 Russian emigrants in Shanghai applied for Soviet citizenship in the immediate aftermath of the German attack, thus rendering themselves liable for military call-up, though none of the applications seems to have been accepted.[10]

Other Shanghai Russians took an intermediate position. While remaining deeply anti-communist, they could not stomach the idea of seeking the defeat of their own country in a defensive war. This was the position taken, for example, by V.D. Jiganov, a well-known Shanghai publicist and author of a pamphlet entitled 'In Defence of the Motherland', published in August 1941. Jiganov denounced defeatist tendencies among Shanghai Russians who, he maintained, were in this respect following the shameful example set by Lenin in the First World War.[11]

Given the USSR's neutrality in the Far Eastern War, the Japanese felt obliged to permit pro-Soviet news organs to continue to operate in Shanghai. The Soviet consulate's bookstore, protected against police raids by its diplomatic status, remained an important centre for the dissemination of communist propaganda. Pro-Soviet newspapers and radio stations functioned freely.

As in the case of other powers, the Soviet propaganda effort merged seamlessly into intelligence activity. In April 1941 the Japanese consul-general in Shanghai reported that the recently appointed director of the TASS News Agency in the city was gradually expanding the Soviet intelligence effort there. He was said to have held a dinner party attended by British and American intelligence chiefs in Shanghai at which it was agreed that the three powers would exchange intelligence at the local level.[12] By 1941 the Soviet intelligence apparatus in the Far East had recovered from the Noulens débâcle and rebuilt a formidable network of spies. By and large they relied on ideological adherents rather than gangsters and petty criminals: the contrast with the Axis powers was striking and at this critical point the Soviet approach yielded by far the more impressive dividends.

上海

On 5 March 1941, Hermann Erben arrived back in Shanghai. Even before calling on his bosom companion Miorini, he went direct from the docks with his luggage to the German consulate, where he was interviewed by the local Gestapo and then taken to see the Abwehr bureau chief, Siefken. The two men had, in fact, met before, in the second-class saloon of a German liner off the coast of Africa in 1939, but Erben appears to have been unaware at that time of Siefken's intelligence connections. Some time later Siefken also introduced him to the head of the German propaganda bureau, Baron Puttkamer, in the latter's penthouse flat at the Park Hotel. They discussed the possibility of Erben taking a job in Puttkamer's organization. Puttkamer offered him 'a nice addition to your income' if he would do so, but Siefken forbade him to work for any other German agency.[13]

Erben was assigned by the Siefken bureau to work on American sailors in the port in order to acquire maritime information. As Erben later described it, his job was:

> to cover the waterfront, to approach, in my capacity as a
> physician, former shipmates, to invite myself aboard ship, to
> get their detailed course from the ship's map, to get the daily
> position if that should be carelessly left there, to contact the
> wireless operators and see if it was possible for them to tell me
> anything about code signals, ships' calling signals, and so on,
> to chart as closely as possible sailing times, arrival dates, cargo
> and ships met and see of what nationality, and so on.

Erben was also ordered to contact the US consulate in his capacity as an

American citizen, with a view to finding some weak link in their security. In addition, he was to watch Major Williams, the local American intelligence chief, who lived in the Medhurst Apartments.[14] Erben's meetings with his controller took place each Sunday at the German Protestant church. The men would signal to each other during the service and then meet outside afterwards. Erben was paid a stipend equivalent to 300 gold marks a month.[15] He continued working on assignments of this sort until 8 December 1941. Meanwhile he practised medicine in Shanghai as a venereal disease specialist and abortionist. Initially he lived at the German School; later he moved in with Miorini.

Siefken's employment of such squalid local agents as Erben gave an opening to his rivals and enemies among the German official apparatus in Shanghai, in particular the newly-appointed chief representative of the SS in the Far East, Colonel Josef Meisinger.

Born in Munich in 1899, Meisinger had been a Nazi since the early 1920s. After Hitler's rise to power he had been summoned to Berlin from his job as a Bavarian police official. In the German capital he served as a henchman of the German security service chief, Heinrich Himmler, and was placed in charge of investigations of homosexuality and abortions. He was said to have 'participated personally in the execution of Captain Roehm' during the Night of Long Knives in June 1934.[16] Following the capture of Warsaw by the Germans in September 1939, Meisinger served as head of the Gestapo there. His ruthless conduct in the Polish capital earned him the sobriquet 'butcher of Warsaw'. Later he returned to Berlin where, on 5 February 1941, he married Catherine Haeder-Quedzuweit-Packheiser.

His wife, a convent-educated, blonde, blue-eyed typist at the Gestapo headquarters in Berlin, was in her late 20s and was described as 'chic and with good taste in clothes'.[17] Rumour had it that she was the discarded mistress of Meisinger's boss, Himmler. Just five days after the wedding, according to Mrs Meisinger, the couple 'agreed to get a divorce, to which, however, the German officials would not agree. Two weeks later [she continued], he tried to put me in an insane asylum.' [18] Mrs Meisinger later recalled that she lived with her husband only for short periods, during which he threatened and abused her to such an extent that she considered suicide.

Meisinger not only was a monster; he also looked like one. An SS colleague described him as 'a frightening individual, a large, coarse-faced man with a bald head and an incredibly ugly face'.[19] An Australian journalist who saw him in Tokyo called him 'a grinning, swashbuckling, donkey-faced scoundrel'.[20]

In the spring of 1941 Meisinger was sent to the Far East with the title of police attaché at the German embassy in Tokyo. Accompanied by his wife, he travelled across Russia on the Trans-Siberian Railway, reaching Tokyo in April 1941 and Shanghai shortly afterwards. Meisinger's authority extended throughout Japan, Japanese-occupied territories and the Far East in general. His task was 'to oversee the activities of all Germans in the Far East, to make sure of their loyalty to the Party and the Fuehrer, and to punish those who were believed to be lukewarm in this loyalty or outright disloyal'. [21] Several suspect Germans were kidnapped and placed on board German blockade runners that sailed from Japan to Europe. As a result Meisinger came to be feared by his fellow-countrymen throughout the region. Although his main base was at Tokyo, he used to spend several weeks at a time in Shanghai. Immediately upon his arrival in the city, he took charge of Kahner's local Gestapo organization.

Like Siefken, Meisinger had uneasy relations with German diplomats in the Far East. Many feared him and resented his diplomatic status. The German ambassador to China, H. G. Stahmer, whose wife was said to be Jewish, was specially apprehensive. The diplomats feared that the police attaché's reports might include damaging information about themselves. On one occasion a report was indeed sent to Berlin from Tokyo 'on the attitude of the members of the consular and diplomatic staff in Shanghai', evoking inquiries by Berlin.[22] Alarmed by Meisinger's activities, Consul-General Fischer pressed the German Foreign Ministry to revoke his diplomatic appointment and the Foreign Minister, Ribbentrop, considered doing so. But in this as in other matters Himmler's contrary opinion prevailed.

Meisinger soon built up a multi-layered intelligence organization, centred in Shanghai, which focused on collecting political information from all parts of the region. Two weeks before Pearl Harbor he scored a minor success for his employers when his ring penetrated the office of the press attaché at the British embassy. But although the achievement was trumpeted proudly to Berlin, no significant seepage of classified information seems to have occurred.[23] Nor was much useful knowledge gleaned from documents handed over to the Germans by the White Russian gangster 'Captain' Pick that he had obtained 'by unknown means' (possibly with the help of Hermann Erben) from the office of the US naval intelligence chief in Shanghai, Major Williams.[24] Meanwhile, even as the Germans celebrated these trivial feats of petty larceny, the Soviets had accomplished a dramatic intelligence coup under the very noses of the Axis intelligence services in the Far East. Their instrument was to be hailed later as the greatest spy of the century.

上海

Richard Sorge was a German citizen, born in Tiflis, Georgia, in 1895. He worked as a journalist in Shanghai from 1930 to 1932. From 1936 onwards he was correspondent for the *Frankfurter Zeitung* and other German newspapers in Tokyo. A well-known and much-liked figure in the German community, Sorge was a trusted adviser to the German ambassador in Japan, Major-General Eugen Ott, who had such a high opinion of him that he was given full access to embassy files. Sorge was also on friendly social terms with Meisinger. When Sorge visited Shanghai in May 1941 to study the attitude of Japanese officials in China towards proposed American mediation between Chiang Kai-shek and Japan, he did so as an official German embassy courier, armed with a Japanese diplomatic pass. In the course of his trip he met senior German and Japanese officials and was able to form an educated view of the movement of Japanese policy in China. His report, submitted to Ott upon his return to Tokyo, was transmitted to Berlin 'without alteration'.[25]

But another copy was sent to Moscow. Sorge's greatest feat, his warning to Stalin of an imminent German invasion, followed a few weeks later.

On 16 October 1941 Sorge, his wife and many others were arrested by the Japanese and charged with espionage on behalf of the Soviet Union. Meisinger was in Shanghai at the time of Sorge's arrest and immediately went to Tokyo. At first, Ott and Meisinger could hardly believe that their compatriot was a Soviet spy and tried to persuade the Japanese to release him. But in prison Sorge confessed that he had been a communist since 1919 and a Comintern agent since 1924. When the truth dawned, the Germans were flabbergasted and deeply embarrassed in their relations with their ally.

Subsequent investigations by the Japanese and the Germans (separately) indicated that Sorge's spy ring had penetrated the office of the Japanese prime minister, Konoye. Intelligence had been dispatched to Russia by means of coded radio messages. The Japanese intelligence service even claimed to have intercepted a message from Moscow thanking Sorge for timely transmission of the date of the German attack on Russia.[26] Sorge was condemned to death on 29 September 1943 and executed shortly afterwards.

The Sorge affair produced a veritable spy hysteria among the Japanese and led to a general tightening of security also by the Germans in the Far East. The episode injected a further element of mistrust into the German-Japanese relationship. Both sides were henceforth less willing to share secret information. In Shanghai special measures were taken by the Germans to enhance the security of cipher materials and political papers. Scissor gratings, steel doors and electric alarms were installed in German government offices. Meisinger, who had been totally bamboozled by Sorge, sought to camouflage his own responsibility by vigorously denouncing Ott and the local Nazi party chief in Japan. Over the objections of Foreign Minister Ribbentrop, Himmler ultimately secured Ott's recall from Tokyo.

The exposure of the communist spy ring at the heart of the Axis establishment in the Far East demonstrated that Russia, although a neutral in the war between Japan and her enemies, was nevertheless a major player in the game of nations. As in the case of the other powers, the nerve centre of her intelligence effort in the region was, almost axiomatically, Shanghai. And in the Russian case too the wider diplomatic struggle was reflected in vicious miniature at the local level.

On 13 September 1941 a Russian journalist, Serge I. Mamontoff, was attacked in the French Concession; he died two days later as a result of his wounds. Mamontoff, who worked on a pro-Axis Russian newspaper, *Far Eastern Times*, had earlier published a pamphlet attacking 'Captain' Pick. According to a later American intelligence report, Pick had succeeded in persuading the puppet Nanking 'Reformed Government' that Mamontoff was a Soviet agent who should be eliminated.[27]* In 'autobiographical notes' that he prepared after the war for the American Counter-Intelligence Corps, Pick claimed that Mamontoff was a Japanese agent who was also working for the French and was killed by a gangster working for the Wang Ching-wei puppet régime.'[29] The truth was that Pick himself hired a Chinese professional killer to kill Mamontoff; the assassin was to be paid 2,300 Chinese dollars (less than US$125 at the then rate of exchange). The money was said to have been provided, for reasons that remain obscure, by the Nanking régime. The killer later complained that he had actually received only 300 dollars. A White Russian officer in the concession police force, Slobodchikov, was assigned to the case. Regarded by his superiors as a brilliant detective, Slobodchikov justified their confidence by rapidly identifying the perpetrators. Both the assassin and Pick were arrested and placed on trial in the Second District Court in the concession. By this time that court was under the control of the Nanking puppet government, but, for the moment, Pick's Japanese connections availed him nothing with the bench. On 24 November 1941 he was found guilty and sentenced to 15 years' imprisonment. His jail term, however, was to be cut short by a sudden change in international – and local – conditions.

上海

Only 750 US marines now remained in Shanghai. On 26 November the *President Harrison*, the US President Line's trans-Pacific liner, arrived to evacuate the last elements of the US 4th Marine regiment. A party at the American Club the next day bade them farewell. On 28 November they marched down the Bund, their regimental band playing 'The Stars and Stripes Forever'. The *President Harrison* successfully disembarked its passengers at Manila a few days later and then turned its prow back towards Shanghai.

---

*A Dutch intelligence report in 1931 had listed Mamontoff, whose real name was said to be Riabtchenko, as an agent in Shanghai of the Soviet GPU.[28]

The Municipal Council announced that, with the departure of the American troops, responsibility for law and order in the former American defence sector of the settlement would 'be placed upon the Shanghai Municipal Police who will request, when necessary, the assistance of the Shanghai Volunteer Corps'.[30] Few deceived themselves that there was now any obstacle to a Japanese takeover. A British intelligence report that month referred to 'an atmosphere of what can only be described as gloomy foreboding as regards the local situation'.[31] Two US gunboats, the *Luzon* and *Oahu*, sailed from Shanghai to Manila at the end of the month, thus virtually dissolving the American Navy's Yangtse River Patrol. Only the USS *Wake* remained at Shanghai and she was reported to be lying at the American naval buoy, prepared to hoist anchor 'at a moment's notice' in order to evacuate American consular officials.[32]

A settlement defended only by the part-time Volunteer Corps represented an open invitation to the Japanese. Recognizing this, the British and Americans, who had been slowly moving out women and children and non-essential civilians since the beginning of the year, undertook a hasty evacuation. The SS *Anhui* of the China Navigation Company was specially fitted out to accommodate several hundred British evacuees who left for Hong Kong and Singapore on 3 December. (They got as far as Manila but were held up there by the outbreak of the Pacific War.) In the growing climate of nervousness, Butterfield & Swire cancelled all sailings for northern ports and diverted ships to Hong Kong instead. The Dutch ship *Tjijilenka* suddenly set sail three days ahead of schedule, before she had even unloaded all of her consignment of goods due to be discharged in Shanghai. On 5 December the *China Press* reported that almost all British ships had left the Yangtse delta 'conceivably for the first time since Shanghai opened up for foreign trade in the early years of the last century'. The next day five Japanese men-of-war stood in the harbour, including the cruiser *Idzumo*, flagship of the Imperial Third Fleet. The only remaining British naval vessel was a small gunboat; like the USS *Wake* she was retained not so much to show the flag as to provide a radio link between consular authorities in Shanghai and the home government.

By now it was almost an open secret in Shanghai that a Japanese attack was impending. 'Like a little Rome awaiting the barbarians',[33] the Shanghailanders made their dispositions as best they could and looked forward with dread to the inevitable.

On 6 December Hugh Collar, local head of Imperial Chemical Industries, received a telegram from the company's Hong Kong office with the message 'The time has come.' He recognized it as a warning that war was imminent.[34]

5 Dark World

JAPANESE OVERTOOK SHANGHAI INCIDENTLESSLY 080100 UP-
CLOSING BANKS BUSINESS INSTITUTIONS WHICH REOPENED LATER
UNDER RESTRICTIONS STOP

was how the United Press began its report on the virtually bloodless seizure of the International Settlement in Shanghai on Monday, 8 December 1941.[1] Shanghai by that date was, in effect, an open city. On previous occasions when the settlement had faced military threats – for example in 1932 and 1937 – British, French and American forces, as well as the variegated national contingents of the Shanghai Volunteer Corps, had drawn up to protect the foreign enclaves. But by December 1941 all British and American troops had been withdrawn, the small French and Italian units were not disposed to resist the Japanese, and the Volunteer Corps was not even mobilized.

The two remaining non-Japanese men-of-war on the Whangpoo, the USS *Wake* and HMS *Peterel*,* were attacked by the Japanese before dawn at 4.00 a.m. – an hour or so after the attack on Pearl Harbor (five time zones to the east, across the international date line). The Allied vessels were overcome in a matter of minutes. The *Wake*, which was commanded by Lieutenant-Commander Columbus Darwin Smith, a former Shanghai harbour pilot, was moored in midstream opposite the Bund. Pre-war plans had been made for scuttling the ship in an emergency, but the captain was in his apartment on shore and the crew were overpowered by Japanese boarders before they were able to resist. The ship was taken without a shot

---

Sic! The misspelling of the correct name, *Petrel*, was originally a mistake by an Admiralty clerk. Over the years it caused endless confusion among officials and, later, historians. But the error, once made, could not, it seems, be corrected.

being fired and the Japanese flag was hoisted. As an account by American naval historians notes, the *Wake* enjoyed the ignominious distinction of being 'the only American naval vessel of World War II to be captured intact and without resistance'.[2] She was subsequently renamed *Tatara Maru* and incorporated into the Japanese navy.

By contrast, HMS *Peterel*, commanded by Lieutenant Stephen Polkinghorn, put up a vigorous but doomed defence. She was moored a little further upstream, opposite the French Bund. The British gunboat had been alerted by a telephone call from the British consulate in time for the crew to get to battle stations. When a Japanese officer boarded the ship and demanded its surrender, Polkinghorn responded, 'Get off my bloody ship!'[3] The Japanese disembarked and opened fire from batteries on shore and on nearby warships, whereupon the *Peterel* responded with her two machine-guns. Meanwhile secret code books were burnt in the boiler room. After the *Peterel* had been hit several times she exploded and keeled over. The order was given to abandon ship. Since the vessel's motor launch had been hit, the men had to swim ashore, some of them being picked up by sympathetic Chinese in sampans. Six of the eighteen crew members on board were killed and all the others wounded (though the Japanese later announced falsely that no British sailors had been killed[4]). Most of the survivors were captured by the Japanese.[5]

All the captured crew members of the *Wake* and of the *Peterel* were interned by the Japanese. Several, among them Smith, later escaped but were recaptured. They were subsequently tried on the strange charge of deserting from the Japanese army and sentenced to prison terms which they served in the Ward Road jail. Two of the American sailors managed to elude capture and escaped from Shanghai to rejoin American forces. Three of the *Peterel's* crew were ashore at the time of the attack; two were soon arrested by the Japanese but one, Petty Officer James Cuming, a radio operator, remained at large. In response to Japanese pressure, Hugh Collar, who had agreed to serve as head of the British Residents' Association in Shanghai, sent word to Cuming that, if he surrendered, he (Collar) would 'accept responsibility towards His Majesty's Government' – an extraordinary arrogation of authority by a civilian, though typical of the Shanghai mind in action.[6] Cuming rightly ignored the appeal and remained underground in

Shanghai under the alias 'Mr Trees'. As a cover, the story was spread that 'Mr Trees' had escaped to Chungking.[7]

Shanghai's first battle of the Pacific War was also its last. From then until the Japanese surrender there was no further conventional fighting in the city. Already, however, battle lines had been drawn for the unconventional struggle that was to be waged in Shanghai over the next four years.

上海

Nothing further prevented the Japanese, on the morning of 8 December, from seizing the richest prize of the entire war in the Far East. Nationalist Chinese guerillas were operating near the city but neither they nor anybody else offered any resistance to the invading army as it entered the settlement. The Japanese forces succeeded within a matter of hours in consolidating their hold on the city. By 10.00 a.m. they had occupied the palatial headquarters on the Bund of the Hong Kong and Shanghai Bank, the greatest symbol of British capitalism in China. The staff were induced to hand over the keys to safes and strongrooms and the enterprise was placed under the control of the Yokohama Specie Bank.[8] Similar measures were applied to all other British and American banks. When they reopened on 11 December, depositors were permitted to make only limited withdrawals. Crowds nevertheless besieged bank premises and long queues of customers clamoured to withdraw money. At the Hongkong and Shanghai Bank alone 2,000 people were dealt with in three hours.[9]

At the American consulate the staff had time to burn papers and code books before the Japanese arrived. Allied diplomatic and consular officials were confined to the Cathay and Metropole hotels and to the Cathay Mansions apartment block. They spent the next few months there at the expense of the Japanese government, pending arrangements for their repatriation in exchange for Japanese diplomats. The relatively luxurious living conditions of these officials aroused a certain amount of resentment among ordinary British and American civilians, most of whom suffered a rude decline in their standard of living.

Allied businesses were taken over by Japanese administrators. The Jardine, Matheson headquarters at No. 27, the Bund, were occupied by the

Japanese navy which installed its intelligence department in the building. One hundred British and American manufacturing concerns were placed under Japanese control, although a shortage of raw materials forced some of them to reduce output or suspend operations altogether. The Jardine-owned Ewo cotton mill, for example, continued to operate until 7 January without interference. It was then placed under Japanese supervision and the only form of further activity was completion of existing orders. The once bustling stock, cotton and bond exchanges closed. Eighty thousand tons of British and American merchant shipping were seized.

Meanwhile, at about 4.00 a.m. on the day of the attack, the chairman of the Shanghai Municipal Council, J. H. Liddell, the acting head of the Municipal Police, Captain H. M. Smyth, and other top officials of the settlement heard by telephone that war had broken out. They were called to a meeting at 6.00 a.m in the council chamber. There they met the Japanese consul-general, Horiuchi Teteki, as well as representatives of the Japanese naval, military and Gendarmerie forces. The consul-general informed them that the Japanese were in the process of occupying the entire settlement area. He asked the council members and officials to carry on in office. The British and American consuls gave their approval and at a further council meeting that evening, the Allied members agreed to continue 'in the interests of the Settlement generally'.[10]

The German consul reported to Berlin that the evening session had been 'dramatic' and that a certain degree of dissension had been visible in the course of the day between the British and American members of the council. For the British, the idea of resignation from the council represented an affront to their traditional imperial role in the Far East, whereas for the Americans such a withdrawal represented merely a loss of their economic and political position; the Anglo-American differences, the consul explained, had been aggravated by the way in which the *Wake* had surrendered that morning without resistance, whereas the *Peterel* had engaged the enemy.[11]

The next day the *Shanghai Times* published a series of proclamations by the city's new masters. All British and American citizens, as well as Filipinos and Indians, were ordered to register at the Japanese Gendarmerie office in Hamilton House, opposite the Metropole Hotel. They were required to give personal particulars and details of all movable property and real estate held in Shanghai. In return they were issued with identification passes. Over the next few days photographers did a roaring trade in pass-photos.

The Volunteer Corps was not immediately disbanded but training was 'suspended until further notice' and all arms and equipment held by volunteers were called in. The British commandant of the corps, Lieutenant-Colonel G. H. Mann MC, was later reported to 'have surreptitiously organized a scheme to turn out and arm the corps when the tide turns and an armed protective force is necessary' – but the day never came.[12]

Eleven Chinese and English newspapers stopped appearing immediately, although three resumed publication after a day or two. From 15 December the two remaining English papers were obliged to submit to formal censorship. Japanese Army 'News Dissemination Trucks' drove round the city distributing leaflets that showed a caricature of Churchill and Roosevelt clinging to each other in terror at a Japanese shell. Army trucks, equipped with loudspeakers, toured the city thundering forth announcements and distributing leaflets. All bookstores and publishing houses were taken over by the Japanese. Large 'war situation boards', measuring 18 feet by 12 feet, were erected by the press section of the Japanese army 'to enable the people to learn the exact news of the war situation as early as possible' – as the *Shanghai Times* put it.[13]

On 30 December 1941 Consul-General Horiuchi summarized the measures that had been taken in the propaganda sphere: 'At the start of the occupation we took over and eliminated all anti-Japanese newspapers, news agencies and radio stations. We confiscated all the anti-Japanese books in the bookstores ... All the news media are totally under our control.' At the same time, Horiuchi noted with concern that residents were listening to shortwave radio broadcasts from Chungking and to overseas stations. As a result 'all kinds of rumours' were spreading and the population was being 'convinced by negative propaganda and false broadcasts'. The Japanese were therefore 'considering taking over all the enemy propaganda institutions, making use of all newspaper and other channels to activate our propaganda, and disposing of the shortwave radios owned by residents'.[14]

At the end of the month the Japanese convened a meeting of prominent British and American citizens at the Metropole Hotel, where the Japanese

Army established its press bureau. According to a report the next day in the *Shanghai Times*, 'eloquent words of encomium were showered by local prominent Britons and Americans on the Japanese forces for their orderly and courteous conduct since their entry into the Settlement'. T. Uno, the head of the press bureau, said: 'If any of you was involved in so-called incidents, like slapping, pushing around or bayoneting, we should like to hear from you.' Whereupon, according to the *Times* report, Mr Gregg of the Asia Glass Company stood up and said that there was no reason for any American to complain about the conduct of the Japanese forces because 'they have been behaving extremely courteous to all of us when the American Club was occupied'. An American missionary made a plea for 'mutual understanding and goodwill'. Among those present was the fiercely anti-Japanese American journalist J. B. Powell. Towards the end of the meeting Uno turned to Powell and asked, 'What did you expect the Japanese forces would do to you when they entered the Settlement?' 'I did not expect anything worse than being shot', Powell replied, occasioning, reported the *Times*, 'an outburst of laughter from the audience'.

There was more hilarity the next day at a press conference convened by the Japanese army spokesman. He warned enemy citizens not to disseminate false rumours or 'disturbing news from Chungking'. When an American correspondent bluntly inquired whether Britons and Americans would be thrown into concentration camps, the spokesman replied: 'The International Settlement is in itself a sort of concentration camp', a declaration that was received 'amid laughter', according to the upbeat report in the *Shanghai Times*.[15]

On 12 December, members of the Shanghai Club on the Bund were interrupted at lunchtime by one of the few Japanese members, accompanied by a Japanese naval officer, and ordered off the premises. The building was taken over for the use of the Japanese Naval Landing Party. Other British and American clubs, formerly centres of expatriate social life, were similarly expropriated.

上海

The French Concession was the only area of the city that was not occupied by the Japanese in December 1941. In his speech at the Concordia Club in November 1940, Major-General Miura had intimated that a more lenient régime was planned for French concessions in China, which, he said, would be regarded as 'territory under the control of a non-belligerent'.[16] On the evening of 6 December Consul-General Margerie received a cable from the French ambassador in Peking instructing him, in the event of the outbreak of war in the Pacific between Japan and the US or Britain, to address himself immediately to the Japanese consul-general and assure him that France would maintain a policy of strict neutrality and, in the spirit of Franco-Japanese collaboration, would repress all anti-Japanese activity in the concession. Margerie was further told that while he should fulfil this undertaking, he should avoid giving his actions 'a spectacular character' that could lead to trouble with 'Anglo-Saxon circles'. Ambassador Cosme added that he was 'aware that there is a certain contradictoriness in the above instructions', but he declared that the only way to protect French interests in the Far East seemed to be to practise a *politique d'équilibre* between the opposing forces in the region.[17]

Faithful to these orders, Margerie gave his 'approval in principle' on the morning of 8 December to the stationing of Japanese Gendarmerie units in the concession.[18] The Japanese did not, in fact, exercise this right immediately. The formal autonomy of the concession was thus upheld for the time being. On 13 December Margerie issued a proclamation announcing that in the event of any acts of terrorism, the *notables du quartier* would be arrested and handed over to the Japanese Gendarmerie for 'severe sanctions'.[19]

In the annual report for 1941, issued by the concession authorities early in 1942, the relationship of the French Political Police to their Japanese overlords was described candidly in terms that, *mutatis mutandis*, might have been applied to the Franco-German relationship in occupied France:

> The principal role of this service remains that of collaboration
> with the local authorities. The service contributes broadly to
> the policy of assistance to the Japanese authorities to the
> extent that the neutral position of France and the statute of
> the Concession do not prevent it. This collaborationist effort

is manifested in numerous inquiries and instances of assistance.[20]

Relations between the Japanese and the French were facilitated by the co-incidence that the French police chief, Commandant L. Fabre, and the head of the Japanese Gendarmerie, General Kinoshita, had been military cadets together at the officers' college at Saint-Cyr.[21]

The Japanese, however, were not altogether satisfied. At a meeting with Fabre in February 1942, Colonel Noguchi of the Japanese Gendarmerie gave him a 'personal and friendly warning' that 'certain Japanese circles' considered that the French were failing to render 'the sincere and spontaneous collaboration expected of them'. Among the officials in the concession, Noguchi alleged, were 'certain Gaullist elements or allied sympathizers'. In response Fabre could do no more than outline all that the French had done to ensure 'harmonious collaboration with the [Japanese] Gendarmerie'.[22]

Yet while subjecting the concession authorities to humiliating treatment, the Japanese found it convenient from time to time to make use of the French as a communications channel. Thus, for example, when they ordered the French broadcasting station to exercise strict self-censorship over all reports arriving from Vichy that might be harmful to Japanese interests, they also asked the French-controlled news agency Havas to supply them à titre privé with unpublishable 'bad news' items.[23] On another occasion the Japanese consul-general visited Margerie and asked him 'confidentially' to transmit a message to Chungking. The message had been written by Sir Frederick Maze, retiring British head of the Chinese Maritime Customs, 'in accord with his Japanese successor', and was addressed to Dr H. H. Kung, Chiang Kai-shek's finance minister. Margerie replied that, on instructions from his ambassador, he had ceased communication with Chungking upon the outbreak of hostilities in the Pacific but that, to render service to his visitor, he would make an exception in this case.[24]

After December 1941 Japanese were for the first time permitted to join the French Club (Cercle Sportif Français) which, in spite of its name, had a very large British membership.* A Canadian businessman recounted that some of the pro-Vichy French 'welcomed the little yellow devils; we wished them joy of their new friends'. He went on to recall with glee an incident in which a Japanese consular official got drunk in the club, tried to kiss French women at the bar, knocked their glasses over, then turned to face the room and urinated on the floor. [25] In July 1942, under Japanese pressure, the club barred the election of new members of Allied nationalities.

上海

Shanghai's riotous nightlife sobered down, not so much because of the puritanism of the New Order as on account of restrictions on transport which prevented merrymakers from travelling out to popular haunts such as Farren's night club on the Great Western Road. The cheap dives on Blood Alley, formerly frequented by American marines, also fell silent. Ciro's on the Bubbling Well Road, which normally closed at 6.00 a.m., now shut at 10.30 p.m. Only along the Avenue Joffre in the concession did some semblance of Shanghai's gaiety survive in the mainly Russian clubs and restaurants: DD's, the Balalaika, the Kavkaz and the Renaissance. Cabarets and ballrooms adjusted to the new conditions by holding *thés dansants* rather than dinner dances. The ready adaptability of the Shanghai entertainment world was exemplified by one 'authoritative source' who declared, 'Why, if the worst comes to the worst, and they find the daily tea dances insufficient to meet overhead expenses, what should prevent them from inaugurating breakfast dances?'[26] Business was not good over the Christmas and New Year holidays. In mock despair, the management of the New Winter Garden advertised: 'Practically no one comes. Come out tonight and enjoy the deep solitude!'[27]

American films continued to be screened though late shows were cancelled: movie-goers could see Basil Rathbone in *The Last Days of Pompeii* at the Uptown, Bette Davis in *Dangerous* at the Doumer, or *Snow White and the Seven Dwarfs* at the Lafayette. Crowds flocked to the movie-theatres, not so much to see the main features as to gape at the Japanese newsreel pictures

---

*Although British far outnumbered French members, the management of the club was in the hands of an exclusively French committee. The French club differed from the British in admitting women. Neither admitted Chinese members.

of the attack on Pearl Harbor.

The scarcity of petrol produced astonishing scenes of tranquillity on Shanghai's normally congested streets. Taxis stopped running and buses, trams and trolley-buses ran limited services. An order was issued on 18 December restricting the use of motor cars to members of essential services.* The one-horsepower motor car made an appearance on the city's thoroughfares (see plate no. 9). Swarms of bicyclists appeared on the streets and rickshaw operators enjoyed a shortlived boom. Traffic lights in the concession were switched off for long periods. Petrol stations were turned into bicycle stands. In the unquenchable Shanghai spirit of free enterprise, Carl Baumann of the Asia Engineering and Iron Works announced that he was accepting orders for the conversion of cars and trucks to operation by charcoal generators. The price, he said, would be $7,000 (presumably Chinese dollars) and it would cost approximately $10.80 to keep a car on the road from the Hungjao Nursery on the outskirts of the city to the Bund. 'On the face of it', he admitted, 'it would seem to be expensive', but he pointed out the 'comforting thought of security and convenience' that the conversion would bring.[29]

The city's industrial economy suffered a severe setback. During the first three weeks of the occupation, 162 of the settlement's 2,310 factories were closed down. By the spring of 1942 only 55 per cent of the factories in the settlement were operating – and these with barely half of their previous workforce. The industrial collapse and the virtual absence of motor traffic changed the atmosphere of the city. 'The air, once polluted with the smoke of countless chimneys, cleared miraculously', wrote one observer. 'Streets formerly grimed with coal dust became strangely clean.'[30] 'Shanghai, once the world's noisiest city, has become strangely silent', wrote a foreign resident a few weeks later.[31]

Shortages soon began to appear in the food supply. The cost of rice soared, amounts for sale were limited and Chinese 'fought with each other

---

*Shanghai had more motor vehicles than any other city in China. The total number of private cars registered in the settlement was 6,457 – among them 1,199 Fords, 595 Plymouths, 284 Studebakers, 19 Cadillacs, 14 Overland Whippets and 2 Rolls Royces.[28]

to secure purchases of the staple product'.[32] Butchers were warned not to sell more than 1 lb of meat to any customer. Butter and sugar became hard to find. From 22 December onwards bakeries were forbidden to produce cakes or biscuits.[33]

On the morning of 28 December, 236 homeless people were found dead of exposure in the streets of the city – though, as the *Shanghai Times* pointed out, 'some allowance' had to be made 'for the well-known fact that many dead children are placed in the streets by impoverished parents who cannot afford even the poorest form of burial'. Some parents were reported to 'throw their children away even before they are dead'. An official of the Public Benevolent Cemetery said, 'Many phone calls which we receive telling us of children lying dead in the streets turn out to be not altogether correct. These children, starving, and just rotten with disease, are still alive – but always beyond recovery.' But this number of corpses was about average for a cold winter night in Shanghai at that period. Over the previous year the cemetery had picked up 29,440 bodies in the streets; of those 20,720 were children.[34]

For a time, traffic on the Whangpoo stopped entirely. Large numbers of vessels regarded as hostile were confiscated by the Japanese navy. The virtual absence of large ocean-going ships was noticeable, but the riverfront nevertheless soon assumed a more normal aspect as Japanese naval and commercial vessels arrived and small Chinese craft plied to and fro across the river between Pootung and the settlement. Junks carrying lumber, hay and coal again moved along the Soochow Creek. Sampans ferried clamouring throngs of Chinese refugees to larger boats that would take them up the Yangtse out of reach of the occupiers.[35] Waterfront pickpockets shifted their main location from the still silent French Bund to the settlement.

Meanwhile the officers and crew of the *President Harrison* which had weighed anchor off the Bund amidst great junketing at the departure of the US Marines on 28 November, suffered an indignity that turned into a nightmare. When war broke out on 8 December, the liner was subjected to a 'hectic chase' by the speedy Japanese T.K.K. liner *Nagasaki Maru*. The American vessel struck a sandbank near the Shaweishan Lighthouse, some 70 miles from Shanghai, and remained marooned there for more than a month. Japanese experts eventually succeeded in refloating the vessel and compelled her to return to Shanghai on 20 January 1942. The 150 Americans aboard were disembarked and interned by the Japanese as enemy aliens.[36]

On 5 January 1942 the four Allied members of the Municipal Council who were still in Shanghai acceded to the 'request' of the Japanese authorities, made a week earlier, to resign. (The American businessman Norwood Allman and two British members of the council were away from the city when the Japanese attacked.) The Japanese consul-general reported that the four councillors had 'thought it was not good for their own governments if they resigned voluntarily, so they wanted to resign at the request of the Japanese government. Their request can be permitted.'[37] The reorganized council now consisted of three Japanese, three Chinese, one Swiss and one German member. Two days later the Japanese vice-chairman of the council, described by a Canadian official of the council as 'highly intelligent and most capable, in addition to possessing a charming manner', was unanimously elected chairman.[38]

While happy to get rid of the British and American members of the council, the Japanese had no desire to accede to their Axis partners' requests for increased representation on the international body. The Germans and Italians had proposed immediately after the occupation that the settlement be handed over to administration by a German-Italian-Japanese triumvirate.[39] The Japanese replied that it 'was too early to think about' these matters.[40] It was also rumoured that the Germans had offered, at the beginning of the occupation, 'to arm two thousand men to patrol the International Settlement' and had 'also offered to use [their] own arms'. The Japanese were said to have 'thanked them – and confiscated all arms the following day.'[41]

The Japanese behaved in a high-handed and insensitive way towards both their their Axis allies and their local Chinese protégés. Barely a week into the occupation, the French consul-general noted that the Japanese military authorities were:

> manifesting utter scorn as much towards the government of
> Wang Ching-wei as towards the Reich and Italy. They [the
> Japanese] have asked us repeatedly not to pay attention to any

request from any source other than themselves, mentioning specifically the Nanking [puppet] authorities and the representatives of the Axis.[42]

Over the following weeks Germans in Shanghai complained with increasing bitterness of the Japanese attitude towards them. German officials were particularly resentful of the freedom allowed to the Soviet radio station in Shanghai which was said to broadcast daily news items unfavourable to the German armies in Russia. Consul-General Margerie commented that it was 'indeed remarkable that the Russian broadcasting station and newspapers continue to receive freely, through the intermediary of the TASS agency correspondent, British propaganda subventions amounting to 35,000 Shanghai dollars per month'.[43]

上海

The occupation of Shanghai was part of a general sweep by the Japanese through British, American and Dutch possessions in China and the Pacific. The British Concession in Tientsin was occupied on the same day. On 10 December the Japanese sank the *Prince of Wales* and the *Repulse*, eliminating at a stroke the British navy's two most powerful capital ships in the Far East. After a doomed resistance, Hong Kong fell on Christmas Day. This triumph was celebrated in Shanghai three days later with a parade by a Japanese military band up the Nanking and Bubbling Well Roads. A French police report noted that it was only as a result of a '*véritable tour de force*' on the part of a senior French police official that the Chinese (puppet) authorities were dissuaded from infringing the neutrality of the concession by holding a demonstration there as well.[44]

The climax of the run of Japanese victories came in mid-February 1942 with the fall of Singapore. Shanghai marked the victory with a 'Rally of East Asiatic People' at the Great China Theatre. Triumphal arches were erected. A banquet was held at the Nippon Club. Japanese flags fluttered everywhere. Tramcars were bedecked with flowers. A hundred thousand Chinese gathered at the racecourse to hail the proclamation of the 'emancipation of East Asia' – or so the *Shanghai Times* claimed (the British journalist H.G.W.

Woodhead later said that such meetings were 'usually attended by only a few hundred obviously mobilized Chinese'[45]). The Japanese added to British humiliation by announcing their intention to transfer administrative control of the British concessions in Tientsin and Canton to Wang Ching-wei's Nanking government. Shanghai remained in a strange limbo – under Japanese occupation, yet theoretically still divided into Chinese, French and international zones.

In the summmer of 1942 a severe cholera epidemic broke out in the city. Food shortages intensified. A black market soon started, with 'rice rustlers' standing in queues to buy the limited amounts available at the official price, and then reselling at a higher price. Shortages led inevitably to inflation.'[46] During the first six months of the occupation, prices rose by more than 300 per cent. In May 1942 a new currency, the Chinese Reserve Bank (CRB) dollar was introduced and residents were compelled to exchange it at a rate of 2 old dollars for 1 new dollar. The new currency found only uneasy acceptance and prices continued to climb steeply. Although the Japanese seemed to succeed in curbing much of the old gang-related racketeering in Shanghai, wartime shortages, rationing and rapid inflation gave rise to new types of crime. The introduction of rice rationing in July led to smuggling from the countryside. Distrust of money values led to hoarding of every conceivable commodity – gold, medicines, cigarettes, 'Sunkist' oranges, even toilet paper.[47]

上海

Yet in these harsh conditions a handful of Shanghai's residents prospered and even enjoyed life. One such was 'Princess' Sumaire.

In spite of the immense wealth of the Patiala family, 'Princess' Sumaire had been reported in mid-1941 to be 'financially in a bad way'. She had moved from the luxury of the Park Hotel to more modest accommodation at 103 Great Western Road, Hubertus Court, Fourth Floor. Her reduced circumstances were 'confirmed to a certain extent by the fact that she is rarely seen in leading local night haunts and hotels which was her previous wont'. [48] Yet by the eve of the Japanese occupation her wheel of fortune had turned again. She was back in the Park Hotel, albeit in a room (405) rather than a suite.

To what did she owe her financial revival? Sub-Inspector McKeown had speculated in November 1940 that 'it is quite possible that she is engaged in highly paid prostitution'. He discarded for the moment 'the political angle', although he warned 'that if her finances dwindle, she may be used by some party in which case her knowledge of India and her so-called rank may be used to advantage'.[49] McKeown's apprehensions soon appeared justified.

On 13 June 1941, as Sumaire's friend Auxion de Ruffe was entering his office immediately opposite the French consulate, several men who were lying in wait opened fire on him and then fled. He died on the way to hospital. His assassins were never captured. Rumour had it that the assassination had been ordered by a local French businessman, Félix Bouvier, proprietor of the immensely popular Jai Alai stadium in Shanghai. Bouvier was a Gaullist and, as president of the French club in the city, had long engaged in a bitter personal and political feud with the baron. Although Bouvier was questioned, no proof could be found against him and he was not put on trial. The police in the French Concession concluded that the assassination had been the work of the quasi-fascist, pro-Kuomintang Blue Shirts whose victims included other prominent Japanese sympathizers in Shanghai.[50]

An anonymous letter sent to Sumaire three months later suggested another interpretation:

> To Her "Highness",
> "Princess" of Patiala,
> Park Hotel,
> Shanghai

Your "Highness",
We warn you. Your running around with Fifth Columnists has completely discredited [you] in the eyes of Public Opinion. It is generally known that you have been relieved of your British passport and this fact together with your present behaviour is only too convicting [sic] for everybody that you could never be a Princess of Patiala but only a shrewd coquette. It might be

known to you that persons that become too well known in China sometimes meet a surprisingly sudden death.

We shall take the liberty of dispatching a copy of this letter to the Editor of "Shopping News" and to other papers that might be interested in activities like yours.

[signed] "Victory Organization"[51]

The missive, with its crudely worded threat, was such as might have been received, read and promptly crumpled up and thrown into the bin by any high-flying socialite. But Sumaire was frightened by it – and with good reason. She was not only acquainted with Don Chisholm, the editor of *Shopping News*. She was also, no doubt, familiar with Chisholm's reputation in Shanghai society as a man whose brand of gossip journalism all too often slipped over the edge into something close to blackmail.

Even more worrying was the clear threat of violence. Given the elimination of Auxion de Ruffe, Sumaire turned for advice to another lawyer, Dr Piero Terni, an Italian who was an anti-fascist and a Jew – although he did not publicize these affiliations. Terni claimed to have worked for British intelligence in Abyssinia but by late 1941 he had been engaged as an informant for the Japanese. Acting on Sumaire's behalf, Terni lodged a complaint with the Municipal Police. He explained to them confidentially that the princess was British by birth and held a British passport which, at the instance of the government of India, had been endorsed valid only for travel to India. He further declared that she was now seeking Chinese citizenship. The police listened to Terni's complaint politely but took no action to discover the source of the threatening letter. Sumaire clearly could not look to the British authorities in Shanghai for protection.

For an Indian holding a British passport to seek to become a naturalized Chinese was, to say the least, unusual. For a member of the princely family of Patiala it was unheard of. The Patialas were notably pro-British and had manifested their loyalty to the raj at the time of the Indian Mutiny and again during the First World War, when they supplied troops and resources for the war effort. As Sumaire's financial lifeline from Patiala dried up, she drifted into the welcoming arms of people who offered not only money but also a new political alignment that seemed more in harmony with the rapidly developing strategic realities in East Asia.

By December 1941 Sumaire had moved definitively into political and social association with the Axis powers. Her friends were now mainly Germans, Italians, White Russians and Japanese. In late December she held a cocktail party 'in her suite at the Park Hotel' to celebrate the birthday of her 'private secretary', a young Russian woman, Olga Yakovlev. The guests included Sumaire's Italian lawyer Dr Terni, an Italian officer, Commandante G. Galletti, a number of Japanese and various titled Germans. The collaborationist *Shanghai Times* published a photograph depicting the princess with some of her guests in what was clearly regarded as a highlight of the post-Pearl-Harbor social scene in Shanghai.[52]

Another foreign resident who did well out of the opening stages of the war was 'Captain' Pick. A few weeks after the Japanese takeover he was released from prison at the instance of his friend in Japanese naval intelligence, Commander Otani. The hired Chinese gunman who had killed Mamontoff remained in detention and died in prison a year later. Pick meanwhile filed an appeal. The hearing was held in camera before the (puppet) Kiangsu High Court, Third Branch, in November 1942 and Pick was represented in court by a renegade half-British, half-Chinese lawyer, Lawrence Kentwell (of whom more later), who secured a reversal of the conviction.

Pick spent the remainder of the war years working for the foreign affairs section of the Japanese Naval Intelligence Bureau under the direction of Otani. Thanks to the generosity of his employers Pick exchanged his prison cell for more comfortable and commodious quarters in room 741 at the Cathay Hotel. In addition, the Japanese provided Pick with a 12-tube shortwave radio receiver, free food, petrol for his Austin car, presents, an expense allowance and a small salary. He supplemented that with much larger sums from racketeering enterprises protected by the Japanese.

A post-war American intelligence report gave the following schedule of Pick's daily activities. He got up before dawn and listened to radio news from Moscow, Honolulu, San Francisco and London on his shortwave receiver. From 6.00 a.m. to 7.00 a.m. he made and received telephone calls concerning local Shanghai intelligence. After that he perused the local Russian papers and ate breakfast. Then he went to his office at the Japanese Naval Intelligence Bureau at No. 27, the Bund (former headquarters of Jardine, Matheson), where he wrote reports and received visitors. Occasionally he visited the Japanese Gendarmerie headquarters to supervise the interrogation of a foreign prisoner. At 1.00 p.m. he ate lunch, always entertaining a visitor. After a nap, he took some more calls and then set off for meetings concerning his theatrical, newspaper, or 'charity' interests. Almost every Sunday evening he 'performed in an important role in either a concert or a play'. He would donate what he said were the profits from these shows to Russian charities, seeking thereby, as one of his Japanese colleagues later put it, 'to suppress the antagonism of the public to his racketeering'.[53] After the show he would dine with friends and admirers and drink vodka in a nearby nightclub. He went home late and rarely slept more than two or three hours.[54] The Japanese seem to have had few illusions about his character but considered him a useful information source. In a post-war deposition, the head of the Japanese naval resident's office declared that Pick was regarded as an 'information broker' of the type common in Shanghai.[55]

At first Pick merely prepared reports on Soviet radio broadcasts but he soon became anxious to broaden his area of responsibility. In a letter to his Japanese handler on 14 January 1942 Pick argued that the Japanese Gendarmerie were incompetent to handle espionage cases and he urged the formation of a special judicial investigation section under navy control. No such section seems to have been created but Pick himself was later assigned to report on the activities of foreign nationals in Shanghai. The naval authorities were the most powerful of the various rival Japanese organs operating in the city and as a result Pick's was a position of real influence. He used it ruthlessly to settle old personal scores. Otani several times warned Pick to keep his personal affairs separate from his official duties – but to little avail. As will be seen, Pick was eventually able to terrorize much of the remaining European community in Shanghai – and in the case of one large group to help determine its wartime fate.

For the time being, however, most foreigners, Allied as well as Axis nationals, were able to continue semi-normal lives – and in some cases to delude themselves that the occupation would make little difference. They were soon to be rudely disabused. As for the Chinese population, they did not enjoy even the minimal courtesies extended to foreign nationals in the city. Their sufferings during the war were infinitely greater than those of their former foreign masters. The Shanghailanders were at least generally acknowledged by the Japanese as fellow human beings; the Chinese were commonly treated like dogs. For the great mass of its native population, occupied Shanghai, grim, silent and fearful, became known during the occupation as a 'dark world'.

6 Oriental Mission

In conventional military terms, Shanghai's war ended after just a few hours on the morning of 8 December 1941. Yet the secret war in the city, waged by unconventional means, continued. True to their traditional role in the settlement, the British at first took the lead. Aware that a Japanese attack was merely a matter of time, British intelligence and subversion organizations had made contingency arrangements before December 1941. Yet when the time for action came, their plans went disastrously awry.

The Special Operations Executive (SOE) was formed in July 1940, shortly after the Dunkirk withdrawal and the fall of France. Churchill, anxious to demonstrate that, even if Britain could not hope to launch a full-scale invasion of Nazi-occupied Europe, it could still play a military role there, had given the famous order, 'Set Europe ablaze!' SOE's objective was to organize subversive operations inside occupied territory with the help of local resistance groups who would be supplied by the British with weapons, technical help, training and advisers. The organization, whose existence remained secret, was placed under the direction of the Ministry of Economic Warfare, headed until February 1942 by Hugh Dalton, and thereafter by Lord Selborne. The 'Ministry of Ungentlemanly Warfare', as SOE was dubbed, never quite fulfilled all of Churchill's hopes, but it played a significant part, mainly in the later part of the war, in stimulating and aiding anti-Nazi resistance, particularly in France, Poland and Yugoslavia.

SOE encountered considerable difficulties at first in laying the groundwork for subversive warfare in occupied Europe in the form of networks of agents, wireless stations, escape routes, arms caches and landing-grounds. Harsh experience taught the value of preparation for secret warfare before rather than after territory had been lost to the enemy. Hence the decision, a year before Pearl Harbor, to set up a branch of SOE in the Far East to prepare for the eventuality of war with Japan.

A. E. Jones, the SOE officer charged with initial planning for Oriental

Mission (OM), as the Far East section was known until 1942, arrived in Singapore in January 1941. He proceeded to establish its headquarters there and set about creating a regional organization. Before leaving London he had been instructed to appoint a 'no.1' in Shanghai who would be responsible for the whole North China area.

> No.1 should never contact agents. He should have no.2s,
> preferably Englishmen, for Russia, Japan, China and general
> contacts. None of these no. 2s should necessarily know what
> the other no.2s are doing. If possible these no.2s should have
> deputies who should be neutrals, who, if Japan occupied
> North China, could continue to act on our behalf.[1]

These orders, redolent of John Buchan and 'Bulldog Drummond' rather than of the real world of the Gestapo and the Kempeitai, reflected the amateurishness of the early British ventures into foreign subversion.

In May 1941 Jones gave way to a permanent head of OM, Valentine St John Killery, a former vice-chairman of ICI in Shanghai, who had served as a member of the Shanghai Municipal Council. Killery was assigned the code-name 'O.100' and arrived in Singapore on 7 May 1941. Jones, who remained in Singapore as Killery's subordinate, seems to have resented his displacement. He did not get on with his boss and later held him largely responsible for Oriental Mission's failure. His criticism had considerable justification, for Killery, although a successful businessman, lacked the sense of urgency, capacity for cutting through problems and ability to inspire subordinates that the job required. He was hampered, moreover, by his own inexperience, by lack of resources, by conflicts among the different British military, diplomatic, and intelligence authorities, and by disagreements about priorities. Shanghai was only one part of Oriental Mission's vast area of responsibility, which included the whole of the Far East. It was distant from the headquarters at Singapore and, in spite of the importance of British interests in north China, inevitably took second place in official thinking to the needs of British possessions such as Malaya and Hong Kong.

Jones and Killery nevertheless succeeded in establishing a rudimentary organization in Shanghai. As the local 'no. 1', Jones appointed W. J. Gande, a 55-year-old local wholesale liquor merchant. Gande, who took the code-name 'O.5000', recruited a small team that would prepare for undercover activities. The other members were John Kenneth Brand, aged 52, a businessman, Joseph Fone Brister, aged 56, a manager of Ilbert & Co, George Duncan Jack, aged 55, manager of the Confederation Life Insurance Company, and Sydney Chilton Riggs, aged 49, surveyor to the China Homeward Freight Conference. Also associated with the group were Edward Elias, aged 41, a stockbroker, and W. G. Clarke, aged 65, president of the Shanghai St Patrick's Society. A former deputy commissioner of the Shanghai Municipal Police, Clarke had retired from the force some years earlier to start his own detective firm, Clarke's Enquiry Agency.

These were men whose loyalty to the crown was unquestioned and whose bravery was tested under the most gruelling conditions. Yet the most obvious deficiency of OM Shanghai was its personnel. A later SOE evaluation noted that it could only have hoped for substantial results 'by training and using Asiatic agents'.[2] Yet the Shanghai team consisted of conspicuous British citizens who were natural targets for Japanese suspicion and investigation.

The members of the team were pledged to refer to one another only by their code numbers although the chief members knew each other's identities. The four main objectives of OM Shanghai were defined as:

1. To compile a complete register of enemy goods stores in Shanghai and, when moved, to trace its destination.
2. To organize sabotage of enemy interests, such as shipping, enemy goods, wireless broadcast propaganda stations etc.
3. To establish depots in Free China, to which Allies of military age might be sent in the event of war spreading to the Far East.
4. To assist Allied propaganda in the form of leaflets, whispering campaigns etc.[3]

In the event, the group was able to achieve only very limited progress towards these ends.

The second task, potentially the most valuable, proved the most difficult to execute. From the outset, British subversive warfare experts were not optimistic about the practicability of sabotage activities in Shanghai. Noting that the Whangpoo was 'a fairly narrow river', they considered the possibility, in the event of war, of blocking it to shipping, but noted that 'even at its narrowest part it would be difficult to cause an effective obstruction unless two or three fairly large steamers were sunk'. But they believed it might be worth sinking dredgers and water barges and attacking oil storage installations, oil lighters and Japanese-owned wharves and warehouses along the river's edge.[4]

In the summer of 1941 Killery received a telegraphic inquiry concerning the pro-Nazi American journalist Karl von Wiegand, star roving reporter for the Hearst Press, whose syndicated reports from Shanghai were 'doing great harm [to the] Allied Cause in America':

> Can you interfere with his activities? Urge special caution
> required since even anti-Nazi journalists would resent
> interference with fellow journalist and disclosure would be
> more dangerous than continuance of Wiegan[d]'s work.
> Emphasize this is purely exploratory. Extreme, extreme
> discretion to be used.

SOE headquarters in London informed its New York representative of the suggestion but warned: 'In view of inevitable press reaction if physical or any other interference with any journalist became known, consider it extremely doubtful if anything can be done in Shanghai, but can you consider influencing your side with view curtailing his publications?' New York, however, replied: 'Hearst thinks highly of this man and would entertain nothing against him.' The message added that it might be possible to arrange for the publication of an attack on Wiegand if evidence could be furnished that he was a German agent. New York also inquired 'if Lady Drummond Hay [Wiegand's British mistress] is in Shanghai, could she be used for scandal affecting v. W.?'[5] In the event the British shrank from taking effective counter-measures, whether 'physical' or scandal-mongering, against Wiegand. He continued his isolationist and pro-Nazi propaganda until the eve of Pearl Harbor, secure in the protection of his patron. The

Hearst influence no doubt also explains his inclusion among American citizens repatriated from Shanghai in September 1943.

The large number of German establishments in Shanghai presented tempting opportunities for British sabotage, and the Italian entry into the war in June 1940 added their economic, military and naval interests in Shanghai to the list of potential targets. But OM Shanghai found itself hamstrung by the traditional view that the International Settlement was 'neutral' territory, by fears that, given the magnitude of Britain's interests in Shanghai, she had most to lose from any subversive warfare campaign, and above all by British diplomatic policy towards Japan which continued to be guided by appeasement attitudes.

In a later assessment of Oriental Mission's record in Shanghai, SOE attributed much of the blame for its failure to the uncooperative attitude of the Secret Intelligence Service:

> The determining handicap was that OM telegrams to the
> Shanghai representative had to pass through the hands of the
> SIS representative at Shanghai. No other secure line was
> available. This representative was very anti-SOE and also
> much disliked handling the new traffic and feared some
> breach of security or other accident would compromise him.
> He went further than that and was a damping influence upon
> the OM representative.[6]

The rivalry between the two organizations in Shanghai reached a climax in September 1941 when the SIS officer, 'using his position as our post-box ... misrepresented to the Counsellor of the [British] Embassy' an SOE scheme that had been mooted for attacking the *Eritrea*, an Italian naval sloop.

The *Eritrea* had arrived in Shanghai from Kobe after Japanese officials had rejected an Italian proposal that it be permitted to attack Russian ships carrying oil from America to the Soviet Union.[7] The boat was anchored in the Whangpoo in midstream off the settlement. British naval authorities approved an order to Gande's Shanghai group to 'examine urgently [the] possibility of destroying or damaging' the ship. Gande was instructed that it was 'essential' that the action 'should not be traced to British agency'.

Before anything could be done, however, the SIS representative in Shanghai protested to the British Embassy in Shanghai* against the proposal. A telegram was dispatched to London pointing out that it would be impossible to keep the source of such an action secret, as 'no other power will or can be credited with requisite motive'. The enterprise might well lead to 'considerable property damage and widespread anti-British feeling, extending to local American community whose cooperation is essential factor in life of the Settlement'. Even more alarmingly, the embassy warned that the 'immediate Japanese reaction' might involve 'the closing of the Whangpoo river and even military occupation of the Settlement'.[8] Echoing these objections, the Foreign Office informed SOE of its opposition to any such operation at Shanghai: 'We have very large interests there and no means of protecting them, and it would therefore be rash for us to disturb the virtual truce now existing in the International Settlement, which, though Chinese soil, has always enjoyed a quasi-neutral status.'[9] As a result, the project was abandoned.

Since sabotage was ruled out, OM Shanghai was left with little to do save compile registers of enemy stores and assist the Allied propaganda effort by distributing pamphlets and organizing whispering campaigns. In August 1941 Brand was sent to Hong Kong to receive instruction in the use of incendiaries, with a view to future sabotage operations. Gande was provided with a budget of £5,000 to cover expenses. Remarkably, the sum was remitted through regular banking channels to Gande's account at the Hong Kong and Shanghai Bank – thus enabling the Japanese liquidator, after the bank had been taken over, to discover the incriminating book entry. This astonishing breach of security was sadly indicative of the amateurishness with which much of the enterprise was conducted.

Little was done to train or equip OM Shanghai, to plan operations or earmark targets. After his appointment by Jones, Gande never even saw another SOE representative before the outbreak of the Pacific War. Upon the

*The British embassy, as well as the diplomatic missions of some other countries, had moved to Shanghai as a result of the Japanese conquest of Nanking.

Japanese occupation, the group was left (as a subsequent appraisal put it) 'without any instructions whatsoever'.[10] In early December 1941 arrangements were in hand for an SOE expert to go to Shanghai to help train the group in sabotage methods – but before he could arrive, the Japanese struck.

OM Shanghai received advance warning of the forthcoming Japanese attack. In a post-war report, Gande stated that he had destroyed all documentary evidence of the group's existence as early as 1 December 1941.[11] But the Japanese already knew about it and had been monitoring its activities for several weeks. Although they appear not to have discovered its real objectives, they knew that it was in some way related to the Ministry for Economic Warfare. Their main source appears to have been a Romanian employee of Gande's firm who had had access to his safe, had taken secret documents from it and had sold them to the Japanese.* Among the documents obtained by the Japanese were copies of telegrams between Gande and the head office of Oriental Mission in Singapore. In addition, Gande's telephone had been tapped and his conversations recorded.

上海

The first member of OM Shanghai to be arrested, on 17 December, was Clarke. He was subjected to torture at the Japanese Gendarmerie headquarters and it may have been as a result of this that the Japanese obtained a clear picture of the group's organization. Such, at any rate, was the opinion of the rest of OM Shanghai, although there is no conclusive evidence that Clarke broke under interrogation. After interrogation and torture, the 65-year-old Clarke, who was so weak that he could hardly stand, was thrown into a cell with the American journalist J. B. Powell:

> They pushed him into the corner alongside me, and I saw he
> was in severe pain. He was suffering from several boils on his

---

* Documentation concerning the betrayal has been made available at the Public Record Office only with deletions; a fuller explanation must await the complete opening of the files.

neck; they had become so infected and swollen, because of lack of medical attention, that his head was pressed over against his shoulder. He grew worse and about midnight he nudged me and asked me if I knew a prayer. He said he had been born in a Catholic home but had drifted away from the faith. 'I think I am going to die,' he said. We repeated the Lord's Prayer together, and as he grew calmer he told me his life's history.[12]

A few days afterwards, during an interrogation session, Powell remonstrated with Lieutenant Yamamoto over Clarke's condition and said he would die if he did not receive medical treatment. 'Yamamoto made a gesture with the edge of his hand across his throat, indicating that he thought Clarke should have his head cut off, but I could see that my words had impressed him.'[13] Later that night Clarke was taken away in an ambulance to the municipal hospital.

Ten days after Clarke's arrest, Gande, Brister and Jack were seized by the Gendarmerie and sent to the Bridge House. This prison and interrogation centre acquired a sinister renown in the course of the occupation. Situated on the northern side of the Soochow Creek in a former Chinese hotel behind the General Hospital, it had been used as a jail by the Japanese before the outbreak of the Pacific War – but in such secrecy that its very existence had not been known. Conditions were frightful. Cells were overcrowded, filthy and infested with rats. Torture, particularly of Chinese prisoners, was routine.

Brand and Elias followed their colleagues to the Bridge House on 13 January 1942 and Riggs on 5 February. Most were arrested early in the morning, while in their beds. Riggs was surprised in his office by 'three gunmen – vicious-looking characters', carrying drawn Colt .45 automatic pistols. They turned out to be plain-clothes Gendarmerie officials. They searched his office and then took him away for interrogation.[14] The Japanese also arrested a number of other British and Americans suspected of involvement in the group. Gande's secret service fund was confiscated by the Gendarmerie for their own use.

Riggs recorded how the men were treated in the Bridge House:

> Interrogations were carried out under hideous conditions ... such a thing as a bath or a shave was unheard of and when dragged from cells and bombarded with questions hour after hour with a very lowered condition of health due to undernourishment and squalid living conditions is an ordeal which to me to-day seems but a bad nightmare.[15]

Talking among prisoners was generally forbidden but Riggs was able to exchange a few words with Brister, who whispered to him: 'Tell them all – they *know*.' A few days later, Riggs:

> caught a glimpse of Gande returning from what I took to be an interrogation as I was being led in for same. He looked extremely ill and worn and his head was swathed in bandaging which from its appearance had been there for many days. I afterwards learned that he had developed an enormous carbuncle on the back of his head ... Whilst at the Bridge House the infection in Gande's head spread to his toes and each big toe was so infected as to loosen the toe nails thereon. It was during one of the rare visits of a Japanese medical officer that they decided to remove these toenails, which was carried out with forceps in a brutal fashion without any anaesthetic whatsoever and with two men holding Gande down in a chair.[16]

Powell, who spent some time in the same cell as Gande, recalled that he 'had so many boils on his neck that he could not lift up his head'.[17]

In March 1942 the SOE organization in unoccupied China dispatched a Chinese agent, 'Dr Chang', to Shanghai. A former employee of ICI, he was highly regarded by SOE. The main purpose of his mission was to find out what had happened to Gande's group, and, if possible, to pass Gande the message: '100 [i.e. Killery] wants news'. 'Chang' arrived in Shanghai on 21 April 1942 and went to the ICI office where he met Hugh Collar and was told that Gande had been arrested. He visited other British businessmen in Shanghai but most were afraid to tell him much. His return to unoccupied

China was by a circuitous route so that he did not arrived at Kunming until 11 September. By then Gande's arrest and something of his subsequent fate had already become known to the British through a news report in the Shanghai press in June.[18]

After several weeks in the Bridge House, Gande's group was removed to the headquarters of the 15th Japanese Army at Kiangwan, about 10 miles away. Before leaving, each prisoner was obliged to sign a statement declaring that he had been reasonably treated and was in good health. At Kiangwan each was placed in solitary confinement. Gande's health meanwhile worsened:

> His much neglected carbuncle on his head was spreading
> poison rapidly all over his body. From his knees to his chest he
> was covered with ugly-looking suppurating sores and his
> health was rapidly failing. His condition was so bad that on
> one occasion we of the group all lined up during the exercise
> period and, through the interpreter, put in a plea to the
> Governor to have him removed to hospital from his awful cell
> before the worst could happen. We were told it was no
> business of ours and that he was receiving adequate medical
> attention. In effect, it was cheerfulness, fortitude and an iron
> will that pulled this brave man through what appeared to us to
> be a hopeless case.[19]

The food at Kiangwan was somewhat better than at the Bridge House. Prisoners' wives were permitted to deliver food packages and some actually reached the husbands – after the greater part had been pilfered by the guards.

All the members of OM Shanghai, except Clarke, were placed on trial before a Japanese military court at Kiangwan on 28 April 1942, charged with 'having operated a secret organization whose activities were detrimental to the interests of Japan and to local peace and order'.[20] Riggs called the trial 'farcical':

> These proceedings commenced with a long diatribe in

Japanese from the man on the extreme left of the bench, presumably the prosecutor and a man ranking, I imagine, as a Sergt. Major.

When this man had finished, we were each questioned in turn by the man second from the right – a man ranking as Captain. His questions were mainly, I thought, irrelevant to the situation and dealt with such matters as our respective family histories, if we were married or not, how many children etc. ...

This part over, the man on the extreme left of us then rose again and delivered what we took to be the sentence, after which we were all filed out to our cells again.

Throughout these proceedings, the Court President had maintained complete silence and we were not allowed any opportunity to offer defence of any kind ...

When we left the court we were under the impression that this session was a preliminary to bigger things to come. But no! This was the trial and we had been sentenced to what we did not then know.[21]

Gande's sentence was four years' imprisonment; his subordinates received lesser terms.

After the trial the men were transferred to Ward Road jail in Shanghai. Administered by a branch of the Shanghai Municipal Police and supposedly the largest prison in the world, this was a large grey-brick building surrounded by an 18-foot wall with watch towers at the angles. Conditions here were much better than in the Bridge House: unusually for the period, the municipal authorities had even provided flush toilets in each cell. Some of the British warders were still on duty and thus found themselves in the extraordinary position of guarding fellow-Britons convicted of espionage against Japan. These warders were able to ease the plight of the imprisoned men to some degree by providing a link to their families outside and by bringing in extra food to supplement the miserable official rations.[22] In the prison, Gande and his men met one British and two American naval officers, among them Lieutenant-Commander Darwin Smith, the former commander of the USS *Wake*. They had escaped from the prisoner-of-war camp at Woosung but were recaptured and sentenced to ten years' imprisonment. Other fellow-prisoners included officials of the British press attaché's office in Shanghai and a member of Egal's Free French movement.

Gande remained in prison until the end of the war. Riggs, Brister, Jack and Brand were exchanged against Japanese prisoners in Lourenço Marques in the autumn of 1942. The British government tried hard to have Gande included in the exchange, but without success. Riggs later wrote a long memorandum on the arrest and imprisonment of the members of Gande's group. A senior SOE official in London commented that it was 'an extremely good report – ghastly to read, restrained and vivid'.[23] Lord Selborne, the ministerial chief of SOE, read it 'with horror and regret', but decided that it could not be shown to the Foreign Office unexpurgated 'because of SOE's own reputation'. He pointed out that the whole of OM Shanghai 'was blown to the Japanese before the Japanese war ever began. In fact, they even had an agent in the office of Gande, the leader of the group.' Riggs was therefore asked to write a bowdlerized version of the report for the eyes of the Foreign Secretary.'[24]

Elias was released in October 1943. After leaving prison he was said to have made attempts 'to form a secret organization among young foreigners', hinting that he was a Chinese intelligence agent; at the same time, according to a statement made by one Karpatlan (himself a Japanese secret agent), Elias, according to a post-war Municipal Police report:

> was working for the Japanese. It might be suspected that E.
> Elias intended to form a secret organization with the purpose
> of giving it away to [the] Japanese Gendarmerie. Posing as a
> Chinese secret agent he was able to collect very much
> information from trusting young people and it must be feared
> that this information ultimately found its way to the
> Japanese.[25]

Clarke recovered from his maltreatment and by the end of 1942 had been released from jail. He decided to remain in Shanghai rather than seek repatriation. This decision was taken, as one British official put it, 'of his own accord and to look after his interests which have always been of a mysterious kind'.[26] His reasons remain unclear. One possibility is that he wished to stay in Shanghai with his wife, who was of Indian birth. Alternatively, since he appeared to have cracked under interrogation, he may have feared repercussions upon returning to Allied territory. A third interpretation is that he had been working for SIS and hoped to continue to do useful work in Shanghai. Clarke had, in fact, been rumoured to be an SIS agent in Shanghai.[27] An SOE message to S.F. Crawford (an SOE official in Chungking) hinted at a mixture of the two latter explanations. Crawford was warned not to seek to establish any connection with Clarke or Jack (who had gone to India after being evacuated with the other repatriates) since 'we hope they will obtain employment independently'.

> The reason for my special warning about Clarke and Jack [the letter continued] is that their behaviour in certain conditions has been criticised. We have not enough evidence yet to make up our minds as to what happened. There is no question that the others behaved grandly; nor is it excluded that Clarke and Jack behaved splendidly too.[28]

Grand or splendid, the failure of OM Shanghai's 'stay-behind' enterprise left Britain with no intelligence or subversion capability under its direct control in Shanghai.

7 Eagles Mew'd

Expatriate social life in wartime Shanghai was a miserably pale reflection of the sophisticated whirl of pre-war Shanghailander society. The tone was now set not by the Anglo-Saxons but by Axis nationals. A favoured Nazi haunt was the Masquée Bar, whose owner was an informant for German intelligence. Another was the Café Federal on the Bubbling Well Road. Busiest of all was the Hungaria restaurant on the Yu Yuen Road in the 'Badlands'. Its owner, S. Silman, a former Jesuit priest, had lost his faith and settled down with a Hungarian accordion-player of doubtful reputation, Stella Szirmay. She was described in a Municipal Police report as 'nothing more nor less than a third-rate type of demi-mondaine who arrived in Shanghai from Bucharest via the night-life haunts of Constantinople, Algiers, Port Said, Singapore, and Hankow'.[1] Her colourful background and exuberant personality made Szirmay a popular figure – except with the police, who suspected her of white slave trading.[2] For a time, in the early 1940s, she reigned as queen of Shanghai's diminished nightlife.

In May 1942 Major-General C. C. Pan, Commissioner of the Western Shanghai Police Force operating in the former 'Badlands', paid personal visits to six of the area's night clubs (the Arizona, Ali Baba, Merry Widow, Argentina, Hungaria and Venezuela) on one night to warn them to observe the 11.00 p.m. curfew. When, a few weeks later, it was pointed out to him that they were nevertheless remaining open into the small hours, he instituted a concerted 'drive' to close them down on time. The *Shanghai Times* reported:

> one hitch was encountered ... at the Hungaria night club ...
> The ground floor of the establishment was closed at the
> specified hour but there was a party going on upstairs. Police
> authorities were told that this was a private party ...
> Commissioner Pan overlooked the case on Thursday night but

pointed out to a representative of the *Shanghai Times* yesterday that although the 'old lady running the Hungaria is very clever, I will find a way to have her abide by the regulations'.[3]

A happy hotchpotch of squeeze and connections explained the impunity with which Szirmay nevertheless remained in business until early 1944 when she sold out to a Frenchman.

The Shanghai Nazis also had their more serious side. A few, such as the journalists Karl von Wiegand and Klaus Mehnert, were men of genuine intellectual standing whose association with the Nazi cause lent it a certain air of respectability. Next door to the Hungaria was the Book Mart, owned by a Hungarian 'countess', where the more literary members of the German community gathered to browse. The German propaganda chief, Baron von Puttkamer, would arrive in a broker's trap driven by his '*ma fu*', accompanied by his Korean bodyguard and a dog. Sometimes German intellectuals would get together to reflect on ideas. 'At the invitation of the head of the German Information Bureau,' the *Shanghai Times* reported in March 1943, 'a very interesting lecture was given on Wednesday evening before a small circle of appreciative listeners by Professor Dr. R. Neumann on the results of his latest research in the field of racial physiognomy.'[4]

Known as the 'butcher of Buchenwald', Neumann had arrived in China in 1940. A graduate of Hamburg University, he had conducted experiments in a shack at the Buchenwald concentration camp in the early part of the war. In post-war questioning Neumann described his work as 'purely pathological', involving autopsies on the bodies of dead patients from the camp hospital. Neumann was sent to China by the German government for reasons that remain unclear. He established a pathology laboratory at the Paulus Hospital in Shanghai and conducted experiments there on dogs, cats and apes. The noise of the animals disturbed patients in the hospital. On one occasion the apes escaped from their cages and visited some of the patients in their rooms. The doctor did not enjoy Shanghai and manifested several signs of discontent. He tried to quit his job in 1943 because 'the roof of my office leaked', but was told that he must continue in the work to which he had been assigned.[5] Neumann would become furious if addressed in English; he denied he spoke the language and insisted that Germans must speak nothing but their native tongue. He quarrelled with his wife frequently and raucously. The story circulated that he set his dog on her 'and derived considerable satisfaction from the fact that the animal bit her finger off.'[6] Mrs Neumann fled to the home of neighbours, declaring: 'He will kill me if I stay in the house with him.'[7] Neumann's violence was not restricted to a domestic setting. He flew into a rage at the slightest provocation: once he fired his revolver at close range at a Chinese watchman in the street. On another occasion, at the golf club, he beat his caddies severely.

On formal occasions during the war the entire German (Aryan) community would gather at the German Garden Club. In April 1943, for example, the birthday of Hitler was celebrated with speeches and parades by the SA sports section, the Hitler Youth and the Bund Deutscher Maedel. K. Huether, leader of the local branch of the Nazi party, led the community in 'three vigorous salutes to the Fuehrer'. All then sang the German national anthem and the Horst Wessel song.[8]

上海

Most of the foreign residents of Shanghai suffered very different fates during the occupation. Shortly after the Japanese takeover of the international Settlement, a census was conducted in the area and in the neighbouring Chinese municipality. The French authorities carried out a parallel count in their concession. This showed that the Japanese had become by far the most numerous foreign nationality in the city: the number of their civilians was now over 33,000. The next two largest categories were Russians and European Jewish refugees – although since both groups included large numbers of stateless persons, no exact figures were available. There were still over 6,000 British citizens and at least 1,300 Americans in Shanghai.

The census was the first step in a security sweep by the Japanese against suspect foreign residents. In addition to the members of Oriental Mission, several other prominent British and American citizens were seized and sent to the Bridge House. Among those picked up in the early wave of arrests were the American journalists Victor Keen, correspondent of the *New York Herald Tribune*, and J. B. Powell, whose Kuomintang-supported *China Weekly Review* had been an irritation to the Japanese for several years. Also apprehended was Ellis Hayim, former president of the Shanghai stock exchange, an Iraqi Jew who held British citizenship. In the summer of 1941 the garden of Hayim's house on the Avenue Haig had been the venue for a series of *soirées* entitled 'Midnight Follies', organized by the British radio station XCDN. Each evening was devoted to one of the Allied countries. No doubt this association in itself was sufficient to render Hayim suspicious in Japanese eyes.

Probably the most hated European in Shanghai in the view of the conquerors was H.G.W. Woodhead, editor of *Oriental Affairs*. In his journal, as well as in his daily column in the *Shanghai Evening Post and Mercury*, he had pursued a resoundingly anti-Japanese line. His twice-weekly broadcasts on radio stations XMHC and XCDN, which he undertook at the request of the British government, increased the venom with which he was regarded by the Japanese. Realizing the danger in which he had been placed by his denunciations of Japanese militarism, the British embassy in Shanghai advised him on 5 December 1941 to leave the city as soon as possible. He immediately booked a passage on a Panamanian steamer scheduled to leave four days later, but the Japanese occupation of the settlement on 8 December prevented his departure.

Determined, if possible, not to be captured alive, Woodhead took refuge in the home of a friend in the French Concession, but after a few days he emerged, returned to his apartment and registered as an enemy national as required by the occupation authorities. Woodhead received indirect assurances that he would not be interfered with but, hearing of the arrest of Powell and other journalists, he took the precaution of concealing a lethal dose of morphia which he carried around with him to be used in case he was tortured.

At 2.45 a.m. on the morning of 5 March 1942 Woodhead was woken by a banging on his door. He was 'confronted by four Japanese in plain clothes who were brandishing pistols'. They arrested him, ransacked his apartment, and drove him to the Bridge House.[9] Upon arrival, he was told to empty his pockets and take off his watch, ring, braces, collar and tie. An officer named Lieutenant Hirano introduced himself and told Woodhead that if he had any complaints or requests to make he should ask for him. 'Asking for Lieutenant Hirano was to become one of the tragic jokes of my imprisonment,' Woodhead later recalled.

He was then led along various corridors and passageways until he reached a barred wooden door. At this point he was ordered to take off his shoes and get in. His description of what followed is one of the more horrifying documents of the war in Shanghai:

> I had to climb to enter the cage in which I was to spend the next three months ... The front consisted of wooden bars, four inches by four inches, with a space of about one-and-a-half inches between them. The three walls were of new and damp cement. Ceiling and floor were of roughly planed boards. The appalling stench which greeted me as I entered came from the sole article of furniture – a wooden bucket, which had to suffice for the sanitary needs of all the inmates, was emptied once a day, and, when there were twenty-three prisoners in the cage, could not be used for several hours before it was emptied. The floor space was 346 square feet which allowed a space of 15 square feet or say 5 feet by 3 per person when the cage had that number of occupants. When I entered, a dozen or so emaciated Chinese were shuffling round and round, and in the dim light I could see three other Europeans whom I afterwards discovered to be two Russians who had been there for several months and a German (the Manager of the Park Hotel) who had been put in just ahead of me. We were joined that morning by several other Europeans and a Honolulu Chinese. When I sat down against the side wall I was warned that this was not permitted. From 6 a.m. until 9 p.m. prisoners, with occasional brief intervals when they were allowed to shuffle around, were supposed to sit cross-legged or kneel in rows facing the bars in strict silence. No reading or any other kind of mental or physical occupation was allowed. One was liable to be beaten up by the guards if one leant against the wall or put one's feet out straight ... The cage was infested with lice ... lights burning in the ceiling all night, the attentions of the vermin, and the awful stench made sleep well-nigh impossible.

For talking or other offences such as sitting in the wrong posture, prisoners were beaten up – sometimes, especially in the case of the Chinese, very savagely – or deprived of food, or compelled to kneel on their heels for an hour or two or to stand up with hands outstretched above the head ... In the older gaol in the main building conditions were even worse. Hardly any daylight penetrated into the cages, which were infested with bugs as well as lice, and women were put into the same cages as the men with no chance of privacy ...

It is very cold in Shanghai in March and as one had to walk along a damp paved corridor every time one left the cage, one's feet were almost always cold and damp and one's socks were soon worn threadbare.

In the main building there was a torture chamber to which unfortunate Chinese were taken and subjected to various tortures day and night. The screams and moans of these men could be heard by the prisoners beneath. The tortures included electrical 'treatment' – attaching wires to the arms or legs and almost electrocuting the victim; the water treatment in which buckets of water were poured up the nostrils until the lungs nearly burst, savage beating and the splitting of finger-nails.[10]

The food was so meagre and abominable that Woodhead lost 15 lb weight in the first ten days of his incarceration. As a result of further ill-treatment he fell into a semi-coma and his right arm and leg became semi-paralysed. He kept himself going by repeating to himself over and over again Kipling's 'If'.

On the same day as Woodhead was arrested, Sir Frederick Maze, former inspector-general of the Chinese Customs, was seized by Japanese gendarmes in the French Concession. He too was taken to the Bridge House. Six other senior customs officials (three British, one American and two Chinese) were also there. Maze's cellmates included 'Chinese thieves, murderers and bandits'; most 'were suffering from various types of loathsome skin diseases and their clothes were alive with vermin'. Maze was 'detained for questioning' for four weeks.[11] The Swiss consul-general, Emile

Fontanel, who represented British, American and Dutch interests in Shanghai, was not permitted to visit the Bridge House and it was some time before the plight of the inmates became generally known.

The general position of remaining Allied nationals in Shanghai meanwhile deteriorated. Restrictions on their businesses and on withdrawals from British and American bank accounts drove many into poverty. In January 1942 a soup kitchen was opened at the American School to feed destitute Americans and Filipinos. The British government provided funds, through the Swiss consulate and the British Residents' Association, to support indigent British citizens. But out of parsimony or the racialism taken for granted in the period, no such relief funds were paid to British subjects of Chinese race. The head of the British Residents' Association, Hugh Collar, protested against this ruling but to no avail.[12]

In June 1942, 639 Americans as well as a few Canadians and citizens of South American states were allowed to leave Shanghai under a repatriation agreement between the United States and Japanese governments. They sailed aboard the Italian liner *Conte Verde* (marooned on the Whangpoo since the Italian entry into the war in June 1940) to Lourenço Marques in the Portuguese colony of Mozambique where they were exchanged for Japanese citizens. In August a similar agreement with the British led to the repatriation of 225 British and other Allied civilians from Shanghai as well as 100 Indians. They reached Liverpool in October. A further batch of 906 British diplomats and Free French officials, as well as several Dutch, Belgians and Norwegians, left in August. The party included the former secretary of the Shanghai Municipal Council, Godfrey Phillips, and the former acting Municipal Police chief, Captain H. M. Smyth. Some prominent Bridge House prisoners were also released and repatriated, including H. G. W. Woodhead, Sir Frederick Maze, Ellis Hayim and four of the members of Oriental Mission. Before their departure the repatriates were warned against 'spreading false rumours'.[13] When American repatriates nevertheless related their experiences to the press, the *Shanghai Times* published a Japanese rebuttal headlined 'USA Repatriates' Tales about Nippon "Cruelties" Branded by Hori as Lies'.[14]

In the summer and autumn of 1942 the hitherto relatively liberal treatment of most remaining British and American civilians began to change.

One small sign of change was the prohibition, in June 1942, of performances by the Amateur Dramatic Society at the Lyceum Theatre of Shake-
speare's *Richard III*. Did the occupiers read a subversive sub-text into the
midsummer reference to a 'winter of discontent'? Perhaps they detected a
subtle commentary on conditions in occupied Shanghai in the lines:

> More pity that the eagles should be mew'd*
> While kites and buzzards prey at liberty

No explanation of the ban was forthcoming.

An 'Anti-Anglo-American Association' conducted fierce propaganda
against the former rulers of the settlement. In October enemy nationals
were ordered to wear red armbands with a letter designating nationality (A
for Americans, B for Britons, etc) and a different number for each person.
The official purchase price of the armbands was set at 3 Chinese dollars.
The *Shanghai Times* on 4 October advertised the availability of 'Armlet Band
Protector Made of Genuine Chinese Silk: Transparent, Waterproof and
Durable': the price of this luxury item was 15 dollars. At the same time Allied nationals were forbidden to enter theatres, cinemas, dance halls, nightclubs, the Jai Alai stadium, the Canidrome or the Race Course. They were
also ordered to surrender radios, cameras and telescopes.

In the early morning hours of 5 November 1942, 350 male foreigners,
including 243 Britons (among them Hugh Collar), 65 Americans, 20
Dutchmen, and assorted Greeks, Canadians and other Allied nationals were
arrested. They were deposited in the former American marine camp on the
Haiphong Road where they were finger-printed by officers of the Shanghai
Municipal Police. The Japanese camp commandant delivered an address
explaining that they had been detained for their own protection and that
any attempt to escape would result in the sentries using their rifles and bay-
onets. Since the departure of the marines, 'the kitchens, plumbing, electrical equipment etc. had been dismantled and the place was therefore not in
a fit condition for the internment of Europeans'.[15] Inmates were crowded

---

*Caged.

into 32 rooms with two washrooms, two toilets, and one shower room. The assigned quarters were filthy and much of the bedding was crawling with bed-bugs.

Meanwhile, the Japanese prepared for the mass internment of enemy civilians in Shanghai. About 7,600 British, American and other civilians, including women and children, were interned in eight camps in the Shanghai area in stages between January and July 1943. The *Shanghai Times*, which first reported the internments in April 1943, explained that the step had been taken 'to prevent fifth-column activities and guarantee stabilized livelihood for the enemy nationals'. The paper reassuringly noted that internees would be allowed to send and receive letters, to read newspapers and listen to the radio, to play tennis and volleyball, and to cultivate vegetables.[16]

The camps – or 'civilian assembly centres', as the Japanese preferred to call them – were scattered over the city: the Girls' Public School on Yu Yuen Road; a former British military establishment, Ash Camp, opposite the school; an old three-storey tobacco godown in Pootung; and four other camps, one outside Shanghai.

The internees destined for Pootung were assembled at a drill hall and marched a half mile or so to the Bund, carrying their hand baggage. One later recalled:

> This so-called hand baggage was of all sorts and kinds, some of
> it too heavy for one man to carry, but in spite of this no
> coolies were provided. However, a few were able to secure
> ricshas for the heavier pieces. It was a pathetic sight to see old
> and young trudging along preceded by gendarmes, gendarmes
> following in the rear, and friends marching alongside helping
> to carry luggage. This procedure was evidently adopted in
> order to degrade the white man and to lower his prestige in
> the eyes of the Chinese.[17]

Conditions in the camps varied: at first, they were generally rough without being deliberately cruel. Food was short, congestion was severe and washing facilities were minimal. As a result diarrhoea, whooping cough and other diseases broke out.

The Haiphong Road camp differed from the rest, being earmarked by the Japanese for political suspects, often former Municipal Police officers and ex-servicemen. It was under military control, whereas the other camps were under the authority of the Japanese consulate-general. Conditions there were markedly worse than in the normal civilian internment camps. Prisoners suspected of espionage or political activity were often brutally treated.

In March 1943 (according to a confidential report received in London from the Swiss chargé d'affaires in Shanghai) Eric Davies, an engineer, was taken away from the camp by the Japanese Gendarmerie, beaten, and subjected to torture by water and by electric currents.[18] Davies (a Welshman) was accused by the Japanese of involvement in underground Free French activities in Shanghai. This was perhaps a case of mistaken identity. Davies had first been arrested in 1942 and thrown into the Bridge House; after his first interrogation he came back to his cell with 'a puzzled look on his face' and told a fellow-prisoner: 'I wonder what those blighters want – I never wrote anything about the Japs in my life.' J.B. Powell, at any rate, was persuaded that he had been mistaken for R.W. Davis, managing director of the *North China Daily News*.[19]

In August 1943 Bill Hutton, a Scottish former chief inspector of the Municipal Police, was returned to Haiphong Road after ten days in the hands of the Gendarmerie. 'He was insane [a fellow-prisoner recalled] and bore marks of ill-treatment and he died two days later after one lucid interval.[20]

Elsewhere conditions gradually improved. In one of the camps, Jimmy James, former proprietor of the Mandarin nightclub, took charge of the catering with mouthwatering results. Eventually schools and libraries were opened, sports and cultural activities were organized, and camp newspapers appeared.

Family members were generally able to live together – although allegedly in one camp Japanese signs separated 'married women', 'attached women' and 'loose women'. For a while prisoners were able to communicate with loved ones outside by means of the personal column of the *Shanghai Times*. Among such messages appearing in February 1943 were:

TED: Be seeing you after the ball is over, with Three Roses. –
Sandy
LULU: Probably leaving shortly. Domestically stored and sold.
Personally prepared.
REGGIE: Realize now nothing can change it. Miss you. Love,
Cubit's m-m.
HELEN: Received package. Regards from family, keeping fine.
Stop flattering through letters. – With love, Joey.[21]

The Municipal Police took note of these messages. Careful textual analysis was applied to the message from 'Sandy': 'As there was or would be no dance (ball) at date of insertion of the advertisement', an enterprising detective reported, the true purport of the message must be: 'Ted, be seeing you after the war, with love'. Since such communications were 'contrary to the wishes of the Japanese authorities', the practice was curtailed.[22]

Thrown together at close quarters, the internees generally got on surprisingly well. By and large, camps did not divide into factions based on nationality or on class. Taipan grandees mucked in with the hoi polloi in the day-to-day tasks of camp maintenance. In some cases, however, other lines of division emerged. In the Chapei camp, for example, the arrival of a large number of up-country American missionaries led to grumbling. In his account of conditions in Chapei, H. E. Arnhold, a leading British businessman and former chairman of the Shanghai Municipal Council, complained that the missionaries would not comply with camp rules, neglected cleanliness in the lavatories, occupied more floor space than they were entitled to, interfered with the distribution of eggs and, most annoying of all, propagated the species:

> Considering the overcrowded and undernourished condition
> of the camp one would have thought that self-restraint would
> have been exercised, so that the camp would not have been
> deprived of most necessary food (eggs and milk) to provide
> for this increase in population, apart from the indecency of
> sexual intercourse in over-crowded dormitories and the
> embarrassment, annoyance and disturbance caused to other

> inmates ... One person went through the nightly performance
> of quoting the Bible to an unwilling spouse until she
> submitted to his importunities.[23]

Overall, conditions in the Shanghai internment camps were spartan but not utterly inhuman. The camp-dwellers were at least able to obtain basic levels of food and shelter and, with notable exceptions, were not subjected to the kind of barbaric cruelty routinely inflicted on Allied servicemen in Japanese prisoner-of-war camps.

上海

The largest group of foreign civilians interned in Shanghai were not, however, Allied nationals but stateless Jews, most of them former German citizens. Some 20,000 Jewish refugees from Nazi Europe had arrived in Shanghai between 1933 and 1941.

The Japanese had contradictory and confused attitudes towards the Jewish question. On the one hand, some were impressed by the *Protocols of the Elders of Zion* and similar publications and adopted antisemitism in a form hardly distinguishable from the Nazis'. General Shioden, a leading figure of this tendency, went so far as to complain in September 1938 that the German embassy personnel in Tokyo were only lukewarm in their hostility to Jews and failed to provide assistance to his 'efforts to acquaint my fellow-countrymen with the principles of the antisemitic world movement'.[24] Many Japanese, on the other hand, were highly suspicious of Nazi racial ideology. Such suspicions arose partly from their traditional resentment of the racialism of the white races towards Asiatics. The Kaiser's warnings against the alleged 'yellow peril' and American immigration laws restricting the inflow of Japanese and Chinese remained near the surface of the Japanese national consciousness in the 1930s. The Nazis' racialism became something of an embarrassment in their relations with Japan: the German ambassador in Tokyo in 1934 called it the single most significant obstacle to German-Japanese relations.[25] German explanations that the Japanese were not regarded as a 'coloured race' had some reassuring effect – but the Japanese remained sceptical and suspicious.

Against this background, some influential Japanese advocated a policy on the Jewish issue that, while affected by antisemitic ideas, was favourable to the idea of promoting Jewish immigration to Japanese-controlled areas of the Asiatic mainland. To some extent this was based on the hope that Jews would provide capital and expertise that might facilitate economic development. The attribution to world Jewry of exaggerated economic and political power also contributed to such policies. The most prominent representative of this tendency, Captain Inuzaka Koreshige, was assigned responsibility for Jewish affairs in Shanghai, representing the Foreign Office, the Japanese navy and the Asia Development Board. In a speech over Tokyo Radio on 13 September 1940, he announced that Japanese policy was set against any discrimination on grounds of race. At the same time, he took exception to the pro-Chungking policy of two Jewish newspapers in Shanghai.[26]

Most of the Jewish refugees reached Shanghai penniless, dispirited and disoriented. Those with no means at all were placed in refugee camps in Hongkew, the first of which was on Ward Road immediately opposite the municipal jail. Upon arrival there each newcomer was handed a blanket, bedding, a spoon, a tin cup and a tin plate. The camps were soon severely overcrowded and living conditions were grim. Overwhelmed by despair, several of the inmates committed suicide.

Yet most soon adapted to their surroundings and the area around the camps in Hongkew acquired a strangely central European flavour. The bearded ultra-orthodox Jews, who continued to wear their traditional garb of long black coats and wide-brimmed hats, oblivious to the summer heat, added a new dimension to Shanghai's cosmopolitanism. Viennese pastry shops and cafés opened and soon acquired a large clientele. The Café Louis and Roy's Roof-Garden above the Broadway Theatre on Wayside Road became popular haunts. Theatrical groups staged performances of *Die Fledermaus* and *The Merry Widow*. A German-language exile press flourished.

After the outbreak of the European war, antisemitic propaganda in Shanghai grew to serious proportions. The two main sources were White Russian and German. In September 1939, for example, a White Russian weekly, *Russian Voice*, published two articles entitled 'Disturbed Israel' that, according to a Municipal Police report, 'display[ed] anti-Semitic feelings in a manner that has no precedent in the local periodic press'. The articles identified Jews with communism and 'red terror':

> Take a closer look at these Jewish refugees from Germany and Austria ... Why, they are the same hangmen of the Cheka! ... The very same people who have enslaved Russia and established their own régime there; who have robbed the entire Russian people and are still destroying the Russian nation in the name of and to the glory of Israel.

Particular exception was taken to animadversions on the purity of Russian women in Shanghai that had appeared in a local Jewish newspaper. By way of rebuttal, the Russian writer admitted that:

> Russian women and girls work in restaurants and bars for their living ... A certain percentage of Russian women cohabit with foreigners ... But it would be unnatural for a Russian woman to cohabit with a Jew and she would get nothing from such a union except sexual perversity ... A Russian emigrant made the acquaintance of a Jewess. He knows the German language a little and they came to terms. The Russian was astounded ... The Jewish refugee woman offered to treat him to such specimens of the 'latest Berlin and Vienna fashion' that the young man was literally put out of countenance. One must possess a purely Jewish imagination in order to be able to invent such bestialities ... We Russians can only envy the Germans. Just think, they have got rid of the parasites in a very short time! Our deliverance, of course, is a matter of the future but it certainly will come ... It is not in vain that Jewish refugees are spreading monstrous lies about Russian nationalist organizations in Germany.[27]

While such attacks were not to the taste of all White Russians, many saw the Jews as potential competitors for jobs or in business and almost instinctively identified the Jew with bolshevism or the Antichrist.

For a time, the Japanese saw some political advantage in the growth of the Jewish population of Shanghai. In March 1940 Japanese agents, accompanied by German interpreters, visited Jewish refugees in Hongkew to urge them to vote for Japanese candidates in the forthcoming municipal elections. Jews were allegedly promised that if they voted the right way their relatives in Europe would be given facilities to enter Shanghai.[28]

After the entry of Italy into the war in June 1940, passage by sea from Europe to the Far East became nearly impossible. Some Jewish refugees travelled on the Trans-Siberian Railway across the USSR to Vladivostok and thence by land through Manchuria, or by sea via Kobe, to Shanghai. The outbreak of war between Germany and the USSR in June 1941 closed that route too, though a trickle of Jews still reached Shanghai in the second half of the year.

By this time the Japanese had decided to close Hongkew altogether to further Jewish refugees. The decision was taken at a conference of army, navy and diplomatic representatives on 21 August 1941. In a memorandum to Ellis Hayim, Captain Inuzaka gave as reasons for the decision the pressure on housing in the area, an outbreak of street fighting between Jews and White Russians, and the lack of response to his proposal the previous summer for the formation of a joint Japanese-Jewish real estate company. Inuzaka also complained of anti-Japanese statements by Sir Victor Sassoon and he warned Hayim (who had been closely connected with the Sassoon interests) that 'before expecting special dispensations from the Japanese authorities, the evils above-mentioned must first be removed'. The British consul-general, forwarding a copy of the memorandum to his ambassador, drew attention to the proposed real estate venture and commented that the Japanese seemed 'particularly surprised and irritated at their failure to browbeat the leaders of the local Jewish community into financing a venture for the profit of the Japanese in exchange for continued "protection"'.[29]

The outbreak of the Pacific War undermined the fragile economy of the Jewish refugee community in Shanghai. Immediately upon the Japanese takeover on 8 December, the subsistence of 8,000 refugees who were totally dependent on charitable relief was reduced from two meals a day to one. A deputation of three Jewish leaders, including Hayim, visited Captain

Inuzaka at his office in the Cathay Hotel and told him that relief funds were almost exhausted. Inuzaka retorted that he would have no dealings with men who had constantly defied him. He 'virtually threw the men out of his office'.[30] Shortly afterwards, as we have seen, Hayim was arrested and sent to the Bridge House. Another deputation, this time headed by the representative of the American Jewish Joint Distribution Committee, Laura Margolis, an energetic young American, visited Inuzaka a few days later and received a more cordial reception. He agreed to a scheme whereby the 'Joint' would borrow money from local neutrals in order to support the Jewish refugees.

Meanwhile, some Jews outside the refugee community worked for the Japanese and a few actively collaborated. Among these was C. Brahn, a businessman engaged in an import-export enterprise of chemicals and medicine. He had come to Shanghai from Germany shortly after the First World War. Brahn had good relations with the Japanese Gendarmerie as a result of his friendship with a Japanese woman who worked as interpreter for the chief of the Gendarmerie. Laura Margolis called Brahn 'a very unreliable, frustrated, sadistic person with a strong desire to dominate and show his power over those dependent on him'.[31]

In the summer of 1942 a Jew named Peretz, described by Margolis as 'a German refugee of very bad reputation', approached Jewish leaders in Shanghai and warned them that some form of Japanese action against the Jews was imminent. 'According to Peretz,' as Margolis later recalled, 'a plan was being evolved whereby the refugees would be loaded on ships, taken out to the ocean and drowned.' In the late 1930s Peretz had been engaged in a racket whereby Jews in Hongkew were sold what purported to be immigration permits to allow relatives to come to Shanghai. His partner in this enterprise was a Japanese named Katawa. In 1942 both Peretz and Katawa were employed on Inuzaka's staff and claimed that as a result they had found out about the impending action. Margolis suspected that Peretz might be attempting some sort of blackmail: 'Knowing the records of both Mr Peretz and Mr Katawa, we all think that they had hoped to get those men present ... to pay some money to stop this action and that in those negotiations they would make their percentage.'[32]

Word of the meeting reached the Japanese through one of the Jewish participants, Brahn, who 'went directly to the head of the Gendarmerie and, not being a very tactful person, told the whole story giving away all the facts about the meeting'. The Gendarmerie chief promptly ordered the arrest of Peretz and Katawa as well as all the Jewish leaders who had participated in the meeting – except Brahn. They were all sent to the Bridge House for questioning. One, a British national named Topaz, later died as a result of his treatment there. Although no immediate action ensued against the generality of Shanghai Jews, the episode heightened anxiety among Jews and suspicion by the Japanese of the political loyalties of Shanghai Jews.

Meanwhile Inuzaka was transferred from Shanghai to the Philippines. His successors did not share his special interest in and relative sympathy for Jews. Japanese policy towards Jews, particularly Jewish refugees, hardened. New and drastic measures came to be regarded as necessary to solve what was seen by the Japanese as a dual problem – one of security and one of public order.

In July a Jewish newspaper, *Unzer Lebn*, referred to a report by the Japanese news agency Domei that the Japanese army and navy, the Asia Development Board and the Shanghai Municipal Council were:

> engaged in working out measures for curbing the unlawful
> economic activity of those members of the Shanghai Jewish
> community who speculate in staple commodities, falsify well-
> known products and perform other commercial operations
> detrimental to the population of Shanghai.

The news was said to have 'provoked bitter feeling amidst the local Jewish circles'. The paper added: 'It is impossible to believe that the Authorities, being fully empowered to demand cooperation under the threat of redress from every individual resident in Shanghai, should prefer to choose the path of racial discrimination hitherto unknown in this part of the world.' [33] Such a public protest was almost unknown in occupied Shanghai: in this case it probably avoided the censor's pencil only by virtue of the Russian (i.e. neutral) ownership of the newspaper, which had only a small circulation.

By early 1943 the economic position of the majority of Jews in Shanghai was desperate. In the refugee camps a shortage of soap accentuated the decline in hygiene. Many camp-dwellers died of hunger, heat exhaustion and diseases such as beriberi. A Municipal Police report on 4 February 1943 stated:

> Due to a gradual impoverishment of Jewish refugees without a regular income or means of their own as well as the decreased aid granted to them by the committees, the number of persons begging has risen considerably. The number of persons who make begging their main occupation is estimated between 150 and 200. The majority are inhabitants of the refugee camp at 961 E. Seward Rd where single males are housed.
>
> The beggars regularly visit Jewish shops and households in all parts of the town. The main begging day is Friday because with approaching 'Sabbath' they expect their co-religionists to be particularly soft-hearted. On such a day a single household is visited by as many as 20 beggars. Among each other the beggars pass around information regarding 'good' or 'bad' places according to the results achieved on previous visits.
>
> Enquiries revealed that a successful beggar may obtain up to $30 on a single day but the average is of course much lower. Instead of money at some places they receive food or old pieces of clothing. Since it has become known that gifts are sometimes misused for drinking or gambling, the Jewish Gemeinde [community] has recently introduced a beggar ticket system ... which has partly remedied the matter. It is of course unavoidable that the ticket may be sold against cash.
>
> One source of information opined that since there were also criminal elements among the beggars, a certain danger exists that they may utilize their knowledge of localities and whether or not people are at home for criminal purposes.[34]

Some refugees resorted to petty crime. Seven women registered as prostitutes and more engaged in sexual commerce without registering. Twenty women are credibly reported to have sold their newborn babies.[35]

The accusation of Jewish racketeering and black-market activity was loudly voiced in the Shanghai press. On 16 February 1943, the *Shanghai Times* carried a prominent article under the headline:

SHANGHAI, HUNTING GROUND OF THRIVING
JEWISH RACKETEERS: PROMINENT BUT SHADY PART
PLAYED BY UNSCRUPULOUS JEWS IN CITY'S
ECONOMIC LIFE AND DEVELOPMENT.

The officially inspired nature of the article was indicated by the fact that it bore the signature of a prominent supporter of the Wang Ching-wei puppet régime, and quoted approvingly antisemitic statements made by Wang himself.

Two days later the press and radio published an official announcement that, 'due to military necessity', all stateless persons (the word 'Jew' was not mentioned) who had arrived in Shanghai since 1937 must move to a 'designated area' in the Wayside and Yangtsipoo sections of Hongkew by 8 May. Some of those affected by the order tried desperately to avoid the inevitable. Over the next few days the personal column of the *Shanghai Times* carried announcements such as:

Young, independent, good looking Viennese lady, Aryan, seeks
acquaintance with well situated Aryan for house-keeping or
business help. Box 6247.
Gentleman 39, good position, wishes to meet lady under 30
(non-refugee). Fond of music, home life. Apply Box 6245.[36]

Was the 'Viennese lady' really an 'Aryan'? And even if so, was she perhaps a political refugee who feared that, given the wording of the decree, she would be lumped together with the Jewish refugees in the ghetto?

The hardest hit by the order were the relatively better-off among the refugees who lived in the French Concession or in areas of the settlement other than Hongkew. They were obliged to dispose of their homes and businesses at give-away prices and to find accommodation in the already grossly overcrowded 'designated area'. By the due date all but a few hundred exempt cases had moved to Hongkew.

The Japanese propaganda machine took some pains to cushion the blow. On 25 February Ossi Lewin, editor of the *Shanghai Jewish Chronicle*, published a fawning interview with T. Kubota, director-general of the 'Office for Shanghai Stateless Refugee Affairs'. Lewin (whose editorial offices were located in Hamilton House, headquarters of the Japanese Gendarmerie) declared that 'a very friendly atmosphere' prevailed in the office. Kubota, 'the directing brain', had disclaimed any antisemitic intention behind the decree and had spoken in a 'serious and engaging manner', leaving 'the pleasant feeling that the fate of our community has been put into the hands of a man who has treated our numerous problems with so great understanding'.[37] In a speech at a banquet at the Shanghai Jewish Club a few weeks later, Kubota reiterated his denial of any antisemitic motive and rebutted rumours that the Japanese decision was a result of German pressure. The true cause, he explained, was the conduct of some Jews: 'I would like to state quite frankly, although it is very regrettable, that there were a certain number of stateless refugees who in their activities hindered and disturbed Japan in her pursuance of the Great East Asia War.'[38] 'The area designated in the Proclamation', he declared in yet another public statement, 'is neither a ghetto nor a jail but an area which is full of hope for the refugees, in which they may build a haven for themselves.'[39]

On one point, at least, Kubota probably spoke the truth. Although Shanghai Jews were convinced that German pressure was behind the Japanese decision, there is no evidence that the Nazi apparatus in Shanghai exercised any influence in the matter. In so far as the Japanese paid attention to outsiders they looked less to the local Nazis than to their chief advisers on such issues, who were White Russians. The two agencies primarily concerned with the matter were, in order of importance, the Japanese Naval Intelligence Bureau, responsible for security, and the Municipal Police Special Branch, responsible for public order. In the former, the central figure advising the Japanese was Eugene Pick; in the latter the officer chiefly responsible for furnishing reports on Jewish affairs, and particularly on the black market, was one of Pick's sidekicks, a Russian detective, Morris Gershkovitch.

Pick's recommendations for handling the Jews were laid out in a letter to his boss, Commander Otani. The document is undated but was probably written in early 1943:

There is no need to stand on ceremonies with the Jews. If you take into the iron fist all Russian, German and Austrian European Jewish refugees and Indian, Arab and British and American Jews all over Asia, you will get in full your subjects in America. [In his fractured English, Pick seems to be suggesting that the Jews might be used by the Japanese as bargaining counters to secure the release or exchange of Japanese internees in the United States.] Control over the Jews should be strengthened. They should be compelled to revive the life of Shanghai. In the meantime they are making money by some ways and means; one could see in any cabaret on the eve of New Year that of those who drank champagne, 60% of the foreigners were Jews ... Measures and friendly handshakes and blankets [?] offered to them would not impress them; they need a good whip and a clenched fist — then they will do everything that is necessary.[40]

Pick remained unrepentant about his role in the internment of the Jewish refugees in Shanghai during the occupation. In a statement to the US Army Counter-Intelligence Corps after the war, he called the Jewish refugees 'maggots' who had 'penetrated into stores and after a year they become the bosses'. Alluding to the common accusation that Jews dominated the black market, he alleged, 'They produced everything from counterfeit dollars to vitamins ... bootlegged vodka and perfume and whiskey from abroad'. 'The Jews,' he added, 'became excellent collaborators of the Japs.'[41]

Unlike the Allied citizens, the Jews were not interned in camps but were merely restricted to the 'designated area' in Hongkew. Whatever its formal title, the district amounted to something very similar to a ghetto. It did not quite conform to the traditional model, since some Chinese continued to live there side by side with Jews. Nor was it quite like a concentration or internment camp, since at first residents were allowed out more or less freely during the daytime to go to work elsewhere in the city. After 10 August 1943, however, Jews were not permitted to leave without a special pass, which was difficult to obtain — though distribution of such documents eventually turned into a typical Shanghai racket. Day-to-day control was the responsibility of a Japanese official, K. Ghoya, a crude and tyrannical figure with a reputation for petulant rages and slapping the faces of Jewish applicants.

With the internment of most Jews, the only non-Japanese foreigners in Shanghai who remained at large were Axis citizens, Russians (Whites, Reds and Russian Jews), and an assortment of Asiatics (Indians, Filipinos and a few others).

上海

Even some friends of the Axis fell foul of the occupying authorities. Sumaire's social connections availed her little when, one night in early 1942, she was awakened at 2.00 a.m. by loud knocking on her door. When she opened it, eight Japanese, some in Japanese Gendarmerie uniform, burst in and ransacked the apartment, removing documents and jewellery. She was humiliatingly forced to get dressed in front of the men and then 'peremptorily bundled downstairs into a car' that took her to the Bridge House. There (according to her later testimony) she was subjected to violent ill-treatment. She was 'brutally cuffed about the head on several occasions' until 'a state of hysteria was produced'. After two weeks of imprisonment she was interrogated and accused of being a British spy:

> They based their allegation on the fact that I had left France
> just about one month before the fall of that country to the
> Germans. This, they said, was suspicious and pointed to my
> guilt. I strongly denied the allegation and was severly [sic]
> manhandled for doing so. They then produced my album of
> photographs, which they removed from my room and which
> contained several pictures of me taken with Major Hamilton
> of the United States Marine Corps, at several Shanghai social
> functions, as well as other photographs containing well-known
> British and American personalities in Shanghai.
>
> Concerning Major Hamilton, the Japanese told me that I
> could not deny the fact that he was an intelligence officer. This
> was unknown to me and I said so. This, of course, caused me

to be beaten, shouted at, and generally treated like an animal.[42]

Sumaire claimed that she had been kicked violently in the stomach as a result of which she suffered a haemorrhage. After about a month she was released. As a consequence of her ill-treatment she later had to undergo an operation at the Country Hospital.

Sumaire's story is uncorroborated by any other source but there is no reason to think that she invented it. In spite of the rumours flying around Shanghai that she was a Japanese or Nazi agent, the truth was almost certainly much more mundane: that she was an amoral, relentlessly self-seeking, social butterfly who fluttered hither and thither, always looking for the brightest lights, the fanciest parties and the richest lovers.

Berrier's activities during the period after the outbreak of the Pacific War are sparsely documented. As in the case of Sumaire, the most readily available evidence is unfortunately suspect, coming as it does from himself in the form of a lengthy and vivid account, presented to American intelligence authorities in Peking after the war, of his arrest and imprisonment by the Japanese. According to this narrative, Berrier received a number of warnings shortly after the outbreak of the Pacific War that he was under suspicion by the Japanese Gendarmerie. One such warning came from Sumaire who said to him, 'You must promise not to try to escape because they know all about your fiancée and her mother and they will be blamed for making the contact for you if you do.' (Was this reference to Rosalynd Kadoorie or to Evelyn Oleaga and her daughter?) The aviator preposterously claimed in his post-war narrative that he had been 'left behind under the orders of the U.S. Government' to act as adviser to the French resistance movement in Shanghai.[43]

A few months after the start of the occupation (still according to Berrier), gendarmes called at his apartment and questioned him, particularly regarding his connections with Shanghai Gaullists. He confessed, so he said, to a 'slight acquaintance' with the Gaullist resistance leader Egal. He admitted to the Japanese that he had volunteered for the Gaullists but said 'that the British had refused to let Monsieur Egal send me'. During the summer and autumn of 1942 he was:

followed continually. I tried to throw Japs off my fiancee and
her family (feared they would be tortured on account of me)
by staying away from their place. Every move watched, I tried
to give impression of lack of political interest. Went around
with one Portuguese woman [Mrs Oleaga?], frequented Jimmy
James' [a night club], smoked opium with a French scholar,
spent time in research on oriental literature.

Even now, it seems, Berrier could not resist the opportunity to spice up his
story with piquant detail.

Berrier was arrested in November 1942 and placed in the Haiphong
Road detention camp for political prisoners – this much, at any rate, was
true since the head of the British Residents' Association, Hugh Collar, recalled seeing him there.[44] With what was perhaps the poetic licence of the
freelance journalist, Berrier gave a colourful account of his interrogation by
a Japanese Gendarmerie officer whom he described as 'about 5 ft. 8 inches,
around 200 lbs, has bullet head, neanderthal or cro-magnon face, receding
forehead, ape lips, no lower jaw, has crescent-shaped scar, like small horse
shoe, on right side of his head, just above ear'. This officer was assisted by
an interpreter, of whom Berrier etched no less arresting a portrait: 'Short,
dapper, may be Eurasian, wore dark blue suit with thin stripe, Rudolph
Valentino haircut – obviously a returned student – sleek, oily, "sheik" type
Japanese. Took off coat and daintily rolled up sleeves. Silk shirt bore monogram YS or SY. Had a number of small blotches, might be called dark, small
unformed moles on right side of face and lobe of left ear.' Berrier's account
of his treatment by these two unprepossessing individuals was artfully de-
vised to indicate that he had had friendly connections with British intelligence in Shanghai. Given the evidence of British hostility to him, this may
be taken as false – probably inserted for the purpose of ingratiating himself
with the American recipients of his narrative. Berrier further claimed to
have been savagely beaten with the handle of a floor-waxing machine (another clever touch of detail) and later to have been subjected to water torture. In further questioning by the Japanese, Berrier was (as he recalled)
accused of being a communist. 'Protested I was a monarchist, member of
French Royalist Party and of noble family.'

While imprisoned, Berrier claimed to have met two British agents named John Cook and Eric Davies. Both were tortured by the Japanese and Cook later died as a result of treatment received during his captivity. According to Berrier, Cook told him 'that it weighed heavily on his mind that the entire "chain" that had served British intelligence through him, running all the way to Hankow, were about to face execution because of his confession. "You must get word someway to Mr Steptoe".'[45] Berrier at least got the names more or less right, since Harry Steptoe had indeed been the SIS chief in the Far East before the war, and men named Davies and Cook were among those arrested and tortured by the Japanese – possibly on account of connections with British intelligence. But the most plausible interpretation is that Berrier had picked up knowledge of these names of suspected British agents and dropped them into his narrative to provide a patina of authenticity that would impress his American readers.

In the curriculum vitae that he prepared in 1957,* Berrier expanded (or exaggerated) these claims. He wrote that at the time of Pearl Harbor he had been 'running [a] Chinese Nationalist underground radio station in Shanghai' and that after the Japanese occupation he 'went into [a] French resistance organization working with the allies'. Upon his arrest in November 1942 he had endured 'eighteen days' of torture. And after the war he had been awarded (so his account continued) 'Chinese citation for radio communications, French Volunteer of the Resistance Cross, Combatant Cross, and Victory Medal' – a jangling collection of gongs of which, given his documented record of pro-Axis activity, he had good reason to boast.[46]

Berrier seems (it is not certain) to have spent the later part of the war interned together with other Americans. If so, he was probably fortunate, since he might otherwise have shared the fate of his former business partner in the 'male brothel', Dr von Miorini. The doctor's various enterprises throve to such an extent during the war that he built up a hoard of gold bars, the most reliable long-term investment at the time. In the course of 1943, however, he came under suspicion of furnishing information pro-

*Berrier submitted the document to the former Shanghai businessman Norwood Allman, apparently hoping that Allman would help him find a job.

cured from his Axis friends to agents of the Chinese nationalist régime in Chungking.

In June 1944 Miorini died suddenly after an operation at the Paulus Hospital. This hospital, in which Dr Robert Neumann's experimental pathology laboratory was situated, was described in a later US intelligence report as 'a veritable house of horror'.[47] The diagnosis of the attending physician was that Miorini had died of para-typhoid, but an autopsy cast some doubt on this and rumours suggested foul play. The disappearance of Miorini's gold bars led some to suspect the hand of Ruby Edwards who was known to be jealous of his liaison with another woman. But post-war investigations by American intelligence authorities suggested that the most likely assassins were Nazi doctors acting under instruction from the local Gestapo. The prime suspect was the 'butcher of Buchenwald', who had performed the autopsy on Miorini. In a post-war deposition, another doctor involved in the case suggested that Neumann, possibly in collaboration with Ruby Edwards, had administered a slow poison to the patient. Neumann himself declared that the post-mortem indicated that Miorini's death had been 'caused by a badly ulcerated stomach and intestinal tract and not by typhus' and he admitted that 'death by intentional poisoning was possible'. A macabre coincidence that came to light subsequently was that at the time of his death Miorini had been working on a book on Chinese poisons. A will was found naming Ruby Edwards as heir to the greater part of the estate, which included ten houses. As for the gold bars, they were never found – or, if they were, the finder never publicized the fact.

Meanwhile Miorini's old schoolfriend, Erben, suffered a no less bizarre fate. He spent much of his time in the early days of the occupation associating with interned American sailors from the *President Harrison* and seemed to be trying to stir up trouble. An American resident concluded that Erben was 'at least pink, if not red'.[48] In fact, Erben was trying to pump the sailors for information that he transmitted to Siefken's office.

Siefken tried to have Erben included on a list of American citizens eligible for repatriation in the projected Japanese-American civilian prisoner exchange. The plan was for Erben to remain in Lourenço Marques, where the exchange would take place, and operate from there as a German agent. On 7 September 1942 Erben registered as an American citizen, took out a red armband marking him as an enemy alien and applied to be placed on a list for possible repatriation to the United States. His departure was apparently vetoed by the Japanese and he therefore remained in Shanghai working for the Abwehr.

At the end of 1942, after a reorganization in the Abwehr office, Erben was given a new controller, Captain Otto Habenicht, who, according to Erben's post-war account, suggested that he should focus on seeking information about escape routes into Free China used by Americans and Britons. Habenicht also asked Erben to 'try and find people who are stigmatized by their habits, men who have something to fear ... drug addicts, men who are homosexuals, who would be easier for me to find out the angles as a physician'.[49]

On 25 January 1943 Erben was called to the Swiss consulate in Shanghai and handed a document notifying him that he had been deprived of his US citizenship with retroactive effect to 1941.[50] When Erben read this he became 'extremely truculent' and said that 'they could not do that to him'. The Swiss consul told senior figures in the American residents' association that he had a thick file on Erben that had been given to him by the US consulate, 'and that they believed that he had been one of the key men in one of the large opium smuggling rings'.

The German intelligence establishment in Shanghai too came to consider Erben 'an extremely questionable person' and instituted inquiries concerning his background.[51] In May 1943 a message arrived from Berlin warning that Erben was an 'impostor, narcotics dealer and American propagandist'.[52] He was consequently dismissed by the Abwehr and sent to the Lunghwa internment camp and later to the camp at Pootung. Habenicht told him that he would remain in the camp for a certain period, then effect an escape with another American and make his way to Chungking where he would work as a German agent.[53] Habenicht probably spun him this yarn in order to keep him quiet while he was in the camp – perhaps also in the hope of using him as bait to discover internees' escape routes.

Upon being handed over to the Japanese Gendarmerie, Erben succeeded in persuading them (or himself) that he could be of use as an informer on fellow internees. He was told to try to identify any American agents or former servicemen, to look out for connections between inmates and Chinese in Shanghai 'so the Japanese could put their fingers on them', and to try to identify any disgruntled Americans who might be useful to Axis intelligence.[54] He was visited regularly in camp by officers of the Japanese Gendarmerie. These visits came to the knowledge of other prisoners and rendered Erben an object of suspicion among his fellow internees. Ultimately he became something of a pariah in the camp. Erben later recalled that Habenicht arranged for him to be given 'the undesirable job of garbage man in the camp in order to be able to receive and send out with the garbage necessary communications'. Erben considered this to be part and parcel of his intelligence duties though the awful suspicion arises that the work assignment may have been a private joke on the part of Habenicht.

Shanghai could boast few more self-sacrificing records of collaboration than Erben's long period of voluntary work for the Axis cause while himself incarcerated in an internment camp. In reality, of course, he could cause little harm to the Allied war effort from behind Japanese barbed wire.

More dangerous were the collaborators of several Allied nationalities who earned exemption from internment by rendering no less devoted, and in many cases much more effective, service to the Japanese cause in occupied Shanghai.

8 Collaborators

Quite early in the Pacific War the British authorities noted a disturbing prevalence of collaboration among their citizens in Shanghai. In May 1942 the British commander-in-chief in India, General Wavell, dispatched a telegram to the War Office in London expressing concern that:

> reports from Shanghai indicate British subjects, many of military age, living more or less normal lives, although good prospects of escape exist if effort made. Reports also indicate some continue serve in Police and Municipal Administration. Fact that extremely few British civilians have so far escaped significant in view of these reports. Our prestige will be still further lowered if British subjects continue serve puppet Municipal Council and if British firms continue to operate by agreement with Japanese as appears to be the case.[1]

Wavell's message, evidently based on intelligence reports, actually understated the extent to which, particularly in the early phase of the occupation, British and other Allied civilians adapted with seeming insouciance to the realities of the New Order in Shanghai.

In fact, virtually the entire British and other Allied staffs of the Shanghai Municipal Council and of the Municipal Police remained at their posts for several weeks, in many cases for months, in some for more than a year after the start of the occupation. They thereby facilitated the smooth handover and functioning of the administration of the International Settlement, with its port, its major industries and other strategic facilities, under Japanese auspices. On 30 December 1941 the Japanese Consul-General, Horiuchi, noted complacently that 'thanks to our generous policies, the Municipal Council staff have started to abide by our orders'.[2]

Although the Allied members of the council were induced to resign their seats in early January 1942, Allied citizens among the senior council staff decided, after consulting their consuls, to remain at their posts. At the end of February Godfrey Phillips resigned; this was on the advice of the British consul-general, A. H. George. Phillips had come 'to the conclusion that as a British subject he could no longer act as the senior executive officer of what had become a Japanese controlled organization'. He was replaced by a Japanese.[3] Most other British officials remained at their desks until the following June. Many British and American citizens who had been thrown out of work by the closure of enemy businesses were employed temporarily by the council's emergency supply offices and by the Revenue Office, helping it 'to cope with the increased work caused by the imposition of new taxes'. The pay was poor but, as the deputy-secretary of the council, J. W. Allen, later put it, such employment 'nevertheless proved a blessing to many of them' since it 'enabled them to carry on without applying to their national associations for relief'.[4] Most of the British and American employees of the council were among those interned in 1943, but a few who were regarded as indispensable by the Japanese were brought by bus daily from the camps to continue their official business.

The conduct of all these men was contrary to guidelines set at a meeting of senior officials from several government departments in London on 3 December 1941. On that occasion it was agreed that while 'no forcible resistance to armed seizure [was] to be offered by the local British authorities [in the Far East], including the British municipal authorities and police', at the same time 'British subjects must not, however, assist the Japanese in the running of the administration or the public utilities, social services and so on'.[5] When the time came, a few days later, British municipal officials, police and utility workers in Shanghai remained at their posts, with very few exceptions, unless or until they were dismissed by the Japanese. The explanation, it seems, was that the London decision was never conveyed clearly to the British population of Shanghai. On the contrary, Consul-General George in Shanghai gave his seal of approval after the Japanese attack to the continued functioning of municipal officials in their posts. The hope was thereby to preserve some simulacrum of the international character of the settlement and to salvage as much as possible of long-term British interests.

Americans in Shanghai were similarly informed that they should carry on unless required to do something contrary to American interests.[6]

The British officers of the Municipal Police stayed at their posts for as long as it suited the Japanese to keep them. In this case they were acting in accord with official instructions that had been distributed confidentially before the occupation to all British members of the force by the commissioner of police, Kenneth Bourne. Responding to requests from some police officers to be released to join the British armed forces, Bourne wrote: 'I can assure you that until this war is over our duty lies in Shanghai...the greater the danger and the more trying the conditions to be faced *where we are needed* the greater the obligation to stick it out until British [sic] is victorious.'[7]*

In February 1942 Bourne was formally replaced as commissioner of police by the Japanese chief deputy commissioner, Watari Sakon, 'owing to the inability [of Bourne] to return to his post'.[8] At the same time ten other senior British officers were retired, though Deputy Commissioner Smyth and one other were retained as 'advisers'. Many British officers, nevertheless, continued to serve in the force for some time longer – 'remembering [as a post-war report put it] that the first duty of this international force was to the community.'[9]

The question that inevitably arose was which community they were supposed to be serving. The issue presented itself in a direct manner early on the morning of 20 December 1941, when Japanese Gendarmerie officers, headed by Sergeant-Major Yamamoto, called at the Municipal Police headquarters and asked for assistance in conducting 13 raids at various addresses in the settlement 'for the purpose of effecting the arrest of eight British subjects, three Americans, one Russian and two Chinese, all of whom were alleged to be engaged in anti-Japanese activities'. The two most senior

---

* A note appended to the copy of this document in the Public Record Office states: 'After this had been issued, Major K. M. Bourne obtained furlough and went to Canada where he joined H. M. Forces.' Sauce for the goose, it seems, was something else for the goslings. In fairness to Bourne, it should be stated that his apparent abandonment of his men in August 1941 was the result of orders from above. For much of the wartime period he worked for the British Security Executive in New York, then in India.

British officers in the force 'gave instructions to the effect that assistance to arrest the Chinese be granted, but that the other [requests for assistance] be withheld pro tem, inasmuch as that it placed the police in a very embarrassing position'.[10] One of the two Chinese turned out to have fled his home the previous night. The other, who was the ex-chauffeur of the naval liaison officer at the British embassy, was arrested by the Gendarmerie with the aid of one Chinese and one British police officer. Police records over the ensuing weeks contain several instances of assistance by British policemen in arrests of Chinese accused of resistance activities.[11] On 26 January 1942 British policemen accompanied a Gendarmerie party, composed of ten Japanese professors, in a raid on the old-established Shanghai bookstore and publisher Kelly and Walsh at 66 Nanking Road, as well as on nine other foreign bookshops suspected of stocking anti-Japanese literature.

At one level, cooperation in repressing resistance activities by citizens of China, an ally of Britain against Japan, might seem like a clear instance of collaboration. Yet these officers were, after all, doing no more than they had done in the period before December 1941 when the Municipal Police Special Branch, like its counterpart in the French Concession, had cooperated on a regular basis with the Japanese in suppressing Chinese terrorism and political activities against Japanese forces in Shanghai.

In July 1942 74 British policemen, including most remaining commissioned officers, were retired, but 187 British citizens remained in the force. Some of these became increasingly perplexed at the false position in which they found themselves. In September a number of them sent a message to the British government, through the Swiss consulate in Shanghai, asking for guidance.[12] They do not seem to have received any reply. Several more British policemen had in the meantime been dismissed, but the rest continued to serve and some were commended by the Japanese commissioner for efficient service. During the winter of 1942–43 some were even promoted. Detective Sergeant Byngs, the Foreign Affairs Section officer responsible for regular reporting on British and American affairs until the spring of 1943, was himself a British citizen: a post-war American intelligence report concluded, however, that 'nothing detrimental concerning his work was known and he appeared to be no more of a malicious collaborator than anyone else in the Section'.[13]

In some cases service in the force terminated with an abruptness in which dark comedy mingled with personal tragedy. A post-war statement by Superintendent J. A. McFarlane, former police quartermaster, describes with indignation how, on 6 January 1943, he was standing in uniform in his office at the Gordon Road Police Depot when:

> about five or six male Japanese in plain clothes entered, and,
> through the Japanese Superintendent who was supposed to be
> in charge of the Department but under my tuition, I was
> informed that the gentlemen who had just entered were
> members of H.I.J.M. Gendarmerie and they were to ask me a
> few questions at Headquarters.

McFarlane's pistol and office keys were taken from him and he was led away for interrogation at the Bridge House. After 12 days of detention there, during which he was beaten on the head with a bamboo cane, he was removed to the Haiphong Road internment camp for political prisoners.[14] Only in the spring of 1943 were all remaining British police discharged and, in most cases, interned.

Some British officials in Shanghai appear to have feigned collaboration under specific orders from London. Such may have been the case of James H. Smart, head of the British wireless monitoring station in Shanghai. Immediately upon the outbreak of the Pacific war the station's equipment was dismantled and hidden. Smart was arrested a week later by the Japanese Gendarmerie but he was released after a fortnight. At the end of January 1942 Smart was summoned to the Cathay Hotel where he met Eugene Pick and Commander Otani. They asked Smart to work for the Japanese. Smart reportedly agreed on condition that he and two other men from his team would be evacuated from Shanghai on the first repatriation ship. For the next six months Smart ran a listening station monitoring the Chungking-San Francisco telegraph circuits and news from United States broadcasting stations.

Smart's activity was approved by his superiors in the British embassy. The object of this extraordinary form of officially sanctioned collaboration appears to have been to maintain in existence the rudiments of a wireless communications capability with a view to creating a 'stay-behind' radio team that might function after Smart left. Smart's hopes in this regard were centred on his stepson, Vyacheslav ('Slava') Toropovsky, aged 17, whom he had trained as a wireless operator and who worked in his station. In August 1942 Smart was included, as promised, in the repatriation programme, leaving behind his Russian wife and stepson. Before going, he showed Toropovsky a means of maintaining secret radio communication with him. But on the very day of Smart's departure his station was closed down. Toropovsky was unable to communicate with him at all and eventually succumbed to Japanese navy pressure to work as a radio expert in the Axis interest.[15]

The one significant exception to the general pattern was the case of the 300 or so British and other Allied staff of the Chinese customs service, headed by the inspector-general, Sir Frederick Maze, who ceased working after about 11 December 1941. They did not, however, resign voluntarily; they were informed that their services had been dispensed with by the Nanking (puppet) government.

上海

If such was the example offered by official and quasi-official Allied citizens in Shanghai, it is hardly surprising that many ordinary civilians, particularly businessmen, followed suit. The origins of economic collaboration can be traced back in part to the phony war period and the deliberate laxity with which economic warfare against Germany was conducted at that time by the British in the Far East.

The Shanghai ICI chief, Hugh Collar, had felt no qualms in joining with German businessmen in a price control committee set up at the request of the Municipal Council early in the war. 'If it sounds a little queer that we should contemplate working with our enemies', he later wrote, 'it must be remembered that we were working for the International Settlement ... for the common good.'[16]

Unfortunately, the line between appeasement and collaboration was not always clear. In May 1941 the British military intelligence chief in Singapore wrote: 'A particularly dreadful aspect of the situation is the number of

British firms in Shanghai and elsewhere which are not above turning a dishonest penny by trading with the enemy.'[17]

At the interdepartmental meeting of officials in London on 3 December, the position of 'industrial plants and public utilities at Shanghai and Hankow' was considered and the decision was reached that 'British companies operating such enterprises and British subjects employed in them should be told that while they are not expected to offer forcible resistance to armed seizure by the Japanese military, they must not work for the Japanese or help them in any way. In fact, British subjects working voluntarily for the enemy would be regarded as traitors.'[18] Again, the decision seems not to have been conveyed clearly before the outbreak of the Pacific War to those most directly involved.

Public utility employees in both Shanghai and Hankow generally remained at their posts after 8 December 1941. In some cases they were threatened by the Japanese with dire consequences if they failed to turn up for work. But even where no intimidation was applied, the result was generally the same.

At Hankow, several British concerns, including the important Hankow Light and Power Company, continued in operation. The British Consul-General in the city later urged prosecution of some of those involved. He described how his efforts to persuade the managers of two large tobacco companies to comply with the Trading with the Enemy Act had been ignored:

> The Manager, Parsons, an American, never came to see me until we had been at war nearly five months. He then excused himself on the grounds that the Japanese had compelled them to work... On the morning of December 8 British and American subjects were assembled at the Hankow Club and told by the Japanese authorities of the restrictions that would be imposed. Eppes, the manager of the factory, also an American, at once got up and asked for a pass to go to the factory. I made a point of getting hold of him after the meeting and remonstrating with him, pointing out that it would in my opinion be trading with the enemy. To this he

replied that he would have a riot on his hands among his Chinese employees if he stopped. I said this was for the Japanese to handle. He then asked me if I ordered him to stop work, to which I answered that I had no legal power to do so … *

Even Parsons admitted that the gendarmes disappeared from their offices after a few weeks and they still went on working. The truth is that the two companies worked very closely with the Japanese before the war, thought by continuing to do so they would save their businesses and the first explanation given to me by third parties was that they had orders from Shanghai to continue working. These orders they certainly did not have on December 8.[20]

In April 1942 the British Residents' Association in Shanghai sent a message to London, through the Swiss, asking 'whether in the opinion of HMG responsible representatives of these [British] firms [still permitted to function by the Japanese] should remain on the spot in order to safeguard British economic interests in general and capital in particular'. The message added that the local heads of the three most important British concerns, the Hong Kong and Shanghai Bank, Butterfield & Swire and Jardine, Matheson, all felt that 'a reduced staff should remain in Shanghai as long as the possibility of doing useful work remains'.[21]

No direct reply seems to have been sent but a Foreign Office comment, in a telegram to Wavell in May 1942, was significantly more lenient than earlier London views: 'Assistance in municipal administration and maintenance essential public services not considered unpatriotic. Any activity which assists enemy war effort considered reprehensible but for consider-

---

* The British consul-general, of course, could claim no authority over American citizens. Even his power to issue orders to British citizens appears to have been limited. This view of the limits of consular authority was subsequently endorsed by the wartime German consul-general in Shanghai, Martin Fischer, who testified to a post-war US military tribunal that 'a consul-general never has any authority or power over his fellow citizens in the community where he resides'. Each of these experienced diplomats no doubt had his own reasons in different circumstances for taking such a narrow view of the matter. Other consuls at other times, particularly in China, had pursued a much more robust policy.[19]

ation whether retention of responsible representatives of British firms at Shanghai not necessary for preservation assets post-war period.'[22] Some such guidance seems to have reached Shanghai, since a letter of around the same time from an executive of the British-American Tobacco Company in the city reported 'British official advices have been received that "voluntary cooperation" should be avoided.' The distinction between 'voluntary' and 'involuntary' collaboration was a nice one, since, as the writer pointed out, 'there would be grave dangers to individuals in open non-cooperation, such as by closing factories. This applies to all foreign enterprises.'[23]

The practical upshot was that, in most economic enterprises, the decision was made not by the Britons or Americans involved, but by the Japanese. Foreign staff at the Ewo cotton mill, for example, remained at their posts under Japanese supervision, without being able to do much work, until they were dismissed on 1 June 1942.[24]

上海

The single most significant case of economic collaboration by a British or American business enterprise in China during the war was that of the Kailan Mining Administration (KMA). The largest coal-mining enterprise in China, the KMA was a joint Sino-British concern, although the chief manager was British and effective control was exercised by a British parent company, the Chinese Mining and Engineering Company, based in London. The KMA, whose headquarters were in Tientsin, employed 47,000 Chinese labourers in its mines, which produced over 6.5 million tons of coal in the financial year 1939–40. Of this, some 2 million tons were supplied to Shanghai, supplying about 40 per cent of the city's entire coal needs – largely used for power generation and industrial purposes rather than domestic heating. Much of the remainder was exported to Japan whose coal imports from China had more than quintupled since 1935: the KMA was the largest single supplier to the Japanese market. But the economist E. B. Schumpeter, writing in 1940, warned that Japanese success in exploiting this asset depended on peaceful collaboration rather than coercion: 'If, however, a Japanese army has to keep the mines running, the cost in the long run will be prohibitive.'[25]

In early 1941 the Kailan Mines were the only ones in Japanese-occupied China that had not been taken over by the Japanese. One reason, no doubt, was the long record of close relations between the company and the Japanese army, who had been helpful since 1935 in curbing industrial unrest among the company's huge workforce.[26] The chairman of the parent company, at the annual meeting in London in 1937, insisted that 'neither the Kailan Mining Administration, nor this company, has any political ends to serve. We are concerned only with the prosecution by the administration of our legitimate business interests.'[27]

The KMA's chief manager, Edward Jonah Nathan, was a British businessman of the utmost respectability who had been awarded the Order of the British Empire before the war. Nathan had worked for the company for more than 30 years. His family had long been associated with the Kailan Mines. His father had also served as general manager (succeeding Herbert Hoover, later president of the United States). Nathan was a competent businessman and, according to his own lights, a loyal British citizen. But his long sojourn in the Far East had cut him off from the general drift of British opinion. In the critical situation with which he was confronted during the war, Nathan fell back on the implicit assumptions and values of the Shanghai mind. He was by no means alone. In his case, however, the consequences were severely detrimental to the Allied war effort – and to Nathan's personal reputation.

Given the supreme importance of coking coal for the Japanese steel industry and therefore for Japan's war effort, the company had sought guidance from the Foreign Office before the war as to what attitude it should adopt in the event of hostilities between Britain and Japan. But the government declined to offer any advice. In August 1941, therefore, Nathan gave the local Japanese authorities, who already effectively controlled the area, an assurance that he 'accepted responsibility for the continued functioning of the mines until such time as the Japanese were able to assume this responsibility if, after war had broken out, they decided to do so'.[28] Nathan wrote a memorandum recording this pledge which he sent to his company's headquarters in London. From there a copy was sent to the government by a director of the company in late September.[29] In mitigation of Nathan's conduct it might be argued that, given the abjectly submissive posture of the British government in the face of Japanese provocation at Tientsin over the previous two years, Nathan had good reason to believe that his undertaking was in accord with official British policy.

At the Kailan Mines after 8 December 1941, Nathan kept the promise he had given to the Japanese the previous August. He and almost all 71 senior British staff of the KMA remained at their posts, with the title of 'advisers', producing coal for the Japanese war effort under Japanese supervision and training Japanese managers to take over their own functions. One British staff member, E. F. Watts, escaped on 19 December 1941 and made his way overland to Chungking. On arrival, he wrote to the company's headquarters in England: 'On more than one occasion prior to the outbreak of war in the Pacific I had asked Mr Nathan to release me for war service. I was in each instance refused.'[30] Nathan's decision to continue to operate the mines under Japanese control was eased by a legal opinion furnished by the company's British lawyer in Tientsin endorsing the legal propriety of such conduct.[31]

In February 1942 Nathan wrote (via neutral Switzerland) to his wife in America:

> KMA affairs are conducted as before with the exception that
> we are now under military control, which is exercised through
> a supervisory staff of Japanese businessmen, most of them
> employees of the North China Development Co., but all KMA
> staff (foreign and Chinese) retain exactly the same positions as
> they did previously with the sole exception of myself as I
> refused the 'offer' to continue as Chief Manager made to me
> by the Japanese military authorities on Dec. 8th and after
> more than a month's negotiation was on Jan. 10th ordered to
> assume the post of 'Chief Adviser' and carry on my duties
> exactly as before. The supervision to which we are subjected is
> by no means excessive nor, so far, unpleasant or unreasonable
> and the Chief Supervisor is an extremely intelligent man with
> sufficient influence in military circles to get his opinions
> respected ... The Joergs [the Swiss consul in Tientsin and his
> wife] dined with us once or twice and I had to give a party

[for] eight men in honour of our Chief Supervisor (Mr Shirakawa).[32]

Over the next few months Nathan repeatedly boasted to Japanese officials and to the Swiss consul in Tientsin that he had 'completely discharged the responsibilities I assumed in virtue of the undertaking I gave to Generals Shiozawa and Tanabe in August 1941'.[33] In February 1943 Nathan was replaced by a Japanese manager. Upon his resignation, the Japanese embassy in Peking wrote to him: 'General Shiozawa appreciates your good faith in carrying out the obligations which you had undertaken and fully understands the army-controlled Kailan Mining Administration must attribute its present smooth operation to your great devotion which you have made [sic] since December 8th 1941.'[34]

Unfortunately for Nathan, the British Foreign Office had a similar understanding of the value of his services to the Japanese war effort. In February 1942 the Foreign Office wrote to the British parent company, objecting to Nathan's conduct in giving 'certain undertakings which appear difficult to reconcile with the duty of a British subject to abstain by all means in his power from giving aid or assistance to the enemies of his country'. The letter went on to point out that 'these undertakings are only explicable on the assumption that they were extorted under pressure'.[35] The directors of the company wrote back, attempting to justify Nathan's behaviour, but the Foreign Office was unconvinced and returned to the charge:

> His Majesty's Government do not regard as unpatriotic the
> participation of British subjects in such maintenance of
> essential services as is for the benefit of the civil population of
> the occupied territory, but ... they do expect patriotic British
> subjects to refrain from assisting the war effort and ... as the
> production of coal is clearly essential to the Japanese war
> effort, His Majesty's Government cannot but regard assistance
> given voluntarily by British subjects to this end as [un]patriotic
> and reprehensible.[36]

Much alarmed by this extraordinary official rebuke, the company made renewed attempts to defend Nathan, arguing that if the British staff had refused to work the Japanese could easily have carried on without them. The
British might as a result have suffered 'grave personal consequences'. The
company added that if British staff had withdrawn the KMA would have
passed into Japanese hands and after the war into full Chinese control,
'with the result of the total loss of the Company's enterprise in China'.[37]
This barely disguised claim to the priority of their business interests over
the national interest evoked an even sharper retort from the Foreign Office:
'Mr Eden is not impressed by the statement of your directors ... These and
the other arguments advanced in your memorandum do not, in Mr Eden's
opinion, excuse the voluntary undertakings.'[38]

Following his resignation, Nathan was interned by the Japanese in
Shanghai for the remainder of the war. Although the Foreign Office refused
to withdraw its criticism of his conduct, he was never prosecuted and he
later assumed control of the English parent company. The Foreign Office
contemptuously rejected Nathan's offer in December 1946 to pay the government £934 15s. 8d., representing 'the total sums received by me from
the Japanese Army-controlled Kailan Mining Administration as honorar-
ium and living expenses ... at the rate current at the outbreak of the war'.[39]

One of the many ironies of this case is that, whereas the British police
and municipal officials in Shanghai might defend their conduct under the
occupation on the basis of the official guidance they had received, Nathan
could lodge, no less sincerely, a defence that was based on the exact opposite: lack of official guidance. Since Nathan, his entire British staff and his
business partners in London remained convinced in their own minds that
they had not acted unpatriotically, their behaviour might be classed as an instance of unconscious collaboration.

上海

Falling into a very different category were those Allied citizens who con-
sciously and deliberately embarked on the collaborationist road. These
were only a small minority among the foreign population of Shanghai, but
several became well-known public figures thanks to their involvement in

the German or Japanese propaganda effort. Neither the English-language press nor English broadcasting in Shanghai could have continued during the war without their participation.

The *Shanghai Times* was taken over by the Japanese Embassy on 9 December 1941. Shortly afterwards, an American-educated Japanese was appointed editor. E. A. Nottingham, the paper's British proprietor, remained in nominal charge but exercised little real authority. Nottingham, a thin, sickly-looking man with a pockmarked face and a hunched back, instead spent his time with a girlfriend in a 'love nest'. The staff of the paper included a Filipino, Conrado A. Uy, who served as city editor, a stateless Armenian born in Japan, Roy Essoyan and some British citizens, among them Sylvia Bradshaw, described as a 'sob sister'. None of the British employees resigned after the outbreak of war; the British Residents' Association instructed them to stay on the job lest they fall on relief funds. One editorial staff member, a stateless Russian Jew, George Leonoff, was confined in the Bridge House in early 1942 because his work was not considered 'in harmony with the present sympathies of the city of Shanghai'. He was accused of being a 'central liaison for British, French, and American intelligence' and held for six months.[40] Upon his release, he was taken back by the paper.

The *Shanghai Times* was the foremost English-language organ of Japanese propaganda in Shanghai during the war. The paper's editorials were written by a Japanese journalist who acted on orders from the Japanese embassy. News reports tended to be bland but the paper published a number of articles accusing the Allies of anti-Japanese atrocities. Typical headlines ran: 'Japanese Internees in New Delhi and Singapore Badly Treated, Says Correspondent', 'British Atrocities in India Seen as Sequel to Long Reign of Terror' and 'Nippon Lodges Vigorous Protest With US Canada, over Cruelty to Internees'.[41] On 22 January 1942 it reported: 'One of the cheerful aspects of Shanghai life today is the spirit of cordiality and friendliness shown by the average Japanese soldier towards foreign children.' On 17 July an editorial pronounced Hong Kong 'an earthly paradise' thanks to the Japanese occupation. On 23 September it made a rare criticism of the Japanese authorities who, it complained, 'show too much leniency towards their war prisoners and enemy nationals'.

The other English-language paper that continued to appear was the American-owned *Shanghai Evening Post and Mercury*. From the violently anti-Japanese tone of its editorials before Pearl Harbor, the paper's line abruptly changed to one more acceptable to the new masters of the city. George C. Bruce, the business manager, kept the paper going under Japanese army auspices. Bruce also broadcast for the Japanese on Radio Station XMHC.[42] He later fell foul of the Japanese, was interned and died after undergoing interrogation. Bruce was assisted by the advertising manager, Jack Howard, a former sailor. A Californian-born Japanese editor, Uno Kazumaro ('Buddy' Uno), exercised editorial control until he went to Tokyo to work for a radio station. After that the paper was edited by David Zentner, a Polish Jew (his American wife was interned briefly in 1943 but released thanks to Zentner's influence with the Japanese). Others who worked for the paper during the war included Gus Johansson, a Swede whose mother was Japanese, Abe Ladar, a Jewish refugee who was said to be a supporter of the Palestinian Jewish terrorist organization *Lehi* (the Stern Gang), and Tom Butler, an Irishman who purchased Portuguese citizenship in 1943. Butler was fired for misspelling the name of the Japanese emperor in a headline. He found a new job as an announcer on radio station XMHC.

Most of the collaborationist journalists seem to have worked for the Japanese mainly in order to make a living, rather than out of ideological motives. The same was true of most of those who worked as announcers on German or Japanese radio stations in Shanghai.

One of the best-known of these broadcasters was the American Don Chisholm. Son of a dean at Johns Hopkins University, Chisholm had built up a considerable criminal record in America before fleeing to the Far East. He had turned up in Shanghai in 1930 as a stoker on an American Dollar Line ship. A contrary, argumentative character who enjoyed controversy, Chisholm seemed to relish notoriety. Soon after his arrival, he began appearing in Municipal Police reports on account of minor incidents of credit fraud. He was also involved in a strange episode involving the use of a tear-gas 'fountain-pen pistol' in a late-night brawl at the Canidrome dogtrack in the French Concession. After a few years on the fringes of respectability, Chisholm founded *Shopping News*, a magazine which had the reputation of trading in scandal – literally so, since potential subjects of articles were reputedly given the opportunity to buy their way out of embarrassment by paying to have stories 'spiked'. Chisholm was not a popular figure in Anglo-Saxon Shanghai. A post-war American intelligence report noted that he had 'made himself generally unpleasant to business people and their friends if advertisements were not forthcoming from them or if they offended him, and it was generally believed that he was using his sheet for blackmailing.'[43] He had probably been the source of the crude attempt to blackmail Sumaire in 1941. Unlike most English-language publications in Shanghai, *Shopping News* was not closed by the Japanese after 8 December 1941. Chisholm continued to publish it quite contentedly under Japanese censorship.

Soon afterwards Chisholm embarked on a career in broadcasting. Starting on 1 February 1942, he read news and anti-British commentaries twice daily in English on radio station XMHA, now under Japanese control. His relations with the Japanese, however, were chequered. In November 1942 he was interned in the Haiphong Road camp for 'politicals'. The following spring he was freed, but was rearrested soon afterwards and held for a time in the Bridge House.

> He did not show any particular effects of being badly treated on his release [US intelligence later reported]. A few days later he was found at the foot of the stairs in his house badly banged up and covered with blood. He explained that he had fallen down the stairs… It was stated by informant that there was a strong feeling that the injuries were believed by many to have been self-inflicted, and that there was a possibility that a deal was made with the attending doctor to continue keeping Chisholm in a cast. The reason being that Chisholm seemed to have taken a change of heart and did not care to play along with the Japanese any longer … He hopes to be repatriated and expects to 'catch it hot'.[44]

His apparent shifts with the wind did not endear Chisholm to the Japanese any more than to his compatriots. By March 1945 he was reported to be back in the Haiphong Road camp.

The chief English-language commentator on the German radio station XGRS from 1940 until the end of the war was a young Chinese-American, Herbert Erasmus Moy. A former student of Columbia University, New York, he had arrived in Shanghai in about 1932. In his early years in the city, according to a Municipal Police report, he 'had funds and did little more than an occasional brokerage job in gold bars or exchange, the while speculating more or less successfully himself'. After that he drifted into radio announcing. Moy was an effective broadcaster and enjoyed a certain following, but he complained of being underpaid, drank heavily and 'often called on his aged parents for assistance'. He was said to be proud of his American citizenship and was not initially friendly to the Axis. But in October 1937, as manager of radio station XMHC, he was warned by the Municipal Police Special Branch not to broadcast programmes 'detrimental to the peace and good order of the International Settlement'. Shortly afterwards, a newsreader on the station mocked both the Japanese and the British, evoking a stern rebuke from the Special Branch, one of whose officers reported that the broadcast 'was spoken in a spirit of levity, and that degree of impartiality which should characterise a public news broadcast was totally lacking'.[45] Moy responded by promising not to include any anti-Japanese materials in the station's broadcasts. A little later he sold the station to the *Shanghai Evening Post and Mercury*.

During the war Moy became the Germans' star broadcaster on XGRS. He was the highest-paid announcer on the station, receiving a salary of RM1,100 per month. He did not see his activity as unpatriotic. He told a friend at Farren's nightclub that most Americans, after all, shared his 'isolationist views'. Before the outbreak of the Pacific War, Moy was deprived of his US citizenship, supposedly on the ground that he had been more than seven years outside the country. Subsequently he applied for, and was granted, Chinese citizenship under the name Mae Gi-chuan. In addition to his radio job, Moy also wrote editorials for the English-language German propaganda sheet *Noon Extra*. His instructions for these editorials were 'to be always friendly to the Chinese – whether Chungking or Nanking'. His behaviour in the later part of the war suggested a certain self-disgust at his work for the Axis.[46] He consoled himself with the bottle and with his mistress, Mrs Marquita Kwong.

Three British citizens also became well-known radio voices in Shanghai during the occupation. A discharged naval gunner, J. K. Gracie, broadcast in a working-class Scottish accent under the pseudonym 'Sergeant Allan McIntosh'. In a post-war statement, Gracie outlined candidly the motives that led him to collaborate. Down and out in Shanghai before the outbreak of the war, he had appealed for help to the British Residents' Association who sent him to the Salvation Army Hostel. Gracie protested against being dispatched to what he said was 'a crummy, broken-down old godown', inhabited by 'gaol birds, dope addicts, bums, sneak thieves, incurable drunks and in general the scum of the earth'.[47] He felt, or so he later claimed, that he was 'being discriminated against because my wife was of Japanese descent, so refused to go to the Hostel in Wayside and consequently found myself without help of any sort'. At that point he was offered a job as an announcer on the German radio station, XGRS, and accepted it, receiving payment in Reichsmarks. Gracie claimed that the texts of his broadcasts were prepared for him by the Germans, but according to the station manager, Flick-Steger, Gracie wrote his own scripts in which he employed a great deal of slang and foul language. Flick-Steger said that Gracie 'was a sincere communist' who broadcast commentaries addressed 'to the poorer classes of the British Peoples [sic], such as the stevedores, mine workers and merchant seamen'. He added that Gracie was 'full of hate against those persons and classes whom [sic] he considered had brought him to the said state of poverty and want'. The Germans were very pleased with Gracie's broadcasts which the embassy radio attaché said were 'noted for their particular vituperation and energy'.

In March 1942 Gracie renounced his British citizenship – though the British authorities afterwards refused to recognize this, as the law forbade renunciation of citizenship in wartime. Later that year he was arrested and interned by the Japanese as an enemy national. After a time he was released and agreed to go back to broadcasting. When he returned to his house, he discovered that his wife and daughter had been sent away to Japan. He never saw them again (Mrs Gracie's home town was Nagasaki, where the second atomic bomb exploded on 9 August 1945). Gracie continued to broadcast political commentaries until the end of the war.[48]

Another British (or, as he claimed, Irish) broadcaster for the Germans in

1. View of the Shanghai International Settlement's famous waterfront thoroughfare, the Bund, in 1937. The domed building in the centre of the picture was the headquarters of the Hong Kong and Shanghai Bank.

John Swire & Sons Ltd

John Swire & Sons Ltd

2. Before the lights went out: the Bund illuminated to celebrate the coronation of King George VI on 12 May 1937

3. On 14 August 1937 the war came home to the foreign enclaves when Chinese warplanes mistakenly dropped bombs on the city's streets, killing 2,000 people. Sapajou (George Sapojnikov), the White Russian cartoonist of the North China Daily News captured the bizarre horror in his 'Danse Macabre'.

From Four Months of War (Shanghai, n.d. [1938?]); courtesy of John Swire & Sons Ltd.

Diaspora Museum Photo Archive, Tel Aviv (courtesy of Yair Hendl)

4. Japanese troops parade in triumph in the International Settlement of Shanghai, December 1941

5. *Thousands of refugees fled Shanghai during the Sino-Japanese hostilities in 1937. This picture was taken on a wharf next to the Whangpoo. The Bund is in the background, right.*

6. *Shanghai in ruins after the fighting of 1937*

7. HMS Peterel, *the British gunboat that put up a heroic but doomed defence at Shanghai on 8 December 1941*

US Naval Institute

8. USS Wake, *seized by the Japanese at Shanghai on 8 December 1941, the only American naval vessel to be captured intact and without resistance in the Second World War*

US Naval Institute

9. *In the early days of the Japanese occupation of the International Settlement, fuel rationing evoked a number of inventive stratagems. Shown here is a 'one-horse-power' motor car, 1942.*

Diaspora Museum Photo Archive, Tel Aviv (courtesy of Horst Eisfelder)

10. *Valentine St John Killery, first head of 'Oriental Mission', established by the British clandestine warfare organization Special Operations Executive in 1941–42*

11. *Tai Li, the 'Himmler of China' (back, centre) with his mother (front, centre), other family members, Milton ('Mary') Miles (front, left), and another American officer, 1944*

12. *William J. ('Tony') Keswick, taipan of the 'muckle house' (Jardine, Matheson), chairman of the Shanghai Municipal Council and senior officer in SOE*

13. *John Keswick, brother of Tony, and wartime head of SOE in China*

14. *Hermann Erben, drug smuggler, monkey expert, Hitler impersonator and German agent, who voluntarily spent two and a half years in a Japanese internment camp*

15. 'Princess' Sumaire, perhaps niece of the Maharajah of Patiala, Schiaparelli mannequin, and Shanghai socialite, with a friend

16, 17, 18, 19. The many faces of Eugene Pick, actor, gangster, 'competent murderer' and freelance intelligence operative

Shanghai was Frank Johnston, who had a long criminal record and had served time in San Quentin penitentiary in the USA. Before the war Johnston had worked for the British station XMHA. Flick-Steger was impressed by his voice and offered him a large financial inducement to cross over to XGRS which he agreed to do. Claiming to be Irish, he adopted the professional pseudonym of 'Pat Kelly'. He read the news and later also broadcast a 'morning gymnastic programme' as well as a magazine programme dealing with local social events, 'Shanghai Wallah Wallah'. Occasionally he performed in dramatic propaganda sketches, playing the parts of President Roosevelt and other well-known figures. In 1942 the Japanese seized Johnston and took him to the Bridge House, where they questioned him about his pre-war work for XMHA. At the intercession of his German employers, however, he was released and allowed to return to his job. At first Johnston was paid a very high salary, but later the Germans became dissatisfied with his work and his pay was reduced. He was obliged to supplement his income by going round to the offices of well-off acquaintances such as Baron von Puttkamer, offering cigarettes and spirits for sale. In 1944 Johnston was dismissed for unpunctuality, but he soon found other jobs, back at his old station, XMHA, now under the control of the Japanese navy, and on XGOO, a satellite station of XMHA. On one occasion Johnston recorded interviews with Allied prisoners of war at Kiangwan and broadcast extracts over XGOO.[49]

A third such case was that of Robert S. (Bob) Lamb, a former Indian Army officer. In 1936 he had founded an English-language monthly political magazine in Shanghai, *The Cathay Cosmopolitan*, in which Paul Paelz, press officer of the local branch of the Nazi party, had acquired a 49 per cent interest. Paelz also offered a subvention for the journal and a salary of $500 per month. In a post-war deposition Lamb claimed that the arrangement had been made with the full knowledge and approval of officials of the British consulate-general, 'their idea being that I could be relied upon to ensure that nothing detrimental to British interests would be published – a guarantee they could not have if I refused the offer and [Paelz were to] engage another, possibly non-British editor.' According to Lamb, the publication flourished with no complaints either from the Nazi party or the British consulate. After the Japanese attack on China in 1937, however, it ceased publication, apparently as a result of a falling-out between Lamb and Paelz. This enterprise, of course, was undertaken long before the outbreak of the war in Europe, and, whatever political view one might take, it could in no sense be regarded as treasonable.

After the British declaration of war on Germany, Lamb (so he later claimed) volunteered repeatedly and insistently for the British forces, but was rejected. In his post-war deposition he further asserted:

> Incidentally, I then put forward the suggestion that if there were any information required in regard to local Germans or the Nazi Party the British Consulate might consider the advisability of enlisting my services in this connection as I had knowledge of practically every individual in the Deutsche Gemeinde and of Nazi personnel and methods.

Lamb stated that he had 'submitted certain confidential reports' to British naval intelligence officers in Shanghai.[50]

Lamb's account of the sequence of events after the Japanese occupation, for all its obvious self-serving intention, has a ring of truth about it:

> Immediately after the outbreak of hostilities here on December 8th 1941, I was called on at the Foreign YMCA (where I was living) by a Mr Jourdain, who informed me that Baron von Puttkamer, Director of the German Information Bureau, wanted to have a talk to me. Jourdain intimated that he had a car with him. (He omitted to mention, however, that he also had a Japanese plain-clothes gendarme with him.) He suggested that I accompany him, as otherwise I would be unable to get through the barricades at Bubbling Well.
>
> On arrival at the Bureau, Puttkamer complimented me on my handling of the *Cathay Cosmopolitan* and proceeded to tell me that they wanted me to 'edit' their propaganda material. Could I start immediately? I pointed out that I was a British subject and reminded him that at the time I was editing the *Cathay Cosmopolitan* our two countries were not at war. He

smilingly retorted that other British and American subjects in the employ of the Municipal Council, the Municipal Police, and every utility company without exception were 'co-operating'. He asked me to let him have my decision before noon on the following day. On enquiry, the Council and utility company employees admitted that they were to be paid C.S.$2,000 monthly and that any balance due would be paid into a special account with the Yokohama Specie Bank. Not a man in any of these services had 'downed tools' voluntarily. Although I appreciated the significance of this, I nevertheless got word through to [the British Consul-General] Mr George (then interned in the Cathay Hotel), of what had happened. His reply was 'force majeure'. My course of action apparently was clear: when the Council, Police and utilities refused to 'cooperate' I would do likewise.[51]

Lamb worked for Puttkamer's organization for several months.

In April 1942, after the arrest of Frank Johnston, Lamb replaced him as English-language announcer at XGRS, using the pseudonym 'Billy Bailey'. His boss, Flick-Steger, admired Lamb's 'deep, sonorous voice' and considered him 'one of our best announcers'.[52] Lamb played the part of Churchill in plays put on by the station's drama department. But one day in the summer of 1942 he arrived for the noon broadcast dead drunk and was fired on the spot. The following November he was interned in the Haiphong Road camp. While there, he defended his conduct to fellow internees, using the 'force majeure' argument. For additional effect he boasted that he had had a job with the British Ministry of Economic Warfare – a lie. He remained interned for the remainder of the war.

The Axis radio stations in Shanghai also employed some women as English-language announcers. Among these was Hilda Edna Glatzel who broadcast on XGRS under the pseudonym 'Diana Hamilton'. She had been born to British parents in China in 1906. Her father, Joseph Ratcliffe, had been a military instructor to the Chinese army. When she was six months old Hilda was adopted by a German, Hermann Schultz, 'a Masonic brother of my father', and Schultz's Peruvian wife. Although German-born, Schultz could not speak German, since he had left his native country at the age of 14 and spent the rest of his life abroad, mainly in the Far East. He worked for the Shanghai Municipal Council until 1924 and then lived on a pension until his death in 1942. Hilda attended British girls' schools in Shanghai and a finishing-school at Bournemouth. In 1925 she married Nicolaus Alfred Glatzel, a German businessman in Shanghai. Glatzel, a Sudeten German who had fought with distinction in the First World War, was strongly hostile to Nazism. In October 1941 he was mobilized and in early 1942 was sent to Germany on a blockade runner. The following June his wife started broadcasting 'Diana Hamilton's Advice to the Lovelorn' on XGRS. She also participated in comedy shows and political sketches, later taking charge herself of the station's drama department. She subsequently defended her conduct on the ground that 'it was hinted to me that it would be greatly to my husband's advantage if I would show my goodwill'.[53]

Among the collaborators was a little group of Australians. Their leader was Alan Raymond. He had arrived in Shanghai from Melbourne in 1928 and pursued a dubious career as an unsuccessful marble salesman. He was also an amateur jockey and horse trainer. In these capacities he accumulated unpaid debts at the Race Club and left a trail of dishonoured cheques made out to business associates. Following the Japanese attack on Shanghai in 1937, Raymond decamped for a time to Hong Kong where he was expelled from the Jockey Club after 'an incident connected with a running of a pony at the Macao Races'.[54] On his return to Shanghai in July 1940, a Municipal Police report characterized him as:

> a capable business man but has always suffered from lack of
> capital to finance his ventures. This failing is partly due to his
> spendthrift nature and his fondness for luxuries, insofar as
> whenever he brought off a good business deal he would
> squander the money on gambling and pleasure seeking. In this
> respect there have been occasions when his clients' money
> became indistinguishable from his own.[55]

In early 1942 Raymond emerged as the moving spirit in an 'Independent Australia League' in Shanghai in which half a dozen other local Australian residents participated. Among these were B. A. MacKenzie, who broadcast over shortwave to Australia under the pseudonym 'Roy Stewart', and Eyn MacDonald, who worked as MacKenzie's assistant and also broadcast her own programme, 'Woman's Hour'. This went out on XMHA over the long-wave transmitter only. According to the station's chief engineer, it 'consisted mainly of persuading local women of the advantages to everyone of being under Japanese control'.[56] Raymond broadcast for the Japanese to Australia and wrote anti-British articles in the press. In addition to his broadcasting and journalistic duties, Raymond also served as a paid employee of the Japanese naval intelligence department in Shanghai.[57]

Raymond's main partner in his propaganda activities was another Australian, John Joseph Holland, an unsuccessful journalist in his early 30s, who had abandoned his wife in Sydney and arrived in Shanghai in 1937. Like Raymond he accumulated numerous debts in the city and dabbled in business ventures. In early 1941 he was reported to be peddling arms on behalf of the legendary British 'General One-Arm' Sutton to the Chinese puppet government. In March 1941 Holland approached the French vice-consul in Shanghai, claiming to represent an American export firm, and proposed selling to the government of Indo-China seven bombers 'which at that time were in Manila'. A subsequent investigation by the French political police concluded that Holland's firm had 'a doubtful reputation in local commercial circles'. Among those involved in it were a number of well-known swindlers. The manager was reputed to have 'special relations with the Japanese' and on this account the French decided that Holland's offer might well be a 'provocation'.[58] The offer was declined.

The inaugural meeting of Raymond's 'movement' took place at the Palace Hotel in Shanghai in March 1942. Eleven people attended, of whom eight were Australians. Among the audience was a member of the foreign section of the Japanese Gendarmerie. The Japanese army's friendly interest was signalled by the presence at a second meeting, a week later, of a representative of the army's intelligence section. The *Shanghai Times*, noting the occasion under the headline 'Australians Urged to End Pointless War', commented that 'the gathering has grown to twice the number of Australians who attended the first meeting'. The paper did not give precise attendance figures.[59] Following the meeting, the military observer, Lieutenant Ueno, wrote a memorandum explaining that it was proposed to broadcast a three-hour daily programme over station XMHA entitled 'Calling Australia' in which Australia would be urged to withdraw from the war. 'Should this programme fail,' Ueno declared, 'it is the intention of the Japanese authorities to contact all Australians in occupied areas and give them a chance to go with the Japanese to Australia and there run the administration.'[60] Although the *Shanghai Times* continued to make extravagant claims for the movement's success, the Municipal Police reported more soberly that the league's activities were confined to 'social meetings among a limited group of supporters'.[61]

The prospect of emerging as the Quisling of Canberra nevertheless seems to have attracted Raymond. In his regular commentaries to Australia over the shortwave transmitter of XMHA, he continued to call upon his countrymen to sever the British connection and withdraw from the war. The Japanese, seem, however, to have had some suspicions of Raymond's good faith. It was noted that during his time in Hong Kong he had been friendly with the owner of an anti-Axis newspaper. During that period he was also said to have been 'on intimate terms with Mrs Elsie Zee, a wealthy Chinese lady, the wife of a high Chungking official'. Holland too was recognized by the Japanese-controlled settlement police as 'an adventurer'.[62] A few weeks after the inaugural meetings of the league, a Municipal Police report observed that the movement, 'contrary to expectations, has not progressed from its embryo state'. No further meetings seem to have taken place but Raymond and Holland carried on their propaganda work until the eve of the Japanese surrender.

上海

Whereas full-blooded collaboration in the British, American and Australian communities was confined to a handful of individuals, the Japanese devoted more serious efforts to promoting support for the New Order among other foreign groups in Shanghai, in particular members of colonial nationalities such as Indians and Filipinos. The Japanese might have built effectively on the anti-colonial resentments of such communities. But here too their approach was uncoordinated and unimaginative, their propaganda crude and, as in their treatment of occupied peoples everywhere, the effort to win support was vitiated by racial arrogance, violence and the transparent hypocrisy of their anti-imperial protestations.

In early January 1942 the Japanese capture of Manila was celebrated at a meeting of 100 Filipinos (magnified to '300' by the time the news reached the Japanese-controlled press in Hong Kong) in the Metropole Ballroom in Shanghai. Those present agreed to form a 'Filipino Association of Shanghai' and elected as its head the journalist Conrado Uy.[63] He later recounted how, a few days after the occupation of the city, he had been called in by Lieutenant Matsuda, an American-educated officer who worked in the army spokesman's office in Shanghai. Matsuda told him that the Japanese had nothing against Filipinos, even if, 'much to our regret', Japanese forces had landed in the Philippines for the purpose of expelling the Americans. 'This is a war of the oppressed Asiatics against their Occidental oppressors,' he said, 'to bring about the emancipation of Greater East Asia from imperialistic domination.' Uy, like many Filipino nationalists in his homeland, swallowed this. 'With this piece of information in my hands,' he later wrote, 'and cognizant of the growing difficulties of living in the city as a direct result of the war, I saw an opportunity for me and a few other civic-minded friends to work out a plan for mutual assistance.'

The association received $2,000 a month from the Japanese and on 31 January 1942 Uy began publication of the *Filipino Clarion*. The subsidy proved miserably inadequate for the purpose. In an effort to raise money for Filipino welfare activities, Uy enlisted the cooperation of local Filipino musicians, 'who constituted more than 80 percent of our community', in holding a 'midnight ball' at the Mee Kao Mee Ballroom. Unfortunately for Uy, 'the Japanese Gendarmerie, acting on a malicious report, prevented us from going ahead with the affair'. As a result, both the association and Uy personally were out of pocket. In his post-war apologia, Uy denied that the organization 'had any political character', though he admitted that he and his chief lieutenant had held private political views 'looking toward the regeneration of our people'.

Other Filipino leaders later disputed Uy's account and insisted that he had participated actively in anti-American and pro-Japanese propaganda and had intimidated and threatened members of the community. Sara Malabanan, a telephone switchboard operator at the *Shanghai Times*, furnished accounts of conversations, some in English, others in Tagalog, that she had overheard. These suggested that Uy had been responsible for the consignment to the Bridge House in 1944 of the leading pro-Allied Filipino in Shanghai, Dr H. Evangelista.

The Japanese nevertheless grew dissatisfied with Uy's leadership and eventually replaced his association with a new body, Lipunang Pilipino. Its leader, Dr Gertrudo Kalambakal, described by Uy as 'a man without scruples', operated in close harmony with the Japanese Gendarmerie. According to Uy, the new organization accomplished nothing 'aside from entertaining Japanese wounded soldiers in a military hospital and cavorting with a number of Japanese officers'.[64]

The Japanese met with a little more success among the 2,000 or so Indians in the city. Most of these, of course, were of very different social background from the Maharajah of Patiala's kinswoman. The largest number were Sikh constables of the Municipal Police ('turbaned number threes'). Before the war they had been hated by many Chinese as collaborators with British imperialism; now many came to be hated by the British as collaborators with the Japanese. In January 1942 an 'Indian Independence League' was formed, under the leadership of B. Bobby. A long-time pro-Japanese enthusiast, he was described in a post-war US intelligence report as 'of the gangster type'.[65] Bobby later delivered broadcasts over station XMHA with titles such as 'Rise Up, Indians – This is the Time!'[66] The league held a number of public meetings which attracted considerable crowds. A rally at the race course in August 1942 was addressed by A. M. Sahay. A close associate of the pro-Axis Indian nationalist leader, Subhas Chandra Bose, Sahay had lived for many years in Japan, where he had been active in Indian nationalist causes. He later served as minister without portfolio in Bose's Japanese-sponsored 'Provisional Government of Azad Hind'. Another speaker was F. Y. Chen, head of the 'Anglo-American Annihilation Association'. Chen was a former associate of the Green Gang boss, Tu Yueh-sheng. An anti-Japanese activist in 1937, Chen had switched to support Wang Ching-wei in 1939. In November 1943 Chandra Bose himself paid a brief visit to Shanghai. He was welcomed at a tea reception at the Cathay Hotel. In his speech he called on the Chungking régime 'to realize the error of its ways and ... withdraw its troops from India. Brother Asiatics should not lay hands on one another.'[67]

The Shanghai Indians were divided both by religion (Hindus, Muslims and Sikhs) and by politics, since some remained loyal to Britain. A separate 'Sikh Society of Shanghai', formed in July 1942, was denounced by a Sikh officer of the Municipal Police as 'a British agency to carry on the evil policy of "Divide and Rule"'. Its promoters were said to be 'all British agents'.[68] Although no evidence of such British influence was adduced, the society fell into disfavour and was dissolved in December 1943. Some Sikh policemen acted as guards in internment camps; a few were hostile to the internees but others were described by an interned missionary as 'loyal citizens of the British Empire [who] hated the Japanese'.[69]

In the later part of the war some Shanghai Indians were recruited into the Japanese-sponsored Indian National Army (INA), which set up a training camp on East Paoshing Road. The INA training programme was headed by Major B. Narain, a former officer in the British army in India. Reluctant recruits were threatened with harsh treatment. As a result, support for the cause waned. The Japanese responded with a round-up of all suspect Indians, among them 18 INA members. One of these, Chanan Singh Sandhu, later recounted the manner of his arrest. When he asked Narain what he had done wrong, 'the commandant jumped at me and shot me point blank in the shoulder. "I am now sending you to a very nice place where you will feel the consequences of being pro-British and of being a spy," he said.' The arrested men were sent to the Bridge House and later to Ward Road prison where, in addition to being deprived of washing facilities and exercise, they were whipped and subjected to the ultimate indignity: Chinese food. 'Even dogs and pigs would not touch it', Sandhu recalled.[70]

上海

One element in the population that was disproportionately prone to collaborate was the mixed-race group known as Eurasians. In the case of the half-Chinese, half-British Lawrence Klindt Kentwell, the psychological motives that led to collaboration are particularly well documented. Kentwell was born in 1882 aboard a British sailing-ship in Hong Kong harbour, the illegitimate son of the ship's captain and a Chinese woman. His father died soon afterwards and he was taken to his mother's home in Honolulu where he was a pupil of Sun Yat-sen, later the leader of the Chinese revolution, at the Mills School. When Kentwell's mother died, he inherited her estate. Regular remittances from this source enabled him to go to university and pursue a professional career. While studying at Columbia University, New York, he became an American citizen, forfeiting his British citizenship. After graduating from Columbia he proceeded to Oxford where he matriculated as an undergraduate at New College. When he failed responsions there in 1910, he transferred to another Oxford college, Lincoln. In 1913 he sat the final university examinations in which he was awarded a fourth-class degree in jurisprudence. The fourth class, which no longer exists, was, in effect, a courtesy degree, often awarded as a consolation prize to sportsmen and aristocratic dullards who could not achieve even a respectable minimum performance in the examinations. Kentwell remained deeply devoted to Oxford, maintaining his wife and family at 159 Woodstock Road there for the following two decades, and sending two of his six children to study at the university. In spite of his undistinguished academic record at Oxford, he succeeded in qualifying as a barrister at the Middle Temple in London. In 1915 he was renaturalized as a British citizen and in the following year he moved to China and was admitted to practise as a barrister in the British Supreme Court in Shanghai.

Over the next few years Kentwell acquired an unsavoury reputation in Shanghai for ungentlemanly behaviour, alleged forgery of banknotes and non-payment of rates. In 1926 he was disbarred by the British court in Shanghai for unprofessional conduct. He had applied to the Spanish consulate for registration of a Chinese client as a Spanish citizen, on the basis of a spurious claim that the man had been born in the Philippines. In the process he had defrauded his client of a large amount of money. Kentwell was so upset that he took the extreme step of announcing in open court that he had torn up his British passport. He declared that he was applying for citizenship of China, 'my motherland', and intended 'to throw myself heartily into her fight for the recovery of her legitimate rights'.[71] He insisted that he was a victim of racial prejudice and 'political considerations'.[72] J. B. Powell of the *China Weekly Review*, for one, took him at his word, and a recent writer has naively accepted this interpretation, calling his case one of 'persecution on an institutional scale'.[73] As Judge Peter Grain, who issued the order for his disbarment, later wrote, in a confidential letter to the British Minister in Peking:

> L. K. Kentwell usually states that he was disbarred merely because he caused a Chinese subject to be registered as a Spanish subject. But the facts against him were far more serious than that. L. K. Kentwell constantly speaks of China as his 'Mother Land' or some such title, but the grave charge against him when the Court was moved to disbarr [sic] him was that he had taken large sums of money from one of his Chinese (?) brothers.[74]

From then onwards, Kentwell bombarded the British judicial and political authorities in Shanghai and London with a stream of impertinent and abusive letters complaining of persecution, denouncing British imperialism and threatening retribution. British consuls in China, he complained, behaved like 'tin gods'.[75] 'My personal experience with British Consular officials in China is that they are God Almighty and I am an humble pie.'[76] His most vituperative personal denunciation was directed against Judge Grain. In one characteristic outburst to the judge in 1927, he wrote:

> You know from the bottom of your stony heart that you have illegally and arbitrarily removed my name from the roll of legal practitioners...Indeed, the loss of Hankow and Kiukiang* is a bitter pill of the first water and a jolly good lesson for you and your kind in this part of the world...Are you a product of Oxford or Cambridge? I suspect you belong to neither, hence refinement and nobility of character and good conscience are not within your reach...the good name of the British nation has been poluted [sic] by you...I will not resort to bombs,

---

* In early 1927 Hankow had fallen under the control of the communist-nationalist faction of the Kuomintang. As a result, Britain had been forced to retrocede her concessions there and at Kiukiang.

dynamites or revolvers, I would soil my hands if I did. I am
content to leave the matter in the hands of the just
Providence...This letter is written in a serious and
determined mood. It is not intended as a joke. The joking
stage is past. It now enters on the tragic platform.[77]

In another communication he prophesied: 'The earthly dissolution of said
Peter Grain will surely be a painful and agonizing one. Even hell fire is too
mild and pure to roast the putrid carcase of the said Peter Grain.'[78]

The British authorities reacted to all this with extreme irritation: 'one of
the worst of the scallywag lawyers practising in that Court', wrote a British
lawyer in Shanghai.[79] More succinctly, a Foreign Office official minuted,
'He is a rotter'.[80] The British consul-general in Shanghai, Sidney Barton,
recommended that the government cancel Kentwell's naturalization on the
ground that 'apart from his bad personal and professional reputation, Mr
Kentwell has during the past two years shown himself to be rabidly anti-
British and disloyal and has maintained close relationship with local subversive elements'.[81] By 1928 the Foreign Office had concluded that he was
'mentally unbalanced and violent'.[82] 'He is at least part scoundrel, part
madman' was the verdict of the Peking legation.[83] British officials, growing
more and more exasperated by Kentwell's raving effusions, almost matched
his capacity for personal abuse: 'the obnoxious "British object"' was how a
Home Office official referred to him.[84]

The *fons et origo* of Kentwell's half-crazed enmity to Britain appears to
have been his experience of racial discrimination: initially at Oxford, then
in relation to service in the British army during the First World War, but
above all in Shanghai. As an undergraduate his application to join the Officers' Training Corps had been rejected, on the grounds 'that I was not a
person of pure European descent. I was classed in the same category as Indian students...In spite of such rotten treatment, nevertheless I joined up
as a private in 1917 and demobilized in 1919.'[85] One of his bitterest complaints was his exclusion, on the ground that he was of mixed race, from the
Shanghai Club. 'The arrogant Englishmen of the Shanghai Club regard me
as an interloper and a step lower in the wrung [*sic*] of the social ladder. This
I will never concede and will fight to the finish. I am a man and not an in-

sect.'[86] The Shanghai Club, he declared, must be pulled down, set on fire, or turned into a lodging-house for rickshaw coolies.*

Kentwell's anti-imperialist political activity had begun early. According to his own account (in a statement in 1945), he served as secretary-interpreter to his former teacher, Sun Yat-sen, in New York in 1905–06. At Oxford he was an active member of the Lincoln College debating society. On 19 May 1912 he spoke against a motion regretting the fall of the Manchu dynasty. On 9 February 1913 he opposed a motion that 'patriotism is a much exaggerated and childish sentiment'.[87] In 1926 he founded the China Courier, an anti-British journal. His partners in this enterprise were Francis Zia, a Jesuit-educated Kuomintang propagandist, and G. R. Graves, another Eurasian, who had been involved in various shady business enterprises and was entered on the blacklist of suspects issued by the (British) commander of the Shanghai Defence Force with the annotation 'thoroughly unscrupulous and untrustworthy'.[88] The Shanghai Municipal Council turned off the paper's electric power; according to one account in order to suppress its opposition to 'the Chinese ratepayers' struggle against taxation without representation'. No doubt the paper's editorial policy was an aggravating factor, but utility switch-offs were a standard sanction applied by the Council to those who failed to pay rates on time.[89]

In 1927 Kentwell was reported to be working as an adviser to Chiang Kai-shek. Two years later he adopted a Chinese name, Kan Teh-yun (he also appeared from time to time under the names Kum Tuck-yen and Keu Wen-loo†), and founded a 'Chinese Patriotic League', based in Macao and devoted to the cause of expelling British imperialism from all its outposts in Asia. In the same year he established another magazine, The China Truth, which was published at Canton, in which there were articles under such titles as 'Extraterritoriality Must Go!'

Over the next decade Kentwell poured forth a stream of anti-British propaganda. In 1931 he was publishing a daily newspaper, the Canton Daily

---

* This was almost prophetic: after 1949 the club became a Chinese seamen's rest home.
† These may have been respectively Cantonese and Shanghainese variants of the Mandarin form of the name.

Sun, and for a short time seemed to pursue a conciliatory line towards the British. The British consul-general in Canton reported that Kentwell had offered to publish 'articles on commercial subjects which we might care to supply to him'.[90] At this period he was said to be 'in close touch with' and 'taking his cue from' the Chinese Foreign Minister, Eugene Ch'en, the Trinidad-born, British-educated lawyer who had negotiated the agreement with Britain on the retrocession of Hankow and Kiukiang. Kentwell had stayed with Ch'en in Hankow for two months in late 1927. But Kentwell's tone soon reverted to extreme hostility to Britain, perhaps as a result of the resignation of Ch'en in early 1932 or more likely because of the final British decision in August 1931, after four years of consideration, to order Kentwell's denaturalization. He declared the impending order 'very ridiculous indeed', and protested that, notwithstanding his 'fit of righteous anger against Judge Peter Grain', he had 'no grudge against the King or the British Government'. 'I have often thought', he confessed, 'of buying an automatic and put [*sic*] a bullet into the infamous Grain's head, but on second thought, I felt I would disgrace the good name of my family and that I would be regarded as a murderer if I did such a thing.'[91]

The failure of the British to respond to an offer 'to bury the hatchet and forget the past' evoked a rage that now knew no bounds. 'My ambition in life is to be your hangman', he wrote to Judge Grain.[92] In 1932 he wrote to the British prime minister on notepaper with the letterhead 'Headquarters of the Retrocession Commissioner for the International Settlement of Shanghai and for Hong Kong and Kowloon'.[93] In 1934 he moved back from Canton to Shanghai and resumed his law practice, though he could not, of course, appear in the British court. The following year he founded *China Outlook*, a monthly magazine that advocated 'a United China against foreign aggression and exploitation'.[94]

In March 1936 he wrote to the French consulate-general in Shanghai, enclosing an article scheduled for publication in *China Outlook*, 'in support of France against German reoccupation of the demilitarized Rhineland zone'. He added that he would 'be pleased to receive materials...that is', propaganda materials in English presenting the case of France to the outside world'.[95] The French had less compunction than the British about paying subventions to obtain press support but, no doubt well-informed about

Kentwell's antecedents, they seem not to have replied.

Perhaps on this account, Kentwell's sympathies moved towards Germany. In November 1936 he wrote to Judge Grant-Jones of the British court in Shanghai, once again airing his old grievances against Judge Grain and confessing candidly:

> I cannot endure it any longer. It seems it would pay me to murder some one and then murder myself and/or get hanged for it rather than continue to watch the rising and setting of the glorious sun...As each year rolls by, my desire for revenge [*sic*] the injustices and wrongs done me by Judge Grain grows stronger and stronger...The undersigned is in the position of Germany, but not so powerful [as] to enable me to enforce my will. Germany has suffered injustices and wrongs under the Versailles Treaty. I have suffered much more than Germany.[96]

A few months later the Japanese invasion of China provided Kentwell fortuitously with a new and willing sponsor. In 1939 he received a subsidy from the Japanese in support of another new magazine. In a printed prospectus, dated 1 July 1939, announcing the launch of the bilingual fortnightly, Kentwell wrote: 'The present wave of anti-British feeling and the anti-British campaign are but the culmination of Britain's own acts of perfidy in this country and the just retribution for the suffering and misery she has caused the Chinese people...New China and Japan cannot ignore Britain's evil role in East Asia. They are prepared to act to suppress such evil.' Not content with endorsing Japanese actions in China as a defence of the country against British imperialism, Kentwell dredged up an old issue and added a paragraph expressing outrage at the 'disgraceful deportation of the German and Austrian communities including women and children in Shanghai and elsewhere in China, at the instigation of Britain, in 1919'.[97] 'He's at it again!' was the half-amused, half-amazed comment of a Foreign Office official.[98] The leaflet was brought to the attention of the Shanghai Municipal Police but a senior officer concluded resignedly:

> With the situation as it is, there is little we can do with him

although he has been seen in Shanghai from time to time. He renounced [*sic*] British nationality some years ago and to bring him before the Shanghai Special District Court [the Chinese court in the International Settlement, still under the control of pro-Chungking judges], especially on a political charge, would embarrass the poor old judges no end.[99]

Meanwhile Kentwell's self-appointment as 'Retrocession Commissioner for the International Settlement of Shanghai and for Hong Kong and Kowloon', a mere letterhead fabrication a few years earlier, received startling official confirmation from the 'Reformed Government of China', the puppet régime established at Nanking by the Japanese in March 1938. Kentwell was acquainted with Wen Tsung-yao, a senior figure in the régime, who (according to Kentwell's later recollection) 'told me, as far as I can remember, to help China to get back all concessions and to advocate the abolition of extrality [*sic*] and the recovery of Hong Kong, that is, I should write articles in my magazine about China's demand for the retrocession of concessions and to make China a complete sovereign country. I told him I would do it.'[100] With this backing, Kentwell printed new notepaper with the words 'Reformed Government of the Republic of China' in Chinese and English at the top, above his title. It is probable that he did receive authorization from the puppet régime to do so: his post-war statement, suggesting that he had merely been invited to publish articles, was presented in order to defend himself against charges of collaboration and cannot therefore be regarded as reliable on this point.

About this time Kentwell happened to share a railway compartment with the British propaganda chief in Shanghai. Kentwell, who was not aware of his travelling companion's identity, happily boasted 'that he was Special Adviser to the Reformed Government Legislative Yuan and was working on the return of extraterritorial rights'.[101]

Decorating his new notepaper with an official-looking red ribbon, Kentwell wrote to the British prime minister, Neville Chamberlain, in August 1939:

Pursuant to instructions and by virtue of the authority vested in me by the Reformed Government of the Republic of China at Nanking, I have the honour to give Your Excellency formal notice of the resolute stand of the Chinese Government in demanding the early retrocession of Hongkong, Kowloon, the adjacent New Territories, and the British concession in Tientsin...These remarks apply equally to the International Settlement in Shanghai, and though this area is not in form a British concession or settlement, it is generally recognized as being under a majority British control, and, as such, it is our earnest desire that Your Excellency's Government will take the initiative in prevailing upon the other Powers interested in the International Settlement to agree to its early retrocession.[102]

The 'Reformed Government' had not, of course, received British recognition – nor any recognition: even Japan was ambiguous on the point. No reply was therefore sent to the 'Retrocession Commissioner' in his office at 17, Drum Tower Villa, Nanking.

The official silence in London was received in Nanking as a crowning insult. Kentwell's letter to Chamberlain had at least been courteously worded. In June 1940 he sent a further letter to the British ambassador in Shanghai in which he rehearsed all his old themes and avowed that his anti-British feelings were 'one hundred times more bitter than Hitler's'.

There is no doubt that I was regarded as a despised Eurasian, a half-cast [sic] outcast with all sorts of hidden indignities heaped upon me like Hitler by the people of my fatherland and as unworthy of their association in spite of the fact that I was British born, a gentleman, an Oxford graduate and a member of the English Bar and father of six wonderful children, two of whom are Oxford graduates. The golden portals of the Shanghai Club dubbed the 'home' of British snobs and racial prejudice may not be soiled by my unworthy feet because I am not a person of 'pure' European descent. Do you think that any human being with any spark of self respect and pride in him will take such outrageous treatment lying down? Never! The worm has at last turned!

It is a great pity that I am too old to shoulder a rifle on the side of Germany against treacherous England. My bitterness is full to the brim. My ultimate goal is the completest destruction of England.

My great sorrow is that my only son born in England, 24 years of age, graduate of New College, Oxford, is now serving in the British forces. I could not prevent that, but I pray for his safety.[103]

For good measure Kentwell sent a copy of this document to the new prime minister, Winston Churchill. A Foreign Office official minuted: 'Hitler might find some use for this embittered madman, e.g. as an assistant to Haw-Haw!'[104]

In normal times Kentwell's bombastic letters and publications might have been consigned to the cranks' file. But in time of war he became an irritation, then a nuisance, and finally placed himself in the category of traitor – paradoxically not to Britain but to his 'motherland', China.

In March 1940 the 'Reformed Government' was replaced by the 'Reorganized Government' of Wang Ching-wei. That month Kentwell was taken by his friend Wen Tsung-yao to visit Ch'en Kung-po, one of the closest confidants of Wang Ching-wei and a senior figure in the puppet government. Ch'en had been one of the founders of the Chinese Communist Party in 1921, though he left it almost immediately. Like Kentwell, he was a graduate of Columbia University. Ch'en told Kentwell (according to Kentwell's later account) that 'he wanted to give me some money to help my magazine, but [as] he himself had no money he would appoint me a member of the Legislative Yuan [parliament] and I could draw $500 a month as salary'. Kentwell recalled that 'after thinking it over I decided to accept his offer, as I would then have the opportunity to find out what the Japanese were doing and what the Wang Ching Wei régime would be doing'. His alleged motive for accepting was certainly a post-war gloss rather than an accurate description of his intentions at the time. The salary was no doubt particularly welcome after December 1941, when his regular allowance from Honolulu suddenly stopped owing to the outbreak of the Pacific War. Kentwell attended a few meetings of the legislative assembly, but since he knew only the Cantonese dialect found that he 'could not understand the discussions'.[105] He continued to draw pay as a legislator and to produce his journal, one issue of which in 1942 carried a portrait of Adolf Hitler on the cover.

In the spring of 1942 Kentwell returned to Shanghai. At first he stayed at the Foreign YMCA on Bubbling Well Road. Hampered no longer, however, by the hostility of the British legal establishment in the city, he resumed his legal practice and found at least one influential client: he successfully represented 'Captain' Eugene Pick in his appeal against his conviction for murder. His affairs prospering, he brought his wife to Shanghai from Nanking and the couple moved into the Palace Hotel on the Bund where they lived until the end of the war. In his post-war deposition, Kentwell claimed that he had worked against the Japanese and had been held for interrogation at the Bridge House for three days in late 1942. The claim remains uncorroborated.

Kentwell was more than a crackpot. His publications, even if bizarre and crude in both conception and expression, were often lively, readable and effective as anti-imperialist propaganda. British officials might scoff and sneer at him, but the Japanese and their Chinese clients found him useful at a certain level. His case illustrates the difficulty of categorizing some of the cases of collaboration in Shanghai during the occupation. Was he a traitor? If so, to whom? Since the British had denaturalized him, he could hardly be accused of treachery against Britain. In moving over to the Japanese, he was following a large body of opinion on what was regarded as the 'left' of the Kuomintang, among whom were Wang Ching-wei and Kentwell's former patron Eugene Ch'en, who was a wartime informant for the Japanese.[106]

Kentwell later defended himself against the charge of treason on the grounds that he was not a Chinese citizen. His citizenship status was indeed questionable since, although regarded by the puppet régime as sufficiently Chinese to serve in its legislature, Kentwell had never formally been granted Chinese citizenship. Even if he were to be regarded as Chinese, it is difficult to regard Kentwell as more guilty, although he was certainly more indiscreet, than large numbers of other Chinese who opted for the path of least resistance.[107] Many Shanghai Chinese factory-owners, in particular, adapted readily to production and profit-making under Japanese rule: their 'overwhelming motivation', according to a recent historian, 'was not patriotism nor collaborationism but survival – to find some method of keeping their enterprises in operation'.[108] Many Chinese generals (42 in 1943 alone) went over to the enemy, taking hundreds of thousands of their troops with them. The great mass of Chinese workers and peasants too – as of the populations of most other occupied countries, whether in Europe or Asia – found themselves compelled by pressures of daily survival to choose the path of least resistance, which often meant a measure of collaboration.

This circumambient atmosphere of acquiescence, as well as the ambiguous guidance from home governments and the difficulty in shifting wartime conditions of discerning how best to safeguard national interests, must all be taken into account when assessing the wartime record of Allied civilians in Shanghai and the descent of some of them into outright treason. Collaboration was surprisingly prevalent but the traitors were a minority. Most Allied citizens in Shanghai, like most occupied populations throughout the Axis dominions in Asia, Africa and Europe, muddled through as best they could. And a few Shanghailanders regrouped to resume the struggle from exile.

9 Shanghailanders in Exile

With the elimination by the Japanese of Oriental Mission, Shanghai, the British resistance effort within Shanghai was reduced to a strength of one. Petty Officer Jim Cuming of the *Peterel*, who had eluded capture in December 1941, remained at large in Shanghai throughout the war. For a while he was supported by some sympathetic British residents. Without the knowledge of the British Residents' Association, he obtained a registration certificate under the name 'John Rogers' which served as identification if he was stopped in the street. The navy tried to persuade SOE to help him escape, but given the absence of an effective British underground organization in Shanghai this proved impossible.[1] With the internment of most British civilians in Shanghai in April 1943, Cuming's position became difficult. He owed his continued freedom to protection by friends in the Municipal Police. During the later part of the war he was able to put his skills as a radio operator to good use by working for a Chinese nationalist underground organization which established long-distance connections with British secret organizations operating in the west of China. With this single heroic exception, Anglo-Saxon Shanghai now fought its secret war by remote control from unoccupied China, often using Chinese or other proxies.

Although only sporadically active in Shanghai, the Anglo-American subversive campaign in China was, nevertheless, still, in a sense, waged by Shanghai. The British and American underground campaigns in China were to a remarkable extent conceived and directed by the businessmen of the Bund, so much so that the China sections both of Special Operations Executive (SOE) and of its American equivalent, the Office of Strategic Services (OSS), seemed almost like the Shanghai Club in exile.

The London director of SOE for the Far East was W. J. (Tony) Keswick, the Jardine, Matheson taipan and former chairman of the Shanghai Municipal Council. For much of the war the senior SOE figure in Chungking was his brother John. They benefited from the automatic deference accorded to them by Shanghailanders on account of their dynastic roots. The Keswicks recruited several other men of similar social origins and Shanghai connections into SOE's China enterprise. Among 'possible personnel' nominated for SOE by Tony Keswick in 1942, for example, were:

> *Peter Probie:* Age about 35. Educated Eton and Trinity; now Captain in Welsh Guards. Member of Jardine, Matheson & Co., and would have been a junior partner if war had not broken out. He is at present interested in musketry. Speaks German and French. Intelligent. Gets on with people easily...

> *Godfrey Phillips:* Head of Harrow School. A 'double' first at Cambridge. President of the Union. Practised at the bar for three years. Went to Mexico Railways for two years, then studied municipal government, eventually going to Shanghai where at the very young age of 34 became Secretary and Commissioner-General of the Shanghai Municipal Council where he showed outstanding ability in dealing with political problems both of the Chinese and Japanese, and daily annoyances from fourteen Embassies and Consulates and from the Powers of the International Settlement. He is now being evacuated to Lourenço Marques. First class man. Salary 3,000 pounds a year.

> *Roger Heyworth:* Brother of the Chairman of Lever Bros. For the last 5 or 6 years has been Lever's representative in the Far East...Intelligent and intelligence-minded. An independent thinker and a man of considerable ability...[2]

Keswick had already written Phillips a letter of welcome:

> I am overjoyed at the thought of seeing you again and rejoice for you in having got away from that wretched place. We must meet at the first possible opportunity. I sent a telegram to

Lourenço Marques, which may or may not have found you.
The Government Department in which I am working is very
short of high powered executives like yourself and I have been
asked to recruit. Therefore before you make any rash decision
about the future I hope you will at least listen to me while I
put a proposition to you.[3]

Soon after his return to England, Phillips joined SOE.

Among other British businessmen in east Asia involved in wartime intelligence were Godfrey Denham of Anglo-Dutch Plantations Ltd, who became Far Eastern Director of MI6 and Colin Mackenzie of Coats Ltd, who
served as head of the SOE group based at Meerut in India. One historian
comments that 'as the war progressed, SOE in particular began to resem-
ble empire trade in khaki'.[4] So pronounced was this tendency that one OSS
official, highly suspicious of 'old China hands', had a report prepared on
the pre-war commercial connections of British officials in China.[5]

Yet the pattern was similar among Americans. Cornelius V. Starr, insurance executive and owner of the *Shanghai Evening Post and Mercury*, was an
early recruit to OSS. On his recommendation, Norwood Allman, the
prominent Shanghai lawyer, businessman and municipal councillor, was appointed to head the Chinese secret intelligence department of OSS in
Washington. Another of Starr's nominees was Arthur Duff, an 'old China
hand' who had been born in China of missionary stock. Before the war
Duff had been in the motor car and insurance business in Shanghai, Hong
Kong and Manila. He escaped from Hong Kong after the Japanese attack
and made his way to Chungking and thence to the USA where he was recruited to the OSS through Starr. Duff's extensive range of Chinese contacts made him particularly attractive to the OSS.[6]

The links between British and American intelligence in China and the
Shanghai Anglo-American business community were not only personal but
also to some degree institutionalized. The major Shanghai merchant firms
such as Jardine, Matheson and Butterfield & Swire continued to operate in
unoccupied China to a limited degree and personnel were sometimes du-
plicated with intelligence organs. Thus G. Findlay Andrew, the head of SOE
operations in China, 'by agreement [did] a certain amount of work with the

firm of Butterfield & Swire, who pay part of his salary'. An SOE report noted that 'Butterfield's office [in Chungking] is on the other side of the Yangtse River and to cross it O.125 [Findlay Andrew] has to go two miles to the bank of the river, descend 320 steps, cross the river in a ferry and then ascend 750 steps'.[7]

Shanghai in exile also recruited several former members of the Shanghai intelligence community. Harry Steptoe, former head of SIS operations in the Far East (he had served in various parts of China, including Shanghai, as well as Tokyo), returned to England before the outbreak of the Pacific War and assumed a senior position in MI6. Tony Keswick pushed for the appointment to SOE of Captain H. M. Smyth, former deputy commissioner of the Shanghai Municipal Police, who was among the British citizens repatriated from Shanghai in the summer of 1942. When he was rejected as unsuitable, Keswick recommended him to MI5.[8] The British military liaison officer in Shanghai, Major S. R. Hunt, and his deputy Captain R. V. Dewar, succeeded in slipping out of Shanghai on 17 December 1941. They set out on an epic journey across China to Chungking. In the course of their trek across Japanese-occupied territory they received help both from Chinese troops nominally under Japanese control and from pro-Chungking guerrillas. 'Our departure from Shanghai and journey through the occupied areas was arranged in cooperation with Puppet troops who, incidentally, were apologetic about their association with the Japanese and protested that their hearts were loyal.' Later, as they were aided by the guerrillas, one of them 'entertained us during a tedious sampan journey with the songs of Josephine Baker'.[9]

Even Shanghai journalism somehow persisted outside Shanghai. While collaborationist newsmen in Shanghai were producing their pro-Japanese version of the *Shanghai Evening Post and Mercury*, the paper's owner, C. V. Starr, set up a New York edition. Later he established a Chungking office and surmounted newsprint shortages and other technical difficulties to produce a regular weekly paper on which some of the paper's former staff found employment. The newspaper provided a useful front for intelligence activity and the paper in fact served as an Allied espionage ring jointly funded by the British MI6 and the American OSS.[10]

But such Anglo-American cooperation was rare. While men like the

Keswicks and Starr, whose wife was British, personified the Shanghai mind, the Shanghailanders were unable to imprint a common outlook or strategy on their colleagues in the secret war. Although the British and American governments were formally committed at the highest levels to a full pooling of intelligence resources and data, the Allies' officers in the field often evinced the utmost suspicion of each other. An SOE evaluation in the early part of the war poured scorn on the amateurishness of the American subversive effort:

> In China I can safely say that American activity has been
> nothing short of senseless. Those engaged neither speak
> Chinese, know the country, or have ever had any dealings with
> the Chinese – all of which suits the Chinese book very well
> indeed. The Chinese apparently sold someone a very good
> story on the advantages of operating through people who
> know nothing about China or the Chinese; the advantages are
> all on one side, and the whole programme is so ridiculous that
> to anyone who knows China such a proposition does not even
> bear discussion.[11]

The British typically complained of 'the ignorant sentimentality of the average American' in China.[12] The Americans for their part tended to view the British as imperialists and snobs.

The first British subversive warfare venture in China was an ill-fated enterprise called China Commando Group (CCG). Its origins went back to early 1941 when the British began to consider ways of giving secret assistance to Chinese guerrillas against the Japanese. These forces were disorganized, uncoordinated, poorly armed, had little liaison with regular forces and in their targets and activities often verged on rural banditry rather than insurgent warfare. Lest the British be implicated at a time when they were anxious not to give the Japanese any pretext for declaring war, two Danes, Erik Nyholm and Hans Tofts, were appointed by SOE leaders of the underground organization, code-named 'ANTIPODES'. The group was initially established under the cover of a Danish-American industrial group, Madsen Corporation. They operated with the sanction of Chiang Kai-shek. Volunteers, like the leaders mainly Danes who knew Chinese, were recruited and trained in commando warfare and the use of explosives at a secret training school in Malaya.

After the outbreak of the Pacific War the unit was renamed China Commando Group and moved into China. Killery, head of SOE's Oriental Mission, entrusted its direction to John Keswick. Seventy Chinese were trained in guerrilla tactics at Chungking. But the organization encountered jealousy and obstruction from the chief of the commando force in Chiang Kai-shek's army. Chinese liaison officers 'were employed chiefly in spying on CCG and, instead of assisting the Group, were sending fantastic reports to Chungking'. A Chinese general who was sent to help arrange for the movement of petrol for the group was caught by the Chinese customs trying to smuggle more than 2 tons of silk and lipstick under the cover of CCG. In March 1942 the commander of the Chinese commando force issued a virtual ultimatum, demanding that all the group's equipment, supplies, lorries and petrol be turned over to him. At the same time he 'made fantastic accusations that the Commando sent secret agents all over China and established clandestine wireless stations'. He demanded the group's immediate withdrawal. The British refused to hand over their stocks and Keswick asked for a meeting with Chiang Kai-shek. But the Generalissimo's only response was to send a curt message to the British ambassador demanding the immediate withdrawal of the British commando force.

Keswick's embroilment in the CCG fiasco led Killery to consider withdrawing him from China altogether. But his local expertise was felt to be indispensable and he was accordingly directed to 'lie very low' with a view to directing future secret activities. In a conciliatory discussion with the British ambassador on 24 April 1942, Chiang Kai-shek agreed that Keswick might remain as SOE representative in China and he undertook to place him 'in contact with his own secret organisations'.[13]

Thereafter the British largely abandoned the hope of organizing subversive operations on their own in China and for the time being limited their secret activities mainly to propaganda and intelligence-gathering. Killery nevertheless remained hopeful that it might be possible, through the British military mission in China, to encourage 'for the present on a small scale only, planned sabotage in the Shanghai area' and Keswick was instructed to cooperate with the British army representatives in Chungking 'and to assist in the development of this work'.[14]

By June 1942 SOE was disenchanted with the limited results produced by Killery's operations. The hard lessons of SOE's early amateurishness in Shanghai and of its even more abysmal failure in Malaya were now absorbed. Oriental Mission was closed down altogether and Killery was sacked. The British intelligence and subversion effort in the Far East was reorganized under new leadership. And the Americans, who, like the British, had failed to retain any 'stay-behind' capability in Shanghai, joined in the effort to project a war of resistance from the remote fastnesses of western China.

The Americans were later off the mark than the British in organizing subversion in China but they devoted larger resources to the enterprise and soon became the dominant partner. The effectiveness in the field of OSS was diminished, however, by personality conflicts and by limitations set by the Chinese. At first the American intelligence effort was headed in Chungking by Commander James McHugh, the US naval attaché. McHugh, who had worked in China for most of the inter-war period and knew the country well, was strongly pro-British and for a time shared a house in Chungking with John Keswick. In October 1942, however, McHugh was superseded by Captain Milton Miles of the Office of Naval Intelligence who secured appointment as OSS director of operations in China. Miles, known as 'Mary' (after a film star of the silent screen), was a former officer of the Yangtse Patrol and a bold, energetic commander. But he was also vain, impressionable and politically naive in his dealings with the host country's leaders.

Miles's chief contact among the Chinese was Chiang Kai-shek's secret service chief, Tai Li, whose evil legend had continued to grow during the war. His network was now said to consist of more than 40,000 men, many of them behind enemy lines. In spite of his sinister reputation, Tai Li had a certain charm and some diplomatic gifts. He took particular care to maintain good personal relations with the heads of the American and British secret organizations in China, while at the same time playing them off against each other. Miles was fascinated, almost mesmerized, by the secret police chief. He had no time for those who talked of the 'Chinese Himmler'. This was a man, said Miles 'who never had anyone shot without proper autho-rization'.[15] When Miles arrived in Chungking, Tai Li turfed a senior Chi-nese official out of a luxury villa in order to accommodate his American guest. Miles was delighted. Later Tai Li accompanied Miles on a trip to the Fukien coastal region to inspect his wireless system and to check the effi-ciency of his agents' network. He took Miles to visit his home village, where he introduced him to his mother and other family members (see plate 11).

A top secret British memorandum (sent to John Keswick with the re-quest that it should be burnt after reading) reported that Tai Li had used other methods to impress Miles:

> He was shown the well-equipped and stocked poison
> laboratory, the torture chamber, equipped with such ancient
> but efficient devices as Spanish Flies, water cure, etc., and he
> was told that O.601 [Tai Li]'s boys could bump off anyone
> they wanted in any part of the world ...
>
> A couple of weeks later O.610 [Miles] appeared with a leg
> and shoulder bandaged. His story is that he was attacked by
> Japanese agents, who inflicted on him five knife wounds, but
> that O.601's shadow bodyguard, the existence of which O.610
> did not even suspect, immediately 'liquidated' the attackers.
>
> WN [US Navy] personnel (or better say one or two of their
> officers, who was [sic] sworn to secrecy) find this story rather
> 'phony', but I have personally seen the wounds, and believe
> that the attack was staged by O.601 in order to impress O.610
> and have him under his thumb. Just a security measure.
>
> O.610 lives now in a state of mortal fear, and wonders
> whether he will ever be able to return home, as he 'knows too
> much'.

The SOE report added that Miles's activities were disapproved of by the American commander in China, General Joseph W. Stilwell, who thought that the naval officer 'was being made a "sucker"' by Tai Li. Stilwell conse-quently refused to grant space on army planes to OSS for the importation of '"silly articles" such as hand grenades at a time when every inch of space had to be reserved for aviation gasoline, bombs and munitions for the WM [US Army] planes successfully operating in China'.[16]

The sceptical British appreciation of Miles's mission arose in large measure from a jaundiced view of Miles's Chinese friend. The British military attaché in Chungking, Brigadier G. E. Grimsdale, suggested in March 1942 that Tai Li's organization could 'legitimately be compared to the Gestapo, on which no doubt it has been modelled'.[17] Grimsdale suspected Tai Li of being 'anti-British and probably anti-foreign, although he is charged with active cooperation with the American Mission, and is suspected of maintaining liaison with German agents'.[18] The latter point particularly worried the British since a German, E.O. Stoelzner, was known to head the communications section of Tai Li's organization. The British were unable to do anything about Stoelzner's presence in this sensitive post, since Tai Li was said to have declared that 'any Chinese who tries to get Stoelzner thrown out would be liquidated'.[19]

As in the case of the British-sponsored CCG, the Chungking authorities insisted that the OSS commando enterprise in China must be under Chinese control. Stilwell was unhappy about this, but Miles eagerly agreed to serve under Tai Li. In the course of several months of negotiation between the autumn of 1942 and spring 1943 the Sino-American Cooperative Organization (SACO) was established, with Tai Li as commander and Miles as his deputy. More than 2,000 Americans were trained at 'Happy Valley' near Chungking and participated in SACO's operations, which included guerrilla, sabotage, propaganda and subversive operations behind Chinese lines. The long arm of Tai Li's organization reached into Shanghai where one of his agents, a Chinese policeman, used time-delay explosive devices, supplied by the British, to burn three Japanese planes at the Hungjao aerodrome – or so Tai Li informed Miles in October 1942.[20]

Suspicion and rivalry between SOE and OSS proved impossible to eradicate and hampered operational effectiveness. Whereas elsewhere the British shared their counter-espionage files freely with the Americans, they would not do so in China. They did not trust American security. The Americans, for their part, regarded the British as competitors rather than allies. In May 1942 the OSS representative in China boasted to the head of the organization, Colonel 'Wild Bill' Donovan: 'I have the jump on the British in many ways.'[21] A large share in the responsibility for the development of such attitudes rested with the Chinese government in Chungking which frequently sought to play off the British and Americans against each other. A secret British analysis in February 1943 referred to 'O.600 [Chiang Kai-shek]'s divide and rule – or better to say – "make trouble and cash the benefits" policy'.[22] Different military and official factions within Chiang Kai-shek's régime allied themselves with specific British or American intelligence organizations or units, adding to the general dissension.

In an effort to solve such problems, Donovan met his SOE counterpart, Sir Charles Hambro, in June 1942 and concluded an agreement to divide up the world for the purpose of subversive operations. China was to be an American sphere, India British. From the beginning, both sides grumbled about the arrangement and sought ways round it.

上海

No case better illustrates the bureaucratic, diplomatic and tactical obstacles that hindered effective subversive action by the Allies than Operation CONWAY, the attempt by SOE to blow up the Kailan Mines. In the autumn of 1941, even as the mines' chief manager, Nathan, was finalizing his collaborative arrangement with the Japanese authorities, SOE was preparing plans for the destruction of key sections of the mines in order to prevent the Japanese from utilizing them for their war effort. The destruction of the mines had already been recognized as a priority by the British government and a secret agent had been dispatched the previous June to look over the target area. He stayed there for a month but 'was so impressed by Japanese security measures and the Japanese contacts of Major Nathan that he dared not take the latter into his confidence'.[23] The sabotage scheme was hatched on 25 September at a meeting in the Thatched House Club in London, a traditional rendezvous for 'old China hands'. Colonel P. C. Young, a director and former general manager of the KMA's parent company, met an SIS officer and proposed that, with the help of the British engineers at the mines, the central power house could be blown up, rendering the entire mines unworkable for a year.

In October 1941 a detailed study of the mines and of available courses of action was prepared in London by SOE. It was noted that the mines were situated in very low-lying country: they were deep pit mines which, if flooded, would be difficult if not impossible to render operational again. Shanghai was 'extremely dependent on Kailan coal' which would be difficult to replace from elsewhere. If the mines were destroyed, the Ministry of Economic Warfare estimated that 'the immediate result might be a reduction of iron production in the Japanese Empire by as much as 50%'. This disruption would last for 'upwards of 2 months' and it would take about six months before 'the situation could be substantially restored'. If Japan were at war at the time of destruction, the effect on Japanese iron and steel production 'would be more critical'. The effect would be to 'impose limits on the size of the armed forces which could be maintained in a war involving any substantial expenditure of material'. The study recognized that the destruction of the mines would result in the loss of a major British and Chinese investment. But 'the material loss would be infinitely greater to the Japanese than to the Chinese and ourselves'.

Although the strategic advantages were plain, there were diplomatic drawbacks. Assuming that the destruction took place in time of peace and were 'attributable to British agents', the incident might be made a *casus belli* by the Japanese or 'an excuse for drastic action against all British rights in China'. But since 'in any case Japan will come into the war when she feels she is strong enough', the deprivation of her access to such a vital supply source might lead her to 'postpone fighting until she had reorganized her coal situation'. Moreover, it was possible that 'the sabotage could be so arranged that it could be plausibly attributed to Communists or Chinese guerillas. In that case, the diplomatic reactions might be slightly different.' The conclusion reached by this study was that action should be postponed until war with Japan seemed inevitable. Meanwhile, plans for demolition and escape should be prepared.[24]

Following this memorandum and the agent's report, an operational plan for the destruction of the mines was ordered to be prepared on 22 November 1941. Further meetings on the subject took place in London and Singapore over the next two weeks but by the outbreak of the Pacific War nothing had been done.

Meanwhile the Japanese, like the British, were preparing plans for action to be taken in the event of war. A document outlining these enemy plans was obtained by British intelligence and considered in London at the beginning of December 1941. The document stated: 'enemy mines are to be seized', which was understood as referring specifically to the Kailan Mines.[25] Yet in spite of this foreknowledge, no action against the mines had been taken by the British by 8 December 1941.

Following the outbreak of the Pacific War, Killery considered various possible methods of attacking the mines. The arrest of the entire SOE team in Shanghai prevented their employment for the enterprise. Killery rejected as impracticable a proposal that the navy should be induced to bring in a submarine to spirit away saboteurs. He suggested that Nyholm's Scandinavian commando team should handle the attack, subject to approval by Keswick and the Chinese government in Chungking. Still nothing was done. But following the débâcle of the CCG, Keswick came to the conclusion that a guerrilla attack would be impossible to organize and that the only hope was aerial bombardment. He despaired of persuading the RAF to undertake such a mission but felt there was 'quite a good chance' that the Americans might carry it out.[26]

In April 1942 Killery wrote that he considered an attack on the Kailan Mines to be 'the most important single project which can be undertaken in China'. But he added: 'It is bristling with difficulties, physical and political: the reluctance of the Chinese to take any action against the Japanese, the fact that the KMA territory can only be approached through Communist areas, and that the Japanese have taken all possible steps to guard the property, means that much time would be involved in delicate negotiations and in planning an attack on the Mines, if it is to be successful.' Killery pointed out:

> in the meanwhile, however, one line of action suggests itself,
> which has not hitherto been seriously contemplated. The
> Chinese Government in Chungking is so opposed to and
> suspicious of the Communist Party, whose headquarters are in
> Northern China, that it is impossible for anybody situated in
> Chungking or in Kuomintang China to make any approach to
> the Communists. Nevertheless, the latter represent such an

important element in China and moreover are so strenuously and ideologically opposed to Japanese attempts to dominate China that it is felt that a definite attempt should now be made to establish contact with them at their headquarters in Yenan, with a view to encouraging and assisting them and their guerrilla armies to take increased action against the Japanese. Such a move will require the most careful and delicate handling and must not be in any way be associated with O.M. in Chungking. In these circumstances the only possible approach to Yenan is through Siberia or Sinkiang. In either case, this will necessitate at least the tacit approval of the Russians, which no doubt may raise additional complications.[27]

After a generation of regarding communism as its prime enemy in China, British intelligence was thus coming to see Mao Tse-tung as its most useful potential local ally in North China against the Japanese.

In the short term this revolution in thinking bore little fruit. Sir Archibald Clark Kerr, the British ambassador in Moscow, was consulted as to the feasibility of organizing an attack on the Kailan Mines by this circuitous means.[28] His reply poured cold water on the idea.[29] As a result, plans for a commando-style raid overland were shelved.

Allied planning now switched to a projected air attack on the central power house of the mines. The British former inspector of power in the mines spent four months in Chungking advising on the technicalities of the mining operations and helping to prepare detailed bombing maps. Meanwhile news arrived in Chungking that the Japanese were taking elaborate precautions against sabotage and were transferring auxiliary generators into disused mine shafts, which would limit the effect of destruction of the power house. Since the British did not have suitable aircraft available in China, the scheme was handed over to the Americans. John Keswick discussed the problem directly with Colonel Donovan in order to secure his support.

On 21 October 1942, more than a year after their destruction had first been proposed, the Kailan Mines were attacked by planes of the US 10th

Air Force, operating from Chengtu. First reports indicated five planes had reached the target area and two or three were said to have been 'manned by old hands who described it as child's play to get their bombs right on target from somewhere around 12,000 feet'.[30] The power house, transformer plant and main pithead shaft were reported to have been hit, causing heavy damage.[31] Photographic evidence appeared to confirm these claims, though not conclusively.

SOE officials in both Chungking and London were elated. S. F. Crawford of the SOE mission in Chungking called the attack 'one of the most gratifying things that have happened'.[32] 'GM 350 [John Keswick] has reaped a handsome dividend on his work at Chungking and New York for SOE', wrote Sir George Moss, regional adviser for the Far East. To which the director of SOE added a note suggesting to Tony Keswick that 'a short telegram of congrats to GM 350 is indicated (from you & I [sic]).' Tony Keswick replied, 'I feel diffident in congratulating my own brother.'[33] The congratulatory message was therefore sent by Moss.

Unfortunately, later reports were much less encouraging to the attackers. SOE eventually concluded that one minehead had been destroyed, killing about 100 Chinese labourers, but the main power plant had been only lightly damaged. Output in the mines was halted only for two days. An American intelligence report forwarded to MI6 in December 1943 stated that the bombing had not halted production 'even for one day'. Forty Belgians and ten British clerks were said to be still working for the enterprise.[34] A British intelligence report in April 1944 noted that the KMA was still operating in four mining areas, employing 70,000 labourers. The bulk of the work was being carried out by the mines' old employees under Japanese supervision. The total daily output of coal was 18,000 tons, of which 16,000 were commandeered by the Japanese.[35] The volume of production was thus being maintained at pre-war levels, albeit with a higher number of workers.

Oriental Mission's failure to take action against the Kailan Mines before 8 December 1941 became the subject of angry post-mortems in London. The main impediment to action appeared to have been the insistence of the Foreign Office 'that before approval of the operation could be given, destruction should not be attributable to the British, if that could be arranged, and that adequate steps should be taken to safeguard the lives and interests of the British and Belgian personnel of the Mines, at the same time insisting that the Chinese Government should not be informed of the project'.[36] As an SOE memorandum in April 1942 put it, the Foreign Office had 'considered and hesitated over our Appreciation for one month and then attached such qualifications to their approval that they rendered the formulation of any practicable scheme impossible'.[37] The Foreign Office's stern rebuke to Nathan's employers, written in May 1942, shortly after SOE's criticism of the Foreign Office's dilatory handling the previous autumn of the sabotage scheme, was evidently born of a guilty conscience on the part of the Foreign Office itself.

上海

By September 1942 at least 15 separate Allied intelligence organizations were said to be operating in China: five British, four American, four Russian, one Dutch and one Free French – this in addition to the several competing secret services of the Chinese themselves. A report by John Keswick noted that, far from cooperating, 'these organizations compete among themselves, do not pool their information except through London and Washington, and are completely uncoordinated, to the delight of the Chinese'. Keswick despaired of recruiting Chinese agents who would be both loyal and reliable:

> It has been proved that the only way to have really trustworthy
> agents is by acquiring complete control over the destinies of
> their families. The Japanese are using this method but it is
> completely out of the question for British and Americans. The
> Russians are believed to employ agents specially trained in
> Moscow. These agents can be trusted as they believe they are
> working for Communism against Chungking Oligarchy and
> not for Russians against the Chinese. We can offer nothing but
> money and there are more and more young Chinese who will
> not be bought for work for foreigners.

Keswick declared pessimistically 'that nothing can be attempted in China of an independent nature during the present war. The establishment of such a system would require years of effort in peace time. We can only work through the Chinese Government and that means through Chiang Kai Shek and Tai Li.'

The virtual elimination of British and American intelligence sources in Shanghai and much of the rest of occupied China forced them willy-nilly to rely on help from their Chinese allies. But Keswick's report noted that Chinese intelligence was hamstrung by a multiplicity of competing services which 'in their lower stages are often merged into or are allied with Smuggler's Bands, Independent Guerillas [sic], Secret Political Societies, Dope and Crime Rings, and even "Puppet" Government Organizations in Occupied China'. A number of senior politicians maintained their own networks of agents, some of these within official agencies. 'The maze of cross currents and influences', the report continued, 'is such that it is impossible to represent in graphic form the flow of intelligence and to understand the correlation of the multiple organs handling it.' The most powerful and notorious Chinese intelligence organization, Tai Li's 'Gestapo', was described by Keswick as the 'mainstay, eyes, ears, and dagger of the present régime'. A separate organization, also loyal to Chiang Kai-shek, was headed by General Wang P'eng-sheng. This was responsible for military and political intelligence, propaganda and sabotage in occupied China. The Kuomintang maintained its own party secret service. In Keswick's view, the large Chinese espionage apparatus produced intelligence that while 'superabundant' was 'inaccurate, belated, and more often than not worthless'. Many of the underground channels to occupied China were 'double circuits' from which 'the Japanese seem to derive more benefit ... than the Chinese'. Agents were untrained and over-imaginative. 'Every Chinese agent', according to Keswick, was 'a salesman at heart and if he has no goods to sell he will fabricate something.' Rumours were often transmitted as reliable information or even eye-witness reports. Exaggeration ran rampant: 'a company becomes a division, an Armed Junk a Warship'. Yet the Anglo-Saxon powers had no choice. 'Chinese intelligence', Keswick concluded, remained 'the principal source of information for the British and American Intelligence in China'.[38]

Keswick's report was generally accepted in London. One intelligence official there commented:

This detailed report by one who has had firsthand knowledge confirms previous reports we have had from M[ilitary] A[ttaché] China and others. I doubt very much if it will prove practicable to apply pressure on China through Lend-Lease Administration, because such action would immediately produce a Chinese squeal which would go straight to the heart of friends of China here and in the US. All we can do seems to be to continue to give an extremely low grading to all Chinese Intelligence reports, and possibly to make that fact increasingly plain to the Chinese themselves, in the hope that our scorn of their Intelligence may make them improve.[39]

Against this background, it is hardly surprising that the results obtained in the field were disappointing.

After the collapse of CCG, the British laid great store by the creation of a new Chinese secret organization known as RII (variously termed Research and Investment Institute or Resources Investigation Institution). The root idea of RII was an exchange of intelligence assets between the British and the Chinese: the British would supply technical and financial help, in return for which the Chinese would collect intelligence from occupied territories. G. Findlay Andrew was appointed to the cover position of press officer at the British Embassy in Chungking in order to take charge of the enterprise. Andrew had lived all his life in China and was well-connected with leading Kuomintang figures. Working under Keswick's direction, he sought to establish close relations with Tai Li's 'Gestapo'. Eventually, however, it was decided to focus instead on the rival intelligence organization headed by General Wang P'eng-sheng, who was thought to have great influence on Chiang Kai-shek in foreign policy matters.

An unusually cultivated and scholarly figure among Chinese generals, General Wang was a Confucian scholar as well as China's leading Japanologist. Chiang Kai-shek had appointed him head of the Institute of International Relations (IIR), a kind of intelligence think-tank, in 1937. Andrew set about finding 'a way in which a bribe could be paid to O.602 [General Wang] without loss of dignity'.[40] The result was the creation of the Resources Investigation Institute (RII) as an offshoot from the IIR. To this end, Andrew was appointed Adviser to the IIR in June 1942.

Andrew was helped by a small non-Chinese staff among whom was a sinologist called Soderbom. Variously described as a Dane and a Swede, Soderbom had been born in Kalgan in Inner Mongolia. His standing in the organization sharply deteriorated a few months later, when, allegedly 'under the influence of drink', he breached security by stating that he had brought out a packet of important papers from the Communist-controlled area of North China.[41] Andrew's office was divided into two departments, the first concerned with research and analysis, the second with 'the despatch of agents to areas behind Japanese lines to collect information and intelligence reports'. The second department, headed by Lo Chien-peh (C. P. Lo) succeeded in establishing 'a number of energetic agents who had been briefed by Mr Lo for many years and were working in the various areas behind the Japanese lines'.[42] As of January 1943 the British enjoyed, through RII, the services of about 20 radio transmitting and/or receiving stations in various parts of occupied China, including two in Shanghai.

The real effect of all this was that the British paid a large part of the bills and called much of the tune, while Chinese agents did the work. A contemporary SOE report described the relationship thus:

> Mr Findlay Andrew's power with General Wang Ping-sheng is derived from his excellent personal relations with, and the monetary subsidies which he obtains for, General Wang Ping-sheng through his clandestine connection with SOE ...
> [General Wang] is estimated to rely on SOE funds ... to the extent of about one-third of his total budget.[43]

The Chinese evinced considerable unease at this arrangement, though it worked with reasonable success.

One of RII's most effective agents was based in Shanghai. During 1943 and 1944 the British received what Andrew described as 'a considerable quantity of extremely valuable intelligence from Mr Hsu Ming-ch'en which emanated from the East China and Shanghai districts'.[44] Hsu was described in another SOE report as being 'particularly able' and as having 'close connections with Puppet officials and enemy personnel connected with various

Japanese official organizations'.[45] But unknown to the British, the head of the Shanghai station was a communist who had worked with Richard Sorge in Tokyo and had escaped detection by the Japanese.[46]

In spite of the OSS-SOE 'treaty', SOE insisted on retaining control of its special relationship with RII. An SOE memorandum in late 1942 defended its position with the argument that OSS was 'not yet properly organized in Chungking' and 'had not asked' to take over RII. Moreover, the memorandum pointed out: 'That the time is not ripe, in spite of the terms of the agreement between OSS and SOE, is due to the overriding fact that the Generalissimo has expressly vetoed active American participation in RII.' Chiang Kai-shek had laid down that he was 'prepared to cooperate in subversive activities with the Americans through General Tai Li's organization – provided the British are excluded – and with the British in respect of RII activities – provided the Americans are excluded'. The British well understood that Chiang's policy was 'to drive a wedge between the British and Americans whilst obtaining benefits from each'. This suited the British well since it gave them an excuse for failing to fulfil the terms of the OSS-SOE agreement regarding China.[47] SOE's continued role in occupied China through RII remained a continuous source of aggravation in relations between SOE and OSS, but the British maintained their support of RII until 1944.

In addition to embroiling SOE with their American counterparts, the RII arrangement also aroused jealousy in SIS. The latter 'consistently pressed us to maintain and expand the RII intelligence service, because it is a better service than they can obtain themselves'.[48] Although the Chinese insisted on security grounds that RII intelligence not be shared with the SIS representative at Chungking, SOE nevertheless passed on RII data to the SIS headquarters in London. At the same time SOE strenuously resisted SIS pressure to take over control of RII themselves.[49] SOE justified their stance on the faintly specious ground that RII was a 'Chinese organization' which could not be transferred without the consent of Chiang Kai-shek, which was unlikely to be forthcoming. Personal differences were also involved. Andrew, one SOE memorandum noted, was 'notoriously a difficult man to work with and, owing to former jealousies, it would be difficult to get senior men such as Steptoe of SIS to serve under him'.[50]

The British did achieve one remarkable success: operation REMORSE.

This was a logical outcome of the Shanghai commercial background of the directors of SOE in China. REMORSE was an effort to manipulate the black market to ensure favourable currency exchange rates for several organizations. The participating organizations or clients were official, voluntary and commercial: they included the British embassy, the SIS, the Red Cross and Reuters. The British controller of REMORSE, W. Fletcher, worked chiefly through a Chinese businessman, Frank Shu, a former employee of BAT (British-American Tobacco Company). The inducement to Shu, according to an SOE report, was that, 'in addition to getting a good profit on each deal, he hopes to be a big man in British business and banking circles after the war'.[51] The operation eventually created a huge trading network throughout enemy-occupied China, including areas as far from Chungking as Tientsin, Manchuria and Shanghai. Apart from currency manipulation, REMORSE also had many useful adjuncts. One was the procurement of intelligence. Another was the acquisition of large quantities of black-market quinine from occupied areas. The quinine was obtained partly through a Persian named Mogra and partly through a trading organization known as the China Syndicate. One-fifteenth of the profits of the quinine trade was earmarked for Tai Li's organization – 'a necessary insurance against guerrillas and obstruction by Customs', as an SOE report put it.[52] The difference between the official rates of exchange (80–160 Chinese National Dollars to the pound) and the black market rate (590 CND to the pound) yielded huge profits to the benefit of the organizers. Altogether REMORSE is said to have produced a revenue of £77 million for SOE.

Otherwise the record was generally unimpressive. The atmosphere of corruption and intrigue in Chungking, the mutual rivalries, suspicions and resentments among the Allies, as well as constraints of supply and strategy, all militated against an effective subversion campaign before the later part of the war. Miles's SACO group made a renewed attempt to attack the Kailan Mines, this time by guerrilla attack from the ground, but the aerial bombardment had alerted the Japanese to take defensive precautions and the sabotage effort failed. SOE expressed some interest in a plan, supervised by the former Shanghai Green Gang boss Tu Yueh-sheng, 'to induce skilled labour to leave Japanese employ in Shanghai, Hongkong and Canton and move to the Interior where arrangements are being made for their maintenance and eventual employment'. Funds for the project were provided by American labour organizations through the United China Relief fund. SOE was sceptical about the effectiveness of such operations since 'the moment large numbers of men fail to report for work in plants etc under Japanese control in Hongkong, Canton, or Shanghai, the Japanese will know how to take effective steps to put a stop to such delinquencies and their ruthlessness will generally prove effective'.[53]

Some desultory consideration was given to proposals for attacks on Shanghai. The Chapei power station was identified as a key target. Possible assassinations were also mooted: it was pointed out that the Japanese would find it hard to find replacements for collaborationist English-language broadcasters such as Herbert Moy, Don Chisholm and Pat Kelly (Frank Johnston).[54] But the difficulty of projecting force over immense distances across Occupied China, added to all the other impediments, prevented any significant sabotage attacks on Shanghai.

A frustrated SOE official commented in July 1943: 'It is now well known that enormous possibilities exist along the China Coast. It is a scandal that the Japanese have been allowed full opportunities to exploit such large centres as Shanghai and Hong Kong without interference on our part except for an inconsequential air raid or two.'[55] Only towards the end of the war did the Anglo-Saxon powers succeed in penetrating any distance towards their former strongholds.

In the meantime, even in the absence of two of its chief contestants, the game of nations was still being played with its customary ferocity within Shanghai.

10 Wars Within Wars

With the virtual elimination of the Anglo-Saxon powers, the chief players in the game of nations in Shanghai from 1942 to 1945 were the Germans and the Japanese. The relationship of these allies in China, even more than the parallel Anglo-American relationship, was poisoned by mutual suspicion, conflicting interests, ambitions and objectives.

The Japanese made little effort to conceal their mistrust of their Axis partners. In March 1942 a Japanese army representative told the acting police chief of the French Concession that he was charged with control of political activities by foreigners in the concession – in particular those of 'German and Italian circles'.[1] A Municipal Police report from about the same time took note of heightened discontent among German and Italian businessmen in Shanghai 'in connection with the restrictions imposed on them by the Nipponese Military Authorities'.

> It was originally believed by these circles that Japan's Axis partners will enjoy right[s] and privileges in Shanghai but now they regard themselves as being treated almost in the same way as enemy nationals.
>
> Thought is gradually gaining ground among prominent Germans and Italians in Shanghai that the Far East will eventually be closed economically and otherwise to all Europeans, including Germans and Italians, and that all trade possibilities will disappear.
>
> The ever-increasing military and economical might of Japan is evidently beginning to worry her Axis partners who consider that there may be no limit to Japan's expansion.[2]

Shortly afterwards a British intelligence report commented on severe fractures in the Axis partnership in China:

As long ago as January the German ambassador in Nanking was complaining that the Japanese Government treated the war in the Pacific as peculiarly their own and acted as if they saw danger in Axis cooperation there, and that in Shanghai they were treating all whites, whether enemies or friends, exactly alike, with the result that German interests were suffering...A report received through a secret Allied source states, for what it is worth, that the Japanese have demanded the recall of the German Consul-General at Shanghai because of his having set up an espionage organisation which is highly unwelcome to them.[3]

The tense nature of the relationship was manifested in things great and small. A repatriated American missionary recalled an incident when 'a German lady on horseback was stopped at the barrier where Great Western Road crosses the R.R. [railroad] to have her pass examined by the Jap sentry. He made her dismount and kept her waiting for some time during which time her horse dropped a lot of dung. Returning, the sentry ordered her to clean up the place, refused to lend her a brush and dustpan, and made her remove the filth with her hands.'[4]

Even senior German officials were treated by the Japanese with a discourteousness verging on hostility. In October 1941, for example, SS Colonel Meisinger decided to go to Tokyo but found it almost impossible to obtain a passage on a Japanese steamer. When he finally got hold of one, the Japanese refused to provide a ticket for his wife, and when at length he procured that, they then made difficulties about furnishing railway tickets from Nagasaki to Tokyo. Meisinger was said to be 'furious over this treatment by the ally of Germany'.[5]

The Japanese were extremely interested in finding out everything they could about their ally's secret activities in Shanghai and even interrogated British Municipal Police detectives on the subject.[6] So concerned were the Japanese that they made a special search for a suitable detective who would specialize in the delicate matter of German affairs. They had great difficulty in finding a suitable candidate, since they did not wish to appoint either a German or a Jewish refugee. Eventually a White Russian named Brauns, a warder in the Ward Road prison, was offered the job. He said he would accept it only if the British head jailer, Hogg, approved his secondment. When told the purpose of the proposed transfer, Hogg 'unhesitatingly forwarded the recommendation'.[7]

According to a post-war American intelligence report, Brauns's

> investigations re German Secret Service, nazi activities, [and]
> attempts on the part of Germans to conduct a pro-Vlasov
> campaign among the Russian emigrants* provoked suspicions
> of [the] German secret service and at one time put the officer
> in [a] difficult position as [the] Germans used every means to
> undermine D[etective] S[ub-] I[nspector] Brauns in the eyes
> of [the] Japanese.[8]

上海

While the Japanese spied on the Germans, the Germans spied on the Japanese. Meisinger's network of agents in Shanghai was headed by Dr Paul Rudolf Klare who had worked for the Gestapo under Meisinger in Berlin. Klare was described in a post-war US intelligence report as 'one of the most brilliant Germans in the Far East'. In 1940 he had been sent to Manchuria to report for the DNB news agency; he probably worked there as an intelligence agent on the side. The following year he was transferred to Shanghai where he lived at the Park Hotel and was employed simultaneously by Puttkamer's propaganda office and the SS. Klare's team provided Meisinger with reports on such subjects as Japanese troop dispositions, Nanking (puppet) government politics, 'anything on the Russians', German merchants trading with Chungking and the Free French underground.[9]

Klare organized a number of agents' rings in Shanghai. One was headed by Frederick Wiehl. Born to German parents at Winfield, New York in

---

* Andrei Vlasov was a Soviet lieutenant-general who, after capture by the Germans,
agreed to lead a 'Russian Liberation Army' on the side of the Nazis.

1902, Wiehl held both German and American citizenship. He had qualified in the USA as a lawyer and for a time had practised law from an office at 55 Myrtle Avenue, Ridgewood, Long Island. In 1940 he received orders from the German government to prepare for work as a spy and propagandist. In June 1941 he moved to Mexico City where the German legation issued him with a German passport in the name of 'Captain Friedrich Awald'. Armed with this new identity, as well as a spare Peruvian passport for emergencies, he travelled by ship to Japan.

Aboard the same ship was another German agent, Herbert Haupt. He was one of eight German saboteurs who later landed from a German submarine on the coast of the United States, were arrested and executed. Haupt suspected that Wiehl was an American spy and at one point tried unsuccessfully to throw him overboard. When he reached Japan, Wiehl was ordered to go to Shanghai, from where he would be sent to Germany on a blockade runner. He arrived in Shanghai in October 1941 and stayed at the Metropole Hotel, but instead of being returned to Germany was retained for work as a propagandist on the German radio station XGRS. His speciality was a weekly broadcast supposedly representing the point of view of the American working-man.

Acting as a kind of under-boss for the Shanghai Gestapo, Wiehl employed a number of sub-agents in Shanghai. Among these was Roland Grutli, also known as 'Guthrie' and 'Kerwyn'. Grutli was about 40, stocky, with blond-brown hair. In November 1941, according to a British intelligence report, Grutli had been working for the Germans in Japan. While lodging at a hotel in Yokohama, he had engaged British and American visitors in conversation, hoping to 'encourage them by his garrulousness to let drop information valuable to Germany'. Grutli, the report continued, became 'involved in a brawl in the bar of the New Grand Hotel in Yokohama with a Finn who was audibly insulting the Nazis. Grutly [sic], who is powerfully built and was drunk, beat up the Finn and was later ordered by the German Embassy not only to apologise but to remove his residence from the hotel.'[10] Wiehl later wrote of him:

> Roland came down from Tokyo where he had just broken the
> jaw of the Danish Consul General...His orders were to cover

the Japanese situation, [an] assignment for which I had no better man. Roland collected information covering all phases of the Japanese position in Shanghai. During this work he often had fights with Japanese whom he used to entertain to excess in order to obtain information. Roland also operated a small prostitution house financed by the German Government for the benefit of Japanese who were interested in White Russian girls. He later became very involved in his work and there were several complications. I was frequently requested to appear before the 2nd Chief Police Commissioner whenever a Japanese was found dead and the suspicion arose that Roland did the killing. Their questions were to find out if I ordered the killings of the Japanese. At that time I was on very friendly terms with the Police Commissioner and was supplied with as many pistols as I wanted for my men...

On the last assignment, Roland got himself into a tight position between the Japanese and the Russians, over a subject being investigated. Roland killed four Japanese on that night and hid in my room until late the next evening when he was planning to leave for Nanking for a rest. However, he was drinking heavy, too heavy, and was last seen being taken from a bar in a totally drunken condition, by two Russians known to have been working for the Japanese. That night he was killed.[11]

Grutli's body was found the next morning in an alley in the French Concession. The exact identities of his killers remained in doubt. Wiehl implied that the Japanese were responsible, but another version, unearthed by American investigators after the war, had it that he was killed by a Gestapo agent on orders from Meisinger and Kahner. Meisinger's estranged wife lent support to that theory by claiming that she had overheard a conversation in which Meisinger indicated that 'Roland' was in disfavour; she concluded that Meisinger had ordered his elimination.[12]

Employment by the Shanghai Gestapo was plainly a far from risk-free undertaking, as is illustrated by the career of another sub-agent recalled by

Wiehl in a post-war deposition:

> Rudolf Mamlock, age about thirty, short, a former reporter on
> the Paris newspaper, *Soir*. He was able to speak French,
> German, English, Chinese, and Japanese. His assignments
> were mostly anti-Russian. His work, generally considered, was
> to contact the Russians on the basis of 'double-crossing' me.
> [Wiehl seems to mean that Mamlock was to act as a double
> agent in the German interest]...
>
>   He was able to get official documents from the Japanese
> authorities' offices and Russian offices. He dressed very flashy
> and created quite a little jealousy among his former pals.
> Mamlock came to me straight from the Ward Road Jail
> without shoes or a decent suit. Soon he had several suits and
> hats, and in fact, I myself looked second-class in appearance
> [compared] to him. His work was very satisfactory. Finally the
> Japanese arrested him while he was working on the Liebig
> case, Mrs Liebig being a Japanese agent. He was placed in the
> Bridge House and after eight months died of dysentery and
> beri-beri. Just a few days before dying, the Japanese released
> him and placed him in a small room in Hongkew where no
> one knew they had sent him. Evidently this was done to avoid
> increasing the toll of deaths in the Bridge House.[13]

Meisinger fell out not only with the diplomats but also with his own subordinates. In January 1943 he transferred Kahner from Shanghai to Tokyo.
Kahner's replacement in Shanghai was SS Hauptsturmführer Franz Huber.
Huber was a professional Gestapo officer who had worked as a German
agent in Hong Kong, Indo-China, Bangkok and Tokyo. His office was in the
sub-station (Dienststelle) of the German embassy at 2 Peking Road. Huber
was jealous of his status and argued with Meisinger as to whether he had the
right to submit reports direct to Berlin without going through Meisinger.
The relative standing of the three top Gestapo officers in the Far East in
March 1942 is indicated by their salaries: Meisinger received RM4,760 a
month, Huber RM1,830 and Kahner RM1,570.[14] Perhaps reflecting

Huber's increasingly autonomous role later, his monthly allotment had risen to about RM5,000 by the end of the war.[15]

Although Meisinger's brief was limited to internal German security in China and Japan, he occasionally sought to prove his usefulness by providing items of external intelligence. Some of this was of questionable value. In August 1943, for example, he reported that wall placards had appeared in a number of Soviet Far Eastern cities, including Vladivostok, with caricatures of Stalin, Churchill and Roosevelt as well as handwritten abuse.[16] This message elicited a rebuke from Ribbentrop, who declared such reports extremely improbable and instructed the German ambassador in Japan in future to discuss Meisinger's reports with him prior to dispatch, since the ambassador, by his signature, took some responsibility for the contents of the telegrams he dispatched.[17]

Meisinger and his men in fact achieved very little in Shanghai. Thuggery was no substitute for serious intelligence warfare. Failing miserably to secure much useful information about Germany's enemies or even her allies, the Gestapo boss turned his attention to his own countrymen. Local Germans were terrorized and a few were forcibly shipped back to the fatherland on blockade runners, put in uniform and dispatched on what generally turned out to be one-way trips to the Russian front. Meisinger scored a few minor successes in his specialized field of exposing homosexuals, securing the dismissal of a handful of German officials on that account. He also uncovered some instances of embezzlement. But his one major victory was over his main rival in the German intelligence field in the Far East, the local Abwehr chief, Louis Siefken.

上海

In late June 1941 Siefken was joined in Shanghai by another Abwehr officer, Major Lothar Eisentraeger. He had travelled from Germany over the Trans-Siberian Railway and reached the Chinese border post eight hours before the German invasion of the Soviet Union on 22 June, thus narrowly avoiding capture and internment. Eisentraeger was slim, muscular, balding and dissipated-looking, with a reputation as a ladies' man. He could claim some knowledge of the region, having worked for a German firm in

Manchuria as far back as 1926. His initial assignment in China ostensibly had a commercial purpose. He was to close a tungsten contract with the Chungking government and arrange for the purchase of other important war materials such as zinc and rubber. It was a sign of the flexible nature of diplomatic alignments in China that the Germans could still pursue such commercial deals with the Chiang Kai-shek régime. But the official German recognition of Wang Ching-wei's Nanking government on 1 July 1941 put a stop to commercial relations between Chungking and Berlin and thus prevented Eisentraeger from carrying out that part of his mission.

The proposed commercial transactions were in any case a cover for other duties. Eisentraeger was an agent of the Abwehr economic intelligence branch and had been sent to Shanghai to set up a reporting station there. Disputes over the demarcation of their respective functions soon broke out between Siefken and Eisentraeger. Siefken could not but resent the order from Berlin that the new arrival was to have his own sources of information and was not to be under Siefken's control. Eisentraeger, for his part, objected to having to pass all his telegrams to Berlin through Siefken, who could add his own comments although he could not alter them. Eisentraeger's dependence on Siefken for funding was, no doubt, another source of friction. In settling accounts and eventually superseding Siefken, Eisentraeger found an ally in Meisinger with whom he established close relations. Although Eisentraeger's initial orders had been confined to the gathering of economic intelligence, he received an order in October 1941 from the head of the Abwehr, Admiral Canaris, to assume control of the entire Abwehr operation in the Far East. Armed with this authority, he moved to destroy his rival.

Siefken's position was weakened by continuing quarrels between his office and the German diplomatic staff in Shanghai. In July 1942 the diplomats won a round when they obtained approval from Berlin for an instruction to be issued to Siefken that henceforth all his telegrams must be laid before them in plain text for encoding. But Siefken refused to comply and instead dispatched his messages in his own codes direct to Germany from transmitters in the Italian embassy buildings in Shanghai and Peking. He proposed to set up a network of transmitting stations in Nanking, Canton, Saigon, Bangkok and Hsingking (Manchuria), all of them to be kept secret from the Japanese. Siefken told the German ambassador, Heinrich Stahmer, that there was no question of his submitting his telegrams openly to the German embassy or the consulate-general. For his part Stahmer complained that the volume of Siefken's transmissions from the embassy transmitter had led to its discovery by the Japanese, with the result that transmissions had been systematically disturbed. Stahmer was now obliged to seek Japanese approval for such transmissions from the German diplomatic transmitters in Shanghai and Peking; he therefore urged that Siefken's proposed network be disclosed to the Japanese. Siefken refused, insisting that his system could remain undetected.[18] Siefken from then on sent most of his messages from the transmitter of the Italian naval radio station in Peking, which was powerful enough to enable him to communicate direct with Berlin. He eventually moved his headquarters to Peking, leaving only a skeleton team in Shanghai. But his departure left the field open for his enemies to intrigue against him.

When Eisentraeger uncovered suspicious-looking relations between the Siefken bureau and the Japanese, he thought he had found Siefken's Achilles' heel. The Abwehr office routinely supplied the Japanese naval intelligence office with reports on Allied ship movements in the south-west Pacific area.[19] Siefken's main contact with the occupying power had been Commander Otani Inaho, who had served since August 1941 as assistant naval attaché and head of the foreign affairs section of the Japanese navy office in Shanghai (and in that capacity had been the patron and employer of 'Captain' Pick). Eisentraeger claimed to have discovered 'that the friendship [between Siefken and] Otani had a commercial basis' and that the two men had been engaged in shady private financial transactions.[20] Exploiting this allegation against Siefken, Eisentraeger achieved a dramatic coup.

In September 1942 Siefken fell ill with typhoid fever, followed by an eye infection, and underwent treatment in a Peking hospital. Meanwhile he was accused of homosexuality; no doubt Meisinger's expertise in this area of criminal investigation proved useful here. Siefken, who enjoyed the support of German naval officers in the Far East, denied the accusation but the charge stuck and was the proximate cause of his downfall. On a trip to Tokyo in late 1942, Eisentraeger was able to persuade the local German naval authorities to recall Siefken. Siefken was so upset at being bundled aside that he destroyed all the records maintained by his office – a serious setback for the German intelligence effort in the region. In November 1942 he was removed from any active role in intelligence work and ordered to return to Germany on a blockade runner. Pleading ill health, he remained in China until the end of the war. The Siefken bureau was thereupon disbanded and entirely replaced by Eisentraeger who took the cover name of 'Ludwig Ehrhardt' (as we shall now call him). His organization was henceforth known as the Ehrhardt Bureau and was assigned a budget of about RM25,000 per month.

By contrast with Siefken, a quiet character, his successor was a gregarious loudmouth. According to a US intelligence report, Ehrhardt 'tried hard to look and act like a Prussian officer, but it is also said that he does not quite succeed in this'. He was 'arrogant and jealous of all possible rivals to his authority'.[21] Ehrhardt's secretary, Gerda Kocher, in post-war interrogation by US counter-intelligence officers, painted a picture of her boss as a fun-loving playboy:

> He is a jolly fellow and he likes a good drink, good food and to
> enjoy life. His house was open to everybody who wanted to
> have a drink and was willing to keep him company. He hated
> to be alone and therefore he was almost always out or had
> somebody at his place. He [was] very talkative, especially
> when he had drunk one too many. He invited almost the
> whole of the German community. During the first two years in
> Shanghai he went very often to the night club Hungaria in Yu
> Yuen Road. He urged me to come with him. I went there
> twice (in 1941), but I disliked the place.[22]

Miss Kocher added that Ehrhardt was a babbler, boaster and spendthrift. She expressed wonder 'how such a man could be appointed to this job'.[23]

In post-war depositions to American investigators, Ehrhardt specified the main tasks of his bureau as espionage against the Soviet Union, observation of Japanese activities and gathering information about raw materials in the Far East. Omitting any mention of the western Allies was probably deliberate. In fact, his assignment included gathering information on

American and British armed forces in China and the Far East in general.[24]

The Ehrhardt Bureau succeeded in acquiring a significant volume of data concerning the Soviet Far East, dealing with such matters as food supply, transportation, manpower, raw materials, river and ocean navigation, harbours and political developments. Ehrhardt later boasted that these reports 'though always of local character and sometimes even very narrow in scope, were nevertheless very accurate in detail'.[25] The bureau also kept an eye on Soviet activities in Shanghai, employing for the purpose a German-Russian agent, V. Heyking. Ehrhardt at first found his reports quite useful, but later considered that they had deteriorated in value. As a result, Heyking was dismissed and pensioned off with German citizenship papers.[26]

Ehrhardt's deposition of Siefken had earned him the hostility of Siefken's alleged Japanese business partner: 'Otani was very embittered against me for this disruption of his dirty dealings ... and he now pursued me with his hatred. As a result I never again succeeded in establishing any kind of contact with the Japanese navy, not even through Tokyo.'[27] To his consternation, Ehrhardt made the additional discovery that his predecessor's connection with the Japanese navy had damned the Abwehr for ever in the eyes of the Japanese army: 'At that time I had not yet realized that the internal rivalry between the Japanese Army and Navy in Shanghai virtually bordered on enmity.'[28]

Only after considerable efforts was Ehrhardt able, through a contact in Berlin, to establish relations with the Japanese army chiefs in Shanghai. To these he complained that he was being 'shadowed by the police and, since my break with Otani, also by the Japanese Navy, and was being considered a spy'. The Japanese army chiefs were unable to do much to help, though they gave him an introduction to the General Staff in Tokyo. Eventually, Ehrhardt recalled, he finally received 'some kind of work permit'. A Japanese officer was appointed as a liaison between the Ehrhardt Bureau and the Japanese army. Ehrhardt appreciated his few Japanese contacts 'as decent and honourable people', though he lamented the continued hostility of the navy and the Japanese Gendarmerie which both considered his bureau 'a nuisance and a dangerous foreign element and did not miss any opportunity to warn the army and cause us difficulties whenever they could'.[29]

With the help of the Japanese army, Ehrhardt established a cryptanalytical branch which sought to decode Allied radio transmissions. Listening stations in Canton and Peking were operational by early 1943. Each employed 30–40 personnel, including wireless experts (mainly ships' radio men) and cipher specialists. Eventually they were able to hear up to 2,000 transmissions each day. Ehrhardt was astounded by the abundance of secret radio traffic intercepted by these stations. Within a few weeks the Germans had identified 80–90 British, American and Russian transmitting stations, often broadcasting *en clair* even though they were putting out secret data. Many coded messages were inadequately ciphered and Ehrhardt's specialists, headed by Captain Otto Habenicht, were easily able to decode them.

Habenicht's team included a Danish turncoat, Arthur Wedel, a former merchant marine wireless operator with 20 years of experience. He found the German set-up in Shanghai 'ridiculously inefficient'. Wedel's contemptuous dismissal of the German radio effort in Shanghai concluded: 'It was not necessary to sabotage, the Germans did it themselves.' He added apologetically: 'I did my part in passive resistance. The harm I did was to collect my salary every month.'[30]

Another turncoat employed by Ehrhardt was T. M. Thyssen, a Dutchman who, like Wedel, was a marine wireless operator. Thyssen had deserted his ship in June 1941 and offered the Germans secret Dutch naval codes. He was later assigned to work for Ehrhardt's organization as a radio operator, but after a time the German came to suspect him of communicating with enemy intelligence and he was sidelined.[31]

The historian of German Abwehr operations in the Far East, Oscar Reile, reports that Habenicht succeeded in breaking the coastal news code of the American navy. This code was never changed and was used by the Americans for all amphibious operations, so Ehrhardt was able to have a rich insight into US naval operations. Valuable information on Soviet military supply movements and on Allied air activity was obtained, as well as messages passing between the Chinese, British and American military units. Ehrhardt passed on the information to the Japanese, although he got the impression that the Japanese did not make full use of it.[32] This picture of cryptanalytical success, however, is probably exaggerated. In post-war interrogation, Habenicht stated that 'very soon after the outbreak of the war with the USA, the easy code-system was abolished, other systems were used and I never again succeeded in translating any messages until the German surrender when my work stopped automatically'.[33]

In addition to the radio operators, Ehrardt engaged agents in Canton, Peking, Harbin and elsewhere. His highest-paid Shanghai agent was Wolf Schenke, officially a correspondent for the *Völkischer Beobachter*. Another Shanghai agent, Hans Mosberg, was of Jewish origin but treated as an 'honorary Aryan' by the Nazis because of his military service in the First World War (he had been wounded eight times). Ehrhardt was unable, however, to establish the countrywide network of agents that would have been required for him to provide Berlin with a comprehensive picture of the war in China.

The replacement of Siefken by Ehrhardt did not improve relations between German diplomats and the Abwehr Bureau. 'There existed considerable tension in the relationship,' Ehrhardt later recalled, 'as the former considered our activities as an uncontrollable and inconvenient competition.'[34] As in the cases of Meisinger and Siefken, much of the acrimony arose over the question of communications. Ehrhardt sent most of his messages home through the German embassy's 'postal radio', but he used special army codes not available to diplomatic personnel, with the result that they were unable to read his messages. Eventually Ehrhardt, like his predecessor, arranged to use the Italian radio transmitter in Peking.

One of the main objects of Ehrhardt's mission was to provide Berlin with reports on the war-waging potential of the Japanese. 'This was the most difficult part of my task,' Ehrhardt later recalled, 'which I had to attend to essentially personally.' Ehrhardt confessed that the quality of intelligence acquired concerning Japan was poor; the effort 'could not be pursued energetically without endangering the whole scope of our activities' – reasoning with which Berlin finally concurred'.[35]

While spying on his ally, Ehrhardt was also supposed to exchange intelligence information with them. Mosberg prepared weekly reports on his behalf for submission to the Japanese. Ehrhardt recalled that Japanese dissatisfaction with what they received was registered in the quality of what they gave in return: 'obsolete military news about Soviet Russia which were generally already known in Berlin' and other low-grade information. Ehrhardt had succeeded in penetrating the Soviet diplomatic establishment in Shanghai by securing the services of a courier at the Russian consulate-general. This man supplied Ehrhardt with information about internal politics at the Soviet consulate as well as observations on developments in the Soviet Union after his frequent trips there.[36] This valuable information was not, however, passed on to Germany's Far Eastern ally.

上海

In 1943 the Japanese discovered what they thought was a reprise of the Sorge affair in the shape of another suspected German-Soviet double agent. Dr Ivar Lissner was a Germa 'half-Jew' who had worked in Germany for the Nazis, concealing his 'non-Aryan' background. After his racial origin was discovered he was allowed to move to China with his family and some of his property. He established himself in Shanghai and later moved to Harbin, ostensibly as a news correspondent for the *Völkischer Beobachter*, in fact as an informant for the Abwehr. He established a highly effective intelligence network in Manchuria and wrote a number of well-received reports on Japanese political activity in the area. Among his achievements was the penetration of the Soviet consulate in Harbin. So highly was he regarded that he was awarded the Kriegs Verdienst Kreuz, 1st class, and, according to Meisinger, was made a Nazi party member, notwithstanding his 'non-Aryan' blood.

Meisinger, who was anxious to avoid any repetition of the Sorge affair, had become increasingly suspicious of Lissner and launched a vigorous investigation of his activities. Meisinger's hostility was given an added edge by reports that Lissner was claiming to be Gestapo chief in Manchukuo, a usurpation of Meisinger's own purported authority over the whole of the Far East. According to Meisinger's account (in a post-war interrogation), the Japanese accused Lissner of collecting intelligence through agents in Japan and passing data on to the Russians. Meisinger reported the Japanese suspicions to Berlin and added his own denunciation of Lissner. The matter was brought to the personal attention of the Führer, who particularly resented the claim that he had issued a decree certifying that Lissner was of Aryan stock. Hitler said he had never heard of the man, that he should be recalled immediately, and that 'the best thing would be to shoot such people straight away'.[37] The Abwehr chief, Admiral Canaris, defended Lissner and insisted that he was not a Soviet agent, that his reports were extremely valuable and that he should be allowed to continue his intelligence-gathering in Manchukuo. Lissner was nevertheless arrested by the Japanese on 5 June 1943 and accused of espionage on behalf of the Soviet Union. The Germans ultimately disavowed him and he disappeared – probably executed, though one account has it that the Japanese released him in early 1945 (Meisinger thought he was still alive in a Japanese prison at the end of the war).[38]

上海

Later in the war the local Russians continued to play a major role in the Shanghai security apparatus. In May 1942 the Japanese reorganized the Municipal Police Special Branch and amalgamated most of its sections to form a new Foreign Affairs Section, headed by Superintendent H. Yamaguchi. This consisted of about eight senior Japanese, 20 foreign detectives, mainly Russians, and a larger number of subordinate Chinese staff. The removal of most of the British police officers in the course of 1942 gave the Russians, many of whom felt that their promotion to senior positions had been blocked by the British, an opportunity to move up in the service. Chief Inspector B. Maklaevsky, the first Russian to attain that rank, told the *Shanghai Times* in January 1943: 'We have finally been given a chance to improve ourselves, as the Japanese authorities have shown their appreciation of the work of the Russians in the S.M.P.'[39] Maklaevsky's press statement was criticized by other Russian officers as tactless and it sharply antagonized his remaining British colleagues, but it undoubtedly expressed a commonly held view among Russian members of the force.

Although the senior Russian officers in the Foreign Affairs Section were relatively well treated by the Japanese, most held back from wholehearted collaboration with the occupiers. A typical and influential case was that of Chief Detective Inspector Prokofiev, whose conduct was analyzed in an American intelligence report:

> One of the oldest Special Branch detectives. A man of
> exceptional integrity and scrupulously honest, he commanded

and commands respect of everyone who had an opportunity
to serve with him. Throughout his service he was connected
with Russian emigrant affairs. Loathing any kind of hypocrisy,
he used every ounce of his influence in [the] Russian
community to prevent cooperation with Japs and Germans.
He is one of those Russians who helped General Gleboff, the
late chairman of [the] Russian Emigrants' Committee, to steer
[the] local Russian community clear of various pitfalls
prepared by the Japs and their sympathizers. An authority in
his field of work, he was tolerated by the Japs in spite of the
fact that on many occasions he flatly refused to be used for
such purposes with which he could not honestly agree.[40]

Some allowance should perhaps be made for hyperbole in this unsigned report which was written partly with the object of rebutting accusations of
collaboration directed against foreign police officers, but at least in
Prokofiev's case the conclusion seems fair.

Other senior Russian detectives earned less brilliant reputations. Inspector Kochetoff, a friend and nominee of Chief Inspector Maklaevsky, 'enjoyed the reputation of a lazy officer'. Inspector Tcheremshansky was
accorded an even less flattering report:

The case of this officer is entirely a special one. It is known
that his father died in a mental home. In [an] early stage of the
Russian revolution he witnessed a brutal murder of [his]
brother by the communists and this apparently upset him
mentally. Not being an insane person in the usual meaning of
the word, nevertheless he shows to an impartial observer
many signs of unbalanced psychology. The mainspring of his
activities and outlook is unlimited and decisive hate [of]
communists. Everything that appears to his unbalanced mind
as related to communism is regarded by him with the same
hatred. Alone from the whole body of foreign detectives he
took part in some public activities with [a] political and pro-
Japanese tint…He lacked everything that a detective should

possess in the way of mental equipment. He was neither astute nor discriminate [*sic*] in dealings with people. His vivid [imagination] prevented him from forming a true picture of any case. His foreign colleagues saw to it that his reports (almost only re communist activities) were taken by the Japs with a large grain of salt. That the grain was really a large one could be seen from the fact that in spite of his many years of experience as a Special Branch detective he was held in little respect by the Jap[s].[41]

In general, the Russian police officers seem to have aimed at a quiet life under the occupation, not exerting themselves too strongly in any particular direction for fear of making enemies.

In spite of – or perhaps because of – the prominent Russian role in the Municipal Police, Russian criminals in Shanghai enjoyed a field day during the war and, in the absence of most of the pre-war Chinese crime syndicates, came to dominate the Shanghai underworld. They operated at several levels. Some took advantage of wartime conditions to perpetrate minor frauds. Others constructed large-scale rackets. None prospered more than 'Captain' Eugene Pick, who acquired several new and colourful recruits to his gang.

One of Pick's closest associates at this period was Morris Gershkovitch who also went by the alias Boris Gregorovich Mejoff. A British citizen, he was born in Singapore in 1913 to Russian émigré parents.*[42] Investigations by US intelligence yielded an informant's statement to the effect that 'Subject's father was a British-Chinese mestizo and his mother was a Russian Jewess. Subject's father was believed to be the owner of a house of prostitution in Swatow, China, while Subject's mother, Berta, was "madam" of that house.' Another informant stated that 'Subject's mother was a Russian prostitute known as "Great Berta"'.[43] But these may be calumnies: accord-

---

* Gershkovitch's statements regarding his origins were inconsistent. In one of his post-war declarations he gave Singapore, in another Shantung as his birthplace. The latter claim may have been to pretend he was not a British subject – and therefore not liable for prosecution for treason.

ing to another account, his father was a barber. His father died before he was born and his mother later became a Chinese citizen. Gershkovitch was educated at British schools in Hong Kong and Singapore. He later averred that he had 'changed my religion when [he] was in Protestant School in Singapore'.[44]

Gershkovitch was a talented linguist: besides English and Russian, he spoke Malay and Javanese as well as seven dialects of Chinese. In the 1930s he worked as a reporter for English papers in Singapore and Hong Kong. He moved to Shanghai in August 1939. At first he worked as a sports reporter for the *Shanghai Evening Post and Mercury* but resigned after a short time and in 1940 enlisted in the settlement police. There he produced influential reports on, among other matters, Jewish refugee affairs. His colleagues in the Foreign Affairs Section, however, considered him 'a doubtful and shady character' and took care to avoid him.[45] In May 1942 he was summoned by Superintendent Yamaguchi, and told that he had been promoted and assigned to investigate the black market which, as Gershkovitch recalled in a post-war deposition, 'was rampant in Shanghai at the time'.[46]

Gershkovitch's first contact with Pick was a telephone call in August 1942 in which Pick said he wanted to meet him. At their first encounter Pick accused him of being a Soviet agent and threatened him with disclosure. If Gershkovitch wanted to stay out of trouble he would have to provide Pick with reports on Russian activities in Shanghai. Gershkovitch asked his superior, Yamaguchi, for guidance and was told to do nothing. But shortly afterwards Yamaguchi changed his mind: he told Gershkovitch that his work was unsatisfactory and ordered him to collect information on movements of opinion among foreigners in Shanghai. Gershkovitch gathered compromising information on foreign nationals from the police files which he passed on to Pick in return for cash. Pick used data from such sources to destroy rival racketeering gangs. Those exposed were imprisoned or executed. On one occasion Pick boasted to the German agent Frederick Wiehl of 'eighteen pieces finished'.[47]

At the time of the mass internment of British citizens in the spring of 1943, Gershkovitch managed to remain free. He sought to be treated as a White Russian rather than a British citizen; in the police statement he submitted that April he declared: 'My present passport is that of white Russian

No. 14957 issued by the Russian Emigrants Committee on November 23, 1943 [*sic*].'[48] A Municipal Police report in January 1945 indicated that his record in the service had been 'exemplary' – but added:

> several complaints were received for indebtedness. These
> complaints were made by various persons including
> moneylenders. Due to his nationality, termination of services
> with the Police Force occurred in [*sic*] December 31st, 1943.
> He then became associated with persons suspected of being
> on intelligence service, connected with one person called
> Pick-Hovans.[49]

Pick does not, however, appear to have paid him much. Following his dismissal, Gershkovitch complained that he was without any means of support and applied to the Swiss consulate 'in order to get into a concentration camp'. The application was rejected. In May 1944 he was summoned by the Japanese Gendarmerie to the Bridge House and asked to explain why, as a foreign national, he was not interned. His answers seem to have been satisfactory for he was soon released and resumed work for Pick.

Another member of Pick's gang was a fellow-Russian, Morris Levitsky, who had collaborated with him in earlier criminal enterprises as far back as 1931. Levitsky worked for the Gestapo in Shanghai, serving as a member of the ring headed by Frederick Wiehl. He secured that job thanks to a recommendation from Pick. Wiehl's account of the relationship, given to American investigators after war, was not a little confused:

> Morris Levitsky was sent to me by Hovans [Pick]. Hovans said
> he could [not] employ him because of personal reasons.
> Levitsky was in jail with Hovans over the Russo-Asiatic Bank
> checks forgery case. For that reason and in view of the fact
> that he was now a big shot with the Japanese Navy Foreign
> Section, Hovans couldn't see his way clear to give Levitsky a
> job. I took Levitsky on knowing that he would betray me at
> once to Hovans [if it were] worth while, but I knew I could,
> by doing this favour to Hovans, get any German information

of value from him if he happened to come into it before I did. With these lines out, Levitsky was found to be already in the employ of the Soviet information service. I found that Levitsky was pretty down on the Japanese. I gave him anti-Japanese assignments and placed Mamlock to watch him. Every morning he reported to Hovans. However, when I went to see Hovans he acted as though he had not seen Levitsky. From this I took it that Hovans was not objecting to what I was doing with Levitsky (Hovans' job being to stop just such work). [Wiehl presumably meant that Pick was supposed to stop anti-Japanese espionage activity, not connive at it.] I treated Levitsky very nicely. When he did a very good job, I gave him a pair of shoes, an overcoat, hat, suit, shirts. Pretty soon I had him dressed up in good style and he then turned on Hovans and gave me the whole inside story on Hovans.[50]

Wiehl, it will be recalled, took great pride in the smart turn-out of his agents.

The so-called 'pretty boy' and thug-in-chief of the Pick gang was one of the best-known sporting figures in wartime Shanghai. Paul Lojnikoff, who was in his late 20s, had formerly served in the Shanghai Russian regiment but he acquired local celebrity as professional lightweight boxing champion of the Far East. He won the title in 1942 by knocking out 'Knocker Nakano'. After that he toured Japan and beat off a succession of challengers there. On his return to Shanghai, however, he was himself knocked out in an engagement at the Burlington Hotel with 'Battling Fester'. Lojnikoff recovered his crown in a return bout at the Canidrome, but the contest gave rise to controversy as both contenders were overweight. In April 1943 Lojnikoff, apparently still too heavy for the lightweight title, challenged 'Kid Teddy', a Polish ex-sailor, for the welterweight championship. Lojnikoff won the fight in the eighth round when his opponent's doctor threw in the towel. But the match was tainted by untoward publicity. The *Shanghai Times* reported:

More than ever before the need of a Boxing Commission was

felt in Shanghai as there seemed to be every indication that
the fight between Kid Teddy, the Welterweight Champion of
China, and Paul Lojnikoff, pretender to the Lightweight
Crown, at the Auditorium last night was not on the level. Paul
Lojnikoff won the fight on a T.K.O. Why? No one in the
Auditorium could answer.

The paper added that more than half a million dollars had been placed on
Lojnikoff, 'this fact tending to strengthen the belief that the fight was
fixed'.[51] A subsequent medical examination by three doctors determined
that 'Kid Teddy' had entered the ring with a shoulder already injured. This
did not deter Lojnikoff's supporters from backing him in his next fight,
against Joe Clara, a Filipino lightweight. In the event, illness prevented Lojnikoff from appearing and his place was taken by his brother Peter who was
defeated on a technical knockout in the sixth round. Paul made a comeback
in May 1943 when he won on points over 'Young George' in what the
Shanghai Times described as 'a less than thrilling fight' at the Palastro
Galeazzo Ciano (the Italian club named after Mussolini's son-in-law, the
former Italian consul-general in Shanghai, who was now serving as foreign
minister).

Paul Lojnikoff also had political interests. He was said to have worked as
an informer for the Japanese since as early as 1937.[52] He was certainly
doing so by mid-1941, when he was employed by the Chung Wo Industrial
Company, a front organization or sub-station of the Japanese Gendarmerie.
His primary intelligence connection, however, was with the Naval Intelligence Bureau, headed by Commander Otani; and his controller there was
Eugene Pick, who used him as his 'muscle-man'.[53] Lojnikoff also acted as a
purchasing agent for the Japanese, dealing in scrap iron, copper and industrial diamonds. His method of operation, as described in a post-war American intelligence report, differed somewhat from standard business
practice:

He is known to have advertised widely that the Japanese
Military desired to purchase certain commodities and these
commodities could be sold through him. Individuals who

desired to sell the previously mentioned articles contact[ed]
Subject who in turn referred them to the proper Japanese
authorities. The Japanese requested the individuals to submit
lists of the items available, after which they were told to return
in a few days for final negotiations. Upon their return these
individuals were told that the items offered for sale by them
were no longer needed by the Japanese. After this the items
listed were usually confiscated and they themselves were often
arrested. Subject received bonuses for transactions conducted
in this manner.[54]

Lojnikoff, far from making any secret of these Japanese connections,
boasted of them – though he insisted that they were merely of a 'commercial character'.

Exactly what he meant by that became public knowledge in January
1943 when he, his brother Peter and two others, were arrested in a joint
sweep by the French Concession police and the Japanese Gendarmerie.
They were accused of having 'confiscated' a fortune in diamonds from a
Mrs Stenewers, Peter Lojnikoff's mother-in-law, by posing as Gendarmerie
agents. In the ensuing trial the two brothers were acquitted on all charges
– except for a $400 fine imposed on Paul for helping to dispose of the jew-
els. Since he lived in some style in a luxury suite at the Cathay Hotel, he had
no difficulty paying the fine. In August that year Paul acquired a further
source of income when he married Baroness Ksenia Girard de Soucanton,
an eccentric and well-off American socialite.

With the assistance of these and other associates, Pick broadened his
realm of activity. While maintaining his criminal empire, his intelligence
connections and his interest in the stage, he embarked on a propaganda
venture. In April 1943 he was involved with a group of fellow-Russians in
establishing a monthly magazine entitled *Nakanune* ('On the Eve'). The
journal's objects were described in an application for police registration as
'propaganda of the ideas of the New Order of Great Eastern Asia amongst
[the] Russian emigrants' colony'. Among Pick's colleagues in this enterprise was a motley crew of pro-Japanese publicists headed by B.F. Ignatenko, a Harbin-born journalist who was an employee of the Japanese

Gendarmerie. Ignatenko had been a member since 1934 of the Russian Fascist Union, where he was 'head of the agitation branch'. He secured approval for the projected publication from the French police and the Japanese Navy Press Bureau. He also applied to the Municipal Police to register the new journal. Inspector Prokofiev later noted that the magazine had secured the approval of the Russian Emigrants' Committee but only on condition that it refrain from personal attacks and also from 'any form of pressure on members of the Russian community in connection with the canvassing for subscriptions and advertisements or in any other manner'. This warning had been necessitated, Prokofiev continued, by virtue of the fact that the main promoters of the publication 'are known in the community on account of their past and/or present connections with certain organs of the Japanese Intelligence Service. Apparently, it was considered that the possibility was not unlikely of an undue advantage being taken of this fact by the said persons or their sub-agents in order to boost their enterprise.'

Before the magazine made its first appearance, a split took place between Pick and Ignatenko, as a result of which Pick issued a public announcement in the Russian press (signed E. Hovans) that he had 'nothing whatever to do with the proposed publication'. Publication of the first issue of the magazine was held up in May 1943, pending approval by the Municipal Police Censorship Office. Meanwhile its contents were analyzed by Inspector Prokofiev. He noted that its main thrust was anti-communist. The paper also contained 'a few rather rude outbursts of a personal character' directed against local Russian newspapermen. Prokofiev commented:

> A number of names are quoted rather unnecessarily in order
> to illustrate the predominance of Jews amongst the
> membership of the local Soviet Citizens' Club. The
> susceptibility of members of the local German community
> may be hurt by a few expressions contained in the section
> devoted to Soviet humour. Otherwise, from the purely police
> viewpoint, there seems to be nothing objectionable in the
> declared policy of the magazine, nor in the contents of its
> issue under review.

Superintendent Yamaguchi commented that 'the founders are dubious figures', though he decided to permit publication. But the Japanese 'Chief of the Fourth Department', to whom the dossier was submitted for a final decision, forbade the magazine's appearance.[55] Just as Pick's support seems to have been behind the initial approval given to the publication, so his falling-out with Ignatenko was very likely the main reason for its failure to see the light of day.

Pick's star, however, was beginning to fade. From early 1943 onwards a change in the political atmosphere began to be discernible in Russian Shanghai. As the meaning of the Soviet victory at Stalingrad sank in, the White Russians lost their happy confidence in the imminent collapse of the hated revolutionary régime. The scent of victory slowly dissipated and a new fear was born: with the USSR's victory in the west might well come their intervention in the war in the east. The Soviet divisions in Siberia, long stationed in a defensive posture, might move to the offensive and advance south against the Japanese. For the local Russians, as for pro-Axis Shanghai in general, the prospect of a communist conquest of Shanghai slowly shifted from the realm of awful phantasmagoria to dreaded anticipation.

11 Endgames

In September 1942 the Japanese dismantled what the *Shanghai Times* called the 'last symbol of Anglo-US despotism' in Shanghai, the statue of the former inspector-general of the Chinese Maritime Customs, Sir Robert Hart.[1] They also destroyed the memorial on the Bund to the Allied dead of the First World War, a strange gesture since they, after all, had been part of the victorious coalition in that war. There were other indications of the end of Anglo-Saxon predominance. The stock of American films, which continued to be shown in Shanghai during the first year of the occupation, began to run down in late 1942. Thereafter, cinema-goers had to make do mainly with Chinese, Japanese and Soviet films. The Grand was reduced to staging 'Chow and Chow, the Whistling Ventriloquists'. These tokens of a new cultural order were the prelude to a diplomatic revolution: the end of the foreign concessions in Shanghai.

The Japanese and the Allies, alike anxious to pose as supporters of legitimate Chinese nationalism, engaged in a curious diplomatic race to surrender the foreign enclaves to their respective Chinese protégés. On 9 January 1943 the Wang Ching-wei régime declared war on Britain and the United States. In return, the Japanese signed a convention formally committing themselves to the abrogation of extraterritorial privileges and the restoration to China of Japanese concessions, of the international settlements at Shanghai and Kulangsu and of the legation quarter in Peking. Two days later the British and the Americans, who had announced in October 1942 that they would begin negotiations with the Chinese on the return of the foreign concessions, signed treaties to that effect with the Chinese. The Japanese press scoffed at these agreements as empty gestures and took the opportunity to sneer: 'Gone today are the Liddells, the Brownes, the Smythes of the Shanghai Municipal Council and the Shanghai Municipal Police. Gone also are Taipans Mitchell, Keswick and their breed, gone on the evacuation boats that carried them back to their home countries.'[2] On 14 March 1943 the

Japanese Prime Minister, General Tojo, visited Shanghai and publicly stressed that Japan really intended to return all the foreign enclaves to China.

In Shanghai, the French Concession was the first to disappear. In the early months of the occupation the Japanese had left the concession more or less to its own devices. Although they had obtained the French consul-general's agreement in principle to the stationing of Japanese gendarmes in the concession, they did not immediately exercise this right. When they did so in early 1942, only a tiny token unit was installed. In April that year, however, the Japanese consul-general, Horiuchi, presented his French colleague with the demand for a more substantial Japanese presence. Margerie believed that the pressure emanated from the Japanese army, an impression that Horiuchi and the Japanese Gendarmerie chief encouraged by hinting that they were more sympathetic to the French point of view. Together with his police chief, L. Fabre, Margerie stalled for ten days, but eventually they were compelled to yield. Margerie consoled himself with some minor Japanese concessions such as a promise that the Japanese would not parade in uniform in the streets and an undertaking that the new arrangement would not be made public. These titbits Margerie attributed to the 'relations of confidence we have been able to establish with the [Japanese] Consulate-General and the Gendarmerie'.[3] The agreement did not take effect until July, when 150 Japanese gendarmes were installed at a post on the Avenue Pétain. Meanwhile, parades and inspections of the French police and military units were orchestrated in a pathetic effort to assert what was left of French pride.

In February 1943 the Vichy French reluctantly announced that they would relinquish their extraterritorial judicial rights and hand over all their concessions in China to the Wang Ching wei régime. These decisions would be put into effect 'as soon as it will be found possible'.[4] Talks opened in Shanghai in May between the French and Wang's foreign minister, resulting in an agreement on the handover to the Chinese of the French concessions at Tientsin, Hankow and Canton.[5] The greatest prize came last. The formal 'rendition' of the concession in Shanghai finally took place on 30 July 1943.

The end of the little French foothold in Shanghai had both local and international consequences. Fabre, perhaps ashamed of his role in these transactions and regretful that he had not joined those of his men who had rallied to de Gaulle in 1940, committed suicide a few weeks later.[6] The Vichy government's decision to hand over their concessions to Wang Ching-wei provoked outrage on the part of the Chungking government. Although the French Ambassador, Henri Cosme, was accredited to the Wang régime, the Vichy authorities had hedged their bets by maintaining a senior representative, Jean Paul-Boncour, at Chungking. When news of the Vichy-Wang agreement arrived there, Paul-Boncour was summoned to receive 'the most emphatic protest possible in diplomatic language'; he suffered the further sanction of being excluded from a number of diplomatic functions.[7] Beyond that only one recourse remained to the Chiang Kai-shek government: in August 1943 they severed relations with Vichy and a few weeks later recognized the French Committee of National Liberation as the legitimate government of France. The one-armed, Russian-born, naturalized Frenchman, General Zinodi Pechkoff (adoptive son of Maxim Gorki), was appointed de Gaulle's personal representative in Free China soon afterwards.

The rendition of the concession was succeeded two days later by the return of the International Settlement to nominal Chinese authority almost exactly a century after its foundation. The retrocession took place on the basis of an agreement between the Japanese and Chinese (Wang Ching-wei) governments – though the authority of the former to grant it and of the latter to receive it were equally questionable.[8] The Shanghai Municipal Council was abolished and its functions and assets were taken over by the puppet régime. The administrations of the former foreign areas were united with those of the Chinese municipality in a single city government. The police forces of all three areas were also amalgamated, although the separate existence and the uniquely valuable file collection of the Foreign Affairs Section (former Special Branch of the Municipal Police) were maintained throughout the Japanese occupation. The Shanghai Volunteer Corps had already been disbanded in September 1942 'in view of the present circumstances' – though the *Municipal Gazette* announced that former members would be permitted to continue to use its dining room.[9] On 2 August 1943 the Japanese chairman of the Municipal Council formally handed over the settlement to the mayor of the pro-Wang Chinese municipal government.

Later the same day 'President' Wang Ching-wei addressed a celebratory meeting at the Grand Theatre. Wang declared that Anglo-American 'economic exploitation and cultural anaesthesia' had made China 'fall deep into spiritual and material slumber'. With Japan's assistance, 'the accumulated evils of a hundred years' had now been swept away.[10] The *Shanghai Times* rejoiced, calling the retrocession 'the most impressive event of the present century'.[11]

In reality, of course, ultimate power, after the renditions as before, remained in the hands of the Japanese. The occupiers retained control of the municipal prison and reserved their position on the issue of extraterritorial rights, including freedom from taxation, of Japanese citizens. In the First District (the former settlement and two adjacent Axis areas) nine out of the top 20 officials and 12 out of the top 20 police officers were still Japanese, generally titled 'advisers' to department chiefs.[12] But if the Japanese gesture in returning the concessions was hollow and hypocritical, the same might be said of the almost simultaneous undertaking by the British and Americans to return their concessions to the Chungking government. They, after all, had already been ejected from all of them and were merely recognizing, *ex post facto*, and not altogether willingly, an uncomfortable reality – without paying any immediate price at all, since Chiang Kai-shek was in no position to exercise his newly recognized rights.

Further symbolic steps followed. In August 1943 the French Club, which had already excluded British and American members, announced that it would admit Chinese citizens to membership for the first time since its foundation in 1905.[13] To coincide with the 'double tenth' celebrations on 10 October 1943, English and French street names were sinicized: Avenue Edward VII became Great Shanghai Road; Avenue Haig became Hua Shang Road; Broadway became Ta Ming Road; and Jessfield Road became Fan Huang Tu Road.

上海

The demise of the concessions was seen as an Axis diplomatic triumph. But hardly had the Wang authorities assumed the cloak of authority in Shanghai than the Axis coalition began to crumble. The publication on 8 September

1943 of the Italian armistice agreement with the Allies had immediate local consequences. The Japanese denounced the decision as a betrayal and took reprisals against Italians in Shanghai. Hitherto regarded as friendly citizens of an Allied power, they suddenly found themselves placed in the same category as British, American and other enemy aliens. The San Marco Battalion of Italian Marines, the diplomatic and consular staff, as well as all Italian civilians, were now liable for internment. Most were rounded up and placed in camps.

Within a matter of weeks, a dramatic reversal occurred. Following Mussolini's escape from custody and his proclamation of the 'Italian Social Republic' under German protection in North Italy, the Japanese government, on 28 September 1943, recognized his new régime as the legitimate government of Italy. Wang Ching-wei followed suit two days later. Consequently some diehards, among them the consul-general in Shanghai, Pagano di Melito, pledged their continued support to the Duce. On 12 December 1943 more than 2,000 born-again fascists assembled at the grounds of the Nagai Cotton Mill to receive 'liberation certificates' marking their release from internment. After an address by the Japanese Consul-General and a speech by Lieutenant-Commander Bordandini Baldassarri, chairman of the Provisional Italian Committee, the crowd gave the fascist salute.

The Italian Ambassador, Marchese Taliani de Marchio, was one of the few who refused to take the oath of allegiance to Mussolini's rump republic. He and his wife were interned, at first in a pleasant house on Kinnear Road, later in less comfortable quarters at 121 Rubicon Road, where they were compelled to do manual labour. 'One of our guards was crazy', the ex-ambassador recalled after the war, 'and the other two were always drunk.' On one occasion, the Marchesa, a niece of the former Habsburg emperor, Franz Josef, was knocked down by a Japanese guard. She slapped him in the face. Another time all three guards got drunk and the 'crazy' one waved his samurai sword before Taliani's face several times as if to slash him. In the end the swordsman sliced his own foot severely, resulting in a two-month stay in hospital.[14]

Another visible sign of the Italian collapse was the decision by the sailors on the *Conte Verde* to prevent their ship being sequestered by the Japanese navy. The Lloyd Trestino liner had been lying idle in Shanghai harbour since the outbreak of the Pacific War, except for her voyage to Lourenço Marques when she carried American civilian exchangees accompanied by Japanese officers. At 7.00 a.m. on 9 September 1943, the crew scuttled the ship within sight of Americans held in the Pootung internment camp. The 615-ton Italian river gunboat *Lepanto* was also sunk. For months the two hulks lay overturned side by side in shallow water opposite the Bund. The crews of both ships as well as of another Italian gunboat, *Carlotta*, were all interned.

The Italian surrender had untoward consequences for the German intelligence effort in Shanghai. The Ehrhardt bureau had hitherto relied on the Italian radio station in Peking for transmission of messages to and from Berlin. Ehrhardt failed to secure permission from the Japanese to operate a station in Shanghai, though he was eventually permitted to do so in Canton. But there were long delays in setting up the Canton transmitter. Scheduled to become operational on 24 July 1944, it actually started working only in October. It turned out in any case to be of little use to Ehrhardt, since outgoing telegrams had to be relayed from Shanghai to Canton by 'air mail', which took up to three weeks. Incoming telegrams arrived by the same slow route. These delays were aggravated by errors in calculating the time difference between Berlin and Canton. Moreover, some messages had to be repeated more than 20 times because of inaudibility, leading to complaints that such repetition offered the Allies obvious interception possibilities.

The disintegration of the Axis was compounded by Japanese requisitions of German firms in Shanghai. The German High Command was so incensed at the 'unintelligible attitude' of their ally on this issue that inquiries were ordered into whether there had been similar German requisitions of Japanese firms in German-occupied territory in Europe that might be used as a bargaining counter in negotiations with Japan.[15]

上海

On the other side of the lines, the Allied coalition in China also cracked at its joints. In August 1943 the heads of SOE and OSS, Hambro and Donovan, loosened the bonds of their 'treaty' of the previous year. The British predominance for operations out of India and the American for those based in China was reaffirmed. But the 'ungentlemanly warfare' chiefs agreed that too hard and fast a delineation of spheres of subversive operations was undesirable. OSS in India and SOE in China would now be permitted to establish such organizations as were necessary for their work – so long as it was with the full knowledge and consent of the other partner.[16] The vague elasticity of this new formulation engendered even more inter-Allied bickering than the rigidity of the old one. One historian comments that 'this was a charter of equal misery' for both the British and the American commanders in the Far East.[17] Both sides broke the agreement. In China, in particular, the British refused to restrict their activities to a purely intelligence-gathering role. Nor would they fully inform the Americans what they were up to. The British SIS representative in New Delhi was not far off the mark in 1944 in suggesting that the 'treaty', in fact, 'was never implemented'.[18]

In the final year of the war the British inaugurated a Chinese counter-espionage unit based in India. The organization took shape under the combined auspices of SOE and the DIB, the Indian government equivalent of MI5. Lieutenant-Colonel Kenneth Bourne, former head of the Shanghai Municipal Police, was appointed to take charge of this new 'China Intelligence Section'. Bourne operated under the nominal direction of the security control branch of the Calcutta Police but worked secretly with SOE. Bourne's organization was known by the code name 'BRISTOL'.[19] Its main objects were to ensure the loyalty of SOE's Chinese agents and to prevent leakage of SOE's operational plans. Agents of 'Bristol' were to be infiltrated into 'the principal Chinese areas in India where intelligence regarding Chinese underground activities could be obtained'. The DIB agreed to pay for administrative costs, provided SOE covered agents' salaries. The DIB 'also made a grant towards a bribery fund'. By August 1945 Bourne had hired five full-time agents and two sub-agents. 'Bristol' gradually extended its field of activity. Like the old Shanghai Municipal Police Special Branch, 'Bristol' acquired 'elements of both an intelligence and a criminal investigation bureau', acting as an internal check on SOE's Chinese agents and as a general watchdog for 'suspected Chinese political agents', smuggling and cross-border criminal activity.[20]

By the last months of the war, suspicions between the main British and American intelligence organizations in China had reached paranoid levels. On one occasion an OSS official told Donovan that he had obtained possession of a document proving 'that one of the British missions in the China Theatre is here to penetrate for counter-espionage purposes OSS and American Army and Air Force units'.[21] On another, the American commander in China complained to the head of the British Military Mission about reports that the British had plans 'to arm 30,000 Chinese bandits'.[22]

The Americans not only fell out with the British. They also quarrelled bitterly with one another. Although the OSS Director of Operations in China, Milton Miles, was formally subordinated to Tai Li, his real loyalty was supposed (by the Americans) to be to OSS. In fact, he refused to obey orders from Donovan and, when the OSS chief tried to bring him into line, Miles used his influence in the navy in Washington to maintain his independence.[23] SACO, as a result, remained virtually a law unto itself. Miles was said to boast of how he attended political trials with Tai Li at the end of which the accused were buried alive. General Stilwell accused Miles of making secret arms deals with Tai Li. And both Stilwell and Donovan despaired that Miles had fallen totally under the spell of his Chinese friend, virtually emasculating the entire American subversive effort in the country. In November 1944 Donovan complained bitterly to the White House that the Chinese had opposed every effort of OSS to establish itself in China.[24]

The dissension in the Allied camp was visible in Sino-American relations, above all, and culminated in a severe crisis at the summit of power. 'Vinegar Joe' Stilwell's blunt manner and his presumptuous insistence that he knew better than Chiang Kai-shek how to organize the Chinese army deeply affronted the Chinese leader. The two men conceived a deep mutual loathing and Stilwell even discussed with Roosevelt plans for Chiang's assassination – at what level of seriousness is unknown.[25] In October 1944 Chiang finally lost patience with Stilwell and ordered him out of the country. His successor as American commander in China, General Albert C. Wedemeyer, was more diplomatic in handling his hosts, but he too complained that SACO amounted to a private army. He told the head of the British Military Mission, Major-General Grimsdale, in December 1944, that he had 'General Marshall working on the US Navy Department to clean this up'.[26]

OSS could nevertheless claim some noteworthy achievements. SACO succeeded in establishing several guerrilla camps behind Japanese lines, one just 200 miles south-west of Shanghai. If Miles's account is to be believed, SACO was responsible for more than 20,000 Japanese killed in the course of 1,326 separate actions between 1943 and 1945.[27] But Miles almost certainly exaggerated the achievements of his organization.[28]

Only one operation of any consequence was carried out in Shanghai. On 4 May 1944, a bomb exploded on the fourteenth floor of the Park Hotel. In earlier days the hotel had been a favourite rendezvous for Nazis in Shanghai, but Gerda Kocher, Ludwig Ehrhardt's secretary, grumbled that after the outbreak of the Pacific War 'Japs poured in and decent foreigners moved out'. The Japanese took a particular liking to the restaurant on the fourteenth floor. Kocher recollected with disgust that the place became 'overcrowded with Japs, often drunk, in slippers and dangling suspenders'.[29] The bomb killed several Japanese officials.

One common objective of British and American subversive organizations was creating effective escape channels for Allied servicemen in China. The most spectacular escape was engineered in October 1944 from Ward Road Prison in Shanghai by Lieutenant-Commander Columbus Darwin Smith, whose ship, the USS *Wake*, had been captured off the Bund on the first day of the Pacific War. He made his getaway together with an American marine corporal and a British naval officer. It was the first successful escape from the prison on record. The two officers had been imprisoned together in a cell which had steel bars on the window and door. The cell was 25 feet above the inner garden of the prison. The men planned their break-out carefully with the aid of outside confederates who managed to throw hacksaw blades over the outer prison wall in a bamboo tube. The escapers made ropes out of canvas sheets. They wove 12-foot poles out of thousands of bamboo sticks brought in supposedly to support string beans in the prison's vegetable garden. Using the hacksaw blades they sawed through the cell bars. They clambered over the outer prison wall with the aid of the ropes and poles. When they got to the top of the wall they found, to their horror, that the street below was crowded with Chinese and also some Japanese. 'It was a lovely fall evening,' Smith later recalled, 'and I never saw so many Chinese in one place. We were scared to death – after being so successful that far. Honestly we were horrified at that point, but we couldn't go back at that stage so we boldly piled down the rope one after another, landing on schedule at 22.30 amid gasping Chinese.'[30] Then they melted into the crowd and bolted. Although they held no identification papers and were unable to change out of their prison clothes, they succeeded miraculously in passing unchallenged through several Japanese checkpoints. During the night and early morning they walked 24 miles, reaching the hills near Shanghai. The Japanese placed a price of US$1 million on Smith's head but none of the Chinese peasants the escapers met betrayed them. Eventually they encountered guerrillas under the control of Tai Li. With their help, they made their way to unoccupied China where Smith joined SACO.

In early 1945 the Americans took steps to tighten control of OSS operations in China and to weaken Tai Li's authority over it. By the summer the number of OSS operatives in China had greatly expanded and the organization's geographical reach was extended. One OSS intelligence team succeeded in penetrating Shanghai. Agents obtained the code used by the Japanese navy operating in Shanghai waters. The X-2 (counter-intelligence) branch of OSS in China built up a master file of 15,000 'black' names of enemy agents and suspects which led to the arrest of several of these at the end of the war.

上海

As the struggle for mastery in East Asia moved towards a climax, members of the foreign criminal underworld in Shanghai began to reorganize their affairs. 'Captain' Pick, ever on the look-out for new opportunities, embarked on a new venture. In June 1944 he set out from Shanghai for the Philippines on a mission for the Japanese Naval Intelligence Bureau. His nominal controller, whom he manipulated with consummate skill, was Ikushima Kichizo, a civilian employee of the section. An episcopal Christian who had studied at Amherst College in Massachusetts and Cambridge University in England, Ikushima had served as a dean at a university in Kyoto. Pick was accompanied by a motley gang of adventurers and desperadoes from Shanghai. These included his sidekick Morris Gershkovitch, his enforcer, the boxer Paul Lojnikoff, a Portuguese black-marketeer, Francisco

Carneiro, who had served as Lojnikoff's manager, and 'Princess' Sumaire's Italian lawyer, Dr Terni.

Another of the group was even more closely connected to the Maharajah's daughter. Among the guests at Sumaire's much-publicized party in the Park Hotel in December 1941 had been a Japanese playboy, Takami Morihiko ('Mori' to his friends). Takami was an American as well as a Japanese citizen. A dark-skinned, square-jawed, bearded young man, well-built and of medium height, he was said to look 'more Hawaiian or Filipino than Japanese'.[31] Like Sumaire and other members of her circle, Takami had a weakness for spurious titles: he called himself a 'count', though he was rumoured to be the son of a pharmacist in Yokohama. In fact, he had been born in New York in 1914, son of a Japanese-American doctor who was head of the city's Japanese residents' association. He was educated at an expensive private school in Lawrenceville, New Jersey, and spent one year at Amherst College. In 1935 he went to Japan, where he enjoyed the patronage of Count Kabayama Aisuko (hence perhaps his pretensions to a title of his own). Two years later was conscripted into the Japanese army, in which he served until December 1940. Apparently in order to avoid further service in the regular armed forces, he then moved to Shanghai, where he joined the civilian staff of the Japanese Naval Intelligence Bureau.

In April 1943 Sumaire, who had still not divorced her husband in India, married Takami in a 'swank' ceremony at the Park Hotel. The marriage was played up as a sign of Indo-Japanese amity. Takami's employers presented the couple with a lavish wedding present: a villa, formerly inhabited by Americans, at 279 Route Culty in the French Concession. Ensconced in her new home, Sumaire became a hostess in grand style. Champagne and black caviar were staples of her parties. Guests were mainly German and Japanese as well as officials of the Wang Ching-wei puppet régime and White Russian and other collaborators.

But Sumaire's second marriage was short-lived. She discovered that her husband had long been enjoying an affair with Marquita Kwong, mistress of the Chinese-American collaborationist broadcaster Hubert Moy. Sumaire and her husband quarrelled frequently and he was said to have beaten her out of the house on several occasions – but she always returned for lack of money. Before his departure for the Philippines with the Pick gang, Takami had a long discussion with his wife in which they considered divorce.

Pick assembled some supplementary personnel for his Manila expedition. These included Hans Egon Fritz Arnheim (or Aronheim), known as Hans Fritz, an Austrian-Jewish refugee and former newspaperman, who had somehow acquired a Swiss passport. Once an informer for the Vienna police, he had been a petty crook in Shanghai. He worked for Pick as 'informer-secretary-valet-stooge' and was assigned to watch Swiss and Germans as well as Jewish refugees.[32] Two Russian youths came along to work as radio technicians. One of these was Vyacheslav Toropovsky, stepson of James Smart, former head of the British wireless monitoring station in Shanghai.

On 15 June 1944 the *Manila Tribune* carried the following news report:

Group of Third Party Aliens
Now in Manila

Several neutral foreigners who, since the outbreak of the GEA [Great East Asia] War have been living in various parts of the Southern regions, arrived in Manila recently, according to authoritative sources. It is understood that they will proceed to their destination after brief sojourn here. The matter was made public to prevent any groundless rumors suggesting that the visitors are prisoners of war or internees.

Over the next few months, wild rumours nevertheless circulated in Shanghai and Manila about the objects of the expedition and the fate of the group. One account even had it that they had all 'been executed by USSR OGPU for espionage work'.[33]

The chief ostensible purpose of the journey was to uncover links between foreign nationals in the Philippines and the local resistance movement. No doubt the expertise in handling foreign civilian affairs that Pick and his companions had acquired in Shanghai recommended them to the Japanese for this task. Little was achieved in that connection, although a few unwary traders in arms, radios and other forbidden materials were entrapped and punished. Arvid Falk Jensen, a Danish gunrunner, was caught, arrested and apparently killed while in custody. An Irish priest, Father Kelly, who had smuggled goods and medicines to American internees, was also captured and, according to one account, 'crucified by the Japanese'.[34] The reports of these two cases, however, are found in post-war interrogations of Filipino witnesses and are not corroborated by other evidence. Almost the only useful work of the group was performed by the two young Russians, whose radio monitoring station intercepted US naval communications. If Toropovsky's own post-war account is to be believed, they also picked up messages enabling them to anticipate American air raid targets in Manila and even to forecast correctly on 16 October 1944 that the Americans would shortly be landing somewhere in the Philippines – but the Japanese, Toropovsky relates, considered such reports 'dangerous thoughts' and refused to act on them. Since their warnings were largely ignored, the radio operators relaxed their efforts and did not even bother to maintain their expensive equipment. They used their Packard Bell disk recorder 'mainly for recording the hit parade'.[35]

Behind the officially sanctioned intelligence purpose of the expedition was its real, quasi-criminal objective, which was the establishment of an import-export link between the Philippines and Shanghai for manufactured goods that were in short supply at either end. The first cargo of such goods was transported with the gang's luggage aboard a boat that sailed from Shanghai on 10 June 1944. It carried 50 crates of Ruby Queen cigarettes, 40 of medicines, and a large quantity of office equipment. A load of electric light bulbs arrived from Shanghai and a cargo of Manila hemp rope and other products was sent in the other direction from Manila.

Having arrived in Manila, the gang took advantage of the opportunity to combine business with pleasure. They spent most of their time in nightclubs, gambling, smoking Ruby Queen cigarettes and associating with local women. The first night, Takami, dressed in a sharkskin suit, went downtown. 'Paul Lojnikoff headed for the night clubs the day after we arrived', recalled one of his companions.[36] Among the gang's favourite haunts were the Gastronome tearoom, the Torino café and the '69 Club'. Pick was particularly fond of the Gastronome because the juke-box there had a record of him singing that he liked to show off to acquaintances. In their off-duty hours in Manila bars, the gang members spoke with surprising freedom about their activities, avowing openly their connections with the Japanese authorities. They told some people that they were working as purchasing agents for the Japanese navy; others that they had been sent to Manila 'to learn what former American property was then in the hands of Filipinos and neutral aliens'. Gershkovitch said that he was a British citizen 'but he hated the British because they had treated him badly'.[37] From time to time they reported Filipinos to the Japanese authorities for minor offences. So far as can be judged, their victims were mainly small fry such as the proprietor of the Empire State Cleaners on Mabini Street. The gang's investigations appear to have developed into a protection racket: in return for payments, Pick and his associates would undertake not to report miscreants.

Soon after their arrival, Lojnikoff took up with an 'actress', Españita de Vidal, who was working in the Royal Room at the Avenue Hotel. One of the gang's Russian radio operators recalled:

> I doubt if Paul knew what he was doing, but he certainly
> struck oil when he met this jane. It seems she knew every man
> worth knowing in the Philippine Islands, all the way from
> Manuel Quezon down through the Chief of the Manila
> Constabulary ... and all the rest of Insular Society. Her
> husband seemed to be no obstacle to her in her jaunts with
> many of these men. She knew José P. Laurel and Ambassador
> Vargas, and she often played 'madame' for them, pimping out
> sweet young things from Manila's better families and
> introducing them to the 'fathers of the country'. This is what
> Lojnikoff made gee-gee eyes at, as he sat at a table in the Royal
> Room. Pretty soon he had Españita handing him information
> by the ream. He didn't understand half of what was in them,
> but anyway passed them on to Ikushima.[38]

In return for the information, the boxer 'provided Mrs de Vidal with protection from unsympathetic Filipinos'.[39]

In mid-June 1944 a meeting took place in a house near the Malacañang Palace between the gang and their Japanese controller, Ikushima. The encounter took place in the residence of the Japanese naval attaché, formerly the compound of the Hong Kong and Shanghai Bank. Ikushima told them that the Filipinos seemed to be adapting poorly to the Co-Prosperity Sphere. The gang was instructed to investigate the causes of disaffection. They were also 'to study the other nationals in the Philippines, to learn what their sympathies were' and to search out corruption in public utilities.

On 8 August 1944 Pick left Manila, complaining of bad health, and returned to Shanghai. He seems to have taken with him much of the money allocated for salary payments to his colleagues. Lojnikoff now 'set himself up as head of the group', but the boxer lacked Pick's magnetic authority and the gang soon began to fall apart. Gershkovitch, who later complained that Lojnikoff had 'bullied him continually', spent most of his time in the '69 Club'. On one occasion he went to Tom's Dixie Inn to collect some money that Lojnikoff explained was a 'commission on a business deal'. Lojnikoff and Carneiro 'spoke deprecatingly' of Gershkovitch who looked 'ragged and poor' in contrast to the prosperous appearance of the other gang members.[40] Lojnikoff continued blackmailing activities and accumulated a considerable fortune. The gang also branched out into other enterprises. At one point Carneiro and Lojnikoff purchased some industrial diamonds – or rather took them and promised to pay later (the money was never forthcoming). They also tried to buy and sell guns and ammunition.

By late 1944 it was plain that an American landing on the main Philippine island, Luzon, was imminent. Leaving Gershkovitch and Takami behind to fend for themselves, Lojnikoff and the others left Manila on 24 December 1944, two weeks before the Americans landed.

In Takami's absence, Sumaire had encountered money problems. For a time she survived by selling furniture and other personal effects. From December 1944 Ikushima arranged for her to receive a stipend of 50,000 Chinese dollars a month from the Japanese Navy Office. In letters from Manila, Takami insisted that he still loved her. As proof of his continued devotion, he sent her several presents with returning gang members, including a leather suitcase in the lining of which he had concealed ten bars of silver which she was able to sell for a high price. The suitcase also contained 24 yards of sharkskin, six pairs of nylon stockings and a box of cigars (a gift for a German-Brazilian acquaintance). Sumaire, however, had lost interest in Takami. She sought consolation from a number of other men – and, it appears, women. 'Subject', noted a post-war American intelligence report, 'in her pursuit of happiness, has often been physically intimate with both sexes concurrently. She evidently runs the gamut of perversion since she had also been known to be both sadistically and masochistically inclined.'[41] Her women-friends included Margot Chan (alias Nakamura) 'who recently owned the shortlived Donald Duck Bar on Yu Yuen Road' and Lydia Milanowska, estranged wife of a German, Karl Munz, 'who was suspected of having been in the employ of the German Gestapo in Shanghai'.[42] Sumaire also had a long and stormy relationship with a journalist, Roger Pierard, who had been in charge of propaganda in Egal's Free French movement in Shanghai in 1940–41. Pierard had earlier been arrested and tortured by the Japanese and sentenced to two years in prison.[43] Sumaire was later accused of having collected compromising information on Pierard with which she blackmailed him. She developed other liaisons with an escaped German prisoner-of-war and a French-Chinese, Vincent Tang, 'described as the Number One man of the French Club'. According to the same American report, Sumaire lived from early 1945 until the Japanese surrender 'as mistress of Sasaki, a Japanese big shot of whom it was said that he could send anybody to Bridge House'.[44]

Shanghai had always been notorious as a refuge for renegades, black sheep and bad hats. But the topsy-turvy morality of occupation seemed to dredge the worst human filth out of the mud of the Whangpoo. Sumaire and her friends were only the most visible examples of a general collapse of standards of decency in a city never celebrated for decorum. A Chinese doctor from Shanghai, who reached Kunming in unoccupied China in May 1944, sought to convey to Allied interrogators some sense of the contaminated social climate of the city: 'The whole moral construction of the people of Shanghai is undermined. Everywhere and in all walks of life extortion, corruption, bribery and blackmail exist.'[45] In this atmosphere, concepts such as resistance and collaboration were almost emptied of meaning and the most elaborate urban society in China was reduced to the morality of the jungle.

上海

The later part of the war was a grim period in Shanghai. Rationing was extended to salt, soap and matches and permitted quantities diminished. The short-sighted Japanese economic policies of plunder and expropriation reduced Shanghai's manufacturing production by early 1945 to barely a quarter of its 1937 level. As the transportation and supply system crumbled, food shortages in the city became acute and prices soared. Money became worthless and gold the favoured store of value.

On the night of 9/10 June 1944 the first Allied air raid of the war hit Shanghai. Another followed on 5 July, a third four days later. After a further raid in November, electricity could be provided only for a few hours in the evening. Much of what remained of Shanghai's industrial production was paralyzed. In the following months many of the raids took place in daylight, carried out by large US super-fortress bombers.

Meanwhile the decline in the military and political might of the Third Reich began to have ripple effects in the Far East. When the Abwehr chief, Admiral Canaris, was implicated in the July 1944 bomb plot against Hitler, his intelligence agency was taken over by Himmler's SS. This institutional rivalry was reflected in Shanghai in relations between the Ehrhardt Bureau and the Gestapo organization headed by Meisinger. Ehrhardt was instructed by Berlin to place his bureau under Meisinger's orders. He contrived to comply nominally, while secretly maintaining the independence of his organization. He was assisted in this manoeuvre by the Japanese, with whom he was by now on better terms and who were highly suspicious of Meisinger.

After the war Ehrhardt described this episode to American interrogators:

> After the plot against the Fuehrer's life on Ju[ly] 20, 1944,
> Gestapo pressure again increased and developed into a
> planned inveiglement campaign of all party circles with the
> object of my deposition...Due to the excessive indecency of
> these intrigues I ... refused any kind of capitulation and
> determined to see the fight through. The Japanese got wind of
> these internal events and got so worked up over the unjustified
> and dirty manner of the attacks on me that I had considerable
> difficulty in restraining them from taking independent action

against the slanderers. Such action could have been used as the basis for justifiable accusations of disloyalty against me.[46]

In December 1944 Meisinger and Huber visited the Japanese General Staff in Tokyo and asked that they be recognized as having authority over Ehrhardt. According to Ehrhardt's later account, the Japanese refused and declared that they had full confidence in Ehrhardt, whereas they did not have the same confidence in Huber. The Japanese threatened that if the German High Command insisted on subordinating Ehrhardt to Huber, they would prohibit any German military information activities whatsoever in territories under their control.

Shortly thereafter, Ehrhardt received 'strict orders from Berlin' to undertake 'collaboration' with Huber, for which purpose a supplementary budget of RM5,000 was placed at his disposal. His position strengthened by Japanese support and by control of this budget, Ehrhardt found that Huber, on his return from Tokyo, adopted a new tack:

> For the first time in several years, he paid me a visit and, in a
> relatively decent and straightforward manner, gave the
> following explanation. He had been to Tokyo to participate in
> a conference on the subject of my deposition and the take-
> over of the [Ehrhardt Bureau] by the Gestapo. However, it had
> been found that most of the accusations against me were
> unfounded. He sincerely regretted having participated in this
> action and tendered his formal apologies.

Ehrhardt accepted Huber's apology and the two agreed to cooperate henceforth.

The touching reconciliation was only paper-thin. In January 1945 the two met again to discuss cooperation in counter-espionage work. Ehrhardt rejected Huber's request for office space at his bureau's building on Ferry Road. He nevertheless agreed to provide RM5,000 funding for counter-espionage work to be conducted under the direction of Huber by an agent called Marcs. This man played skat with Huber, but Ehrhardt considered him loyal to the Abwehr rather than the Gestapo.

The joint Abwehr-Gestapo enterprise secured 'only one alleged "success"', according to Ehrhardt – the destruction of a Free French resistance group headed by Georges Rivelain-Kaufman. A former judge in the French Concession, Kaufman, a Jew, had been dismissed from his position in 1941 following the decision of the French authorities to apply Vichy anti-Jewish laws. Thereafter Kaufman established contact with the Free French underground in Indo-China and also, using Chinese couriers, with Allied representatives in Chungking. Kaufman's group was said to have prepared plans 'to seize and destroy forty ammunition factories and ten water and power sub-stations' in order to weaken the Japanese defences of Shanghai. The German agents succeeded in uncovering the activities of the group. On 10 August 1944 Kaufman's home was raided by ten Chinese. He was trussed up, beaten and questioned. Meanwhile the house was ransacked and 'a priceless collection of gold watches ... and a fortune in gold bars, US dollars and pounds sterling' were removed. The raid was later identified as the work of the Wang Ching-wei political police operating out of 76 Jessfield Road.[47] Presumably they had been tipped off by the Germans.

In return for the money and the vague cooperation agreement, Huber and Meisinger left Ehrhardt relatively free until the end of the war. Ehrhardt was not altogether happy about the compromise but felt that it was the only way to square Huber 'with his petty party intrigues and his mud-slinging while at the same time utilizing and guiding into productive and harmless channels his ambition and craving for importance'.[48]

From the autumn of 1944 German consulates throughout China, on instructions from the German embassy, began burning confidential papers, fearful that they might be taken over by the Japanese. As their own position in Europe deteriorated, the Germans became increasingly worried about the reliability of their one remaining major ally. In January 1945 a telegram from the German military attaché in Tokyo was circulated within the German High Command. This reported that Russia and Japan had reached an agreement to reduce their forces facing each other in the Far East: as of 1 February the Red Army would station no more than ten divisions between Vladivostok and Novosibirsk while Japan would limit her forces to six divisions plus the Manchurian army. The military attaché noted, however, that this information was based only on a Shanghai agent's report conveyed by the Shanghai Police attaché (Huber), uncorroborated by any other source, and thus was to be 'treated with caution'.[49] The military attaché's scepticism regarding this report was probably justified: no other evidence has been found to substantiate it. At the same time, it may not have been totally baseless. The previous September, the Japanese government had approved a proposal by Foreign Minister Shigemitsu for the dispatch of a special representative to Moscow to negotiate an agreement in which such a mutual force reduction was one element: the Soviets refused even to receive the emissary and at the same time informed Washington of the approach.[50]

British intelligence reports in the spring of 1945 noted that the Japanese were taking defensive measures in Shanghai in anticipation of an attack. In March three 'suicide battalions' of 500 men each were formed by the local army authorities. In early April underground tunnels were being dug on the Route Cardinal Mercier (renamed Kueilin Road) to be used both as air raid shelters and for potential street fighting.[51] An MI6 report in late April 1945, based on information from 'a responsible Chinese official', referred to 'rumours … to the effect that representatives of Chungking and of the Japanese High Command in Shanghai were discussing the possibility of declaring Shanghai an open city'.[52]

On 8 May news reached Shanghai of the German surrender. At Lunghwa internment camp inmates learned the news from an American plane that flew overhead and traced 'V.E.' in the sky. In Chapei Camp H. E. Arnhold wrote that the news 'caused much excitement and rejoicing in the camp. It was immediately assumed that the collapse of Japan was imminent and that we should soon be out of camp.'[53] These hopes proved to be cruelly premature.

After the German surrender, Meisinger's official activities seem to have been restricted mainly to moving around large sums of money between Tokyo and Shanghai.[54] Allegedly these sums were to be used to support 'welfare activities' on behalf of German citizens in the Far East. As for Ehrhardt, he later claimed that he had issued a demobilization order to all his men on 12 May 1945. At the same time he arranged for them to use a communal kitchen at his office each day. A Japanese officer visited Ehrhardt shortly after the German surrender and asked him and his staff to continue to operate in the Japanese interest. According to a later statement by a sympathizer with Ehrhardt (probably Baron Jesco von Puttkamer), 'Ehrhardt's answer was evasive. He said that he was too sick to do so but he would ask his former staff members which he did not do.'[55] Meanwhile Ehrhardt took the precaution of burning his organization's records to prevent them falling into the hands of his allies.

It was not until 11 June that the Japanese government informed the German ambassador in Tokyo that German diplomatic and consular missions could no longer continue official activity. The personal status of German diplomats would not, however, be affected and the German economic delegation headed by Helmut Wohlthat would be permitted to carry on essential business, though it could no longer be recognized as an official representative body.[56] Germans in Japan – but not in Shanghai – were subsequently rounded up and interned.

In late July and early August the German Residents' Association in Shanghai held elections in which opposing slates of Nazi and anti-Nazi candidates were fielded. About 720 individuals and 60 firms voted, producing a solid victory for the Nazis, who won all but one of the seats on the association's board of directors.[57] The result was a striking testimony to the blinkered loyalty of the majority of Shanghai Germans (the 'non-Aryan ones, that is) to the ideals of their dead Führer.

The German collapse in Europe had other effects in the Far East, notably on the position of the French. In spite of the return of the French Concession to China in mid-1943, the French had been permitted to retain their small military force in Shanghai – if for no other reason than that it had nowhere else to go. At that time the garrison consisted of 1,400 men, of whom 320 were French, 200 African and 880 Annamite (Indo-chinese). Four hundred of the Annamites rejected French discipline and volunteered to serve under the Japanese. The remainder mouldered in their barracks. But the Normandy landings and the subsequent eclipse of the Vichy régime made the Japanese less complaisant in this regard. As in the case of the Italians a little earlier, they now turned against erstwhile friends. On 9 March they launched a surprise attack on the French garrisons in Indo-China; those who resisted were massacred, the rest interned. The next day, the Japanese announced that they would no longer recognize the French diplomatic and consular representatives in China. At the same time the Japanese army authorities in Shanghai demanded the immediate disarmament of the French forces in the city. The recently appointed commander of the French garrison, Colonel A.J.F. Artigue, described as '*un officier de très grand choix, énergique, sportif, ancien international militaire de rugby, aimé et admiré de tous*' felt that to agree without resistance would be an act of dishonour.[58] He consulted his diplomatic colleagues who advised him to submit. The alternatives were terrible. The previous day the commander of the French garrison at Lang Son in Indo-China had been confronted with a similar demand. He refused to comply – whereupon he and the French administrator of the province were decapitated with sabres and the entire French garrison was massacred. 'Given the impossibility and pointlessness of resistance', as a French consular account put it, 'the French authorities in Shanghai were obliged to agree' to the Japanese demands.[59] The disarmed French troops henceforth mouldered in the Bernez-Cambot barracks on the Route Frelupt. Their commander brooded on his decision, with ultimately tragic consequences.

Upon the German surrender, radio station XGRS was transferred by its German owners to the Japanese. According to the broadcaster Herbert Moy, the Germans handed it over in return for six bottles of whisky. Most of the previous employees resigned, but Moy continued to broadcast – and to drink heavily. He told cronies that his elder brother was a general in the Chungking forces and his younger one a lieutenant in the American army. 'He made some feeling remark about "their fighting like hell for our country" and here, goddamit, am I, getting tight as all blazes.'[60] Deprived of many of the former German announcers, the Japanese juggled their remaining Allied collaborators: Frank Johnston ('Pat Kelly') returned to his old microphone at XGRS, while J. K. Gracie ('Sergeant Alan McIntosh') was transferred to the Japanese station XGOO.

On 7 July 1945, the Allied 'political' internees who had been held at the Haiphong Road camp since November 1942 were suddenly moved to Peking. The journey took five days and, in the extreme summer heat, was a considerable ordeal.[61] The Swiss chargé d'affaires reported to Berne the alarming news that these men now appeared to be considered as 'hostages' by the Japanese.[62]

In the financial confusion of the summer of 1945, some Shanghai residents took refuge in strange delusions: one was the sudden popularity of old Russian rouble notes of the Tsarist period. Large quantities of such notes had been brought to Shanghai by White Russian refugees at the end of the Russian Civil War. At one point they had seemed almost worthless and were used to light cigarettes. But now some people calculated that they might recover value. Self-styled experts explained that closer relations between Britain and the USSR would be likely to produce an agreement between London and Moscow over the repayment of the old Russian debt, repudiated by the Soviets shortly after the revolution. Such an agreement, it was suggested, would restore value not only to old Russian bonds but also to currency notes. A police report noted that, as a result of such optimistic calculations, people were 'opening up old trunks in a frantic search for old Rouble notes'.[63]* Can one detect the directing brain of 'Captain' Pick behind this fantastic notion? Or was this another example of long-distance currency manipulation by the SOE's 'REMORSE' group? Whatever its source, the rouble bubble grew into a manic speculation – until it ultimately and inevitably burst.

On 17 July a Japanese radio station in Hongkew was bombed. Some bombs missed their target and landed in the nearby Jewish refugee area: 30 people were killed. On 20 July the Australian turncoat Alan Raymond broadcast one of his last commentaries: 'Despite the approaching battle,' he said, 'Shanghai continues as usual. In point of gaiety and amusements, there is no other community anywhere in the world like it.'[64]

News of the Russian entry into the Far Eastern war on 8 August caused a panic on the Shanghai markets. Many Shanghai Russians now changed their tune opportunistically and applied for Soviet citizenship. The old White Russian Club closed down. At the Yar restaurant on the Route Cardinal Mercier a drunken gaggle of bar-girls, known as 'Lojnikoff's Harem', indulged in a final orgiastic party with Russian and Japanese friends. Eugene Pick held a melancholy farewell dinner in his room at the Cathay Hotel

---

* The hoped-for debt agreement was finally concluded in 1986 when the USSR agreed to pay $120 million in compensation to British holders of pre-1917 Russian bonds. The agreement had no noticeable effect on the value of imperial rouble banknotes.

with the Japanese naval attaché. Also present was Pick's young Russian radio operator Vyacheslav Toropovsky and the latter's mother (wife of James Smart, former chief of the British radio monitoring station in Shanghai). At one point Pick whispered to Toropovsky that he had reason to believe that the Japanese were trying to kill him. The young man disgustedly suspected that his host was preparing the ground for his disappearance from Shanghai. Pick, in fact, left the city soon after.[65]

Reports of the explosion of nuclear bombs at Hiroshima and Nagasaki on 6 and 9 August drifted only gradually across the China Sea. Japanese troops and civilians in Shanghai therefore reacted with horror and incredulity as they listened on 14 August to the radio broadcast of the emperor's 'rescript', ordering his nation to surrender. The non-Japanese staff at station XGRS held a party the following evening to celebrate. Herbert Moy drank half a bottle of whisky and then went with Frank Johnston to his office. After a while, Johnston left and Moy remained alone. He locked the door and then slit his throat and wrists with a razor. He sat down at his desk and smoked a last cigarette as his blood coursed out. Finding himself, after a time, still alive, he went to the window and threw himself out. His corpse was found on the pavement the next day. According to his mistress, Marquita Kwong, he had been talking about suicide for several days, ruminating that 'when a man has been playing the type of game I have, there is only one thing for him to do should he lose'.[66]

For several weeks Shanghai hovered in a strange limbo as it waited for the arrival of Allied troops. An OSS project to land 'mercy teams' in a number of occupied areas, including Shanghai, proved premature when the Shanghai team, code-named SPARROW, parachuted safely into the city but was immediately arrested and interned by the Japanese. On 18 August an American C47 cargo plane made several low sweeps over Shanghai and then landed at the Kiangwan aerodrome. It unloaded a goodwill mission with medical and other supplies for Allied internees. The Swiss consulate took over responsibility for the internment camps in Shanghai. It was some time, however, before the inmates were able to leave. Most, in any case, had as yet nowhere to go.

Internal hatreds within various national groups erupted in outbreaks of violence. On 10 August a group of Italian self-styled 'anti-fascists', headed by one Elia Garzea, seized the Italian embassy in Shanghai and tore down the fascist emblems from the front of the building. Garzea, it turned out, was a late convert to the democratic cause. He had been a fascist party member since 1937 and had participated in various fascist bully-boy activities. He had also attempted to blackmail a local Italian. A secretary at the embassy, Pasquale Prunas, later declared: 'The last time I saw him he was peddling color pictures of Mussolini around the Embassy. We told him we didn't want any. I suppose he's peddling pictures of Stalin now.' Garzea nevertheless organized an 'Anti-Fascist Association' and tried to secure election as president of the Italian community in Shanghai.[67]

On 19 August 15 men wearing French police uniform raided the house on Kinnear Road of Georges Rivelain-Kaufman. He was not at home, having taken refuge in the home of a Baghdadi Jewish millionaire. The judge's house was ransacked: furniture, antiques and precious porcelain were destroyed. The homes of other former French officials were raided the same night and 20 men were arrested and charged with 'inciting Annamite troops and the local French community to rebellion'.[68]

The transfer of authority was agonizingly slow. Far from the fighting lines, and apparently forgotten by the belligerents, Shanghai waited, like a patient old horse, for its masters to return. On 24 August the new Chungking-nominated deputy mayor of the city appeared with an entourage of thirty officials. Chiang Kai-shek's military representative had arrived a few days earlier, but in the absence of significant Allied military forces the Japanese remained formally in charge of the city. It was not until 7 September that the deputy chief of the Japanese 13th Army formally surrendered Shanghai to the commander of the Chinese 3rd Chungking Army. Japanese arms and equipment handed over in Shanghai included more than 100 aircraft, 494 field guns, 181 heavy machine-guns, 16,500 rifles, 2,262 horses, 626 carrier pigeons, 368 axes and 29 waterproof food bags.[69] In this manner, the Second World War, which had begun in China exactly 98 months earlier, also reached its terminus there.

12 Twilight of Old Shanghai

'Hello everybody!' announced the Argentina Nite Club in the *Shanghai Herald*. Once the haunt of Nazi agents and Japanese officers, the Russian-owned Argentina now styled itself as 'Shanghai's only American-run Night-Club and Cocktail Lounge' and featured the husband-and-wife American dance team of 'Cheetah and Billy Carroll', who had recently been released from internment.[1] American films, flown in from Chungking, reappeared on the cinema screens, beginning at the Roxy with *Naughty Marietta*, starring Jeannette MacDonald and Nelson Eddy, and at the Nanking Theater with Dorothy Lamour in *Aloma of the South Seas*. MGM made special arrangements to rush in a print of *Thirty Minutes over Tokyo*, depicting the Doolittle raid in 1942.

American sailors on port leave, 'their pockets bulging with wads of puppet currency', raided the shops rather like locusts. 'Silk stockings and filmy black lace panties and brassières were the first things the sailors bought. These were depleted in short order. Their attention then turned to silk hand-embroidered slips, night-gowns, bed-jackets, Chinese pajamas and slippers.' Like manna from heaven, goods of every description suddenly descended on the Shanghai markets: electric kettles and toasters, typewriters, cameras, radios, aluminium pressure cookers, waffle irons, trinkets, fake curios of every description – and even crated automobiles. One sailor from Brooklyn declared: 'This is an unbelievable spot for us guys who have been out there around those Pacific islands for three years. Brother – this is heaven!'[2]

Unlike most of the great cities of Japan and many of China, Shanghai bore few physical marks of war. 'The town is shabby. The Bund looks well enough, although hawkers have begun to establish their stalls on the pavements – doubtless the shape of things to come,' reported the reopened office of Butterfield & Swire.[3] The Allied internees, cocooned from the outside world for the previous three years, had lost touch not only with family and friends but with the rapid development of language under wartime conditions. 'What's a jeep?' asked one?[4] Another described his impressions upon release. On the face of things, it was 'just the same old Shanghai', he wrote, except that the street fortifications and air raid shelters 'looked like ugly scars on the city's face and the general air of having undergone hard wear and tear was upon everything'.[5] Sudden release had traumatic and sometimes tragic effects: one British lawyer committed suicide by jumping from the fifth floor of the Embankment Building shortly after returning from the Weihsien internment camp.

Bizarrely, the 100,000 Japanese troops in the city remained on duty, under Allied orders, to prevent a breakdown in law and order. They still stood guard over essential utilities, government offices and even the Foreign YMCA. As the transfer of power took effect, many changed their uniforms for civilian clothes and quietly melted into the Japanese civilian population of Hongkew. Others remained in uniform under Chinese command and guarded the railway carrying coal to Shanghai from the Kailan Mines.

Behind the scenes, Tai Li, Tu Yueh-sheng and Milton Miles (newly promoted to rear-admiral) were rumoured to have made arrangements with the Japanese and the Chinese puppet authorities to provide for a smooth transition in the city – one, that is, in which there would be no danger of a communist takeover. The rumours had considerable basis in fact. When Tai Li introduced Miles to Tu, the American officer rather took to the ageing gangster: 'a mannerly and ostensibly amiable old gentleman with a long, cadaverous face and snaggle teeth'.[6]

On 19 September Admiral T. C. Kinkaid's flagship, the USS *Rocky Mount*, arrived at the head of an armada of American navy ships, with vast stores originally assembled for the projected invasion of Japan. Cheering crowds lined the river banks. Three entire US fleets, the 4th, 6th and 7th, assembled outside the mouth of the river and were soon joined by a British naval task force. By 23 September more than a dozen American and British warships had returned, recreating the pre-1941 Warship Row on the Whangpoo.

Miles and Tai Li held a reception to welcome the Allied admirals. Among the American naval personnel who returned to Shanghai in triumph was Captain Columbus Darwin Smith who had escaped so daringly from the city a year earlier. He was placed in command of the Shanghai harbour pilots. Signs of the new pecking order of the great powers were soon visible. By tradition, before the war, the British had always retained the right to use the no. 1 buoy for mooring ships opposite the Bund. Now, Miles, in his capacity as port director, scored a subtle point off his ally and assigned the berth to the biggest ship in port: an American cruiser. The Americans established their naval headquarters in the Glen Line Building, formerly British-owned, and only recently vacated by the German embassy.

In order to help forestall any threat of a communist takeover, American planes airlifted tens of thousands of Chinese troops into the Shanghai area. At the same time the US authorities did not wish to appear publicly to be intervening in Chinese politics. General Wedemeyer was therefore angered by Miles's continued involvement with Tai Li and by the publicity that the two attracted. Miles, fearful of a plot against him, became dependent on pills and showed signs of mental instability. The climax of the row came with a press conference, called by Miles in Shanghai, at which he intended to announce that he did not recognize Wedemeyer's authority. In his memoirs, published some years later, Miles admitted that he had been 'all wound up' and 'already a little off my rocker'.[7] His career in China ended abruptly. On Wedemeyer's orders he was placed in the charge of navy doctors who removed him unceremoniously to Washington. The Chinese awarded him Medal No. 90 of the Order of the White Cloud and Golden Banner and accorded him the rank of lieutenant-general. The United States demoted him to captain.

On 26 September the *Shanghai Herald* celebrated the arrival of the US naval hospital ship *Refuge* with 29 'companionable and pretty' nurses aboard. The influx of Americans and American money helped stimulate a revival of all the pre-war rackets. On 3 October the paper reported that a large number of bars and restaurants in the city had been placed out of bounds to US military and naval personnel, as had 'all Shanghai brothels, regardless of their size or location', one of the more spectacularly unenforceable orders given to the victorious soldiery. Italian sailors from the scuttled liner *Conte Verde* happily continued their enforced holiday, dining at the Senet on Avenue Joffre (apparently returned to its old name) to music from the refugee pianists 'Gino and Gizza'. Shanghai in the late 1940s was like a long-running hit musical with a new cast gamely performing the old routines.

Not everybody could participate in the jollifications. Although the Allied internees were free, including the 'politicals' from the Haiphong Road camp who were liberated at Peking, many had nowhere to go. Two months after the Japanese surrender 20 per cent of the internees were still living in camps. Former employees of the Shanghai Municipal Council or of the settlement police no longer had jobs and many returned from internment to find home and household effects all gone. Most of the police felt bitterness at the consequences of having followed official instructions to remain in Shanghai before December 1941: 'Now the war is over and the Allies are nominally the victors but here in Shanghai we are in the anomalous position of having won the war whilst losing everything else not through enemy action but by reason of the action of our own Government and that of our ally, the Chungking Government.'[8] A few found police jobs in Hong Kong or other colonies. Most, like Allied civilians in general, waited impatiently for arrangements to be made for their repatriation. The first Allied vessel to sail with repatriates was the USS *Refuge*, which left for Okinawa on 27 September. It carried 443 passengers, mainly American ex-internees. On 3 October HMS *Guardian* and HMS *Glenearn* left for Hong Kong with over 300 British repatriates.

Retribution followed hard on the heels of liberation. Japanese civilians in Shanghai, who had increased to nearly 100,000 during the war, were subjected to unpleasant treatment that most other foreigners regarded merely as a dose of their own medicine. They were compelled to wear armbands and were segregated in Hongkew. Eventually they were all compulsorily repatriated, part of a great multitude of more than 5 million Japanese from all over the former 'Co-Prosperity Sphere' who were bundled off to their homeland.

Denunciations of all kinds flew around among the foreign communities. Hardy R. Grubb, a former chief inspector in the Municipal Police, accused his ex-colleague Harry Robertson of collaboration with the enemy. Grubb related that Robertson, after being dismissed from his post of deputy commissioner, had 'voluntarily consented to act as an adviser in police matters' to his Japanese successor. Grubb added that 'when treated with contempt for his pro-Japanese actions by several senior police officers', Robertson had 'threatened to report to the Japanese commissioner, which threat if carried out would probably have led to investigations from or confinement in the Bridge House'. Other ex-police officers corroborated Grubb's account and further accused Robertson of threatening behaviour towards fellow internees in the Yu Yuen Road and Yangtsepoo internment camps.[9] Of course, except for the alleged threats, Robertson's conduct did not differ essentially from that of other senior police officers. All were shielded by the pre-war instruction to remain at their posts. None was prosecuted after the war.

The equivocal behaviour of many of the French in wartime Shanghai led some to look for a settling of accounts at the end of the war. But although resistance leaders like Roderick Egal were rehabilitated and honoured, there was little in the way of a Far Eastern '*épuration*'. In November 1945 two French officers, one of them Captain Jacques Guillermaz, a member of the DGER (Direction Générale des Etudes et Recherches, the French intelligence service), arrived in Shanghai to deal with what he called the 'miserable remnant of our "occupation force" in China', disarmed by the Japanese the previous spring. They found the troops in a 'distressing situation'. Nothing had been done for them since the Japanese surrender and the soldiers felt 'morally and materially abandoned'. Guillermaz concluded that it was necessary 'to put an end to their situation immediately, as much for reasons of national prestige as for their own sakes'. During their period of enforced disarmament, their commander, Colonel Artigue, had grown steadily more agitated over what he felt was the shame of his submission to the Japanese the previous spring. He said to Guillermaz: 'They deceived me. We should have fought!' Guillermaz assured him that in the circumstances he would have taken the same decision. That evening at dinner, there was some discussion of the suicide of the former French police commissioner, L. Fabre. '*Il s'étonnait d'un geste qu'il n'aurait lui-même jamais accompli. Déclaration sincère? Appel désespéré que nous ne comprîmes pas?*' The next day Artigue shot himself in the head on the terrace of his office. The shot left him critically wounded, though still conscious. Guillermaz informed Paris and, at his suggestion, de Gaulle sent Artigue a message assuring him of his sympathy and understanding. Artigue lingered on for another two years, then died. Guillermaz noted sadly that a Russian journalist claimed that he had been specially sent from Paris to settle accounts with Colonel Artigue whom he had supposedly forced to commit suicide. '*Pénibles absurdités qu'explique le climat de l'époque.*'[10]

Fabre's former deputy, Roland Sarly, who had served the Chinese puppet régime since 1943, was arrested by the Chinese on 14 December 1945 and charged with collaboration with the Japanese. Reflecting the changed mood in the French community, the committee of the French Club asked the consul-general to 'request that R. Sarly abstain for the time being from appearing' in the club.[11] The French authorities nevertheless protested vigorously against Sarly's arrest, claiming that they had not yet formally relinquished their extraterritorial rights.[12] The treaty of 1943 with the Wang Ching-wei régime had not, after all, been regarded as valid by Chungking. The French chose to regard the surrender of authority by the French consul-general as having been 'on a municipal not on a governmental level'. Judicial proceedings in the Sarly case dragged on for three years before the Chinese Supreme Court in Nanking finally cleared him of all charges.[13]

Germans in Shanghai were at first allowed to continue their lives freely. After October 1945 about 200 out of the 2,000 or so non-refugee Germans in Shanghai were rounded up and placed in the Kiangwan Segregation Center, a former Japanese high school. They were maintained in part by a small stockpile of gold bars that representatives of the local German community had entrusted for safe keeping to the Swiss consul-general shortly after Stalingrad. The rest remained at liberty. The Shanghai Municipal Government formed a German Affairs Commission that registered and eventually repatriated most of them to Germany. But as an American intelligence report noted,

> The internment of Germans by the Chinese in Shanghai can only be described as an absolute farce. Some of the leading Nazi Party members, intelligence agents and officials and propagandists have not been interned. Some who had been interned were released and others have been able to secure passes to visit Shanghai almost any time they desire.[14]

The explanation appeared to be the susceptibility of officials of the German Affairs Commission to offers of squeeze.

War criminals were rounded up and placed in detention. Japanese torturers from the Bridge House jail faced war crimes charges before Allied courts. Josef Meisinger, the former Far Eastern Gestapo boss, was classified by US Counter-Intelligence as 'public enemy number one of Nazi war criminals in the Far East'.[15] He was captured at Kawaguchi, near Tokyo, on 6 September 1945. The American war crimes office in Tokyo reported the arrest to General MacArthur and, no doubt as a result of some poetic garbling of intelligence records, added that Meisinger was 'reputed to be a friend of Heydrich and Himmler and a homosexual'.[16] While held at the Kawaguchi View Hotel, Meisinger talked of shooting himself. Later he made a half-hearted suicide attempt by slashing his wrists with a razor. The attempt failed and he was sent for interrogation by US investigators. The Americans eventually decided to turn him over to Poland for trial as a war criminal. Found guilty of mass murder, he was sentenced to death on 3 March 1947 by the Supreme National Tribunal of the Polish People's Republic. He was executed four days later.

Also arrested were other German officials, among them the former ambassador to China, Stahmer, and the 'butcher of Buchenwald', Dr Robert Neumann, who had latterly been ekeing out his pathological living as a piano teacher. Letters and reports began to appear in local newspapers denouncing Germans as war criminals and demanding action against them. Some Germans made public protestations of their innocence of the Nazi taint and even many former party members, officials, propagandists and agents claimed to have had democratic sympathies. Walter Schmalfuss, a former translator in Baron Puttkamer's propaganda bureau, offered the following evidence of his anti-Nazi views in response to a denunciation in a local Russian paper:

> What made me a definite anti-Nazi is through the snubbing directed against my wife. She is ¾ Spanish and ¼ Filipino. When she came here in August 1941 in order to get married, we had to overcome many obstacles in order to get married at all. The Nazi[s] here in Shanghai were strictly enforcing a rule not to marry Germans to foreigners…What made me

> especially sore is the fact that my wife not only has the finest
> education that money can buy but her family tree boasts of
> such famous names as the Mcmahons, one of whom was
> President of the French Republic after Napoleon III abdicated
> in 1871. Naturally I felt more than indignation to be snubbed
> by men in Nazi uniform who only a little while ago had been
> practically nobody.[17]

Schmalfuss admitted that he had known the head of the Shanghai Gestapo
agents' network, Dr Klare, but insisted that their acquaintance had been
limited to 'a standing date to play Mahjong at the German Club'.

Among the most brazen efforts at self-exculpation was a letter to President Truman submitted in June 1946 by Klare's deputy, the former XGRS
broadcaster and agents' outfitter, Frederick Wiehl:

> During the war between the United States and Germany, I was
> in a tight spot. I sought the middle way of a compromise
> between the United States and Germany...When you took
> over the presidency ... I put on a series of ten radio
> commentaries praising your record over the local 'Radio
> Shanghai', a German government radio station.
>
> I wish to offer my services to you and the American people.
> For you, I wish to work in the internal German field. There, I
> would like to materialize in peacetime what the military failed
> to accomplish in wartime by military methods. I want to
> advise and assist the American Military Government in
> Germany to this end...Today, my wife and myself want to do
> our share towards the establishment of a permanent
> democratic German government.[18]

Some former Nazi agents did succeed in securing employment by their former enemies. For example, Otto Habenicht, the former decoding chief in
the Ehrhardt Bureau, who had failed to decipher a single Allied intercept
since the outbreak of the Pacific War, was given a job as a code expert by the
Chinese government.

Another ex-Nazi who found a niche under the new dispensation was the late Dr Miorini's old classmate and bosom companion. Hermann Erben was released from Pootung internment camp on 17 August 1945. Remarkably, after more than two years of detention, his loyalty to the Axis was undimmed. His first port of call upon release was the former German consul, Dr Hoops, to whom he reported that he had returned 'from military assignment by the Bureau Ehrhardt from the Pootung Assembly Center after two and one-half years, and asked for further orders'. Perhaps he hoped to obtain accumulated back pay due to him: he had received no remittances from his German employers since April 1943. But the substantial funds being administered by Meisinger for 'welfare activities' seemed to have evaporated. At any rate, nothing was available for this most deserving of cases. Hoops told Erben that he was no longer officially German consul. He suggested that Erben contact Ehrhardt at his office in Ferry Road and obtain his 'discharge orders and whatever' from him.[19] Erben thereupon telephoned Ehrhardt whom he found in a rather cross frame of mind. The former Abwehr officer in effect gave his loyal employee the brush-off, telling him 'that there was no reason for me to be indignant that I was not met by a reception committee. They were not sleeping. They had been with their boots on, up to the last minute active.' A few days later Erben paid a call on his former German controller, Hans Mosberg, in his flat on the Yu Yuen Road. Mosberg told Erben he shared his resentment against the Japanese and 'could understand that I was quite sore about the two and half years I had spent there [in internment]'.[20]

The realization that his service to the Axis cause as a volunteer internee had been an exercise in self-deception and futility began to exercise Erben's mind. On his release he had also begun to investigate the death of his friend Miorini and soon concluded that the most likely cause was murder by the Shanghai Nazi apparatus. His old loyalties consequently turned to thoughts of revenge – and the revolutionized political situation in Shanghai afforded him an opportunity to wreak it.

Soon after the Japanese had surrendered, Erben visited the American consulate-general and applied for repatriation to the USA as an ex-internee, admitting at the same time that his citizenship was in question. On 8 October 1945 Erben obtained employment with a malaria control unit of the US Army Medical Corps at a salary of $90 a month. A month later he was arrested by the US provost marshal and lodged in the Ward Road jail. He was investigated by the US Army War Crimes Branch but was saved from prosecution as a traitor by the fact of his American denaturalization in 1941. Upon his release in January 1946, he resumed work with the US government. His duties, however, had changed. He was now assigned at the same rate of pay to the US Army Counter-Intelligence Corps under the orders of Captain Jerome Farrell, a former journalist. Erben later claimed that he was employed 'as an investigator' and he added: 'My orders were to follow the case of Dr von Miorini.'[21]

Erben remained a US Army civilian employee until July 1946. His prime role during this period was to advise the American authorities about the wartime activities of Shanghai Germans. His object was to ingratiate himself with the Americans and to 'gain absolution for his past sins as a traitor' – as his American contact put it.[22] His new employers, like his old, regarded him with suspicion. An American intelligence official warned that an extensive file existed on Erben 'and none of the material is of a complimentary nature'.[23]

Erben was dismissed by the US army in July 1946, but refused to give up work. In April 1947 he reappeared in Shanghai in American uniform 'minus insignia', claimed to be working once again for American intelligence and questioned Polish citizens about communist contacts.[24] A little later Erben was reported to be 'blackmailing Jewish refugees, especially those who have applied for visas to the United States', warning that 'if they do not follow his requests he will inform against them and see that they are not granted permission to enter the United States'.[25] Erben himself hoped to go and live in America but in August 1947 he was arrested by the Chinese Gendarmerie and deported to Germany. He was held in an American-administered detention centre at Ludwigsburg, where he became well-known 'due to the fact that [as a protest against his detention] he habitually walked around wrapped in nothing but U.S. Army blankets with a rope tied round his waist'.[26] Upon release, he resumed the practice of medicine, taking up residence in a number of exotic locations, including Teheran, Jiddah and Tandjung Priok (Indonesia). His dead body was found frozen in his unheated apartment in Vienna in January 1985.

Although Erben was not taken very seriously by the Americans, they utilized him to help build a case against his former colleagues in the German intelligence bureau. In April 1946 Ludwig Ehrhardt and other former members of his organization were arrested in Shanghai. The substance of the charge against all of them was that 'they furnished Japan with military intelligence and disseminated propaganda detrimental to the United States and other Allied nations' between the German surrender on 8 May 1945 and the Japanese collapse three months later. All the accused pleaded not guilty.

Proceedings in *United States of America* v. *Lothar Eisentraeger alias Ludwig Ehrhardt et al.* opened before a US military tribunal sitting at Shanghai in August 1946. Besides Ehrhardt, 22 Germans were accused. Another four, members of the Peking offshoot of the bureau, were later added, making a total of 27 accused in all, including most of Ehrhardt's chief operatives as well as other prominent German officials who had served in China, among them Ernst Woermann, a former German ambassador to the Wang Ching-wei régime, and Baron Jesco von Puttkamer, the former German propaganda chief in Shanghai.

The first witness for the prosecution was Ehrhardt's disgraced predecessor, Louis Siefken, no doubt inwardly rejoicing in the opportunity to turn the tables on his former rival. The second prosecution witness was Erben, 'who freely admitted his activities as a German agent but sought to give the impression that he was in reality working for the Allied interests' – as an American diplomatic report put it.[27] The third witness was more damning since, unlike the first two, he had no obvious axe to grind: Lieutenant-Colonel Mori Akiri, former head of the intelligence branch of the Japanese Army Office in Shanghai, who was brought back from Japan to give evidence. He testified that his office had continued to receive intelligence information from the Ehrhardt Bureau after the German surrender and 'that voluntary agreements to continue working with the Japanese were signed by each member as well as by Baron von Puttkamer for the German Information Bureau'.[28] He believed these compromising documents had been burned together with other documents after the Japanese surrender. This evidence was corroborated by other Japanese witnesses as well as by three Italian radio operators for the bureau and by Chinese and German witnesses. Gerda Kocher, Ehrhardt's former secretary, testified that in July 1945 the Japanese had offered each member of the bureau 2 ounces of gold for services rendered 'and that she believed all members of the staff except herself and Habenicht signed receipts for this gold'.[29]

Upon conclusion of the prosecution case in November 1946, charges against six of the defendants were dismissed. In the cases of Woermann and four others the verdict was given because they were diplomats, in the case of Schenke it was on the ground that the prosecution had failed to establish that he had continued to engage in anti-Allied activity after the German surrender. The six were nevertheless held in custody pending repatriation to Germany.

When the trial resumed for presentation of the defence, Japanese and German witnesses gave evidence tending to show that the Ehrhardt Bureau had not continued to work after 8 May 1945 but had merely gathered to partake of free meals. Hermann Gerhard, an assistant cook at the bureau's premises at 225 Ferry Road, testified that 'he had never seen Ehrhardt do any work either before or after the German surrender'. Ehrhardt's valet confirmed this, saying that 'he never saw any paper work being done there, that the Germans simply took their meals and sat around playing games and talking together'.[30] Testimony was also given by the non-Nazi pastor of the Lutheran Evangelical church in Shanghai who appeared as a character witness for Hans Mosberg. He paid tribute to Mosberg's 'character and high ideals', stressing particularly his admiration for the United States and his Christian attitude (Mosberg, it will be recalled, was of Jewish origin).

In early 1947 Ehrhardt was sentenced to life imprisonment. Puttkamer and one other received 30 years' hard labour. The rest were given prison terms of 5–20 years. The prisoners were repatriated to serve their sentences at Landsberg prison in Bavaria. All were released, however, in 1950 after further investigation of the case by a US army inquiry commission.

The Germans' former opposite numbers in Allied intelligence scattered. Some of the British businessmen resumed control of their companies in Shanghai; others went home. Valentine Killery, former head of SOE's Oriental Mission, returned to England to become a director of ICI. W. J. Gande, former head of Oriental Mission Shanghai group, was awarded the King's Commendation 'for his unflinching courage and devotion to his country in the face of nearly four years of bitter Japanese oppression'. The ceremony at the British consulate in Shanghai, on 9 April 1947, was attended by several of his former associates and fellow-prisoners, including S. C. Riggs and Eric Davies.[31] Godfrey Phillips, former chief civil servant of the Shanghai Municipal Council had no job to go back to in Shanghai at the end of the war. He became head of Lazard Brothers in the City of London and a director of several companies.

The taipan brothers John and W. J. ('Tony') Keswick returned to Shanghai in 1946 to run Jardine, Matheson. They remained there until after the communist takeover, John Keswick's wartime contacts in Chungking with Chou En-lai proving useful at that juncture. Later, however, the firm lost all its assets in mainland China. Jardines shifted their centre of operations to Hong Kong, where they prospered greatly. Although they maintained substantial holdings in Hong Kong, the legal domicile of the firm was moved to Bermuda in the 1980s in anticipation of the return of Hong Kong to Chinese sovereignty in 1997. John died in 1982 and Tony in 1990.

While most former enemies and allied citizens were repatriated, one group of foreigners seemed for a time to flourish in Shanghai:

> Another bitter pill for the former internees to swallow [an American intelligence report noted] is the sight of scores of foreign collaborators of various nationalities, still scot-free and with pockets full of money, promenading Nanking Road and Bubbling Well Road, frequenting the reopened hotels and night-clubs. Their obvious prosperity and arrogance contrast sharply with the gaunt looks and threadbare clothes of the camp residents.
>
> Many of these traitors and collaborators are well known throughout the foreign community. They are now conspicuous chiefly through their cultivating the company of the American armed forces, particularly officers, in Shanghai. Especially the women are seen in public with American officers, in the hotels, cabarets, at moving-picture shows, or riding in official motor cars. Some of the men are working for various American agencies, mostly in minor capacities.

Among examples cited were two women: the Scottish wife of a Chinese collaborator and 'Princess' Sumaire, described as 'an outcast member of the ruling family of the Indian state of Patiala and a former German agent in France and Japanese and German agent in Shanghai'. This almost certainly gives too much political credit to Sumaire's flamboyant but mainly apolitical activities. 'It goes without saying', the report added, 'that both these extremely dangerous women are also extremely good-looking.' Among other collaborators mentioned were the broadcasters Don Chisholm and Frank Johnston, the hit-man Nathan Rabin and Paul Lojnikoff ('was a section chief of the Japanese Gendarmerie and is now working full-time for the Chinese Gendarmerie'[32]).

These complaints had some basis in fact. On 28 October the *Shanghai Herald* announced that Lojnikoff, who had been absent from the ring for more than a year, would shortly face 'Slugger' Tommy Foster of the USS *Dixie*. The pugilist, it seemed, had adjusted rapidly to the new realities, since he was reported by American intelligence to be 'driving about the city in a large motor car bearing the Soviet flag'. In November 1945 Lojnikoff was arrested by the American authorities in Shanghai and 'held for investigation in connection with war criminal activities'.[33] A short time later, however, he was released 'for lack of evidence'.[34] Over the following months he resumed black market dealing – but developed new contacts. He was reported to be trading in stolen American tires and motorcycles and to be acting as an informer for the Shanghai-Woosung garrison command of the Chinese army.[35] The 'pretty boy' of the Pick gang eventually moved to the USA where he continued his boxing career. He died as a result of blows received in the ring.

The Filipino collaborator Conrado Uy stated to American intelligence officials:

> Between the Japanese and the Americans I would take the Americans any time…A student who used to be thrilled at the mere sight of George Washington's picture on the wall, would not suddenly open his arms to Emperor Hirohito in later years. A man who still loves to shout Patrick Henry's 'Give me liberty or give me death', could not be so easily persuaded to

> become a brainless willing tool of militaristic tin gods who
> came running roughshod over my country and over China, my
> father's native land.

Hard pressed to say why he had nevertheless become an instrument of the Japanese, Uy explained his wartime conduct as the result of 'compulsion of circumstances beyond human control'.[36] Uy's eloquent nationalism found its eventual reward: in 1949, at the time of the fall of Shanghai to the communists, he was serving as administrative officer at the Filipino consulate in the city.

The British Foreign Office agonized for some time over the case of E. A. Nottingham, former owner of the *Shanghai Times*. At the liberation his paper had been seized by the Chinese nationalists and was thenceforth published under Chinese management as the *Shanghai Herald*. Nottingham appealed to the British authorities for support in reclaiming his property. Given his pre-war and wartime record of cooperation with the Japanese, he encountered a far from sympathetic reaction but, it seemed, evidence of his collaboration was legally inconclusive.[37] His age and poor state of health eventually enabled him to escape prosecution.

Edward Nathan, whose wartime cooperation with the Japanese army at the Kailan Mines had so exercised Anthony Eden and the Foreign Office, continued to enjoy the full confidence of the Chinese Mining and Engineering Company, of which he was appointed chairman. The company continued its efforts to clear his name, but in April 1946 the Foreign Office wrote that 'Mr Bevin has nothing to add to Mr Eden's letter'.[38] After the communist victory in the Chinese Civil War, the company was compelled to relinquish its interest in the Kailan Mines and ceased operations in China.

Don Chisholm, the blackmailing former editor of *Shopping News*, was arrested by American forces in Shanghai on 6 September 1945, but was released 24 hours later without being charged. In the course of the following weeks he claimed to be employed by US naval intelligence 'which', reported the *China Press*, 'United States authorities here neither confirmed nor denied'. Chisholm was certainly acting as an informant, probably for pay. On 30 October, after what the *China Press* described as 'nearly two months of procrastination and indecision', he was rearrested and placed in

the municipal jail, charged with suspected collaborationist activity.[39] The
ensuing investigation was protracted for nearly two years. In the end it was
decided to release Chisholm without pursuing the charges against him.[40]

Among the former associates on whom Chisholm provided US counter-
intelligence authorities with information was 'Princess' Sumaire. After the
liberation, she had encountered renewed financial problems. She sold her
house and moved to the suburb of Hungjao. She took up with an American
newspaperman and started to cultivate a new set of friends. American officers and immigration officials from the United States consulate now figured
on her cocktail party guest list.[41] In October 1945 Sumaire wrote a long letter to her kinsman the Maharajah of Patiala setting out her sad financial situation and begging for money. 'After a lifetime of tears and loneliness', she
began, 'I have at long last made up my mind to approach you in all earnest-
ness and with all the decency in my heart that only suffering in huge doses
could bring.' She recounted her story of imprisonment by the Japanese during the war, confiding that she had 'survived this tragic incident of my life
stronger in thoughts and mind but utterly weak from a physical point of
view'. She intended, she continued, 'to persue [sic] a literary career under a
pen name, without any desire of disclosing any relationship with you'. At the
same time she planned to buy a farm in South America, 'pay back my debts
of honour and get out of this miserable city of Shanghai that has the most
unbearable memories for me. I am almost lost in this strange town amongst
people who are mercenary and unkind.'[42] The maharajah apparently
heeded this maudlin appeal and sent her the £20,000 that she requested.
Sumaire did not, however, leave Shanghai – apparently for lack of a valid
passport. Instead she bought a curio shop in the Continental Building on
Kiukiang Road. In May 1946 she was said to be planning to marry an American ex-army officer and hoped to move with him to America. Meanwhile
she was 'living a more or less quiet life'.[43] The Chinese authorities considered arresting and deporting her but eventually decided to leave her alone.[44]
In December 1946 she was still in Shanghai, her American fiancé no longer
in evidence. Despairing of making much money out of her antique shop, she
wrote to the British War Crimes Commission, claiming compensation for
her treatment by the Japanese at the Bridge House, which, she said, necessitated treatment at the Mayo Clinic in the United States.[45]

Sumaire's former boyfriend Hilaire du Berrier found work as an informant for US counter-intelligence authorities in Shanghai. Under the name Abdullah De Berrière, he submitted reports on some of his wartime associates, notably Sumaire. Later he resumed work as a journalist, specializing in Indo-Chinese affairs. According to the curriculum vitae he prepared in 1957, Berrier served as adviser on Vietnam to the Geneva Conference of July 1955.[46]

Not all the Shanghai collaborators escaped punishment. Pick's hit-man, Nathan Rabin, was arrested by the Chinese and charged with arms dealing and acting as an informer. Morris Gershkovitch was arrested by the Americans in the Philippines and committed to the Bilibid Prison, Muntinglupa, for investigation on charges of collaboration and espionage. The Australian broadcaster John Holland, who was in Japan at the time of the surrender, went into hiding on the island of Hokkaido from which he planned to return to China. When three Eighth Army counter-intelligence officers arrived at the Grand Hotel, Sapporo, to arrest him, he was reclining in the barber shop being shaved by a female barber while another manicured his nails. He was escorted back to Australia to face the music.

In October 1945 the British Foreign Office was informed by the British Naval Intelligence organization at Shanghai that 'there were some twenty British subjects there against whom there was a prima facie case for a charge of collaboration with the Japanese'. Their continued presence in Shanghai was said to be 'resented by those members of the British community who had suffered internment'.[47] The Foreign Office and MI5 ruminated for some time whether to attempt to have them brought back for trial. Eventually, in December 1945, it was decided to ask the Chinese to hand over the six most serious cases. The number was subsequently further whittled down to three. the broadcasters, J. K. Gracie ('Sergeant Alan McIntosh'), Robert Lamb ('Billy Bailcy') and Frank Johnston ('Pat Kelly'). At that time Johnston was reported by American intelligence authorities to be:

> trafficking in cameras obtained from Germans and Japanese.
> His procedure is to approach enemy nationals and offer his
> assistance as a neutral. In the case of one Shimizu, a Japanese
> who does not wear an arm-band and circulates all over town,

he obtained a camera, a watch and other goods to the value of
several hundred dollars. Shimizu now claims that he has been
tricked and is looking for Johnston.[48]

The Chinese did not respond to the British request until April 1946: they
then arrested the three men, who were placed in Ward Road jail. The Chinese nevertheless refused to hand them over for trial unless the British, by
way of 'reciprocity' returned to China 42 Chinese alleged traitors from
Burma as well as additional suspects from other British territories in the
Far East. The British were reluctant to accede to this demand and protested
that 'they could not acquiesce in a position where three British subjects in
Shanghai were apparently being held as hostages'. The British then tried
unsuccessfully to persuade the Chinese to try the three men in Shanghai. It
was not until early 1947 that the issue was resolved by their deportation to
face trial in Hong Kong.

In addition to the three accused men, German witnesses, including Carl
Flick-Steger, former head of radio station XGRS, and Baron Jesco von
Puttkamer, were also sent to Hong Kong to give evidence. Gracie was found
guilty and sentenced to eight years' imprisonment. Johnston's claim to Irish
citizenship was not recognized by the court and he received a ten-year sentence. Various British authorities tangled themselves up in knots over the
case of Lamb. On legal advice it was decided not to pursue the case against
him since, unlike his two fellow-broadcasters, his treasonable actions all
dated from the period before the retrocession of the International Settlement in 1943. This fact was regarded as likely to impede a successful prosecution. In spite of this technical legal obstacle, he was brought to Hong
Kong anyway, 'due to the very natural desire of both His Majesty's Consul-
General and the Chinese Government to rid that city of a man with so unsavoury a record and of such dangerous potentialities'.[49] Lamb was held in
Hong Kong for several months while officials wrangled over what should be
done with him. In the end he was released, whereupon he immediately
lodged a suit for wrongful imprisonment. The Hong Kong government
'somewhat quixotically', as the presiding judge observed, 'disbursed more
than HK$1,700 for the plaintiff's board and lodging since his release to en-
able him to take the present proceedings against itself'. Judgement was

found in favour of Lamb but he was awarded only nominal damages.[50]

Lawrence Kentwell was arrested by the Chinese authorities in December 1945 and charged with collaboration. He vigorously protested his innocence, pointing to his long campaign for retrocession of the foreign enclaves as proof of his patriotism. His recent pro-Axis views faded from his memory as he avowed: 'I am personally grateful to China's brave and gallant Allies for defeating Japan – China's deadly enemy. Now that victory is with us, let us all unite and rejoice, as one big family of nations and with toleration and goodwill all round.' He complained that he suffered from 'rheumatism of the left leg and stomach trouble' and appealed for 'humanitarian treatment'.[51]

Kentwell was arraigned in the Shanghai High Court in January 1946. Predictably, and disastrously, he undertook his own defence. A newspaper reporter commented that 'he appeared quite gay and light-hearted in spite of the fact that he was facing a very grave charge'. Kentwell pointed out to the court that he could not be held guilty of collaboration as he was not a Chinese citizen. He had merely pretended to be one, he said, in order 'to please his Chinese friends', even though he had not, in fact, been naturalized. This was, in fact, the truth – but it was not accepted by the court. The judge told him that since his mother had been Chinese he would be considered as having held Chinese citizenship since 1931, the date of his denaturalization by the British. On the central issue, Kentwell delivered a long speech denying that he had ever collaborated. On the contrary, he argued, 'in view of the shabby and uncivil treatment he had received at the hands of the British Government on account of his not being an Englishman of pure European descent, he [had] decided to help China against the imperialistic oppression of the British'. As an exhibit for the defence he produced a signed photo of appreciation from Chiang Kai-shek.[52] The *China Weekly Review* (resurrected under the editorship of J. B. Powell's son) commented unkindly: 'Perhaps Kentwell's defense would not have been so unexpectedly ludicrous had he been an illiterate coolie. But for one who studied law, the only wonder is that he ever had a client. Certainly no sane man would entrust his defence to a lawyer who defended him in the way that Kentwell is defending himself.'[53] He was found guilty and sentenced to seven years' imprisonment. The judgement was, however, subsequently set aside by the

Chinese Supreme Court and Kentwell was sent back for a new trial. This time, wisely, he did not defend himself – though his lawyer had difficulty in restraining him from delivering a 'melodramatic speech'.[54] His ultimate fate is unknown.

During the autumn of 1945, the American authorities in China conducted an intensive and fruitless search for Eugene Pick. He was reported to have been seen in a barber's shop in Shanghai, in a Russian Orthodox mission in Peking and elsewhere, but every lead turned out to be a false trail. In fact, Pick had flown in a small plane to Tsingtao on 14 August. From there he succeeded, by bribing a Japanese official, in securing passage on a boat to Japan just before the Japanese surrender. The ship hit a mine and exploded. Pick suffered a leg injury but survived. In a later submission to US intelligence officials, he claimed that his motive in going to Japan was 'to disclose to the Americans all I knew'. 'Besides', he added, he had wanted to 'see the monkeys on their knees'.[55] When he arrived in Tokyo Pick received treatment for his leg wound and then went on crutches to the navy ministry to seek help. He had the good fortune to find there his former employer in the Shanghai Naval Intelligence Bureau, Commander Otani, who put him up at an inn and transferred 1 million yen from confidential navy ministry funds to a bank account in the name of 'Koji', one of Pick's many *noms de guerre*. At Otani's suggestion, Pick considered using the money to open a Russian nightclub in Tokyo.

In February 1946, sensing that the Americans were closing in on him, Pick decided to take the bull by the horns. He went to see the chief of the counter-intelligence section of the American occupation forces in Tokyo and offered to provide information about covert activities by former Japanese naval intelligence personnel, including Otani. Given the extent of the help he had received from Otani, this was, of course, a shocking act of betrayal – though perfectly in keeping with Pick's character and previous history. In private letters to former acquaintances he railed against many of his old comrades whom he now regarded as traitors: Morris Gershkovitch, for example, was denounced as a 'Jewish pig'.[56] On 11 February 1946, as Pick and Otani were dining together at the Takahashi Hotel, they were arrested by American military police. Otani was soon released but his companion was held for investigation.

Pick was sent to be examined by Captain Dr James F. Bing, neuropsychiatrist. Dr Bing noted that the patient talked to himself and still complained of his leg injury. He ate normally, but had recently been smoking and drinking more than usual. Pick seemed otherwise to be in normal physical condition save for a 'slight muscular twitch of the right Orbicularis Oculis muscle'. During the examination Pick constantly drummed his fingers together or tapped nearby objects. After administering various psychological tests, Dr Bing reported:

> This 47 year old civilian…appears to be about 15 years older
> than his actual age…Although he was oriented to time, place
> and person, he had a great deal of difficulty performing simple
> arithmetic tests. For this reason psychometric examination
> was performed. Results of which show he had a mental age of
> 11 years, 9 months and I.Q. of 86 (Wechsler Mental Ability
> Scale). Since the patient has done post-graduate work, it is felt
> the poor performance of this test is a result of cerebral or
> arteriosclerotic or senile changes.[57]

Pick's poor performance in these psychological tests may have been deliberate. In other ways he gave evidence around the same time of an animated and far from senile mind.

Under extensive interrogation by Counter-Intelligence Corps officers, Pick responded with enthusiasm, reeling off names and stories and recounting a long, sensational and semi-fictional account of his life. He claimed credit for arranging the wartime release and repatriation of the American journalist J. B. Powell and of the British radio expert James Smart. He also produced memoranda concerning intelligence activities in Shanghai, the Soviet danger and anything else he thought his captors might appreciate. In addition, he claimed knowledge of a complex subversive plot of former Japanese navy officers, masterminded by Otani. Some American officials were taken in: an official telegram from the senior responsible officer of the US Counter-Intelligence Corps, discussing plans for Pick to be sent back to Shanghai to face trial for war crimes, suggested that 'in view of his extensive knowledge of espionage activities and personalities in Shanghai … careful consideration be given his case if your evidence against him is not conclusive as he may be of considerably greater value to you in the role of employee informant'.[58] Investigation of Pick's allegations produced no evidence of any untoward activity by the Japanese he had named, except for the large disbursements to Pick himself by Otani from secret navy funds and a payment of 100,000 yen to Pick's former control officer, Ikushima, to enable him to set up a geisha house. American officials soon concluded that Pick was 'a lying opportunist of the first magnitude and that he was guilty of double-dealing all along the line'.[59]

Pick was brought to Shanghai under military escort in April 1946. He was held in the Ward Road prison and tried by a special US military tribunal which found him not guilty of involvement in the killing of Catholic priests in the Philippines. The Americans then turned him over to the Chinese authorities who charged him with espionage and collaboration with the Japanese. Proceedings against him dragged on for two years. In 1948 he was found guilty and sentenced to five years' imprisonment.

On 1 December that year Pick submitted a long, rambling memorandum to the American authorities in Shanghai, purporting to demonstrate, with great circumstantial detail, that all his actions since his defection from Comintern in 1927 had been governed by a concern to further the interests of the United States. He accused various Japanese, White Russians and Chinese, as well as an American officer, of framing him.[60] Shortly afterwards he was released from jail. The official explanation was that he had been freed in recognition of the amount of time he had already served. But according to a US intelligence report, 'local American CIC [Counter-Intelligence Corps] representatives paid half amount squeeze necessary to effect release'.[61] What motive the Americans may have had for such a payment is hard to fathom – unless perhaps they were concerned to buy Pick's silence. He succeeded in escaping to Taiwan in early May 1949, just before Shanghai fell to the communists. Characteristically, he tried to ingratiate himself with the Taipei police, posing as an expert on Soviet communism. He also wrote to an American intelligence contact claiming that he had 'valuable information' about American officials who had been working on behalf of the USSR in China. 'I lived in Asia for many years and I know all the Soviet monkey treaks [sic]', he declared.[62] Pick soon fell foul of the Taiwan au-

thorities and was again arrested. Rumours floated that he had been liquidated but an American intelligence report in the summer of 1950 stated
that he was still alive in a prison in Taiwan.[63] Earlier that year he had been
reported to be in possession of an entry visa to Siam.[64] Whether he succeeded in making his way there is unknown. At any rate, after the summer
of 1950 he disappeared.

上海

The end of the war did not bring about any restoration of Shanghai's old
cosmopolitan character. The foreign communities soon disintegrated. Jewish refugees emigrated to the United States, Australia, Brazil and, after May
1948, Israel. About 2,500 returned from Shanghai to West Germany, the
only organized group of Jews to return there from any country. At least 100
returned to Austria. By November 1948, when Mao Tse-tung's armies
began to close in on Shanghai, there were still 5,000 Jews in the city. The
wealthy Sephardi plutocracy fled to Hong Kong. The Israeli government
sent a consul to Shanghai to organize the emigration of most of the remaining Jews. By 1956, when the last synagogue closed, only 173 were left.

The Russians too disappeared. The Auxiliary Detachment of the Municipal Police, last relic of the Shanghai Volunteer Corps (and, at some further
removes, of the anti-Bolshevik military formations during the Russian Civil
War), was finally disbanded on 12 September 1945. Many of the White
Russians fled to Hawaii. Some, lured by the seductive rhetoric of Russian
patriotism and promises of amnesty for anti-communists, returned voluntarily to their homeland. Astonishingly, even leaders of the White Russian
far right, among them Konstantin Rodzaevsky, head of the Russian Fascist
Party, did so; he was later tried and shot as were several of the others. The
evacuation of many of the Jews from Shanghai by the International Refugee
Organization in 1948–49 led to a final outburst of antisemitic feeling by
White Russians, who themselves were desperate to leave before the communists arrived. A crowd stormed the office of the International Refugee
Organization, demanding facilities to emigrate. In early 1949 about 5,000
White Russians were evacuated to the Philippines. Many subsequently
moved on to Australia, the United States and Canada.

A few vestiges of the international character of the city remained. Until 1949 municipal decrees continued to be printed in English as well as Chinese. Some Sikh constables continued to work in the Shanghai police as they had done throughout the war. Others returned to India.

Occupiers, internees and collaborators thus all left town. Yet the Shanghai party hardly missed a beat. In November 1945 the Amateur Dramatic Society revived its production of *Richard III*, which had been banned by the Japanese in June 1942. The Shanghai Club was initially appropriated by the British navy, but after a while its members regained possession and the 'long bar' resumed its function as a strictly graduated, upper-class, white man's watering-hole. The brass foot-bar from the floor, which had been removed by the Japanese, was restored. Holy Trinity Cathedral was restored to the Church of England. The foreign concessions were only a memory, but the Hong Kong and Shanghai Bank recovered its palatial building and enjoyed the exquisite revenge of supervising the liquidation of its own former liquidator, the Yokohama Specie Bank. A new generation of American and British 'griffins' arrived, and Anglo-American capital once again poured into the great enterprises along the Bund. The government enacted a new Chinese company law to limit the activities of foreign-registered firms, but the Keswicks and their fellow-taipans adapted and business revived. The neon lights were rekindled and Shanghai's night life resumed its wicked intensity.

Between 1945 and 1949 Shanghai became once again the intelligence centre of the Far East. The chief foreign players were now the Americans and the Russians, with the British reduced to a subsidiary role. As in the past, foreigners waged their secret war through local surrogates. And as in the past, the Chinese protégés of the powers refused to be mere pawns in the diplomatic game and insisted on playing independent roles and pursuing their own distinctive interests. During the Chinese Civil War, as during most of the Second World War, Shanghai remained on the sidelines of the military conflict, a bride waiting and watching while her suitors fought to the death for her hand. All the while, the guests from abroad carried on with the party, semi-oblivious to the mayhem around them.

The show went on for four more years. Then the curtain descended for the last time. As Mao's troops surrounded the city in the spring of 1949 a chaotic flight took place. The most valuable commodity in the city, information, was sold at a high price: the archive of the special branch of the former Municipal Police, with its thousands of files on communist personalities and activities, was purchased by American intelligence agents. The documents were loaded on to a ship within range of gunfire and some boxes fell into the Whangpoo. Others had been taken in the preceding weeks of chaos and were reported to have been offered for sale to the Soviet Union by six shady underworld figures of various foreign nationalities.[65]

On 27 May 1949 Shanghai was occupied by communist forces. The remnants of Chiang Kai-shek's régime fled to Taiwan. Communist victory brought the gaieties to an abrupt halt. Nearly all remaining foreigners left. The *North China Daily News* declined miserably into a communist propaganda sheet, then faded out of existence altogether. Powell's *China Weekly Review*, which had waged a gallant battle against Kuomintang censorship, lasted a bit longer by abasing itself to the New Order. It ceased publication after a couple of years, whereupon the younger Powell returned to America to face ruin after accusations of disloyalty from McCarthyites. The great British trading houses tried, at first, to adapt to the new reality but found that China's new rulers had no interest in perpetuating their role. One by one they too departed: Jardine, Matheson in 1952, Butterfield & Swire two years later.[66]

Apart from Shanghai's distinctively European architecture, little remained of the foreign presence in Shanghai. One of the few relics was the heavy roller on the front lawn of the British consulate on the Bund. The new masters of the city, not knowing quite what to do with it, left it where it stood. Forty years later a British visitor found it still there, 'half sunk in the mud, the handle gnawed by termites, and, like Shanghai itself, decaying slowly in the heat'.[67]

Conclusion

It is almost impossible to say who won and who lost the secret war in Shanghai. Even to assess the comparative effectiveness of the various great powers involved is difficult. Their interests and objectives were all different, the resources at their disposal varied tremendously and the necessary data, particularly in the cases of the Russians and the British, are not yet fully available.

One interesting attempt at such an appraisal was nevertheless made after the war in a report prepared for the X-2 (counter-intelligence) branch of the OSS by the former head of a Japanese intelligence organization in North China. He rated the British Secret Intelligence Service (SIS) most highly – at any rate in the period before December 1941, when he estimated it had had 300 agents in Shanghai alone. He also held British propaganda in China in high esteem. The American intelligence services, he wrote, were big spenders but their security was bad. German intelligence was skilful and systematic but its various branches 'reject and dislike each other', a penetrating and accurate observation, as we have noticed. As for the Japanese themselves, all their intelligence activities had been undertaken within the military organs of the various armed services. Their 'great weak point' had been the absence of an independent intelligence service on the model of the British SIS.[1]

None of the powers emerged with much honour from the wartime experience in China. The Germans there made no significant contribution to their nation's war effort, nor to that of their allies. The British record was tainted by collaborationism and a primary concern with preserving its position of economic primacy. The Americans' heavy investment of men and resources was vitiated by arrogance, naiveté and lack of clarity of purpose. The French in China, as in their other Far Eastern possessions, clung with faintly ridiculous obsessiveness to the shadow of imperial power long after its reality had disappeared. The behaviour of the Soviets was even more manipulative and cynical than that of the rest. As for the Japanese, they threw away a stunning initial military victory and great political opportunities by descending into savagery and inhumanity — a collective crime committed in their name that, as a society, they (unlike the Germans) still refuse to acknowledge properly.[2]

The wars within wars in China were strongly coloured by racial and class attitudes. Combatants against the Japanese shared a world of implicit assumptions with the collaborationists. As we have seen, the decisions to collaborate of many Allied citizens in Shanghai often arose from perceived social or racial slights. Likewise, British and American guerrilla warfare impresarios in China engaged each other in a contest of 'gentlemen versus players'. One reason for the fierce OSS-SOE conflict in China was that a man like Miles despised the pretensions of a taipan grandee such as Keswick. Similarly, among the Germans, a diplomat like Consul-General Fischer or a veteran officer like Siefken looked down on Nazi guttersnipes like Meisinger and Kahner. The Shanghai mind, in its many forms, infected and corrupted relationships between individuals and between collectivities.

It would be tempting — but mistaken — to conclude that the game of nations in Shanghai during the Second World War had no real meaning, nor any definitive outcome. True, the political warfare and subversive operations of all the powers in China were gravely weakened by inter-agency bickering and inter-allied suspicions and intrigues, often absurdly petty in nature. True, none of the antagonists won a clear victory or even any significant tactical advantage for all the effort invested. The Japanese and Germans spent more time investigating each other than they did coordinating their strategy or sharing information. The British and the Americans, in a strange mirror-image of their enemies' behaviour, competed more than they cooperated. All the powers used their Chinese protégés instrumentally, treating them as pawns rather than as genuine allies.

In the final analysis, then, was the pecking and scratching and mutual bloodletting in the Shanghai cockpit by Tai Li, Otani, Ehrhardt, Meisinger, Keswick, Miles, Pick and their henchmen merely an exercise in futility — a game and nothing more? Or was there, underlying it all, a fundamental conflict, however dimly perceived, among different conceptions of national, economic and individual freedoms?

Old Shanghai is gone. But over the half century after 1949 Hong Kong assumed something of the economic role of pre-war Shanghai. Butterfield & Swire, Jardine, Matheson, the Hong Kong and Shanghai Bank, Baghdadi Jewish capitalists from Shanghai and a new generation of Chinese entrepreneurs, many of them also of Shanghainese origin, created an economic power house in the British colony that, like the International Settlement in former times, aroused a mixture of nationalist resentment and imitative envy in the rest of China. Under pressure from the Chinese that was oddly redolent of the old arguments over Shanghai, the British reluctantly acquiesced in the reversion of Hong Kong to Chinese sovereignty in 1997. The handover was marked by a gigantic party, fireworks and oratory that combined mawkish sentimentalism and humbug – all reminiscent of the smaller-scale wartime handovers of the foreign concessions to the Chinese. But as in the case of Shanghai in 1943, the troubling question remained: would the end of colonialism mean genuine liberation or merely the installation of a new form of oligarchic domination?

As the Japanese discovered, no victories are final. The apparent triumph of the Soviets in China in 1949 was belied little more than a decade later by the beginning of the Sino-Soviet rift. Then, a decade after that, the antiwestern excesses of the Cultural Revolution gave way to the Sino-American rapprochement. In 1989 Chinese communists smashed a democratic quasi-revolution with tanks, blood and lies. Yet the country soon resumed its advance on the road to capitalism. And in spite of savage repression by Tai Li's heirs in the secret police apparatus of the 1990s, the idea of freedom persisted obstinately in the Chinese consciousness. It lingers still – and, albeit in different form, with different players and using different methods, the political struggle in China and the related game of nations continue to revolve around the attempt to define and attain that fundamental, instinctive and inexpugnable human aspiration.

Notes

Abbreviations used in notes

AA	Archives of the German Foreign Ministry, Bonn
AMAE	Archives du Ministère des Affaires Etrangères, Nantes
BAP	Bundesarchiv, Potsdam
CAHJP	Central Archives for the History of the Jewish People, Jerusalem
CIC	Counter-Intelligence Corps
FOIA/CIA	Documents released to the author by the US Central Intelligence Agency under the Freedom of Information Act
FOIA/FBI	Documents released to the author by the US Federal Bureau of Investigation under the Freedom of Information Act
FOIA/SD	Documents released to the author by the US State Department under the Freedom of Information Act
FOIA/USAISC	Documents released to the author by US Army Intelligence and Security Command under the Freedom of Information Act
HIA	Hoover Institution Archives, Stanford, California
IOR	India Office Records, British Library, London
JFM	Captured Japanese Foreign Ministry records (microfilms), Library of Congress, Washington DC
PRO	Public Record Office, Kew
RSHA	Reichssicherheitshauptamt
SMP	Shanghai Municipal Police records, United States National Archives, College Park, Maryland (Record Group 263)
SOAS	School of Oriental and African Studies, London University
USNA	United States National Archives, College Park, Maryland

Introduction

1   Gail Hershatter, *Dangerous Pleasures: Prostitution and Modernity in Twentieth-Century Shanghai,* Berkeley, 1997, p. 40.

2   Quoted in introduction to Frederic Wakeman Jr and Wen-hsin Yeh (eds), *Shanghai Sojourners*, Berkeley, 1992, p. 5.

3   Entry on Keswick by John Swire in *Dictionary of National Biography 1980–1985.*

4   Quoted in J. H. Haan, 'Origin and Development of the Political System in the Shanghai International Settlement', *Journal of the Hong Kong Branch of the Royal Asiatic Society*, vol. 22, 1982, pp. 31–64.

5   Unpublished memoirs of Brigadier L. F. Field, Imperial War Museum archives, London.

6   Maître Barraud, doyen of French corps of advocates in Shanghai, quoted in AMAE, Consulat Shanghai, rép. num. 333, Services de Polices, bulletin mensuel, September 1941, pp. 340–41.

7   See Frederic Wakeman Jr, 'Policing Modern Shanghai', *China Quarterly*, 115, September 1988, pp. 412, 435; and Wakeman, *Policing Shanghai 1927–1937,* Berkeley, 1995, *passim.*

8   Quoted in Brian G. Martin, 'Tu Yüeh-sheng and Labour Control in Shanghai: The Case of the French Tramways Union, 1928–1932', *Papers on Far Eastern History*, 32, 1985, p. 109.

9   G. E. Miller [pseud. Mauricio Fresco], *Shanghai: The Paradise of Adventurers,* New York, 1937.

10   See Percy Finch, *Shanghai and Beyond,* New York, 1953, pp. 72 ff.

11   See Frederic Wakeman Jr, *The Shanghai Badlands: Wartime Terrorism and Urban Crime, 1937–1941,* Cambridge, 1996, pp. 10–11.

12   'Extract from letter dated 12 October 1937 from Colonel Graham', PRO, WO 208/201.

13   Quoted in Nicholas R. Clifford, *Spoilt Children of Empire: Westerners in Shanghai and the Chinese Revolution of the 1920s,* Hanover, NH, 1991, p. 240.

14   Papers of R. Maurice Tinkler, Imperial War Museum archives, London.

15   'Notes on Shanghai 1928' (printed), Appendix E, IOR, L/MIL/17/20/6.

16 Quoted in Alvin D. Coox, 'Flawed Perception and its Effect upon Operational Thinking: The Case of the Japanese Army, 1937–1941', in Michael I. Handel (ed.), *Intelligence and Military Operations,* London, 1990, p. 241.

17 Quoted in Mark R. Peattie, 'Japanese Treaty Port Settlements in China, 1895–1937', in Peter Duus, Ramon H. Myers and Mark R. Peattie (eds), *The Japanese Informal Empire in China, 1895–1937*, Princeton, 1989, p. 187.

Chapter 1

1 Robert Gullain, *Orient Extrême: Une vie en Asie*, Paris, 1986, p. 34.

2 A. Wilbur (Shanghai Foreign YMCA) to Eugene Barnett, 31 December 1937, YMCA archives, University of Minnesota.

3 Edna Lee Booker, *News is My Job: A Correspondent in War-Torn China,* New York, 1940, pp. 295–97.

4 Rhodes Farmer, *Shanghai Harvest: A Diary of Three Years in the China War,* London, 1945, p. 91.

5 Harriet Sergeant, *Shanghai: Collision Point of Cultures 1918–1937,* London, 1990, p. 310.

6 John Hunter Boyle, *China and Japan at War 1937–1945: The Politics of Collaboration*, Stanford, CA, 1972, p. 283.

7 Quoted in Christopher Thorne, *Allies of a Kind: The United States, Britain and the War against Japan, 1941–1945,* London, 1978, p. 68.

8 Wen-hsin Yeh, 'Dai Li and the Liu Geqing Affair: Heroism in the Chinese Secret Service during the War of Resistance', *Journal of Asian Studies,* 48, 3, August 1989, pp. 545–62.

9 See Carl Crow, *Foreign Devils in the Flowery Kingdom,* New York, 1940, p. 126.

10 Sir A. Clark Kerr (Shanghai) to Foreign Office, 14 October 1938, PRO, WO 208/201.

11 MI2 memorandum, 12 May 1939, PRO, WO 208/273.

12 Transcript of remarks on 25 February 1939, enclosed with Butterfield & Swire, Shanghai, to John Swire & Sons, London, 3 March 1939, Swire papers, SOAS, JSSII 2/17, box 53.

13 John Swire & Sons, London, to Butterfield & Swire, Shanghai, 21 April 1939, Swire papers, SOAS, JSSII 2/17, box 53.

14 Butterfield & Swire, Shanghai, to John Swire & Sons, London, 19 May 1939, Swire Papers, SOAS, JSSII 2/17, box 53.

15 Unsigned, undated memorandum [November 1939], SMP, D 9114(C).

16 *Shanghai Municipal Council Report for the Year 1939* Shanghai, 1940, p. 103.

17 OSS X-2 Branch, 'Shanghai: Counter-Espionage Summary', 12 August 1945, FOIA/CIA.

18 Norwood F. Allman, *Shanghai Lawyer*, New York, 1943, p. 228.

19 Commissioner F. W. Gerrard to Secretary, Shanghai Municipal Council, 6 June 1933 (printed copy), PRO, WO 208/184.

20 Text of communiqué in Sir A. Clark Kerr (Shanghai) to Foreign Office, 14 March 1939, PRO, WO 106/2372.

21 W.H. Auden and Christopher Isherwood, *Journey to a War,* New York, 1939, pp. 240–52.

Chapter 2

1   John W. M. Chapman, 'Tricycle Recycled: Collaboration among the Secret Intelligence Services of the Axis States 1940–1941', *Intelligence and National Security,* 7, 1992, pp. 268–99.

2   'Background Material' in HIA, N.F. Allman papers, box 12, file 45; memorandum for the 'family record', 25 June 1941, in Hilaire du Berrier papers, State Historical Society of North Dakota, Bismarck, ND.

3   Report dated 13 July 1937, SMP, D 8000.

4   G. M. Liddell to Sir E. W. E. Holderness, 1 October 1936, copy with accompanying minutes in PRO, FO 371/20580 W 13429/9549/41.

5   Report dated 13 July 1937, SMP, D 8000.

6   Letter dated 28 May 1937, Berrier papers.

7   Letter dated 1 July 1937, Berrier papers.

8   Memorandum dated 25 June 1941, Berrier papers.

9   Report by Detective Sergeant Larby, 10 December 1937, SMP, D 8000.

10 Letter dated 1 July 1937, Berrier papers.

11 Berrier to 'Helen', 28 September 1941, Berrier papers.

12 SMP reports dated 9 and 10 February 1938, D 8000.

13 SMP report, 11 March 1938, D 8000.

14 Letter dated 8 May 1939, Berrier papers.

15 SMP, D 8986 (C).

16 Berrier letter to 'Helen', 8 May 1939, Berrier papers.

17 Memorandum dated 25 June 1941, Berrier papers.

18 *Ostasiatischer Lloyd*, 17 March 1940.

19 'German Intelligence in China and Japan', Strategic Services Unit memorandum, 21 August 1945, FOIA/CIA.

20 OSS X-2 branch report on death of Miorini, 15 October 1945, quoting SMP report, 16 June 1941, FOIA/CIA.

21 Ibid.

22 Ibid.

23 HIA, N.F. Allman papers, box 5.

24 Most of the information in this section is based on materials on Erben released to the author by the CIA, the FBI and the USAISC, under the Freedom of Information Act. For a full account of Erben's career see Rudolf Stoiber, *Der Spion der Hitler sein wollte,* Vienna, 1989. See also evidence given by Erben in the trial of Lothar Eisentraeger et al., Shanghai, October 1946, USNA, RG 153, case 58-137, book 1.

25 Investigation on Erben, file 65-682, FOIA/FBI.

26 Ibid.

27 Ibid.

28 Ibid.

29 US Vice-Consul, Buenos Aires, to Consul-General, 23 January 1940, FOIA/SD.

30 Evidence given by Erben in the trial of Lothar Eisentraeger et al., Shanghai, October 1946, USNA, RG 153, case 58-137, book 1, p. 119.

31 Report by D.S.I. McKeown, [15 ?] November 1940, SMP, H 656(C).

32 Report by 'YEX-55', 27 February 1946, USNA, RG 226, entry 182A, box 10, folder 74.

33 SMP report by McKeown, [23?] November 1940, H 656 (C).

34 Report by 'YEX-55', 27 February 1946, USNA, RG 226, entry 182A, box 10, folder 74.

35 Report dated [23?] November 1940, SMP, H 656(C).

36 See newspaper reports, August 1925, and India Office memorandum, May 1918, in IOR, L/P&S/206.

37 *Patiala and its Historical Surroundings* (3rd edn), Patiala, 1987.

38 Letter to 'Berjee', 10 October 1945, USNA, RG 226, entry 182A, box 10, folder 70.

39 Frederic Wakeman Jr, *The Shanghai Badlands: Wartime Terrorism and Urban Crime: 1937–1941*, Cambridge, 1996, pp. 124–25.

40 Memorandum by 'Don' (probably Don Chisholm), no date (probably 1945), USNA, RG 226, entry 182, box 1, folder 7.

41 Lampson to Sir A. Chamberlain, 26 August 1927, PRO, FO 405/255.

42 See minutes, PRO, FO 371/12422/72ff.

43 OSS report, Peking, 9 October 1945, FOIA/CIA.

44 Unsigned American intelligence memorandum, November 1949, FOIA/USAISC.

45 Statement by Frederick Anton Wiehl among papers on Pick, FOIA/USAISC.

46 'Information Concerning Hovans', OSS report, unsigned, undated [1945/46], USNA, RG 226, entry 182, box 12, folder 78.

47 JICA/China report, 23 October 1945, FOIA/USAISC.

48 Memorandum of conversation with Otani Inaho, 24 June 1950, FOIA/USAISC.

49 OSS report, 12 October 1945, FOIA/CIA.

50 OSS report, 12 [?] October 1945, FOIA/CIA.

51 Report by 'Saint' for US Strategic Services Unit, 12 April 1946, FOIA/CIA.

Chapter 3

1 Carl Crow, *Foreign Devils in the Flowery kingdom,* New York, 1940, p. 134.

2 *Shanghai Times*, 10 September 1939.

3 Butterfield & Swire, Shanghai, to John Swire & Sons, London, 15 September 1939, Swire papers, SOAS, JSSII 2/17, box 53.

4 *Shanghai Times*, 10 September 1939.

5 Bohle to German Consulate-General, Shanghai, 1 April 1940, AA, 27198.

6 *China Press*, 12 October 1939.

7 Donald M. McKale, 'The Nazi Party in the Far East, 1931–1945', *Journal of Contemporary History*, 12, 1977, pp. 300, 310.

8 OSS X-2 branch report on Frederick ('Fritz') Wiedemann, 24 October 1945, page 61, FOIA/CIA.

9 'History of the Nazi Party in China', undated memorandum forwarded within US State Department, 23 April 1946, USNA, RG 59, State Department decimal file 862.20293/4-2346.

10 'German Intelligence Activities in China During World War II', Strategic Services Unit memorandum, 1 March 1946, section III B 2, FOIA/CIA. Much of the information in this chapter on the Siefken and Ehrhardt burcaux is derived from this source.

11 John W.M. Chapman (ed. and trans.), *The Price of Admiralty: The War Diary of the German Naval Attaché in Japan 1939–1943,* 2 vols, Ripe, East Sussex, 1982–84, vol. 1, p. 85 (entry dated 29 January 1940; translation slightly adapted).

12 'German Intelligence Activities in China During World War II', Strategic Services Unit memorandum, 1 March 1946, section III B 7, FOIA/CIA.

13 John W.M. Chapman, 'Japanese Intelligence 1919–1945: A Suitable Case for Treatment', in Christopher Andrew and Jeremy Noakes (eds), *Intelligence and International Relations 1900–1945,* Exeter, 1987, pp. 160–61; John W.M. Chapman, 'Tricycle Recycled: Collaboration among the Secret Intelligence Services of the Axis States 1940–1941', *Intelligence and National Security*, 7, 1992 pp. 268–99, esp. p. 284; and Stephen Roskill, *A Merchant Fleet at War: Alfred Holt & Co. 1939–1945,* London, 1962, pp. 65–73.

14 Chapman (ed. and trans.), *The Price of Admiralty*, pp. 582–83.

15 Translation of notes found among papers of Stanislaus Klimek, German Embassy, Tokyo, 1945, attached to CIC case file on Kahner, USNA, RG 319 07/17/11.

16 Himmler to Foreign Ministry, 28 June 1940, USNA, RG 319 07/17/11.

17 Altenburg (Peking) to Berlin (relaying message from Fischer), 15 June 1940, AA, Inland II A/B 83-60E Sdh I.

18 Foreign Ministry to Müller, 22 June 1940, AA, Inland II A/B 83-60E Sdh I.

19 'German Intelligence in China and Japan', US Strategic Services memorandum, 9 August 1945, FOIA/CIA.

20 Naval and Military Intelligence Summary, 14 October 1939, PRO, WO 208/293.

21 Butterfield & Swire, Shanghai, to John Swire & Sons, London, 15 September 1939, Swire papers, SOAS, JSSII 2/17, box 53.

22 'Instructions for the Commander, Shanghai Area', 16 December 1939, PRO, WO 106/2373.

23 Hallett Abend, *My Years in China 1926–1941,* London, 1944, p. 333.

24 Butterfield & Swire, Shanghai, to John Swire & Sons, London, 15 September 1939, Swire papers, SOAS, JSSII 2/17, box 53.

25 Butterfield & Swire, Shanghai, to John Swire & Sons, London, 22 September 1939, Swire papers, SOAS, JSSII 2/17, box 53.

26 Ibid.

27 Butterfield & Swire, Shanghai, to John Swire & Sons, London, 25 October 1939, Swire papers, SOAS, JSSII 2/17, box 53.

28 SMP report, 10 January 1940, D 9639.

29 Report for February 1940, AMAE, Consulat Shanghai, rép. num. 330, Services Polices, bulletins mensuels, January–June 1940.

30 SMP report, 16 November 1939, D 8155B(C).

31 A. H. George to British Ambassador, Shanghai, 10 December 1940, PRO, FO 371/27631.

32 Reports dated 13 and 20 December 1939, SMP, D 9483.

33 A. Henschel to Press Attaché, German Embassy, Shanghai, 3 March 1941, AA, P3-3a.

34 Memorandum by editor of *Ostasiatischer Lloyd*, 15 May 1941, and accompanying documents, AA, P3-3.

35 For a full survey see Rudolf Löwenthal, 'The Jewish Press in China', in *The Religious Periodical Press in China,* Sinological Series no. 57, published by the Synodal Commission in China, Peking, 1940.

36 German Consul-General, Shanghai to German Embassy, Shanghai, 24 January, 19 February 1940, AA, D Pol 3-1.

37 Engelmann (SS) to German Foreign Ministry, 16 December 1940, AA, D Pol. 3-1.

38 'German Diplomatic and Consular Personnel in China', 28 January 1946: a US intelligence report based on 'Japanese documents found in the files of the Shanghai Municipal Police', FOIA/CIA.

39 'German Intelligence in China and Japan', US Strategic Services Unit memorandum, 21 August 1945, FOIA/CIA.

40 Memorandum on German propaganda in Shanghai, 22 April 1940, USNA, State Department decimal file 862.20293/104.

41 Shanghai Secret Intelligence Service report, 20 February 1940, PRO, WO 208/294.

42 Shanghai Naval and Military Intelligence Summary, 1–15 May 1940, PRO, WO 208/294.

43 Randow (Shanghai) to Foreign Ministry, Berlin, transmitting message from Baron Jesco von Puttkamer, 25 November 1941, AA, 29559.

44 Shanghai Secret Intelligence Service report, 4 April 1940, PRO, WO 208/294.

45 A. T. Steele, *Shanghai and Manchuria, 1932: Recollections of a War Correspondent,* Tempe, AZ, 1977, p. 3.

46 Carroll Alcott, *My War With Japan*, New York, 1943, esp. pp. 298–99.

47 Shanghai Secret Intelligence Service report, 4 April 1940, PRO, WO 208/294.

48 Undated [1945/46], unsigned US intelligence report on German propaganda in Shanghai, FOIA/CIA.

49 Shanghai Secret Intelligence Service (Naval) report for 1–31 August 1941, PRO, WO 208/296.

50 Quoted in Edward E. Rice, US Consul-General, Stuttgart, to State Department, 28 December 1954, FOIA/SD.

51 Statement by Mehnert, 13 [August?] 1946, FOIA/USAISC.

52 Klaus Mehnert, *Ein Deutscher in der Welt: Erinnerungen 1906–1981,* Stuttgart, 1981.

53 Report by Detective Sub-Inspector J. A. Pitts, 3 September 1941, SMP, N 1077.

54 OSS X-2 branch report, 'Propaganda in Shanghai', 21 September 1945, USNA, RG 226, entry 182, box 23, folder 126.

55 Berrier to 'Helen', 28 September 1941, Berrier papers.

56 Berrier to 'Helen', 6 September 1939, Berrier papers.

57   Berrier letter to 'Helen', 20 May 1940, Berrier papers.

58   Memorandum dated 25 June 1941, Berrier papers.

59   Report by Detective Sub-Inspector Logan, 26 July 1940, SMP, D 8000.

60   'German Intelligence in China and Japan', Strategic Services Unit memorandum, 21 August 1945, FOIA/CIA.

61   Report by Detective Sub-Inspector Logan, 26 July 1940, SMP, D 8000.

62   Ibid.

63   SMP report, 7 April 1941, N 765 (C).

64   Ibid.

65   Report by Detective Sub-Inspector McKeown, [15 ?] November 1940, SMP, H 656(C).

66   SMP report, 26 July 1940, D 8000.

67   Letter dated 20 November 1940, Berrier papers.

68   French political police, bulletin mensuel, AMAE, Consulat Shanghai, rép. num. 332, leaf 105, February 1941.

69   'Paddy' [Sir A. Noble], Shanghai, to Frank [Roberts], Foreign Office, 22 August 1940, PRO, FO 371/24361/173.

70   R. L. Speaight for W. H. B. Mack to Sir A. Noble, 20 October 1940, PRO, FO 371/24361/174.

71   Unsigned appreciation by Fischer, 16 December 1942, AA, Botschaft China Prot 2a1.

72   *Journal de Shanghai*, 3 January 1941.

73   Undated US intelligence report [1945], USNA, RG 226, box 57, entry 140, folder 464.

74   'Paddy' [Sir A. Noble] to Frank [Roberts], 22 August 1940, PRO, FO 371/24361/173.

75   R. L. Speaight to H. Somerville-Smith, 3 December 1940, PRO, FO 371/24361/175.

76   See British intelligence report, Shanghai, 1–30 April 1941, PRO, WO 208/296; *Shanghai Times*, 4, 8 and 16 January 1941.

77   See India Office to Government of India, 10 April 1941, IOR, L/P&S/12/499.

78   Le Rougetel (Shanghai) to Singapore, 26 September 1941, IOR, L/P&S/12/499.

79   See E. M. Gull, *British Economic Interests in the Far East,* London, 1943, p. 34.

80 David Smurthwaite (ed.), *The Forgotten War: The British Army in the Far East 1941–1945,* London, 1992, p. 173.

81 War Office to General Officer Commanding Hong Kong, Malaya, repeated to Shanghai, Tientsin, n.d. [7 or 8 August 1940], PRO, WO 106/2396.

82 British intelligence report, 26 November 1940, PRO, WO 208/273.

83 Butterfield & Swire, Shanghai, to John Swire & Sons, London, 15 September 1939, Swire papers, SOAS, JSSII 2/17, box 53.

84 Alcott, *My War With Japan*, p. 318.

85 Norwood F. Allman, *Shanghai Lawyer*, New York, 1943, pp. 221–23.

86 SSIS (Military) report, 1–31 January 1941, PRO, WO 208/296.

87 Ernest O. Hauser, *Shanghai: City for Sale,* New York, 1940, p. 289.

88 Allman, *Shanghai Lawyer*, pp. 221–23.

89 Frederic Wakeman Jr, *The Shanghai Badlands: Wartime Terrorism and Urban Crime: 1937–1941*, Cambridge, 1996, pp. 101–02.

90 French police reports, May and June 1941, AMAE, Consulat Shanghai, rép. num. 332 and 333, Services Polices, bulletins mensuels.

91 *Shanghai Times*, 7 February 1941.

92 Allman, *Shanghai Lawyer*, p. 229.

Chapter 4

1 Frederick S. Litten, 'The Noulens Affair', *China Quarterly*, 138, June 1994, pp. 492–512.

2 See Patricia Stranahan, 'Strange Bedfellows: The Communist Party and Shanghai's Elite in the National Salvation Movement', *China Quarterly*, 129, March 1992, pp. 26–51.

3 Reports by Prokofiev, 6 November 1937 and 22 April 1942, SMP, D 8157-F2.

4 Translation by Shanghai Municipal Police (slightly amended) of extract from article in Russian weekly, 'Back to the Fatherland', 17 July 1939, SMP, D 8149 F6.

5 *China Press*, 26 September 1940.

6 *Shanghai Times*, 5 January 1941.

7 *Shanghai Times*, 7 January 1941.

8   French police monthly bulletin, September 1941, AMAE, Consulat Shanghai, rép. num. 333.

9   *Shanghai Zaria*, 26 December 1942.

10 See French Concession monthly police report for July 1941, AMAE, Consulat Shanghai, rép num. 333; Japanese Consul-General Horiuchi Teteki to Foreign Minister, 17 January 1942, JFM, UD 47; SMP file D 8157-F2; and reports in SMP, D 8149.

11 The original pamphlet has not been found; this description is based on a report by the usually reliable Municipal Police Inspector A. Prokofiev, dated 28 February 1944, in SMP, U 441.

12 Horiuchi (Shanghai) to Prime Minister Konoye et al., 7 April 1941, JFM, UD 46.

13 Evidence given by Erben in the trial of Lothar Eisentraeger et al., Shanghai, October 1946, USNA, RG 153, case 58-137, book 1, p. 146.

14 Ibid., p. 122.

15 Ibid., p. 123.

16 'Enemy activities in Japan', PRO, HS1/204.

17 OSS X-2 Branch report on Mrs Meisinger, 7 December 1945, FOIA/CIA.

18 Ibid.

19 Walter Schellenberg, *The Labyrinth: Memoirs of Walter Schellenberg,* New York, 1956, pp. 14–15, 160–61.

20 Richard Hughes, *Foreign Devil: Thirty Years of Reporting from the Far East,* London, 1984, pp. 34–35. On Meisinger see also my *The Secret Lives of Trebitsch Lincoln* (2nd rev. edn), London, 1989, pp. 313–17 and p. 378.

21 'German Intelligence in China and Japan', US Strategic Services memorandum, 9 August 1945, FOIA/CIA.

22 'Organizations of the German Government in Shanghai', 27 September 1945, PRO, WO 208/28.

23 Randow (transmitting message from Puttkamer) to German Foreign Ministry, 25 November 1941, AA, PA 29559.

24 Statement by F. Huber, Shanghai, 21 July 1946, USNA, RG 226, entry 182, box 16, folder 122.

25 F W. Deakin and G. R. Storry, *The Case of Richard Sorge*, New York, 1966, p. 228.

26 Meisinger interrogation report, annex III, 'Richard Sorge', 25 May 1946, USNA, RG 238, World War II War Crimes Records, microfilm series M1270, roll 25.

27 OSS report, 5 March 1946, FOIA/USAISC.

28 'List of Revolutionary Elements in Shanghai', July 1941, forwarded to Secretary of State, Washington, by K. S. Patton, US Consul-General, Batavia, 14 November 1931, file 893.00B/859, Central Decimal File, 1930–1939, State Department Records, Record Group 59, USNA.

29 Autobiographical Notes by Eugene M. Clige' (Pick), part I, n.d. [1945/46], FOIA/USAISC.

30 *Municipal Gazette* (Shanghai), 28 November 1941.

31 Naval and Military Intelligence Summary, 13 November 1941, PRO, WO 208/296.

32 *China Press*, 3 December 1941.

33 George Woodcock, *The British in the Far East,* London, 1969, p. 223.

34 Hugh Collar, *Captive in Shanghai,* Hong Kong, 1990, p. 15.

Chapter 5

1 *China Weekly Review*, 6 December 1945.

2 H. Grover and Gretchen G. Grover, 'Night Attack at Shanghai', *Naval History*, 5, 4, Winter 1991, p. 37.

3 Ibid., p. 37.

4 *Shanghai Times*, 13 December 1941.

5 Peter Oldham, *Lieutenant Stephen Polkinghorn DSC, RNR,* Auckland, NZ, 1984, pp. 5–6.

6 Hugh Collar, *Captive in Shanghai,* Hong Kong, 1990, pp. 25–28.

7 See Desmond Wettern, *The Lonely Battle,* London, 1960; 'O/X' (Sir George Moss) to 'O.111' (Major S. F. Crawford), 18 March 1943, PRO, HS1/163.

8 Frank H. H. King, *The Hong Kong Bank Between the Wars and the Bank Interned 1919–1945,* vol. III of *The History of the Hong Kong and Shanghai Banking Corporation*, Cambridge, 1988, p. 575.

9 *Shanghai Times*, 12 December 1941.

10 J.W. Allen, 'Report on the Shanghai Municipal Council', 20 September 1942, PRO, FO 371/46191; see also *Shanghai Times*, 9 December 1941.

11 Zinsser (Shanghai) to German Foreign Ministry, 8 December 1941, AA, PA 29559.

12 J.W. Allen, 'Report on the Shanghai Municipal Council', 20 September 1942, PRO, FO 371/46191.

13 *Shanghai Times*, 23 December 1941.

14 Memorandum by Consul-General Horiuchi, Shanghai, 30 December 1941, JFM, UD 47.

15 *Shanghai Times*, 13 December 1941.

16 British intelligence report, 26 November 1940, PRO, WO 208/273.

17 French Ambassador, Peking, to Margerie, 6 December 1941 (recd. 7.00 p.m.), AMAE, Consulat Shanghai, inv. 1844-1952, carton 130, file 8.VI 'Conflit dans le Pacifique'.

18 Margerie (Shanghai) to French Ambassador, Peking, 8 December 1941 (dispatched 9.40 a.m.), AMAE, Ambassade Pékin, carton 254, dossier 'Concession Française Shanghai: Historique depuis 1869'.

19 *Conseil d'Administration Municipale de la Concession Française de Changhai, Compte-rendu de Gestion pour l'Exercice 1941*, Shanghai, 1942, p. 86.

20 Ibid.

21 See Joseph Shieh with Marie Holzman, *Dans le Jardin des Aventuriers*, Paris, 1995, p. 153.

22 French police memorandum, 21 February 1942, AMAE, Consulat Shanghai, inv. 1844-1952, carton 130, file 8.VI 'Conflit dans le Pacifique'.

23 Margerie to French Ambassador, Peking, 16 December 1941, AMAE, Consulat Shanghai, inv. 1844-1952, carton 130, file 8.VI 'Conflit dans le Pacifique'.

24 Margerie to French Ambassador, Peking, 19 December 1941, AMAE, Consulat Shanghai, inv. 1844-1952, carton 130, file 8.VI 'Conflit dans le Pacifique'.

25 Undated memorandum by F. Sullivan, PRO, WO 208/378A.

26 *Shanghai Times*, 28 December 1941.

27 *Shanghai Times*, 13 January 1942.

28 *Municipal Gazette*, 30 January 1942.

29 *Shanghai Times*, 30 December 1941.

30 Eleanor M. Hinder, *Life and Labour in Shanghai* (2nd edn), New York, 1944, p 17.

31 Censorship, Bermuda, intercept of a letter from World's YWCA, Geneva to Miss M. Marianne Mills, World's YWCA, Washington, 5 June 1942, quoting a letter of 5 February 1942 from a YWCA worker in Shanghai, PRO, WO 208/378A.

32 *Shanghai Times*, 9, 11 December 1941.

33 *Shanghai Times*, 21 December 1941.

34 *Shanghai Times*, 30 December 1941.

35 *Shanghai Times*, 18 December 1941.

36 See David H. Grover and Gretchen G. Grover, *Captives of Shanghai: The Story of the* President Harrison, Napa, CA, 1989. See also *Shanghai Times*, 22 January 1942.

37 Horiuchi, Shanghai, to Foreign Minister Togo, Tokyo, 5 January 1942, JFM, S 542.

38 J.W. Allen, 'Report on the Shanghai Municipal Council', 20 September 1942, PRO, FO 371/46191; *Municipal Gazette*, 30 January 1942; *Hong Kong News*, 9 January 1942.

39 Margeris, Shanghai, to French Ambassador, Peking, 10 December 1941, AMAE, Consulat Shanghai, inv. 1844-1952, carton 130, file 8.VI, 'Conflit dans le Pacifique'; see also 'Intelligence Report on the Situation in the Shanghai Area', unsigned, enclosed in dispatch dated 25 September 1942 from former British Consul-General, Shanghai, to former Chargé d'Affaires, Shanghai, 25 September 1942, PRO, FO 916/730.

40 Horiuchi, Shanghai, to Togo, Tokyo, 5 January 1942, JFM, S 542.

41 Repatriated American businessman from Shanghai quoted in 'Analysis of Gripsholm Questionnaires: Far Eastern Propaganda Objectives and Techniques', US Office of War Information Bureau of Overseas Intelligence, February 1944, PRO, ADM 223/72.

42 Margerie to French Ambassador, Peking, 15 December 1941, AMAE, Consulat Shanghai, inv. 1844-1952, carton 130, file 8.VI, 'Conflit dans le Pacifique'.

43 Margerie to French Ambassador, Peking, 26 December 1941, AMAE, Consulat Shanghai, inv. 1844-1952, carton 130, file 8.VI, 'Conflit dans le Pacifique'.

44 French police report for December 1941, AMAE, Consulat de Shanghai, rép. num. 333.

45 *Shanghai Times*, 19–24 February 1942; H.G.W. Woodhead, 'The Japanese Occupation of Shanghai: Some Personal Experiences', address to Royal Institute of International Affairs, 21 November 1942, PRO, WO 208/378A.

46 See 'Intelligence Report on the Situation in the Shanghai Area', encl. in A. H. George to Le Rougetel, 25 September 1942, PRO, FO 916/730.

47 See Poshek Fu, *Passivity, Resistance and Collaboration: Intellectual Choices in Occupied Shanghai, 1937–1945*, Stanford, CA, 1993.

48 SMP report, 22 May 1941, H 656 (C).

49 Report dated [23?] November 1940, SMP, H 656(C).

50 French police report, November 1941, AMAE, Consulat Shanghai, rép. num. 333.

51 Translation of letter (original language unknown), SMP, H 656(C).

52 *Shanghai Times*, 28 December 1941 and 4 January 1942.

53 Statement by former Naval Attaché Fukuhara, quoted in unsigned US intelligence report, [19?] February 1946, FOIA/USAISC.

54 'Information Concerning Hovans', OSS report, unsigned, undated [1945/46], USNA, RG 226, entry 182, box 12, folder 78.

55 US intelligence report on 'Eugene Hovans', [19?] February 1946, FOIA/USAISC.

Chapter 6

1 'Note on Conversation with Mr A. E. Jones', 23 November 1940, PRO, HS1/202.

2 'O/X' (Sir George Moss) to 'C.D.' (Sir Charles Hambro), 13 June 1942, PRO, HS1/226.

3 Memorandum by S. C. Riggs, n.d. [around October 1942], PRO, HS1/181.

4 Far Eastern Activities', undated SOE memorandum, PRO, HS1/181.

5   Exchange of telegrams, 9–19 June 1941, PRO, HS1/204.

6   'History of SOE Oriental Mission (May 1941 to March 1942)', PRO, HS1/207.

7   John W. M. Chapman (ed. and trans.), *The Price of Admiralty: The War Diary of the German Naval Attaché in Japan 1939–1943*, 2 vols., Ripe, East Sussex, 1982–84, vol. 2, pp. 490, 493, entries dated 28 August, 5 September 1941.

8   Le Rougetel, Shanghai, to Foreign Office, 19 September 1941, PRO, HS1/340. See also Gladwyn Jebb to P. M. Loxley, 20 and 27 September 1941 and accompanying documents, PRO, HS1/340. Also Charles Cruikshank, *SOE in the Far East*, Oxford, 1986, p. 76.

9   Loxley to Jebb, 14 October 1941, PRO, HS1/340.

10   'C.D.' (Hambro) to to 'O/X' (Sir George Moss), 13 June 1942, PRO, HS1/226.

11   Gande to J. K. Brand, British Consulate, Shanghai, 23 October 1945, PRO, HS1/112.

12   John B. Powell, *My Twenty-Five Years in China*, New York, 1945, p. 386.

13   Ibid., p. 387.

14   Memorandum by S. C. Riggs, n.d. [around October 1942], PRO, HS1/181.

15   Ibid.

16   Ibid.

17   Powell, *My Twenty-Five Years*, p. 388.

18   SOS memorandum, 'W.T. Chang', 17 October 1942, PRO, HS1/163.

19   Memorandum by S. C. Riggs, n.d. [around October 1942], PRO, HS1/181.

20   *Shanghai Times*, 3 June 1942.

21   Memorandum by S. C. Riggs, n.d. [around October 1942], PRO, HS1/181.

22   Hugh Collar, *Captive in Shanghai*, Hong Kong, 1990, p.31.

23   'A/DU' (W. J. Keswick) to 'C.D.' (Hambro), 1 November 1942, PRO, HS1/181.

24   'AD/S' to 'C.D.' (Hambro), 26 November 1942, PRO, HS1/181.

25   'Re Political Prisoners in S[hanghai] M[unicipal] Gaol', unsigned, undated [post-war] document, SMP, U 208.

26 A. G. N. Ogden (Kunming) to S. F. Crawford (Chungking), 7 December 1942, PRO, HS1/181.

27 See Frederic Wakeman Jr, *Policing Shanghai 1927–1937*, Berkeley, 1995, p. 145.

28 'O/X' (Sir George Moss) to Crawford, 5 January 1942 [actually 1943], PRO, HS1/181.

Chapter 7

1 Report by Detective Sergeant Pitts, 28 June 1939, SMP, D 8264/290.

2 See SMP, D 9290.

3 *Shanghai Times*, 19, 20 May, 10, 11 July 1942.

4 *Shanghai Times*, 20 March 1943.

5 *China Press* and *Shanghai Herald*, 25 October 1945.

6 OSS report, 8 October 1945, USNA, RG 226, entry 182, box 12, folder 79.

7 OSS report, 15 October 1945, FOIA/CIA.

8 *Shanghai Times*, 21 April 1943.

9 Woodhead address at Chatham House, 21 November 1942, PRO, WO 208/378A.

10 Ibid.

11 Maze to J. H. Cubbon, 17 December 1943, SOAS Maze papers, vol. XVI, fol. 51.

12 Hugh Collar, *Captive in Shanghai*, Hong Kong, 1990, p. 56.

13 *Shanghai Times*, 4 August 1942.

14 *Shanghai Times*, 12 September 1942.

15 'Shanghai 1941–1945' by H. E. Arnhold (unpublished typescript written in Shanghai, 1944, in Hoover Institution Library, Stanford, CA), p. 4.

16 *Shanghai Times*, 22 April 1943.

17 Arnhold typescript, pp. 9–10.

18 Norton (Berne) to Foreign Office, 15 May 1943, PRO, WO 208/378A. See also J.H.H. Berckman to Ernest Nash, 19 January 1944, PRO, FO 916/1044.

19 John B. Powell, *My Twenty-Five Years in China,* New York, 1945, p. 378.

20   Stephen Douglas Sturton, *From Mission Hospital to Concentration Camp*, London, n.d., p. 105.

21   *Shanghai Times*, 21, 22, 23 February 1943.

22   SMP report, 26 February 1943, D 8149-F13.

23   Arnhold typescript, p. 38.

24   Memorandum by 'Schwarz' to chief of the Kanzlei Rosenberg, 29 September 1938, copy in archive of Centre de Documentation Juive Contemporaine, Paris, CXLVI.9b.

25   Dirksen, Tokyo, to German Foreign Ministry, 10 January 1934, BAP, Botschaft China 2325.

26   *Israel's Messenger*, 20 December 1940.

27   Amended translation of articles appearing in issues of 3 and 10 September 1939, in SMP report, 15 December 1939, D 8149 F52.

28   French political police bulletin mensuel, March 1940, AMAE, Consulat Shanghai, rép. num. 330.

29   British Consul-General, Shanghai, to British Ambassador, 2 October 1941, enclosing translated copy of memo by Inuzaka, 17 September 1941, in PRO, FO 371/29235/W15226/12102/48.

30   Copy of report to American Jewish Joint Distribution Committee by Laura Margolis, headed 'Report of Activities in Shanghai, China, from December 8, 1941 to September 1943' (henceforth 'Margolis report').

31   Margolis report; 'German Intelligence in China and Japan', Strategic Services Unit memorandum, 21 August 1945, FOIA/CIA.

32   Margolis report.

33   *Unzer Lebn*, 31 July 1942.

34   SMP, D 5422(a)-10(8).

35   See Felix Gruenberger, 'The Jewish Refugees in Shanghai', *Jewish Social Studies*, XII, 4, October 1950, pp. 329–48.

36   *Shanghai Times*, 21–23 February 1943.

37   *Shanghai Jewish Chronicle*, 25 February 1943.

38   *Unzer Lebn*, 2 April 1943.

39   *Unzer Lebn*, 14 May 1943.

40   Pick to Otani, unsigned, undated [probably early 1943], FOIA/ USAISC.

41 'Cooperation between Japanese and Foreigners during the War' by 'Eugene M. Clige', FOIA/USAISC.
42 Sumaire to British War Crimes Commission, Shanghai, December 1946, USNA, RG 226, entry 182A, box 10, folder 74.
43 See OSS report, Peking, 9 October 1945, FOIA/CIA.
44 Collar, *Captive in Shanghai*, p. 99.
45 OSS report, 13 October 1945, USNA, RG 226, entry 182A, box 8, folder 64; also memorandum by Berrier, allegedly written in March 1943, USNA, RG 226, entry 140, box 57, folder 464.
46 'Background Material', undated [around 1957], HIA, Allman papers, box 12, file 45.
47 OSS X-2 branch report on death of Miorini, 15 October 1945, FOIA/CIA.
48 'Saint' to 'Links', 4 March 1944, FOIA/CIA.
49 Evidence given by Erben in the trial of Lothar Eisentraeger et al., Shanghai, October 1946, USNA, RG 153, case 58-137, book 1, p. 111.
50 Ibid., pp. 122, 151.
51 Huber, Shanghai to RSHA, Berlin, 19 April 1943, AA, Inland II g 488.
52 RSHA to Foreign Ministry, 24 May 1943, forwarded to Shanghai, 25 May 1943, AA, Inland II, g 488.
53 Evidence given by Erben in the trial of Lothar Eisentraeger et al., Shanghai, October 1946, USNA, RG 153, case 58-137, book 1, p. 112.
54 Ibid., p. 114.

Chapter 8

1 Wavell to Chief of Imperial Staff, 14 May 1942, PRO, WO 208/378A.
2 Memorandum by Horiuchi, 30 December 1941, JFM, UD 47.
3 J.W. Allen, 'Report on the Shanghai Municipal Council', 20 September 1942, PRO, FO 371/46191; *Municipal Gazette*, Shanghai, 27 February 1942.
4 J.W. Allen, 'Report on the Shanghai Municipal Council', 20 September 1942, PRO, FO 371/46191.
5 Unsigned SOE memorandum, 3 December 1941, PRO, HS1/340.

6   Minute by P.D. Coates, 26 June 1947, PRO, FO 371/63288 F8952/28/10.

7   Undated memorandum, PRO, FO 371/69562.

8   *Municipal Gazette*, 27 February 1942.

9   Unsigned, undated memorandum, 'The Outline Activities of the Foreign Affairs Section, Police Headquarters, during the period of the Japanese occupation of Shanghai', USNA, RG 226, entry 182, box 12, folder 77.

10   'Assistance to Foreign Section of Japanese Gendarmerie Headquarters', 20 December 1941, SMP, D 8299/364.

11   See, for example, 'Assistance to Japanese Gendarmerie', 30 December 1941, SMP, D 8299/374.

12   R. M. Moi[r] et al. to Swiss Consulate-General, 7 September 1942, PRO, FO 371/53592.

13   Unsigned, undated memorandum, 'The Outline of Activities of the Foreign Affairs Section, Police Headquarters, during the period of Japanese occupation of Shanghai', USNA, RG 226, entry 182, box 12, folder 77.

14   Statement dated 30 August 1945, USNA, RG 226, entry 140, box 57, folder 463.

15   No British files relating to this case have been found in the PRO. This account is based on a statement made by Vyacheslav Toropovsky to US counter-intelligence authorities in Shanghai, 7 December 1945, FOIA/USAISC.

16   Hugh Collar, *Captive in Shanghai*, Hong Kong, 1990, pp. 11–12.

17   'Extract from letter from Col. G. E. Grimsdale, GSO1, Intelligence, Singapore', 17 May 1941, PRO, HS1/339.

18   Unsigned SOE memorandum, 3 December 1941, PRO, HS1/340.

19   Report on trial of Lothar Eisentraeger et al. enclosed with US Consul-General, Shanghai, to US Ambassador, Nanking, 30 December 1946, USNA, RG 59, State Department decimal file 862.20293/12-3046.

20   'Notes on the behaviour of some firms and individuals in Hankow after the outbreak of war', memorandum by J. L. O. [?] Davidson, Hankow, 11 May 1942, PRO, FO 369/3790.

21 Copy of telegram from Berne to Foreign Office, London, 18 April 1942, China Association papers, SOAS, CHAS/MCP/44.

22 CIGS (dispatching Foreign Office view) to Wavell, 29 May 1942, PRO, WO 208/378A.

23 Copy of letter (writer's name not given) in China Association papers, SOAS, CHAS/MCP/44.

24 Summary of replies received from repatriates from China who arrived at Liverpool on 10 October 1942, PRO, HS1/150.

25 E. B. Schumpeter (ed.),*The Industrialization of Japan and Manchukuo 1930–1949: Population, Raw Materials and Industry*, New York, 1940, p. 428.

26 See Jürgen Osterhammel, 'British Business in China, 1860s–1950s', in R. P. T. Davenport-Hines and Geoffrey Jones (eds), *British Business in Asia since 1860*, Cambridge, 1989, p. 11.

27 E.M. Gull, *British Economic Interests in the Far East*, London, 1943, p. 198.

28 Memorandum of conversation with General Shio[z]awa, head of China Affairs Board, Peking, 8 August 1941, Nathan papers, Bodleian Library, Oxford, MSS Eng. Hist. c. 452, folios 19–23.

29 P.C. Young to Sir Edward Crowe, 23 Septembe 1941, PRO, HS1/175.

30 E.F. Watts (Chungking) to Chinese Mining and Engineering Company, Exeter, 14 February 1942 (copy forwarded to Foreign Office by British Embassy Chungking), PRO, WO 208/378A.

31 P.H.B. Kent to E.J. Nathan, 22 December 1941, Nathan papers, Bodleian Library, c. 452 folios 92–101.

32 Postal and Telegraph Censorship Extract from letter from Mrs E. J. Nathan, Lantern Hill Homestead, Mystic, Conn., to Lady Nathan, Granby Hotel, Bradford-on-Avon, Wilts, 12 July 1942, itself containing an extract 'from Teddie's letter dated February 18th, which reached here on July 7th, sent by the Swiss Consul, Mr Joerg, through his business office in Geneva', ibid.

33 Nathan to Consul G. Joerg, 10 March 1943, Nathan papers, Bodleian Library, c. 453, folios 87–89.

34 Japanese Embassy, Peking, to Nathan, 12 March 1943, Nathan papers, Bodleian Library, c. 453, folios 91–92.

35 Ashley Clarke (Foreign Office) to Chinese Mining and Engineering Company, 26 February 1942, Nathan papers, Bodleian Library, c. 452, folio 182.

36 Foreign Office to Chinese Mining and Engineering Company, 13 May 1942, Nathan papers, Bodleian Library, c. 452, folio 207.

37 Memorandum to Foreign Office, 1 June 1942, Nathan papers, Bodleian Library. c. 453, folios 2–4.

38 Foreign Office to Chinese Mining and Engineering Company, 13 June 1942, Nathan papers, Bodleian Library, c. 453, folio 5.

39 Nathan to Foreign Office, 23 December 1946, Nathan papers, Bodleian Library, c. 453, folio 196.

40 Interview with George Leonoff, Jerusalem, 10 February 1995.

41 *Shanghai Times*, 2, 10 September, 7 November 1942.

42 OSS record card, HIA, N. F. Allman papers, box 7, file 95.

43 Report dated 16 March 1946, USNA, RG 226, entry 182, box 16, folder 121. See also undated unsigned OSS report, FOIA/CIA.

44 'Shanghai Counter-Espionage Summary', 12 August 1945, FOIA/CIA.

45 Reports dated 19 and 24 October 1937, SMP, D 8113.

46 Statement by Alfred Lewis Meyer, 20 November 1945, USNA, RG 226, report no. YKX-617.

47 Gracie to British Ambassador, Nanking, 3 January 1947, PRO, FO 369/3791.

48 Statements by Gracie, 5 February 1946, Carl Flick-Steger, 16 May 1946, Rudolf Grau, 16 May 1946, and related documents, PRO, FO 369/3791.

49 Statements by Carl Flick-Steger, 16 May 1946, Rudolf Grau, 16 May 1946, Baron Jesco von Puttkamer, 1 May 1946, PRO, FO 369/3791.

50 Deposition by Lamb, 19 January 1946, PRO, FO 369/3790.

51 Deposition by Lamb, 19 January 1946, PRO, FO 369/3790.

52 Statement by Flick-Steger, 16 May 1946, PRO, FO 369/3791.

53 OSS X-2 Branch report, Shanghai, 11 October 1945, USNA, RG 226, entry 182, box 16, folder 182.

54 SMP report, 13 April 1942, N 1457 (C).

55 SMP report, 15 July 1940, N 163(C).

56 Statement by A. V. Cattel, 1 December 1945, PRO, FO 369/3791.

57 US CIC interrogation of Ikushima Kichizo, Sugamo Prison, 20 March 1946, FOIA/USAISC.

58 Report by French Political Police, Shanghai, 5 March 1941, SMP, D 9532 (C).

59 *Shanghai Times*, 13 March 1942.

60 SMP report, 13 March 1942, N 1457(C).

61 SMP report, 20 April 1942, N 1457 (C).

62 Ibid.

63 *Shanghai Times*, 5 January 1942; *Hong Kong News*, 7 January 1942.

64 Statement by Uy, 15 October 1945, and statements by Malabanan and other witnesses, USNA RG 226, entry 182, box 10, folder 66.

65 Report on 'Indian Independence League', 26 October 1945, USNA, RG 226, XL 24487.

66 *Shanghai Times*, 13 August 1942.

67 *The China Annual 1944*, Shanghai, 1944, pp. 218–21.

68 Report by N. Singh, 5 March 1943, SMP, U 225.

69 Stephen Douglas Sturton, *From Mission Hospital to Concentration Camp*, London, n.d., p. 103.

70 *Shanghai Herald*, 1 November 1945.

71 Kentwell to Registrar of British Supreme Court, Shanghai, 22 January 1927, PRO, FO 372/2486.

72 Kentwell to Judge P. Grant-Jones, 19 November 1936, PRO, FO 656/221.

73 Harriet Sergeant, *Shanghai: Collision Point of Cultures 1918–1937*, London, 1990, pp. 158ff.

74 Grain to British Minister, Peking, 23 August 1930, PRO, FO 372/2647.

75 Kentwell to British Home Secretary, 2 January 1928, PRO, FO 372/2486.

76 Kentwell to British Consul-General, Shanghai, 23 November 1927, PRO, FO 372/2486.

77 Kentwell to Grain (copy), 9 August 1927, PRO, FO 372/2486.

78 Kentwell 'to whom it may concern', 7 March 1928 (copy), PRO, FO 372/2486.

79 A. F. Martin to Sir Miles Lampson, 11 January 1929 (copy), PRO, FO 372/2647.

80 Minute by G. Mounsey, 14 April 1927, PRO, FO 372/2387/276.

81 Barton to Foreign Office, 12 December 1927, PRO, FO 372/2486.

82 Minute dated 8 August 1928, PRO, FO 372/2486.

83 E.M.B. Ingram (Peking) to G.S. Moss (Canton), 21 January 1930, PRO, FO 372/2647.

84 Whitelegge (Home Office) to Forbes (Foreign Office), 24 December 1928, PRO, FO 372/2486.

85 Kentwell to Stanley Baldwin, 22 March 1929, PRO, FO 372/2580.

86 Kentwell to British Consul-General, Canton, 2 October 1931, PRO, FO 676/90.

87 Archives of Lincoln College, Oxford.

88 Black List no. 4, 2 August 1927, PRO, FO 371/12409 (F7494/2/10).

89 See Frederic Wakeman Jr, *Policing Shanghai 1927–1937*, Berkeley, 1995, pp. 61, 336.

90 Sir Herbert Phillips to Sir Miles Lampson, 8 June 1931 (copy), PRO, FO 372/2749.

91 Kentwell to Home Office, 23 July 1931, PRO, FO 676/90.

92 Kentwell to Grain, 5 October 1931, PRO, FO 676/90.

93 See Kentwell to Prime Minister, 19 October 1932, PRO, FO 371/16237/306.

94 Kentwell statement, undated, 1945, USNA, RG 226, entry 182, box 2, folder 12.

95 Kentwell to Pierre Francfort (Consul Suppléant, Shanghai), 16 March 1936, AMAE, Consulat Shanghai, Liste 1844–1952, 'cartons noirs', carton 171, file 10.1 'Propagande Français'.

96 Kentwell to Judge Grant-Jones, 19 November 1936, PRO, FO 656/221.

97 Printed circular from Kentwell, 1 July 1939, PRO, FO 371/23406.

98 Undated, unsigned notation, PRO, FO 371/23406.

99 Copy of letter to Dr A. D. Wall, signature indecipherable, 15 July 1939, SMP, D 6876.

100 Statement by Kentwell, n.d. [1945], USNA, RG 226, entry 182, box 2, folder 12.

101 British Embassy, Shanghai, to Far Eastern Department, Foreign Office, 5 October 1939, PRO, FO 371/23407/272.

102 Kentwell to Neville Chamberlain, 8 August 1939, PRO, FO 371/23406/131-2.

103 Kentwell to Sir A. Clark Kerr, 1 June 1940, PRO, FO 371/23407/274-5.

104 Minute by B. Gage, 21 July 1940, PRO, FO 371/23407/273.

105 Statement by Kentwell, n.d. [1945], USNA, RG 226, entry 182, box 2, folder 12.

106 John Hunter Boyle, *China and Japan at War, 1937–1945: The Politics of Collaboration*, Stanford, CA, 1972, p. 311.

107 On the dilemmas of Chinese intellectuals and businessmen in Shanghai during the occupation, see Poshek Fu, *Passivity, Resistance and Collaboration: Intellectual Choice in Occupied Shanghai, 1937–1945*, Stanford, CA, 1993, and Parks Coble, 'Chinese Capitalists and the Japanese: Collaboration and Resistance in the Shanghai Area, 1937–1945, in Wen-hsin Yeh (ed.), *Wartime Shanghai*, London, 1988, pp. 62–85.

108 Coble, 'Chinese Capitalists', p. 79.

Chapter 9

1   See Desmond Wettern, *The Lonely Battle*, London, 1960; 'O/X' (Sir George Moss) to 'O.111' (Crawford), 18 March 1943, PRO, HS1/163; also 'O/X' to 'D/Navy', 1, 19 March 1943, PRO, HS1/163.

2   'AD/U' (W. J. Keswick) to Sir George Moss, 18 September 1942, PRO, HS1/182.

3   W. J. Keswick to Phillips, 11 September 1942, PRO, HS1/182.

4   Richard Aldrich, 'Imperial Rivalry: British and American Intelligence in Asia, 1942–6', *Intelligence and National Security*, 3, 2, 1988, p. 10.

5   Christopher Thorne, *Allies of a Kind: The United States, Britain and the War against Japan, 1941–1945*, London, 1978, p. 314.

6   On Starr's recruitment of old Shanghai business contacts to OSS, see Maochun Yu, *OSS in China: Prelude to Cold War*, New Haven, 1996, pp. 60–63.

7   Unsigned, undated SOE report, PRO, HS1/227.

8   See memoranda to and from Keswick, August–October 1942, PRO, HS1/182.

9   Report, January 1942, PRO, WO 208/387.

10 See Yu, *OSS in China*, pp. 105–06, 301.

11 Unsigned, undated SOE memorandum on 'Sabotage', PRO, HS1/165.

12 'O. M. China', memorandum by Valentine Killery, 29 April 1942, PRO, HS1/164.

13 Ibid.

14 Memorandum by John Keswick, 13 April 1942, PRO, HS1/164.

15 Quoted in Michael Schaller, *The U.S. Crusade in China, 1938–1945*, New York, 1979, p. 234.

16 'O.4020' to 'AD/O' (John Keswick), 9 February 1943, PRO, HS1/158.

17 Memorandum by Brigadier G. E. Grimsdale, Chungking, 20 March 1942, PRO, HS1/204.

18 'RII', Unsigned, undated SOE memorandum, PRO, HS1/165.

19 Grimsdale memorandum, 20 March 1942, PRO, HS1/204.

20 'O.4020' to 'AD/O' (John Keswick), 9 February 1943, PRO, HS1/158; see also Milton E. Miles, *A Different Kind of War*, Garden City, NY, 1967, p.96.

21 Thorne, *Allies of a Kind*, p. 180.

22 'O.4020' to 'AD/O' (John Keswick), 9 February 1943.

23 Undated [1942] SOE memorandum, PRO, HS1/175.

24 SOE memorandum, 25 October 1941, PRO, HS1/175.

25 Ashley Clarke, Foreign Office, to Gladwyn Jebb, SOE, 2 December 1941 and enclosure, PRO, HS1/340.

26 Memorandum by John Keswick, 13 April 1942, PRO, HS1/164.

27 'O.M. China' by Valentine Killery, 29 April 1942, PRO, HS1/164.

28 Copy of cipher telegram dispatched to Moscow, 29 July 1942, PRO, HS1/175.

29 See Thorne, *Allies of a Kind*, p. 184.

30 Keswick to Mackenzie, 28 November 1942, PRO, HS1/175.

31 Air Attaché, Chungking, to RAF HQ, India, 24 October 1942, PRO, HS1/175.

32 Keswick to Mackenzie, 28 November 1942, PRO, HS1/175.
33 'O/X' (Moss) to 'C.D.' (Hambro) with notes by Hambro and Tony Keswick, 24–26 October 1942, PRO, HS1/175.
34 Report dated 29 December 1943, PRO, HS1/152.
35 Report dated 17 April 1944, PRO, HS1/152.
36 Ibid.
37 SOE memorandum, 23 April 1942, PRO, HS1/152.
38 'Notes on General Aspects of Military Intelligence in China', unsigned memorandum, Chungking, 23 September 1942, PRO, HS1/163. An MI2 memorandum attributed authorship of the report to Keswick: see 'Intelligence in China', 28 December 1942, PRO, WO 106/3582A.
39 'Intelligence in China', MI2 memorandum, 28 December 1942, PRO, WO 106/3582A.
40 Unsigned, undated OSS memorandum, section VI, 'China', PRO, HS1/227.
41 SOE report, 22 December 1943, PRO, HS1/161.
42 G. Findlay Andrew to General Cheng Kai-Min, 3 February 1945, PRO HS1/146.
43 'RII', unsigned, undated SOE memorandum, PRO, HS1/165.
44 Report by 'O.119' (J. C. McMullen), Chungking, 30 June 1945, PRO, HS1/146.
45 Undated memorandum, 'RII Intelligence Reports' by J. C. McMullen, PRO, HS1/146.
46 Yu, *OSS in China*, p.305.
47 'RII', Unsigned, undated SOE memorandum, PRO, HS1/165.
48 Ibid.
49 See, for example, 'Future of RII', SOE memorandum, 18 July 1943, PRO, HS1/165.
50 'O/X' to 'A.D.4', 22 May 1943, PRO, HS1/165.
51 Ibid.
52 Ibid.
53 Unsigned, undated SOE memorandum on 'Sabotage', PRO, HS1/165.
54 'BB232' to 'BB100', 7 April 1944, PRO, HS1/172.

55 Unsigned 'Plan for Sabotage Operations along the China Coast', 3 July 1943, PRO, HS1/165.

Chapter 10

1 Margerie to French Ambassador, Peking, 13 March 1942, AMAE, Consulat Shanghai, inv. 1844-1952, carton 130, file 8.VI, 'Conflit dans le Pacifique'.
2 SMP report, 25 March 1942, N 361 (C).
3 Undated, unsigned, 'most secret' report forwarded to V. Cavendish-Bentinck et al. by T. Haddon on 29 April 1942, PRO, HS1/344.
4 Ibid.
5 HIA, diary of Karl von Wiegand, entry for 25 October 1941.
6 Statement by former Sub-Inspector F. A. Pitts, 31 August 1945, USNA, RG 226, entry 140, box 57, folder 463.
7 'The Outline of Activities of the Foreign Affairs Section, Police Headquarters, during the period of Japanese occupation of Shanghai', unsigned, undated [autumn 1945], OSS memorandum, USNA, RG 226, entry 182, box 12, folder 77.
8 Ibid. Minor errors in spelling and punctuation have been corrected.
9 'German Intelligence Activities in China During World War II', Strategic Services Unit memorandum, 1 March 1946, FOIA/CIA, p. 79.
10 'Enemy Activities in Japan', 5 November 1941, PRO, HS1/204.
11 Statement by Wiehl, 15 October 1945, contained in OSS report, Shanghai, 16 October 1945, FOIA/CIA.
12 'German Intelligence Activities in China During World War II', Strategic Services Unit memorandum, 1 March 1946, FOIA/CIA.
13 Statement by Wiehl, 15 October 1945, contained in OSS report, Shanghai, 16 October 1945, FOIA/CIA; see also OSS X-2 Branch report on Wiehl, 16 October 1945, FOIA/CIA.
14 Panzinger (RSHA) to Foreign Ministry, 1 April 1942, AA, Inland II A/B 83-60E Sdh I.
15 'Organizations of the German Government in Shanghai', 27 September 1945, PRO, WO 208/2862.
16 Stahmer to German Foreign Ministry relaying message from Meisinger to RSHA, 25 August 1943, AA, Inland II 17a.

17 Thadden (Berlin) to German ambassador, Tokyo, 1 [?] October 1943, AA, Inland II 17a.

18 Stahmer to German Foreign Ministry, 25 July 1942, AA, PA 29559.

19 CIC interrogation of Ikushima Kichizo, Sugamo Prison, 20 March 1946, FOIA/USAISC.

20 'German Intelligence Activities in China During World War II', Strategic Services Unit memorandum, 1 March 1946, section III B 6, FOIA/CIA.

21 'German Intelligence in China and Japan', Strategic Services Unit memorandum, 21 Aug. 1945, FOIA/CIA.

22 Statement by Gerda Kocher, 29 September 1945, in OSS X-2 Branch 'Report on Abwehr activities in China, Ehrhardt Bureau', 10 October 1945, FOIA/CIA.

23 Undated (post-war), unsigned memorandum, apparently by Gerda Kocher, FOIA/CIA.

24 See Oscar Reile, *Geheime Ostfront: Die deutsche Abwehr im Osten: 1921–1945*, Munich, 1963, pp. 423–24.

25 Ibid. (translation amended).

26 Ibid.

27 Ibid.

28 Ibid.

29 Ibid.

30 Statement by Wedel, 20 September 1945, in OSS X-2 report on 'Abwehr Activities in China, Ehrhardt Bureau', 10 October 1945, p. 79, FOIA/CIA.

31 John W.M. Chapman (ed.and trans.), *The Price of Admiralty: The War Diary of the German Naval Attaché in Japan 1939–1943*, 2 vols., Ripe, East Sussex, 1982–84, pp. 466, 610.

32 Reile, *Geheime Ostfront*, pp. 426–27.

33 Statement by Habenicht, 29 September 1945, in OSS X-2 report on 'Abwehr Activities in China, Ehrhardt Bureau', 10 October 1945, p. 42, FOIA/CIA.

34 'Translation of Report on "K.O." by "Ehrhardt"', 7 October 1945, USNA, RG 226, entry 182, box 10, folder 67.

35 Amended 'Translation of report on "K. O." by "Ehrhardt"', 7 October 1945, USNA, RG 226, entry 182, box 10, folder 67.

36 Reile, *Geheime Ostfront*, p. 424.

37 Extract from note to Ribbentrop by German Foreign Ministry liaison officer attached to Hitler's staff, 30 May 1942, quoted in F.W. Deakin and G.R. Storry, *The Case of Richard Sorge*, New York, 1966, p. 307.

38 Ibid., p. 314; 'German Intelligence in China and Japan', Strategic Services Unit memorandum, 21 August 1945, FOIA/CIA; interrogation report on J. Meisinger, 25 May 1946, USNA, RG 238, microfilm series M1270, roll 25; Bernd Martin, *Deutschland und Japan im Zweiten Weltkrieg: Vom Angriff auf Pearl Harbor bis zur deutschen Kapitulation*, Göttingen, 1969, p. 123.

39 *Shanghai Times*, 30 January 1943.

40 'The Outline of Activities of the Foreign Affairs Section, Police Headquarters, during the period of Japanese occupation of Shanghai', unsigned, undated [autumn 1945], OSS memorandum, USNA, RG 226, entry 182, box 12, folder 77.

41 Ibid.

42 Statements by Gershkovitch, n.d. [1945], FOIA/USAISC.

43 CIC report, 30 July 1945, FOIA/USAISC.

44 Gershkovitch to Officer-in-Charge, Foreign Affairs Section, Shanghai Municipal Police, 5 April 1943, SMP, U 229.

45 'The Outline of Activities of the Foreign Affairs Section, Police Headquarters, during the period of Japanese Occupation of Shanghai', unsigned, undated (Autumn 1945) OSS memorandum, USNA, RG 226, entry 182, box 12, folder 77.

46 Statement by 'Boris Gershkovitch Mejoff' to US CIC, Manila, n.d. [1945], FOIA/USAISC.

47 Extract from statement by Wiehl, n.d. [1945/46], FOIA/USAISC.

48 Gershkovitch to Officer-in-Charge, Foreign Affairs Section, Shanghai Municipal Police, 5 April 1943, SMP, U 229.

49 Report dated 3 January 1945, SMP, U 636.

50 OSS X-2 Branch report, Shanghai, 16 October 1945, FOIA/CIA.

51 *Shanghai Times*, 11 April 1943.

52 *China Press*, 16 November 1945.

53 OSS report, 12 October 1945, FOIA/CIA.

54 'BH215' to Col. Moscrip, 9 November 1946, USNA, RG 226, entry 182A, box 9, folder 66.

55 Reports and minutes, April–May 1943, SMP, D 8149/F152.

Chapter 11

1 *Shanghai Times*, 10 September 1942.

2 *Syonan Sinbun*, 1 January 1943, quoted in F. C. Jones, H. Borton and B. R. Pearn, *The Far East 1942–1946*, London, 1955, p. 18.

3 Margerie to French Ambassador in China, 3 and 8 April 1942, AMAE, Ambassade Pékin, carton 254, dossier 'Concession Française de Shanghai: Historique depuis 1869'.

4 *Shanghai Times*, 24 February 1943.

5 Text of Franco-Chinese agreement, 18 May 1943, in *China Annual 1944*, pp. 226–27.

6 See Joseph Shieh with Marie Holzman, *Dans le Jardin des Aventuriers*, Paris, 1995, pp. 164–65.

7 See OSS record card on Henri Cosme, 24 May 1943, HIA, Allman papers, box 12, file 6.

8 Text of agreement, 30 June 1943, *China Annual 1944*, pp. 229–30.

9 *Municipal Gazette*, 25 September 1942.

10 *China Annual 1944*, p. 230.

11 *Shanghai Times*, 2 August 1943.

12 *China Annual 1944*, pp. 1110–11.

13 *Shanghai Times*, 17 April, 10 June, 23 July 1942, 17 August 1943.

14 *China Press*, 14 October 1945.

15 OKW, Feldwirtschaftsamt Ausland to German Foreign Ministry, 8 August 1944, USNA, captured German documents, microfilm T82, roll 92, serial 129, folder GD 622.

16 Paraphrase of agreement in Richard Aldrich, 'Imperial Rivalry: British and American Intelligence in Asia, 1942–6', *Intelligence and National Security*, 3, 2, 1988, pp. 17, 22.

17 Aldrich, 'Imperial Rivalry', p. 17.

18 SIS representative, New Delhi, to 'C', 29 February 1944, PRO, HS1/184.

19 See documents in PRO, HS1/181.

20 SOE memorandum, 9 October 1945, PRO, HS1/181.

21 Aldrich, 'Imperial Rivalry', p. 27.

22 Ibid., p. 33.

23 See Maochun Yu, 'OSS in China – New Information about an Old Role', *International Journal of Intelligence and Counterintelligence*, 7, 1994.

24 *War Report of the OSS, vol. 2, The Overseas Targets*, Washington DC, 1976, p. 441.

25 Dick Wilson, *When Tigers Fight: The Story of the Sino-Japanese War, 1937–1945*, New York, 1983, p. 221.

26 Aldrich, 'Imperial Rivalry', p. 33.

27 Milton E. Miles, *A Different Kind of War*, Garden City, NY, 1967, p. 478.

28 See Yu Shen, 'SACO: An Ambivalent Experience of Sino-American Cooperation During World War II', unpublished Ph.D. thesis, University of Illinois at Urbana-Champagne, 1995, pp. 223–24.

29 Statement by Gerda Kocher, 29 September 1945, in OSS X-2 report on 'Abwehr Activities in Shanghai, Ehrhardt Bureau', 10 October 1945, p. 53, FOIA/CIA.

30 *Shanghai Herald*, 18 October 1945.

31 Statement by V. I. Toropovsky, n.d. [1946?], FOIA/USAISC.

32 Statements by V. I. Toropovsky and 'Boris Gershkovitz' (Morris Gershkovitch), n.d. [1945/46], FOIA/USAISC.

33 SMP report, 3 January 1945, SMP, U 636.

34 Statement by Bert Poblete, quoted in US Army CIC report by William L. Boyce Jr, 23 January 1946, FOIA/USAISC.

35 Statement by Vyacheslav Toropovsky, n.d. [1946?], FOIA/USAISC.

36 Ibid.

37 CIC report, 30 July 1945, FOIA/USAISC.

38 Statement by V. I. Toropovsky, n.d. [1946?], FOIA/USAISC.

39 'BH215' to Col. Moscrip, 9 November 1946, USNA, RG 226, entry 182A, box 9, folder 66.

40 CIC report, 30 July 1945, FOIA/USAISC.

41 Report by 'YEX-55', 27 February 1946, USNA, RG 226, entry 182A, box 10, folder 74; see also undated, unsigned report, RG 226, entry 182, box 13, folder 81.

42 OSS report, Shanghai, 28 December 1945, FOIA/CIA.

43 See Peter Elphick, *Far Eastern File: The Intelligence War in the Far East 1930–1945*, London, 1997, pp. 281–2.

44 Memorandum by 'Don' [Chisholm?], USNA, RG 226, entry 182, box 1, folder 7.

45 Interrogation report, 18 May 1944, PRO, HS1/137.

46 Amended translation of report by Ehrhardt, 7 October 1945, USNA, RG 226, entry 182, box 10, folder 67.

47 *China Weekly Review*, 10 November 1945. See also Shieh with Holzman, *Dans le Jardin*, pp. 170–71, 174.

48 Amended translation of report by Ehrhardt, 7 October 1945, USNA, RG 226, entry 182, box 10, folder 67.

49 Military attaché, Tokyo, to OKW, 25 January 1945, USNA, captured German records, microfilm T52, serial 159, roll 113, GD 987.

50 F. C. Jones, *Japan's New Order in East Asia: Its Rise and Fall 1937–1945*, London, 1954, pp. 420, 427.

51 'CX Report: Source UX', 24 May 1945, PRO, WO 208/201.

52 MI6 Political Report, 24 April 1945, PRO, WO 208/378A.

53 Arnhold typescript, p. 46.

54 Meisinger to Wohlthat, 4 July 1945, Wohlthat to Meisinger, 16 August 1945, and Meisinger to Dr Witting, Deutsche Bank für Ostasien, Tokyo, 23 August 1945, AA, PA R 27918; Naval Staff Office, Shanghai, to London, 6 November 1945, PRO, WO 208/2862.

55 Unsigned legal memorandum, probably by Baron Jesco von Puttkamer, around 1947, HIA, Karl von Wiegand papers, box 61, p. 3.

56 Notification by German Ambassador, Tokyo, to members of German embassy, 13 June 1945, AA, PA R 27918 (Handakten Wohlthat Ostas. Bd. 10, 1942–46).

57 'History of the Nazi Party in China', enclosed in US State Department file, USNA, RG 59 862.20293/4-2346.

58 Jacques Guillermaz, *Une Vie pour la Chine: Mémoires 1937–1989*, Paris, 1989, p. 136.

59 Library of Shanghai Academy of Social Sciences, Bulletin d'Information[s] Economiques, 10 April 1945 (typescript carbon), French Consulate-General, Shanghai.

60 Statement by Alfred Lewis Meyer, 20 November 1945, USNA, RG 226, report no. YKX-617.

61 Arnhold typescript, p. 46.

62 Norton (Berne) to Foreign Office, 16 August 1945, PRO, FO 916/1339.

63 SMP report, 2[4?] June 1945, U 4.

64 Transcript in USNA, RG 226/5-126-8.

65 Statement by Toropovsky, n.d. [1946?], FOIA/USAISC.

66 Statement by Marquita Kwong, 3 November 1945, USNA, RG 226, report no. YKX-466.

67 *China Press*, 11, 17 October 1945.

68 *China Weekly Review*, 10 November 1945.

69 SOE Chinese Intelligence Reports, 21 and 30 September 1945, PRO, HS1/147.

Chapter 12

1   *Shanghai Herald*, 23 September, 8 October 1945.

2   *Shanghai Herald*, 25 September 1945.

3   Butterfield & Swire, Shanghai, to J. Swire & Sons, London, 30 November 1945, Swire papers, SOAS, JSSII, 2/19, box 205.

4   *Sydney Morning Herald*, 8 September 1945.

5   *Shanghai Herald*, 23 September 1945.

6   Milton E. Miles, *A Different Kind of War*, Garden City, NY, 1967, p. 508.

7   Ibid., p. 559.

8   Bernard Francis Warman to Sir Archibald Clark Kerr, 15 November 1941, PRO, FO 371/53540.

9   OSS report, 3 October 1945, USNA, RG 226, entry 182, box 13, folder 84.

10 Jacques Guillermaz, *Une Vie Pour la Chine: Mémoires 1937–1989*, Paris, 1989, p. 136.

11 See Paul Premet to French Consul-General, 2 July 1946, AMAE, Consulat Shanghai, inv. 1844-1952 (série noire), carton 27, file II.I, 'Cercle Sportif 1938–1952'.

12 *Shanghai Herald*, 17, 18, 19 December 1945.

13 W. R. Fishel, *The End of Extraterritoriality in China*, Berkeley, 1952,
    p. 296; Marie-Claire Bergère, 'The Purge in Shanghai, 1945–6: The
    Sarly Affair and the End of the French Concession', in Yeh (ed.),
    Wartime Shanghai, pp. 157–78.

14 Unsigned, undated [1946] American intelligence report, FOIA/CIA.

15 'Listing of Possible German War Criminals', US Navy Department
    intelligence Report, USNA, RG 226 XL 39875.

16 Col. A. McGoff to MacArthur, 12 September 1945, USNA, RG 153,
    records concerning J. Meisinger, 100-1046-8.

17 Statement by W. Schmalfuss, Shanghai, 27 September 1945, USNA,
    RG 226, XL 26904.

18 USNA, RG 59 Department of State records 862.20293/6-546.

19 Evidence given by Erben in the trial of Lothar Eisentraeger et al.,
    Shanghai, October 1946, USNA, RG 153, case 58-137, book 1,
    p. 116.

20 Ibid. p. 117.

21 Ibid. p. 161.

22 Moscrip to R. A. MacMillan, 15 April 1947, FOIA/CIA.

23 'BH/216' to 'BH/210', 20 March 1947, FOIA/CIA.

24 'BH/216' to Chief of Mission, 7 April 1947, FOIA/CIA.

25 'BH/216' to Chief of Mission, 12 April 1947, FOIA/CIA.

26 [Signature illegible] to Commanding Officer, 60th CIC, 5 January
    1950, FOIA/USAISC.

27 Report on Ehrhardt trial proceedings to 13 November 1946
    forwarded as enclosure with M. B. Davis (US Consul-General,
    Shanghai) to US Ambassador, Nanking, 2 December 1946, USNA,
    RG 59, State Department decimal file 862.20293/12-246.

28 Ibid.

29 Ibid.

30 Account of proceedings, enclosed with US Consul-General, Shanghai,
    to US Ambassador, Nanking, 30 December 1946, USNA, RG 59,
    State Department decimal file 862.20293/12-3046.

31 Ossi Lewin (ed.), *Shanghai Almanac 1946–7*, Shanghai, 1947, p. 23.

32 JICA/China memorandum, 20 October 1945, USNA, RG 226, entry
    182, box 14, folder 87.

33 *China Weekly Review*, 16 November 1945.

34 Moscrip to R. A. MacMillan, 15 April 1947, FOIA/CIA.

35 Ibid.

36 Statement by Uy, 15 October 1945, USNA, RG 226, entry 182, box 10, folder 66.

37 See discussion in PRO, FO 371/53573 and 53574.

38 Nathan papers, Bodleian Library, Oxford.

39 *China Press*, 31 October 1945.

40 Dossier on Chisholm case, USNA, RG 226, entry 182, box 16, folder 121.

41 Memorandum by 'Don' [Chisholm?], USNA, RG 226, entry 182, box 1, folder 7.

42 Letter to 'Berjee', 10 October 1945, transcript in USNA, RG 226, entry 182A, box 10, folder 74.

43 'Memorandum to the files', 18 May 1946, transcript in USNA, RG 226, entry 182A, box 10, folder 74.

44 British Embassy, Nanking, to Government of India, New Delhi, 11 July 1946, PRO, FO 371/53758.

45 Sumaire to British War Crimes Commission, Shanghai, December 1946, USNA, RG 226, entry 182A, box 10, folder 74.

46 Allman papers, HIA, box 12, file 45.

47 'Memorandum on the arrest and detention in Shanghai of Messrs. Gracie, Lamb and Johnston', n.d. [1947], PRO, FO 369/3791; see also Chungking to Foreign Office, 5 December 1945, and related documents, PRO, FO 369/3175.

48 William S. Crawford, US Strategic Services Unit, China Theatre, to Capt. Ogle, British Consulate-General, Shanghai, 11 December 1945, PRO, FO 369/3791.

49 'Memorandum on the arrest and detention in Shanghai of Messrs. Gracie, Lamb and Johnston', n.d. [1947], PRO, FO 369/3791.

50 Judgement of Chief Justice H.W.B. Blackall in case of Robert Sandeman Lamb (plaintiff) and A.D. Monkhouse (Hong Kong Immigration Officer, defendant), 12 September 1947, PRO, FO 369/3791.

51 Kentwell statement, undated (1945), USNA, RG 226, entry 182, box 2, folder 12.

52 *Shanghai Herald*, 16 January 1946.

53 *China Weekly Review*, 2 February 1946.

54 *Shanghai Tribune*, 5 and 18 July 1946.

55 Undated statement by Pick, FOIA/USAISC.

56 Intercepted, undated [1946?], unmailed letter to Vladimir Kedrolivansky from Eugene M. Clige [Pick], FOIA/USAISC.

57 Report dated 28 February 1946, FOIA/USAISC.

58 CIC, Tokyo to 'COMJEN CHINA', telegram dated 29 April 1946, FOIA/USAISC.

59 Historical Division to General Dager, 'Information on Eugene Hovans', 24 June 1950, FOIA/USAISC.

60 Memorandum signed E. Clige-Hovans, 1 December 1948, FOIA/USAISC.

61 Memorandum by Lt. Col. R. J. Delaney, 10 January 1949, FOIA/USAISC.

62 E. Clige-Hovans to 'John', 21 May 1949, FOIA/USAISC.

63 Reports dated 14 June and 14 July 1950, FOIA/USAISC.

64 Undated US intelligence report, around January 1950, FOIA/USAISC.

65 'Sale of Shanghai Police Files', US intelligence report, 20 April 1949, USNA, RG 226, entry 182, box 12, folder 77.

66 See Aron Shai, *The Fate of British and French Firms in China 1949–1954: Imperialism Imprisoned*, Basingstoke, 1996.

67 Simon Winchester, 'Shanghai, city without hope', *Manchester Guardian Weekly*, 23 July 1989.

Conclusion

1 'Appraisal of Intelligence and Espionage Systems of Various Countries by the Japanese', 27 January 1946, USNA, RG 226, entry 182, box 7, folder 51.

2 See Ian Buruma, *Wages of Guilt: Memories of War in Germany and Japan*, London, 1994.

Bibliography

1. Unpublished sources

Archives du Ministère des Affaires Etrangères, Nantes (AMAE)
   Shanghai Consular records
Berlin Document Center (now under the control of the Bundesarchiv)
   Records concerning G. Kahner and J. Meisinger
Bodleian Library, Oxford
   Diaries and papers of E. J. Nathan
British Library, London
   India Office Records (IOR)
Bundesarchiv Potsdam (BAP)
   Records of the German Embassy in China
Central Archives for the History of the Jewish People, Jerusalem (CAHJP)
   Archive of the Far Eastern Jewish Central Information Bureau for
      Emigrants
German Foreign Ministry Archives, Bonn (AA)
   Records of the German Foreign Ministry and of the Consulate-General
      in Shanghai
Hoover Institution Archives, Stanford, California (HIA)
   N. F. Allman papers
   Randall Gould papers
   Karl von Wiegand diaries and papers
Hoover Institution Library, Stanford, California
   'Shanghai 1941–1945' (typescript memoir and diary) by H. E. Arnhold
Imperial War Museum, London
   Papers of R. Maurice Tinkler
   Autobiography of Brigadier L. F. Field
Library of Congress, Washington DC
   Microfilms of captured Japanese Foreign Ministry records

Public Record Office, Kew (PRO)
  ADM 223
  FO 228
  FO 369
  FO 371
  FO 372
  FO 405
  FO 656
  FO 676
  FO 916
  HS 1
  WO 106
  WO 208
Royal Institute of International Affairs, London
  Chatham House Shanghai Study Group papers (1938)
School of Oriental and African Studies, London University (SOAS)
  Butterfield & Swire records
  China Association papers
  'From Confucius to Lenin', typescript by Robert Magnenoz (pseud. =
    R. Jobez, head of French Political Police in Shanghai in early 1930s)
  Papers of Sir Frederick Maze
Shanghai Academy of Social Sciences
  'Bulletin d'Information Economique sur la Chine' (cyclostyled serial
    produced during the war by the French Consulate-General in Shanghai)
State Historical Society of North Dakota
  Papers of Hilaire du Berrier
US National Archives, Washington DC (USNA)
  State Department records (Record Group 59)
  Eisentraeger/Ehrhardt trial records (Record Group 153)
  OSS records (Record Group 226)
  Shanghai Municipal Police files (Record Group 263)
  Records of the Army Staff (Record Group 319)
  Microfilms of captured German Records

US Government records obtained by the author under the Freedom of Information Act (FOIA)

Records concerning German and Japanese intelligence organizations in North China during World War II

Individual case files concerning Lily Abegg, Hermann Erben, Morris Gershkovitch, Klaus Mehnert, Josef Meisinger, Albert von Miorini, Hans Mosberg, Eugene Pick, Walter Schmalfuss and others

University of Minnesota

YMCA archives

Other unpublished sources

W. G. Braidwood, 'Report of the Activities of the British Residents' Association Relief Association of Shanghai Dec. 1941–June 1943' (typescript)

Christine Cornet, 'The Bumpy End of the French Concession 1943–1946', paper presented at conference on 'Wartime Shanghai 1937–1945', Lyon, October 1997

H. (Peter) Eisfelder, 'Chinese Exile: My Years in Shanghai and Nanking', typescript memoirs, 1972

Laura Margolis, 'Report of Activities in Shanghai, China, from December 8, 1941 to September 1943', typescript

Yu Shen, 'SACO: An Ambivalent Experience of Sino-American Cooperation During World War II', Ph.D. thesis, University of Illinois at Urbana-Champaign, 1995

2. Published sources

A. Contemporary newspapers and journals published in Shanghai

8-Uhr Abendblatt

Bulletin Municipal

China Press

China Weekly Review

Israel's Messenger

Journal de Shanghai

Municipal Gazette

Noon Extra

North China Daily News

Oriental Affairs
Ostasiatischer Lloyd
Shanghaier Morgenpost
Shanghai Evening Post and Mercury
Shanghai Herald
Shanghai Jewish Chronicle
Shanghai Woche
Shanghai Zaria
Shopping News
Unzer Lebn/Nasha Zhizn
XX Century

B. Books and articles

ABEND, Hallett, *Japan Unmasked*, New York, 1941.
— *My Years in China 1926–1941*, London, 1944.
ALCOTT, Carroll, *My War With Japan*, New York, 1943.
ALDRICH, Richard, 'Imperial Rivalry: British and American Intelligence in Asia, 1942–6', *Intelligence and National Security*, 3, 2, 1988, pp. 5–55.
ALLEN, Louis, *The End of the War in Asia*, London, 1976.
ALLMAN, Norwood F., *Shanghai Lawyer*, New York, 1943.
AUDEN, W. H. and ISHERWOOD, Christopher, *Journey to a War*, New York, 1939.
BARBER, Noel, *The Fall of Shanghai: The Communist Take-Over in 1949*, London, 1979.
BARNETT, Robert W., *Economic Shanghai: Hostage to Politics, 1937–1941*, New York, 1941.
BEHR, Edward, *Hirohito: Behind the Myth*, New York, 1989.
BERGÈRE, Marie-Claire, 'The Other China', in Christopher Howe (ed.), *Shanghai: Revolution and Development in an Asian Metropolis*, Cambridge, 1981.
BICKERS, Robert A., *Changing Shanghai's 'Mind': Publicity, Reform and the British in Shanghai, 1927–1941*, London, 1992.
BOOKER, Edna Lee, *News is My Job: A Correspondent in War-Torn China*, New York, 1940.
BOYLE, John Hunter, *China and Japan at War 1937–1945: The Politics of Collaboration*, Stanford, CA, 1972.

BUNKER, Gerald E., *The Peace Conspiracy: Wang Ching-wei and the China War, 1937–1941*, Cambridge, MA, 1972.

BURUMA, Ian, *Wages of Guilt: Memories of War in Germany and Japan*, London, 1994.

CALDWELL, Oliver J., *A Secret War: Americans in China, 1944–1945*, Carbondale, Ill., 1972.

CAREY, Arch, *The War Years at Shanghai 1941–45–48*, New York, 1967.

CHABOT, François, 'La fin de la présence politique française à Shanghai 1937–1943', in Jacques Weber (ed.), *La France en Chine 1843–1943*, Nantes, 1997, pp. 233–45.

CHAN, Anthony B., *The Western Armaments Trade in Warlord China 1920–1928*, Vancouver, BC, 1982.

CHAPMAN, John W. M. (ed. and trans.), *The Price of Admiralty: The War Diary of the German Naval Attaché in Japan 1939–1943*, 2 vols, Ripe, East Sussex, 1982–84.

— 'A Dance on Eggs: Intelligence and the "Anti-Comintern"', *Journal of Contemporary History*, 22, 1987, pp. 333–72.

— 'Japanese Intelligence 1919–1945: A Suitable Case for Treatment', in Christopher Andrew and Jeremy Noakes (eds), *Intelligence and International Relations 1900–1945*, Exeter, 1987, pp. 145–90.

— 'Tricycle Recycled: Collaboration among the Secret Intelligence Services of the Axis States 1940–1941', *Intelligence and National Security*, 7, 1992, pp. 268–99.

The China Annual 1944, Shanghai, 1944.

CLIFFORD, Nicholas R., *Retreat from China: British Policy in the Far East 1937–1941*, London, 1967.

— *Shanghai, 1925: Urban Nationalism and the Defense of Foreign Privilege*, Ann Arbor, 1979.

— *Spoilt Children of Empire: Westerners in Shanghai and the Chinese Revolution of the 1920s*, Hanover, NH, 1991.

COLLAR, Hugh, *Captive in Shanghai*, Hong Kong, 1990.

COOX, Alvin D., 'Flawed Perception and its Effect upon Operational Thinking: The Case of the Japanese Army, 1937–1941', in Michael I. Handel (ed.), *Intelligence and Military Operations*, London, 1990, pp. 239–54.

COPELAND, Miles, *The Game of Nations: The Amorality of Power Politics*, London, 1969.

CROW, Carl, *Foreign Devils in the Flowery Kingdom*, New York, 1940.

CRUIKSHANK, Charles, *SOE in the Far East*, Oxford, 1986.

DAVIDSON-HOUSTON, J. V., *Yellow Creek: The Story of Shanghai*, London, 1962.

DRAGE, Charles, *Two-Gun Cohen*, London, 1954.

DEAKIN, F.W., and STORRY, G.R., *The Case of Richard Sorge*, New York, 1966.

DREIFORT, John E., *Myopic Grandeur: The Ambivalence of French Foreign Policy Towards the Far East 1919–1945*, Kent, Ohio, 1991.

DUUS, Peter, MYERS, Ramon H. and PEATTIE, Mark R. (eds), *The Japanese Informal Empire in China, 1895–1937*, Princeton, 1989.

EASTMAN, LLOYD E., 'Nationalist China During the Sino-Japanese War 1937–1945', in John K. Fairbank and Albert Feuerwerker (eds), *The Cambridge History of China*, vol. 13, *Republican China 1912–1949, part II*, Cambridge, 1986, pp. 547–608.

ELPHICK, Peter, *Far Eastern File: The Intelligence War in the Far East 1930–1945*, London, 1997.

FALIGOT, Roger, and KAUFFER, Rémi, *Kang Sheng et les Services Secrets Chinois*, Paris, 1987.

FARMER, Rhodes, *Shanghai Harvest: A Diary of Three Years in the China War*, London, 1945.

FEUERWERKER, Albert, 'The Foreign Presence in China', in John K. Fairbank (ed.), *The Cambridge History of China*, vol. 12, *Republican China 1912–1949, part I*, Cambridge, 1983, pp. 128–208.

FINCH, Percy, *Shanghai and Beyond*, New York, 1953.

FISCHER, Martin, *Vierzig Jahre deutsche Chinapolitik*, Hamburg, 1962.

FISHEL, W. R., *The End of Extraterritoriality in China*, Berkeley, 1952.

FONTENOY, Jean, *The Secret Shanghai*, New York, 1939.

FOOT, M. R. D., *SOE: An Outline History of the Special Operations Executive 1940–1946*, London, 1984.

Four Months of War, Shanghai, n.d. [1938?].

FREYEISEN, Astrid, 'Das Kriegsende und seine Auswirkungen für die Deutschen in Shanghai', *Newsletter Frauen und China*, 9, August 1995, pp. 18–32.

FU, Poshek, *Passivity, Resistance and Collaboration: Intellectual Choices in Occupied Shanghai, 1937–1945*, Stanford, CA, 1993.

GOULD, Randall, 'Shanghai During the Takeover, 1949', *Annals of the American Academy of Political and Social Science*, vol. 277, September 1951, pp. 182–92.

GREAT BRITAIN: NAVAL INTELLIGENCE DIVISION, Geographical Handbook Series, *China Proper*, 3 vols, printed for official distribution, London, 1945.

GROVER, David H. and Gretchen G., *Captives of Shanghai: The Story of the President Harrison*, Napa, CA, 1989.

— 'Night Attack at Shanghai', *Naval History*, Winter, 4, 5, 1991, pp. 34–40.

GRUENBERGER, Felix, 'The Jewish Refugees in Shanghai', *Jewish Social Studies*, XII, 1950, 4, pp. 329–48.

GUILLAIN, Robert, *Orient Extrême: Une vie en Asie*, Paris, 1986.

GUILLERMAZ, Jacques, *Une Vie pour la Chine: Mémoires 1937–1989*, Paris, 1989.

GULL, E. M. *British Economic Interests in the Far East*, London, 1943.

HAAN, J. H. 'Origin and Development of the Political System in the Shanghai International Settlement', *Journal of the Hong Kong Branch of the Royal Asiatic Society*, 22, 1982, pp. 31–64.

HAHN, Emily, *China To Me*, Philadelphia, 1944.

HAUSER, Ernest O., *Shanghai: City for Sale*, New York, 1940.

HERSHATTER, Gail, *Dangerous Pleasures: Prostitution and Modernity in Twentieth-Century Shanghai*, Berkeley, 1997.

HINDER, Eleanor, *Life and Labour in Shanghai* (2nd edn), New York, 1944.

HOGAN, Pendleton, 'Shanghai After the Japs', *Virginia Quarterly Review*, 22, 1946, pp. 91–108.

HSIA, Ching-lin, *The Status of Shanghai*, Shanghai, 1929.

HUEBNER, Jon W., 'The Shanghai Bund's Missing Monuments', *American Asian Review*, VIII, 1, 1990, pp. 88–97.

HUGHES, Richard, *Foreign Devil: Thirty Years of Reporting from the Far East*, London, 1984.

IRIYE, Akira (ed.), *The Chinese and the Japanese: Essays in Political and Cultural Interactions*, Princeton, 1980.

JOHNSTONE, William Crane, *The Shanghai Problem*, Stanford, CA, 1937.

JONES, F. C., *Shanghai and Tientsin*, London, 1940.

— *Japan's New Order in East Asia: Its Rise and Fall 1937–1945*, London, 1954.

JONES, F. C., BORTON, H. and PEARN, B. R., *The Far East 1942–1946*, London, 1955.

KING, Frank H. H., *The Hong Kong Bank Between the Wars and the Bank Interned 1919–1945*, vol. III of *The History of the Hongkong and Shanghai Banking Corporation*, Cambridge, 1988.

KOUNIN, I. I., *Eighty-five Years of the Shanghai Volunteer Force*, Shanghai, 1938.

KRANZLER, David, *Japanese, Nazis, and Jews: The Jewish Refugee Community of Shanghai, 1938–1945*, New York, 1976.

KREISSLER, Françoise, *L'Action culturelle allemande en Chine: De la fin du XIXe siècle à la Seconde Guerre mondiale*, Paris, 1989.

LETHBRIDGE, H. J. intr., *All About Shanghai: A Standard Guidebook*, Hong Kong, 1986 (reprint of 1934/35 edn.).

LEVERKUEHN, Paul, *Der geheime Nachrichtendienst der deutschen Wehrmacht im Kriege*, Frankfurt am Main, 1964.

LEVY, Roger, LACAM, Guy and ROTH, Andrew, *French Interests and Policies in the Far East*, New York, 1941.

LEWIN, Ossi (ed.), *Shanghai Almanac 1946–7*, Shanghai, 1947.

LING, Pan, *In Search of Old Shanghai*, Hong Kong, 1983.

LITTEN, Frederick S., 'The Noulens Affair', *China Quarterly*, 138, June 1994, pp. 492–512.

LOWE, Peter, *Great Britain and the Origins of the Pacific War: A Study of British Policy in East Asia, 1937–1941*, Oxford, 1977.

MAAS, Fritz, *Von Jerusalem nach Schanghai: Abschied vom Konfessionalismus*, Denzlingen, 1987.

McKALE, Donald M., 'The Nazi Party in the Far East, 1931–1945', *Journal of Contemporary History*, 12, 1977, pp. 291–311.

MARTIN, Bernd, *Deutschland und Japan im Zweiten Weltkrieg: Vom Angriff auf Pearl Harbor bis zur deutschen Kapitulation*, Göttingen, 1969.

MARTIN, Brian G., 'Tu Yüeh-sheng and Labour Control in Shanghai: The Case of the French Tramways Union, 1928–1932', *Papers on Far Eastern History*, 32, 1985, pp. 99–137.

—— 'The Green Gang and the Guomindang Polity in Shanghai 1927–1937', *Papers on Far Eastern History*, 42, 1990, pp. 59–96.

—— 'The Green Gang and the Guomindang State: Du Yuesheng and the Politics of Shanghai, 1927–37', *Journal of Asian Studies*, 54, 1, February 1995, pp. 64–91.

—— *The Shanghai Green Gang: Politics and Organized Crime, 1919–1937*, Berkeley, 1996.

MEHNERT, Klaus, *Ein Deutscher in der Welt: Erinnerungen 1906–1981*, Stuttgart, 1981.

MEO, L. D., *Japan's Radio War on Australia 1941–1945*, Melbourne, 1968.

MILES, Milton E., *A Different Kind of War*, Garden City, NY, 1967.

MILLER, G. E. [pseud. Mauricio Fresco], *Shanghai: The Paradise of Adventurers*, New York, 1937.

MURPHEY, Rhoads, *Shanghai: Key to Modern China*, Cambridge, MA, 1953.

OFER, Dalia, 'The Israeli Government and Jewish Organizations: The Case of the Immigration of Jews from Shanghai', *Studies in Zionism*, 11, 1990, 1, pp. 67–80.

OLDHAM, Peter, *Lieutenant Stephen Polkinghorn DSC, RNR*, Auckland, NZ, 1984.

O'LEARY, Cedrick Patrick, *A Shamrock Up a Bamboo Tree: The Story of Eight Years Behind the 8-Ball in Shanghai, 1941–1949*, New York, 1956.

OSTERHAMMEL, Jürgen, 'British Business in China, 1860s–1950s', in R. P. T. Davenport-Hines and Geoffrey Jones (eds), *British Business in Asia since 1860*, Cambridge, 1989, pp. 1–30.

PAL, John, *Shanghai Saga*, London, 1963.

PERRONT, Nadine (ed. and trans.), *Shanghai. Opium, Jeu, Prostitution,* Paris, 1992.

POWELL, John B., *My Twenty-Five Years in China*, New York, 1945.

QUIGLEY, Harold S., *Far Eastern War 1937–1941*, Boston, 1942.

REILE, Oscar, *Geheime Ostfront: Die deutsche Abwehr im Osten 1921–1945*, Munich, 1963.

ROSKILL, Stephen, *A Merchant Fleet at War: Alfred Holt & Co. 1939–1945*, London, 1962.

ROWE, William T., 'The Qingbang and Collaboration under the Japanese, 1939–1945: Material in the Wuhan Municipal Archives', *Modern China*, 8, 1982, 4, pp. 491–99.

RUTLAND, Suzanne D., '"Waiting Room Shanghai": Australian Reactions to the Plight of the Jews in Shanghai after the Second World War', *Leo Baeck Institute Year Book*, XXXII, 1987, pp. 407–33.

SCHALLER, Michael, *The U. S. Crusade in China, 1938–1945*, New York, 1979.

SCHELLENBERG, Walter, *The Labyrinth: Memoirs of Walter Schellenberg*, New York, 1956.

SCHENKE, Wolf, *Mit China allein: Entscheidende Jahre 1939–1947*, Hamburg, 1971.

SCHUMPETER, E. B. (ed.), *The Industrialization of Japan and Manchukuo 1930–1940: Population, Raw Materials and Industry*, New York, 1940.

SERGEANT, Harriet, *Shanghai: Collision Point of Cultures 1918–1937*, London, 1990.

SEYWALD, Wilfried, *Journalisten im Shanghaier Exil 1939–1949*, Salzburg, 1987.

SHAI, Aron, *Origins of the War in the East: Britain, China and Japan 1937–39*, London, 1976.

—— *The Fate of British and French Firms in China 1949–1954: Imperialism Imprisoned*, Basingstoke, 1996.

Shanghai Municipal Council Report for the Year 1939, Shanghai, 1940.

SHIEH, Joseph with HOLZMAN, Marie, *Dans le Jardin des Aventuriers*, Paris, 1995.

SHILLONY, Ben-Ami, *The Jews and the Japanese: The Successful Outsiders*, Rutland, Vt, 1991.

SMURTHWAITE, David (ed.), *The Forgotten War: The British Army in the Far East 1941–1945*, London, 1992.

STAHMER, H. G., *Japans Niederlage – Asiens Sieg: Aufstieg eines Grösseren Ostasien*, Bielefeld, 1952.

STEAD, Mary, et al., *Stone-Paper-Scissors: Shanghai 1921–1945: An Autobiography*, Deddington, Oxfordshire, 1991.

STEELE, A.T., *Shanghai and Manchuria, 1932: Recollections of a War Correspondent*, Tempe, AZ, 1977.

STEPHAN, John J., *The Russian Fascists: Tragedy and Farce in Exile, 1925–1941*, New York, 1978.

STILWELL, Joseph W., *The Stilwell Papers*, Theodore H. White (ed.), New York, 1948.

STOIBER, Rudolf, *Der Spion der Hitler sein wollte*, Vienna, 1989.

STRANAHAN, Patricia, 'Strange Bedfellows: The Communist Party and Shanghai's Elite in the National Salvation Movement', *China Quarterly*, 129, March 1992, pp. 26–51.

STRIPP, A., *Codebreaker in the Far East*, London, 1989.

STURTON, Stephen Douglas, *From Mission Hospital to Concentration Camp*, London, n.d.

TAIRE, Lucian, *Shanghai Episode*, Hong Kong, 1957.

THORNE, Christopher, *Allies of a Kind: The United States, Britain and the War against Japan, 1941–1945*, London, 1978.

— *The Issue of War: States, Societies, and the Far Eastern Conflict of 1941–1945*, New York, 1985.

UNITED STATES WAR DEPARTMENT, Strategic Services Unit, *War Report of the OSS*, 2 vols, Washington DC, 1976.

WAKEMAN, Frederic Jr, 'Policing Modern Shanghai', *China Quarterly*, 115, September 1988, pp. 408–40.

— *Policing Shanghai 1927–1937*, Berkeley, 1995.

— 'Licensing Leisure: The Chinese Nationalists' Attempt to Regulate Shanghai 1927–49', *Journal of Asian Studies*, 54, 1, February 1995, pp. 19–42.

— *The Shanghai Badlands: Wartime Terrorism and Urban Crime: 1937–1941*, Cambridge, 1996.

WAKEMAN, Frederic Jr, and YEH, Wen-hsin, (eds), *Shanghai Sojourners*, Berkeley, 1992.

WANG Ke-Wen, 'Collaborators and Capitalists: The Politics of "Material Control" in Wartime Shanghai', *Chinese Studies in History*, 26, 1, 1992, pp. 42–62.

WASSERSTEIN, Bernard, *The Secret Lives of Trebitsch Lincoln* (2nd rev. edn), London, 1989.

WEI, Betty Peh-t'i, *Shanghai: Crucible of Modern China*, Hong Kong, 1987.

WELAND, James, 'Misguided Intelligence: Japanese Military Intelligence Officers in the Manchurian Incident, September 1931', *Journal of Military History*, 58, July 1994, pp. 445–60.

WETTERN, Desmond, *The Lonely Battle*, London, 1960.

WHITE, Theodore H. and JACOBY, Annalee, *Thunder Out of China*, London, 1947.

WILCOX, Robert K., *Japan's Secret War*, New York, 1985.

WILLOUGHBY, Charles A., *Shanghai Conspiracy: The Sorge Spy Ring*, New York, 1952.

WILSON, Dick, *When Tigers Fight: The Story of the Sino-Japanese War, 1937–1945*, New York, 1983.

WOODCOCK, George, *The British in the Far East*, London, 1969.

WRIGHT, Tim, 'Shanghai Imperialists versus Rickshaw Racketeers: The Defeat of the 1934 Rickshaw Reforms', *Modern China*, 17, 1991, 1, pp. 76–111.

YEH, Wen-hsin, 'Dai Li and the Liu Geqing Affair: Heroism in the Chinese Secret Service During the War of Resistance', *Journal of Asian Studies*, 48, 3, 1989, pp. 545–62.

— (ed.) *Wartime Shanghai*, London, 1998.

YU, Maochun, 'OSS in China – New Information about an Old Role', *International Journal of Intelligence and Counterintelligence*, 7, 1994, 1, pp. 75–96.

— *OSS in China: Prelude to Cold War*, New Haven, 1996.

ZHANG, Zhong-Li, CHEN, Zeng-nian and YAO, Xin-rong, *The Swire Group in Old China*, Shanghai, n.d. [1994?].

Acknowledgements

Like all labourers in the vineyard of wartime intelligence studies, I owe a special debt to John Taylor of the US National Archives. Robert Bickers, Parks Coble, Poshek Fu and David Wasserstein read and commented most helpfully on the manuscript. I also wish to thank many others who have encouraged and helped me in my research: Avraham Altman, Chiara Betta, Geoffrey Bolton, Geoffrey Brooks, Jeremy Brown, Ronald M. Bulatoff, Nicholas R. Clifford, Sherman Cochran, Robert T. Crowley, Irene Eber, Celia Fassberg, John Freely, Jonathan Goldstein, Pan Guang, Marilla B. Guptil, Ambassador Wilhelm Haas, Professor Murayama Naoki, Larry McDonald, Frederic Wakeman Jr and Wen-hsin Yeh. I am grateful to Betty Barr, Fiona Eberts, Rose Horowitz, Sasson Jacoby, George Leonoff, George Wang and many others for sharing with me their memories of old Shanghai. I also wish to express appreciation to the staffs of all the archives and libraries in which I worked, to Charlotte Havilland of John Swire & Sons for assistance with material from the company's archives and for making available photographs of Shanghai, and to all other suppliers of photographs. For research assistance I thank Sandra Gereau, John Hill and Mark Rosenberg. For translations from Chinese and Japanese I am indebted to Xianju Du. A grant from the Special Acquisitions Fund of the Brandeis University Library made it possible for the library to purchase 63 microfilm reels of documents from the archive of the Shanghai Municipal Police. I also wish to acknowledge grants received from the Committee for Scholarly Communication with the People's Republic of China and the Brandeis University Center for International and Comparative Studies. The former enabled me to visit China in 1990 where I enjoyed the hospitality of the Shanghai Academy of Social Sciences. Finally, I owe special thanks to my publisher, Andrew Franklin, my editor, Nicky White, my literary agent, Bruce Hunter of David Higham Associates and my daughter, Charlotte.

Index